THE INSPIRATION AND TRUTH OF SCRIPTURE

SERIES EDITORS

Pablo T. Gadenz
Mount St. Mary's University and Seminary, Maryland

Gregory Y. Glazov
Immaculate Conception Seminary School of Theology
Seton Hall University

Jeffrey L. Morrow
Immaculate Conception Seminary School of Theology
Seton Hall University

EDITORIAL BOARD

ISBN: 978-0-8132-3687-2
eISBN: 978-0-8132-3688-9

Imprimi potest
Very Rev. Thomas Greene, SJ, Provincial
United States Central Southern Province, Society of Jesus

The paper used in this publication meets the minimum requirements of
American National Standards for Information Science—
Permanence of Paper for Printed Library Materials, ANSI Z39.48-1984.

Cataloging-in-Publication Data on File at the Library of Congress

Printed in the United States.
Book design by Burt&Burt
Interior set with Minion Pro and Astoria

The Inspiration and Truth of Scripture

TESTING THE RATZINGER PARADIGM

AARON PIDEL, SJ

The Catholic University of America Press
Washington, D.C.

In memory of
Joseph Ratzinger (1927–2022) and
Avery Dulles (1918–2008),
who modeled the theologian's vocation for me

Contents

Acknowledgments // ix

Abbreviations // xiii

Introduction: Setting the Scene // 1

1 The Search for a New Paradigm
  of Biblical Inspiration and Truth // 15

2 Ratzinger on Scripture as God's Word // 53

3 Ratzinger on the Truth of Scripture // 101

4 The Ethically Normative Interpretation of Scripture:
  Jesus' Teaching on Divorce // 145

5 The Historicity of the Gospels through the Lens
  of the Last Supper // 183

Epilogue: Three Achievements // 231

Bibliography // 247

Index // 269

Acknowledgments

I owe gratitude to many for their generous help to me in completing this book. I received material support from several sources. Marquette University's Faculty Summer Fellowship allowed me to dedicate the summer of 2018 to drafting the first chapter of this book. A Humboldt Postdoctoral Fellowship spanning the 2020–2021 academic year gave me the leisure and impetus to draft the four remaining chapters. The Jesuit Community attached to the Kunst Statio Sankt Peter in Cologne offered me food and lodging during the darkest days of the pandemic. I am very grateful for all these very human supports.

But I am no less grateful for all the personal and intellectual helps I received along the way. This project began as a licentiate thesis about Joseph Ratzinger on biblical inspiration and inerrancy written under the direction of Khaled Anatolios and the much-missed Dan Harrington, SJ. They did much to point me in the right direction. It was Matthew Levering, however, who later pitched to me the idea of a book-length project on the same theme, planting the seed for this book. I am grateful for all their encouragement and mentorship along the way.

There are many who helped in the writing process itself, most of which happened in Germany. My Humboldt *Gastgeber*, Herr Prof. Thomas Söding, chair of New Testament Studies at the Ruhr University of Bochum, managed to be a gracious and humane presence despite the pandemic-related restrictions. He opened his virtual *Oberseminar* to me, allowing me to present my chapters-in-progress to and establish living contact with such hospitable *Doktoranden* as Aleksandra and Lukas Brand, Miriam Pawlak, and Pater Thaddaeus Hausman, OCSO. In a less formal way, many other families helped me keep my sanity. Peter Marx and Sophie Taubert gave me an insider's view of the German Church and academy. David and Linda

Hickson, FOCUS missionaries in Düsseldorf, "adopted" me for all the major American holidays. I am grateful to all who opened not only their minds but their lives to me.

The other pole of my rather limited social life in Germany lay with my religious *Mitbrüder*. The Jesuits at the Kunst Statio Sankt Peter received me warmly and indulged my halting German: Peter Conrads, Heribert Graab, Götz Werner, Klaus Jochum, and Stephan Kessler. I am especially grateful to Klaus for the *Korrektur* of my German homilies and lectures and to Stephan for incorporating me into the liturgical life of the parish. During my occasional sojourns to the community of Sankt Georgen in Frankfurt, Bernhard Knorn, Stephan Hoffman, and Niccolo Steiner all extended warm hospitality. I hope to repay their kindness someday.

Also deserving of acknowledgment are those who have helped me in the refinement of this project. Many of the ideas found in chapters 2 and 3 appeared in germ in previous publications: "Joseph Ratzinger on Biblical Inerrancy," *Nova et Vetera* 12, no. 1 (2014): 307–33; "*Christi Opera Proficiunt:* Ratzinger's Neo-Bonaventurian Model of Social Inspiration," *Nova et Vetera* 13, no. 3 (2015): 693–711. A more focused treatment of Ratzinger on the dating of the Last Supper, a section of chapter 5, recently appeared in the proceedings of the 2020 Msgr. Quinn Bible Conference hosted by St. Paul Seminary: "Ratzinger on the Historicity of the Gospels: A Case Study of the Last Supper Narrative," in *Word of Truth, Sealed by the Spirit: Perspectives on the Inspiration and Truth of Sacred Scripture*, ed. Kevin Zilverberg and Matthew Genung (St. Paul: St. Paul Seminary Press, 2022): 86–108. I benefited greatly from the feedback of both anonymous reviewers and conference participants. I tested out some of the ideas from chapter 4 in a paper titled "Ratzinger's Cross-Cultural Biblical Ethics," delivered at a conference at Mundelein Seminary on "Ratzinger and the Future of African Theology." Matthew Levering's (very) critical feedback helped me improve it greatly. Michael Cover at Marquette University and Nathan Eubank at the University of Notre Dame both lent me their exegetical expertise when I strayed out of my depth in chapter 5. Sr. Maria Veritas Marks, OP, and Emily Barnum encouraged me to think more deeply about prophecy and canonicity, respectively. John Martino at Catholic University of America Press was encouraging and responsive throughout the whole process. One of my anonymous readers went above and beyond the call of duty, reviewing my manuscript in great detail, rescuing me from numerous infelicities, and helping me sharpen my arguments. I alone am responsible, of course, for the remaining blemishes.

Last, but not least, I thank God. He has given us his word in human words, and he has called me to the Society of Jesus, an apostolic body dedicated to the "ministry of the word." Of neither of these gifts am I remotely deserving.

AMDG

Abbreviations

AAS	Acta Apostolicae Sedis
AB	The Anchor Bible
ADA	*Acta et Documenta Concilio Oecumenico Vaticano II Apparando Series I (Antepraeparatoria).* 4 vols. Vatican City: Typis Polyglottis Vaticanis: 1960–61.
ADPSJ	*Archiv der Deutschen Provinz der Gesellschaft Jesu.* München.
AL	*Amoris Laetitia.* Post-Synodal Apostolic Exhortation of the Holy Father Francis (2016). https://w2.vatican.va/content/vatican/en.html.
ANRW	*Aufstieg und Niedergang der römischen Welt*
AP	*Aeterni Patris: Encyclical of Pope Leo XIII on the Restoration of Christian Philosophy* (1879). https://w2.vatican.va/content/vatican/en.html.
AS	*Acta Synodalia Sacrosancti Concilii Oecumenici Vaticani II.* 6 vols. Vatican City: Typis polyglottis Vaticanis, 1970–78.
BK	Bibel und Kirche
CBQ	*Catholic Biblical Quarterly*
CCC	*Catechism of the Catholic Church.* https://w2.vatican.va/content/vatican/en.html.
CCSL	Corpus Christianorum Series Latina
CD	Barth, Karl. *Church Dogmatics.* 4 vols. Edited by G. W. Bromiley and T. F. Torrance. Translated by G. W. Bromiley. Edinburgh: T&T Clark, 1932–88.

Chr mag   Bonaventure. *Christus unus omnium magister.*
In *Bonaventurae Opera Omnia,* 567–73. Vol. 5 of
Opuscula Varia Theologica. Quaracchi: Collegii S.
Bonaventurae, 1891.

CIC   *Code of Canon Law.*
http://www.vatican.va/archive/cod-iuris-
canonici/cic_index_en.html.

Coll.   Cassian, John. *The Conferences.* Translated and
annotated by Boniface Ramsey, OP. Ancient
Christian Writers 57. New York: Paulist, 1997.

DAS   *Divino afflante Spiritu: Encyclical of Pope Pius
XII on Promoting Biblical Studies* (1943). https://
w2.vatican.va/content/vatican/en.html.

De Principiis   *Origen: On First Principles.* 2 vols. Edited and
translated by John Behr. Oxford Early Christian
Texts. Oxford: Oxford University Press, 2017.

DF   First Vatican Council. *Dei Filius* (24 April
1870). In *Trent to Vatican II,* edited by Giuseppe
Alberigo, translated by Norman Tanner, SJ,
804–11. Vol. 2 of *The Decrees of the Ecumenical
Councils.* New York: Sheed & Ward and
Georgetown University Press, 1990.

DH   Peter Hünermann, Helmut Hoping, Robert L.
Fastiggi, Anne Englund Nash, and Heinrich
Denzinger. *Compendium of Creeds, Definitions,
and Declarations on Matters of Faith and Morals.*
San Francisco: Ignatius, 2012.

DV   *Dei Verbum: Dogmatic Constitution on Divine
Revelation* (1965).
https://w2.vatican.va/content/vatican/en.html.

EKKNT   Evangelisch-Katholischer Kommentar zum
Neuen Testament

GCS   Die griechischen christlichen Schriftsteller der
ersten Jahrhunderte

Gn. litt.   Augustine. *The Literal Meaning of Genesis.* 2 vols.
Translated by John Hammond Taylor. New York:
Newman, 1982.

| GNT | Grundrisse zum Neuen Testament |
| Greg | Gregorianum |

| HeyJ | Heythrop Journal |
| *HThKZVK* | *Herders Theologischer Kommentar zum Zweiten Vatikanischen Konzil* |

| ICC | International Critical Commentary |
| *IVSS* | *Inspirazione e verità della Sacra Scrittura*: Document of the Pontifical Biblical Commission (2014). https://w2.vatican.va/content/vatican/en.html. English translation: *The Inspiration and Truth of Sacred Scripture: The Word that Comes from God and Speaks of God for the Salvation of the World*. Translated by Thomas Esposito, OCist, and Stephen Gregg, OCist. Collegeville, MN: Liturgical, 2014. |

JES	Journal of Ecumenical Studies
JJT	Josephinum Journal of Theology
JN 1	Ratzinger, Joseph. *From the Baptism in the Jordan to the Transfiguration*. Translated by Adrian Walker. Vol. 1 of *Jesus of Nazareth*. San Francisco: Ignatius, 2007.
JN 2	———. *From the Entrance into Jerusalem to the Resurrection*. Vol. 2 of *Jesus of Nazareth*. San Francisco: Ignatius, 2011.
JN 3	———. *The Infancy Narratives*. Vol. 3 of *Jesus of Nazareth*. New York: Image Books, 2012.
JRGS 1	*Volk und Haus Gottes in Augustins Lehre von der Kirche: Die Dissertation und weitere Studien zu Augustinus und zur Theologie der Kirchenväter*. Edited by Gerhard Ludwig Müller. Joseph Ratzinger Gesammelte Schriften 1. Freiburg: Herder, 2011.

JRGS 2   *Offenbarungsverständnis und Geschichtstheologie*
            Bonaventuras: Habilitationschrift und
            Bonaventura-Studien. Edited by Gerhard Ludwig
            Müller. Joseph Ratzinger Gesammelte Schriften 2.
            Freiburg: Herder, 2008.

JRGS 4   *Einführung in das Christentum: Bekenntnis—*
            Taufe—Nachfolge. Edited by Gerhard Müller
            and Rudolf Voderholzer. Joseph Ratzinger
            Gesammelte Schriften 4. Freiburg: Herder, 2014.

JRGS 7/1   *Zur Lehre des Zweiten Vatikanischen Konzils:*
            Formulierung—Vermittlung—Deutung. Edited by
            Gerhard Müller. Joseph Ratzinger Gesammelte
            Schriften 7 no. 1. Freiburg: Herder, 2012.

JRGS 9/2   *Glaube in Schrift und Tradition: Zur*
            Theologischen Prinzipienlehre. Edited by Gerhard
            Müller. Joseph Ratzinger Gesammelte Schriften 9
            no. 2. Freiburg: Herder, 2016.

LThK³   *Lexikon für Theologie und Kirche.* Edited by
            Walter Kasper. 3rd ed. 11 vols. Freiburg: Herder,
            1993-2001.

Mansi   *Sacrorum Conciliorum nova et amplissima*
            collectio. 53 vols. Edited by L. Petit and J. B.
            Martin. Arnhem-Leipzig: Hubert Welter, 1901–27.

MIPB   *Mitteilungen.* Institut Papst Benedikt XVI.
MMIPB   Monographische Beiträge zu den Mitteilungen.
            Institut Papst Benedikt XVI.

NBf   New Blackfriars
NTAbh   Neutestamentliche Abhandlungen
NTS   New Testament Studies

Pascendi   *Pascendi dominici gregis: Encyclical Letter of Pope*
            Pius X on the Doctrines of the Modernists (1907).
            https://w2.vatican.va/content/vatican/en.html.
PD   *Providentissimus Deus: Encyclical of Pope Leo*
            XIII on the Study of Holy Scripture (1893). https://
            w2.vatican.va/content/vatican/en.html.

QD   Quaestiones Disputatae

RET   Revista española de teología
RHR   Revue de l'histoire des religions
RTL   Revue théologique de Louvain

SA   *Sacrorum Antistitum: Pii Pp. X motu proprio*
                quo quaedam statuuntur leges ad modernismi
                periculum propulsandum (1910). https://
                w2.vatican.va/content/vatican/en.html.
SBAB   Stuttgarter Biblische Aufsatzbände
SBS   Stuttgarter Bibelstudien
SC   Sources Chrétiennes
ScTh   Scripta Theologica
Sent.   Bonaventure, *Commentaria in Quatuor Libros*
                Sententiarum Petri Lombardi. Vols. 1–4 in
                Bonvaenturae Opera Omnia. Quaracchi: Collegii
                S. Bonaventurae, 1882–89.
SME   *Santa mater ecclesia: Instruction of the Pontifical*
                Biblical Commission on the Historical Truth of
                the Gospels (1964). Latin text: https://w2.vatican.
                va/content/vatican/en.html. English translation
                with commentary: Fitzmyer, Joseph A., SJ.
                "The Biblical Commission's Instruction on the
                Historical Truth of the Gospels." *Theological*
                Studies 25 (1964): 402–8.
SNTSU   *Studien zum Neuen Testament und seiner Umwelt*
SP   *Spiritus Paraclitus: Encyclical of Benedict XV on*
                St. Jerome (1920). https://w2.vatican.va/content/
                vatican/en.html
ST   Thomas Aquinas. *Summa Theologiae*
                ("Blackfriars" ed.). 61 vols. Various translators.
                London and New York: Eyre and Spottiswoode
                and McGraw-Hill, 1963–80.
StZ   *Stimmen der Zeit*
Super Ioannem Thomas Aquinas. *Super Evangelium S. Ioannis*
                lectura.
                https://www.corpusthomisticum.org/iopera.html

Super Psalmos	Thomas Aquinas. *In psalmos Davidis expositio* (Parma, 1863). https://www.corpusthomisticum. org/cps00.html. Partial English translation: *Thomas Aquinas: The Gifts of the Spirit.* Edited and introduced by Benedict M. Ashley, OP. Translated by Matthew Rzeczkowski, OP. New York: New City, 1995.
Super Sent.	Thomas Aquinas. *Scriptum super Sententiis.* https://www.corpusthomisticum.org/iopera. html.
ThTo	Theology Today
TQ	Theologische Quartalschrift
TRev	Theologische Revue
TS	Theological Studies
VC	Vigiliae Christianae
VD	*Verbum Domini: Post-Synodal Apostolic Exhortation of Benedict XVI on the Word of God in the Life and Mission of the Church* (2010). https://w2.vatican.va/content/vatican/en.html.

THE INSPIRATION AND TRUTH OF SCRIPTURE

Setting the Scene

M y purpose in writing this book has been to treat in a more sophisticated way questions that it nowadays seems unsophisticated to
pose. What does it mean to say that the Bible is the word *of* God,
not just words *about* God? Just how true is the Bible? To what extent can the
Word of God be expected to transcend the cultural level of its day? Most
reflective Christians are aware that Scripture contains ideas deficient from
the point of view of modern thought: for example, primitive astronomical
models, lax historical conventions, and incomplete views of social relations
(e.g., man-woman,[1] slave-master). Raised in an era of historical consciousness, many Christians reflexively identify such ideas as products of a less
enlightened age and ignore them without much fuss. But this reading strategy, once ingrained, makes it natural to assume the Bible deficient in every
matter where it collides with modern sensibilities. Accepting the biblical
vision of reality thus comes to seem an all-or-nothing prospect. One may
adhere blindly to what the Bible contains, to the point of accepting, as did
the Victorian father of marine biology Philip Gosse, that God planted fossils
to test our faith in hexameral creation.[2] Or one may accept a unidirectional
criticism of Scripture from the perspective of a modern worldview to the
point of abandoning Scripture as a revealed norm for thinking and acting.
Joseph Ratzinger (1927–2022), later Benedict XVI,[3] dedicated considerable

---

1 The Pontifical Biblical Commission's *Inspiration and Truth of Sacred Scripture* identifies
the biblical theology of woman as socially conditioned (*IVSS*, no. 132). Few would deny
this altogether. The real question is, How much?

2 Philip H. Gosse, *Omphalos: An Attempt to Untie the Geological Knot* (London: John Van
Voorst, 1857).

3 For the most part, this book refers to its subject as Joseph Ratzinger because it draws from
his works as private theologian rather than from official teaching documents. However, this

energies to escaping the horns of this dilemma. This book will argue, in fact, that he brought more than a century of Catholic reflection on the inspiration, truth, and normative interpretation of Scripture to a new and stable configuration.

The era of reflection that Ratzinger crowns is a complex one. It begins arguably with a shift of "adversaries." In the first half of the nineteenth century, Catholic theologians were principally concerned to demonstrate Scripture's lack of diaphanous "perspicuity," thereby vindicating the Catholic principle of Scripture-plus-tradition against the rival Protestant principle of *sola Scriptura*, or "Scripture alone." This preoccupation manifests itself in the emphasis, shared by theologians as diverse as the Jesuit Giovanni Perrone (1794–1876) and Tübingen divine J. A. Möhler (1796–1838), on tradition as the indispensable norm of biblical interpretation.[4] Starting in the latter half of the nineteenth century, however, the intellectual front shifts palpably. Faced with geological and archeological findings difficult to square with biblical cosmology and history, Catholic theologians began to insist not so much on the text's opacity as on its veracity, and that despite all appearances. Perrone's student, for instance, the Jesuit Cardinal Johann Baptist Franzelin (1816–1886), would feel obliged to develop the notion of biblical inerrancy at much greater length than his teacher, taking care to exclude all error at least "in those things that pertain to the principal objective [*scopum*] of the book."[5] In this new phase of reflection, reconciling divine authorship of Scripture with the contemporary state of human knowledge would become the overriding concern.

This is nowhere more evident than in the reflections of the English Catholic convert John Henry Newman (1801–1890), whose efforts in this regard foreshadow Ratzinger's own. In his later years, Newman found himself facing the same scholarly paradigms that still dominate our social imaginary. His

---

does not exclude personal commentaries on such documents, such as those prefacing statements of the Congregation for the Doctrine of the Faith and personal works dating from his papacy, such as the *Jesus of Nazareth* trilogy.

4 See Johann Adam Möhler, *Unity in the Church or The Principle of Catholicism: Presented in the Spirit of the Church Fathers of the First Three Centuries*, ed. and trans. Peter C. Erb (Washington, DC: The Catholic University of America Press, 1996), 96–98; Giovanni Perrone, *Continens tractatus de locis teologicis partes secundam et tertiam*, vol. II, no. 2, of *Praelectiones theologicae* (Rome: Typis Collegii Urbani, 1842), 105–54.

5 Johann-Baptist Franzelin, *De Divina Traditione et Scriptura* (Rome: S. C. Propagandae Fidei, 1896), 304. My translation.

friend Edward Pusey (1800–1882) had studied theology and oriental languages at the University of Göttingen, bringing back with him the so-called higher criticism.[6] In 1859, Darwin's *Origin of the Species* proposed an account of human origins seemingly incompatible with the creation narrative of Genesis. Sensing a growing disquiet among educated Catholics, Newman confessed in private writings dating from the early 1860s that he desired to do his part in "destroying the feverishness and nervousness which is abroad, the vague apprehensions of some coming discoveries hostile to faith, that spontaneous unwelcome rising of questionings and perplexities in the secret heart, which cut at the root of devotion and dry up the founts of love, homage, loyalty, admiration, joy, peace and all the other best and noblest attributes of religion."[7] Newman wanted to narrow the field of potential conflict between faith and reason, in short, without diminishing Scripture's authority, or the basic credibility on which its transformative power depends.

Already in these unpublished papers, Newman saw the need for a theory of inspiration that would change the unit of analysis from the individual oracle, narrative, or even book to that of the whole of Scripture. "Though a portion of [Scripture] is in its first instance *or* origin the word of man, as the speeches introduced into the historical and other portions, yet He has, as it were, spoken the whole of it over again and made it His, even in those human parts, by the new sense *or* drift which he has put into them. This is the inspired sense."[8] If God puts into the Scriptures an overarching "drift," Newman reasons, then this divine intention would relativize all regional intentions as a criterion for identifying Scripture's revealed content. Though Newman saw already in the early 1860s the need for a theory of inspiration that would account for such a unifying "drift," he kept his ideas to himself, deeming them still unripe for publication in a rather defensive ecclesial climate.

The mounting tension between faith and reason, however, would eventually move Newman to publish. In the early 1880s, Ernest Renan caused

6 Stephen Thomas, *Newman and Heresy: The Anglican Years* (Cambridge: Cambridge University Press, 1991), 42.

7 See Newman's posthumously published reflections, "Essay on the Inspiration of Scripture (1861–1863)," in *Newman's Doctrine on Holy Scripture: According to His Published Works and Previously Unpublished Manuscripts*, ed. Jaak Seynaeve (Louvain: Publications Universitaires de Louvain, 1953), 70*.

8 Newman, "Essay on the Inspiration of Scripture," 129*.

an international sensation by renouncing his faith on the grounds that the "Roman Catholic Church admits no compromise on questions of Biblical criticism and history."[9] Newman responded by revisiting his earlier thoughts, now emphasizing the purpose of inspiration. He noted how Catholic theologians had long ago restricted the infallibility of dogmatic statements to matters of faith and morals and, even then, to targeted ethical or doctrinal affirmations.[10] He suggested the same thing might be said of Scripture, provided one accounts for the unique interwovenness of biblical faith and historical fact: "Scripture is inspired, not only in faith and morals, but in all its parts which bear on faith, including matters of fact."[11] Such a teleological view of inspiration and narrative, however, implied the "possible presence of *obiter dicta* in inspired Scripture."[12] If Scripture has a main point, Newman reasoned, then it may also contain ideas that are beside the point, or ideas that enjoy divine guarantee only so far as they bear upon the point. New scholarly discoveries, he predicted, would never contradict anything truly to the point in Scripture.

Though warmly welcomed by a few, Newman's insights remained largely unreceived for several reasons. For one thing, they lacked systematic integration. Newman never really provided what one might call a causal analysis of inspiration. Though he intuited that a satisfactory theory of inspiration would explain how God had spoken the sayings of individual authors "over again," imbuing them with a new sense, he never provided a theoretical account of how God communicates his own sense through human intermediaries. More decisively, his proposal was widely thought to have fallen under papal censure. Not long after Newman's death, Leo XIII's encyclical *Providentissimus Deus* (1893) put on notice those who "concede that divine inspiration regards the things of faith and morals, and nothing beyond."[13] Though Leo probably did not have Newman in mind, and though Newman expressly denied the "nothing beyond," the English cardinal nevertheless

---

9 Newman, "Inspiration in Its Relation to Revelation," in *On the Inspiration of Scripture: John Henry Newman*, ed. Derek Holmes and Robert Murray (Washington, DC: Corpus Books, 1967), 102.

10 Newman, "Further Illustrations," in Holmes and Murray, *On the Inspiration of Scripture*, 133.

11 Newman, "Further Illustrations," 140.

12 Newman, "Further Illustrations," 141.

13 *PD*, no. 20.

showed up regularly in early twentieth-century theology manuals among the ranks of "adversaries."[14] Theologians would shy away from any solutions along Newman's lines for decades—that is, until Joseph Ratzinger proposed a reprised model. We will return to this point later.

In the meantime, we do well to observe a second inflection point, one falling between Newman and Ratzinger. Throughout the early part of the twentieth century, the question of reconciling inspiration with scientific and historical reason continued to dominate the horizon of biblical theology, generating, as we will see in the first chapter, several philosophically sophisticated models of biblical inspiration and inerrancy. But by the dawn of the post–Vatican II era, the question ceased, by and large, to interest professional exegetes. The roots of this change are deep and complex, but a couple lie nearer to the surface. Perhaps most obviously, the Catholic magisterium gradually relaxed its surveillance of biblical interpretation over the course of the twentieth century. With Pius XII's *Divino afflante Spiritu* (1943), the Church cautiously endorsed the value of historical-critical study, giving additional impetus to an already burgeoning Biblical Movement. After Vatican II the Catholic magisterium largely left off policing exegetical opinion. Pope Paul VI's motu proprio *Sedula cura* (1971) institutionalized this change by decommissioning the Pontifical Biblical Commission as an official magisterial organ, reconstituting it instead as a consultative body of biblical experts linked to the Congregation (now Dicastery) for the Doctrine of the Faith. This signaled the dawn of an era of disciplinary autonomy for exegetes, making the questions of biblical inspiration and truth less professionally relevant and existentially urgent.

But this arrangement did not so much resolve the question of inspiration as defer it. In exchange for autonomy, historical-critical exegesis agreed to limit itself to the task of historical description, thus tacitly surrendering its claim to direct relevance for theology. The American exegete Raymond Brown created waves not long after the Council, for instance, by arguing

---

14 See Robert Murray and Derek Holmes, introduction to Newman, *On the Inspiration of Scripture*, 85–86. The French exegetes François Lenormant and Maurice d'Hulst have been suggested as more likely targets. See H. J. T. Johnson, "Leo XIII, Cardinal Newman and the Inerrancy of Scripture," *Downside Review* 69 (1951), 411–12. Though Jared Wicks perhaps correctly lists Newman's exploratory essays from the 1860s as bearers of "rejected concepts" (*concetti rispinti*), it seems unlikely that *Providentissimus Deus* had these still unpublished manuscripts in mind. Jared Wicks, SJ, *La Divina Rivelazione e la sua trasmissione,* 3rd ed. (Rome: Editrice Pontificia Università Gregoriana, 2008), 152–153.

that the Bible gives us little historical warrant for thinking that only priests and bishops presided over early eucharistic celebrations. But he hastened to add that the Church may validly define the conditions for the valid celebration of the Mass "no matter who celebrated the Eucharist in NT times."[15] Even more striking than the ecclesiastical positivism is the division of labor implied therein. For Brown, the exegete's job is no longer to generate normative conclusions. It is rather to inform theologians concerned with normative questions just how clearly the historical record, critically sifted, attests a given belief or practice.

A generation later John P. Meier would arguably scale the normative ambitions of academic exegesis back even further. The methodological preface to the first volume of *A Marginal Jew* distinguishes sharply between the search for the "historical" Jesus and the search for the "real" Jesus. According to Meier, scholars applying the canons of critical historiography cannot claim to reconstruct even the "real" Julius Caesar, let alone the "real" Jesus. After all, the contemporaries of each figure would have known so much more about them than any historian could reliably reconstruct.[16] A critical biography of Jesus thus offers not a behind-the-scenes exposé but, at most, the artifact of an abstractive procedure. Meier cannot himself seem to decide how this resultant artifact stands vis-à-vis the "real Jesus." Does it relate like an X-ray image to a patient—incomplete, but accurate in what it recovers? Or does it relate more like the image in a funhouse mirror to passers-by—not only incomplete, but disfiguring as it captures? Meier hedges with language suggestive of both possibilities, admitting that the application of historical criticism to Jesus will "produce a narrow focus, a fragmentary vision, perhaps even distortions."[17] It is worth noting how frankly Meier admits the uncertain bearing that historical-Jesus research has not only on Christian doctrine but on historical reality itself.

Yet only someone aiming to pronounce on reality would need to engage the traditional doctrines of biblical inspiration and inerrancy. After Vatican II, in short, considerations of biblical inspiration and inerrancy became

15 Raymond Brown, "Difficulties in Using the New Testament in American Catholic Discussions," *Louvain Studies* 2 (1976), 154.

16 For a clear articulation of the distinction between "real" and "historical," see John Meier, *The Roots of the Problem and the Person*, vol. 1 of *A Marginal Jew: Rethinking the Historical Jesus* (New York: Doubleday, 1991), 21–40.

17 Meier, *Marginal Jew*, 1:2

methodologically irrelevant precisely to those who might most be expected to take a professional interest in them—namely, biblical scholars. Expelled from the precincts of exegesis, the topics of inspiration and truth suffered a period of relative neglect.[18]

Even at the height (or depth) of the post-inspirational era, however, Joseph Ratzinger, the subject of this book, continued to call loudly for their retrieval. Under his leadership, the Congregation for the Doctrine of Faith took the occasion of the publication of *Ad tuendam fidem* (1998), John Paul II's *motu proprio* on the profession of faith, to rank the "absence of error in the inspired sacred scriptures" (*absentia erroris in scriptis sacris inspiratis*) among the Church's most authoritative doctrines—that is, among the truths divinely revealed, whose denial qualifies as material heresy.[19] Soon after assuming papal office in 2005, Ratzinger dedicated the 2008 Synod of Bishops to "The Word of God in the Life and Mission of the Church." Because the synodal dialogue revealed that the concepts of biblical inspiration and truth remained both vital and contested, the assembled bishops recommended them for further study by the Congregation for the Doctrine of the Faith.[20] Ratzinger amplified this *desideratum* in the post-synodal apostolic exhortation *Verbum Domini* (2010), calling upon theologians to reclaim "inspiration and truth as two key concepts for an ecclesial hermeneutic of the sacred Scriptures."[21] He went so far as to assign the topic to the Pontifical Biblical Commission.

But the Commission's response arguably only underscored the disciplinary divisions that their labors were meant to bridge. One of its members recalls the collective anxiety the Commission felt upon receiving the papal mission to prepare a document on biblical inspiration and truth: "There was an audible murmur in the meeting room: 'We are exegetes; we know little about this; this is a theological topic.'"[22] Feeling out of its depth theologically,

---

18 To my knowledge, there are no book-length treatments of inspiration by Catholic exegetes for decades after. See Bruce Vawter, *Biblical Inspiration* (Philadelphia: Westminster, 1972).

19 Congregation for the Doctrine of the Faith, "Nota Doctrinalis *Professionis Fidei* Formulam Extremam Enucleans," *AAS* 90 (1998), 549.

20 Pablo T. Gadenz, "Magisterial Teaching on the Inspiration and Truth of Scripture: Precedents and Prospects," *Letter & Spirit* 6 (2010), 67, 79.

21 *VD*, no. 19.

22 Denis Farkasfalvy, *A Theology of the Christian Bible: Revelation, Inspiration, Canon* (Washington, DC: The Catholic University of America Press, 2018), 98.

the Commission opted simply to parcel out the biblical canon among its members, leaving all to comb their allotted books for any "self-attestation" (*auto-testimonianza*) of divine origin.[23] The resulting document, *The Inspiration and Truth of Sacred Scripture*, consists mostly of a catalogue of such internal testimonies. The Catholic Church's recent efforts to make Scripture living and effective for Christians have thus revealed two things. First, those charged with pastoral renewal of the Church see a need for a normative hermeneutic that goes beyond historical description. Second, those most familiar with the biblical text are often those least comfortable with such a normative hermeneutic.

This book addresses this disjunction by showing what has often gone unnoticed—namely, that Ratzinger himself laid a groundwork for a comprehensive theory of biblical inspiration and truth. Ratzinger's intensive study of Bonaventure, which has been published in its entirety only relatively recently, provided him with the seminal intuitions on revelation that he would gradually elaborate into a theory of inspiration. And though Ratzinger's insights lie scattered throughout his extensive writings, when assembled they reveal a consistent theology of Scripture, one that addresses the kind of questions that used to be handled in the traditional neo-scholastic tract *De sacrae scripturae inspiratione*. As we shall see by the book's end, Ratzinger's theological instincts are in many ways similar to Newman's. He too shows himself sensitive to the difficulties that scientific and historical reason pose to an uncomplicated trust in Scripture, acknowledging the corresponding need to follow its overall "drift." But he also provides a systematic integration lacking in Newman. Ratzinger builds on Bonaventure, adding the insights of twentieth-century theologies of biblical inspiration, tracking the later findings of biblical exegesis, and bringing all this into conversation with subsequent statements of the Catholic magisterium. Ratzinger proposes, in short, a new synthesis.

Though this book will certainly explore this synthesis, it aims at more than exposition. It also argues that Ratzinger's theology of Scripture is more "serviceable" than others on offer. "Serviceability" implies, of course, a certain degree of success. And success implies standards of evaluation. Given the nature of Ratzinger's own project, I consider the key standards of evaluation to be the following: the standard of faith, represented especially by *Dei Verbum*, Vatican II's Dogmatic Constitution on Divine Revelation; the

---

23 Farkasfalvy, *Theology of the Christian Bible*, 99.

standard of reason, represented especially by the deliverances of historical-critical exegesis; and the comparative standard of alternative theologies of inspiration. I consider the following to be the most influential theologians of inspiration active after *Providentissimus Deus*: the French Dominican Pierre Benoit (1906–87), the German Jesuit Karl Rahner (1904–84), and the American diocesan priest David Tracy (1939–). Ratzinger's approach can be considered more "serviceable" because it responds better to the exigencies of faith and reason than others on offer.

The grand narrative of the book reflects the nature of its argument. The first chapter will begin not with Ratzinger but with the principal alternative models of biblical inspiration and truth: Benoit's Thomist-instrumental model, Rahner's Molinist-predefinitive model, and Tracy's Heideggerian-disclosive model. The list of interlocutors perhaps calls for some explanation. The ecumenically minded will notice immediately that I have put Ratzinger in conversation with fellow Catholics rather than with Protestant theologians. This option for an intramural Catholic conversation has its ground not in indifference to the cause of ecumenism but in the option for *Dei Verbum* as an evaluative standard, which applies much more naturally to Catholic theology.

If non-Catholics do me the honor of reading the first chapter, however, they will find that the Catholic authors surveyed do not lack analogues in Protestant theology. Benoit's model would doubtlessly receive a warm welcome among American evangelicals and Reformed theologians, whose commitment to the "infallibility" of Scripture found classic form in the writings of A. A. Hodge and B. B. Warfield.[24] Even those who continue to defend the central role of authorial intention will perhaps find appealing his Thomistic version of this common-sense approach.[25] Tracy's understanding of Scripture as a religious "classic" resonates in many ways with the disclosive models of biblical revelation proposed by the American H. R. Niebuhr[26] and the

---

24 See A. A. Hodge and B. B. Warfield, "Inspiration," *Presbyterian Review* (1881): 225–60; Paul Helm, "B. B. Warfield's Path to Inerrancy: An Attempt to Correct Some Serious Misunderstandings," *Westminster Theological Journal* 72 (2010), 38.

25 See, for instance, Francis Watson's chapter, "Literal Sense, Authorial Intention, and Objective Truth: In Defense of Some Unfashionable Concepts," in *Text and Truth: Redefining Biblical Theology* (Grand Rapids, MI: Eerdmans, 1997), 95–124.

26 See Niebuhr's conclusion that "revelation means divine self-disclosure rather than communication of truths about God." *The Meaning of Revelation*, 2nd ed., Library of Theological Ethics (Louisville, KY: Westminster John Knox, 2006), 95.

French Reformed philosopher Paul Ricoeur,[27] whose reflections on the non-propositional veracity of narrative continue to influence a different segment of Protestant interpreters.[28] Rahner's approach, because of its heavy reliance on the consciousness of the Church, finds fewer counterparts in Protestant theologies of inspiration. For some, however, it will recall Schleiermacher's insistence on a God consciousness imparted through a "divinely-effected corporate life,"[29] or, more recently, the Lutheran Peter Stuhlmacher's call for an "ecclesial hermeneutic of the Bible."[30] At all events, his neo-Molinist model of divine-human cooperation finds its staunchest English-language champions now among evangelical philosophers of religion.[31] Non-Catholic Christians reading this scene-setting chapter are likely to find their view of the normativity of Scripture approximated by one of the Catholic models consulted.

Catholics may have their own questions about the figures excluded. Where is the French Jesuit Henri de Lubac, the great reviver of the fourfold sense of Scripture? Or, from a different angle, where are the eminent American priest-exegetes such as Raymond E. Brown, Joseph Fitzmyer, and John P. Meier, all of whom saw their scholarship as a service to the Church? And

27 In an illuminating analogy, Ricoeur compares the power of Scripture to the power of an abstract painting: "It depicts no object in the real world, but it generates an emotional model which reshapes our whole world view." Paul Ricoeur, *Essays on Biblical Interpretation*, ed. Lewis Mudge (Philadelphia: Fortress, 1980), 45. For more reflections on this theme, see my "Ricoeur and Ratzinger on Biblical History and Hermeneutics," *Journal of Theological Interpretation* 8, no. 2 (2014), 42–44.

28 Although not uncritical toward Ricoeur, Kevin Vanhoozer and Daniel Treier likewise focus on narrative's power to "reconfigure" self and community, making it the foundation for a "narrative continuity" in Christianity without "conceptual sameness." See their *Theology and the Mirror of Scripture: A Mere Evangelical Account* (Downers Grove, IL: IVP Academic, 2015), 95–96, 188.

29 Friedrich Schleiermacher, *The Christian Faith*, ed. H. R. Mackintosh and J. S. Stewart (Philadelphia: Fortress, 1976), 358.

30 Peter Stuhlmacher, *Biblische Theologie des Neuen Testaments*, 2 vols. (Göttingen: Vandenhoeck & Ruprecht, 1992–99), 2:329. For a brief treatment of Stuhlmacher's ecclesial hermeneutic, see also Eckart D. Schmidt, *". . . das Wort Gottes immer mehr zu lieben:" Joseph Ratzingers Bibelhermeneutik im Kontext der Exegesegeschichte der römischkatholischen Kirche*, SBS 233 (Stuttgart: Katholisches Bibelwerk, 2015), 166. Jesuit Luther expert Jared Wicks has pointed out that Luther's *De servo arbitrio* (1925) speaks of Scripture's "two-fold clarity": God's interior word to conscience and the church's external judgment. "Biblical Criticism Criticized," *Gregorianum* 72, no. 1 (1991), 122.

31 See, for instance, Alvin Plantinga's "Free Will Defense" of God's existence, despite the persistence of evil, in *The Nature of Necessity* (Oxford: Clarendon, 1974), 165–95.

where are the more recent Catholic theologies of inspiration? Here I will add just a couple of words about my criteria for selection. First, to avoid comparing apples and oranges, I chose theologians who offer a theory of biblical inspiration developed in philosophical categories. None of the figures just mentioned is so comprehensive.[32] Second, we will meet them all anyway, whenever their more occasional thoughts on inspiration or truth intersect instructively with Ratzinger's proposal. Finally, I have attempted to assemble a representative rather than an exhaustive list of thinkers. The approaches of Benoit, Rahner, and Tracy typify the interpretive styles still prevalent today.[33]

The second chapter will treat what I call Ratzinger's Bonaventurian-ecclesial model of biblical inspiration. Taking as its point of departure Ratzinger's *Habilitationsschrift* on St. Bonaventure, the second chapter will show how Ratzinger creatively extends the Seraphic Doctor's thinking on inspiration, repackaging it as a principally—albeit not exclusively—communal charism. By means of this Bonaventurian retrieval, Ratzinger arguably brings the individual strengths of Benoit, Rahner, and Tracy into a new combination. Despite its many advantages, Ratzinger's theory of social inspiration is not beyond criticism. I will also entertain objections, defending him against some charges while elsewhere indicating lacunae in his account.

The third chapter will show how Ratzinger understands the implications of his model of the Word of God for the question of biblical truth, in both its privative and its positive aspects. Ratzinger continues to defend Scripture's truth in the sense of immunity from error, albeit in a more qualified sense than his neo-scholastic forebears. This he does by transferring the intention governing Scripture's inspired meaning from the level of the individual

---

32 Brown comes closest, but even those who admire him admit that, as far as hermeneutical theory goes, he went lightly clad. See Donald Senior, CP, *Raymond E. Brown and the Catholic Biblical Renewal* (New York: Paulist, 2018), 63.

33 Joseph Gordon draws heavily on Lonergan and thus shares a common parentage with David Tracy. See Gordon, *Divine Scripture in Human Understanding: A Systematic Theology of the Bible* (Notre Dame, IN: University of Notre Dame Press, 2019). Matthew Levering extends a Thomistic line of thinking, much like Benoit, in *Participatory Biblical Exegesis: A Theology of Biblical Interpretation* (Notre Dame, IN: University of Notre Dame Press, 2008). Philip Moller continues in a recognizably Rahnerian line in "What Should They Be Saying about Biblical Inspiration? A Note on the State of the Question," *Theological Studies* 74 (2013): 605–31. Without surrendering his independence of judgment, Abbot Denis Farkasfalvy came to many of the same conclusions as Ratzinger. See especially his *Inspiration and Interpretation: A Theological Introduction to Sacred Scripture* (Washington, DC: The Catholic University of America Press, 2010).

authors to that of a corporate author, the People of God. Recalling the various stages of this community's historical pilgrimage, Ratzinger develops a series of criteria for discerning just how far Scripture intends to affirm formally the ideas it contains materially. I will illustrate how these criteria operate, presenting Ratzinger's argument that the existence of the Devil, unlike a geocentric cosmos, belongs to Scripture's formal affirmations.

The same corporate model of inspiration also allows Ratzinger to account for the inexhaustible depth of meaning and irreducible multivalence ascribed to the Bible from the beginning of the Christian tradition. Scripture abounds in truth in this positive sense precisely because its corporate author has survived its individual authors and continues to accrue historical experience. Ratzinger's attempt to show how the Marian dogmas can be found "in" Scripture will illustrate this more positive aspect of the biblical truth. In developing a method that limits the truth claims of Scripture in certain respects and expands them in others, I argue, Ratzinger offers a less inadequate account of Scripture's preeminent veracity.

Because the third chapter already contains practical applications of Ratzinger's theory of Scripture to disputed questions of science and doctrine, the last two chapters will turn to nettlesome issues of ethics and historicity. The fourth chapter, taking up a fraught question in theological ethics, will study Ratzinger's evolving assessment of the permanently normative content of Jesus' teaching on divorce. Though Ratzinger gradually comes to see less room for maneuver for divorced Christians, he both forms and revises his judgment with reference to a consistent set of criteria—the same criteria laid out in the third chapter. It is arguably by an increasingly consistent application of these hermeneutical tests that he comes to see the so-called Matthean unchastity clauses (Matt 5:32, 19:9) not as exceptions to Jesus' prohibition of remarriage after divorce but as a "case-type" adumbrating the Catholic canons on annulment. Here, as elsewhere, the bimillennial reception of Jesus' teaching proves the key to identifying its normative content and rescuing it from ambiguities irresolvable by strictly historical methods.

The fifth chapter will bring us to Ratzinger's late-career intervention in the question of Gospel historicity, as represented especially by his *Jesus of Nazareth* trilogy. Framed as a negotiation between faith and historical reason, the chapter will begin by revisiting *Dei Verbum*'s teaching on Gospel historicity and Ratzinger's philosophical critique of historical-critical "worldview." The study will then follow closely how Ratzinger forms his judgment on the historicity of the Last Supper narrative. The focus will be twofold: the chronological discrepancies between Mark and John, and the verbal discrepancies between the Markan-Matthean and Pauline-Lukan traditions. The chapter will then show how Ratzinger applies his hermeneutical "tests" analogously even to historical questions, all the while keeping in mind *Dei Verbum*'s guidelines and correcting for philosophical bias in critical historiography. Unsurprisingly, Ratzinger concludes that the Last Supper goes back in substance to Jesus himself. Perhaps more surprisingly, he maintains this substantial historicity while conceding irreconcilable differences in Johannine and Synoptic chronologies and significant post-Resurrection redaction of Jesus' words and deeds at the Last Supper.

Since the *Jesus of Nazareth* trilogy represents Ratzinger's most sustained engagement with the question of the historicity of Scripture, it is hardly surprising to find that it also drew the most criticism from exegetes. The chapter will therefore conclude by staging a sort of conversation between Ratzinger and his critics. It will concentrate on two recurrent reproaches: that Ratzinger approaches the Gospels in a naively historical way, and that he reads Scripture in an excessively harmonizing way. I conclude that these typical objections to Ratzinger's exegetical style reflect standards of evaluation that are themselves never critically examined. This explains in part why Ratzinger still refuses to equate exegetical consensus with the standard of reason as such. His attitude recalls that of the great Dominican theologian, Yves Congar: "Je respecte et j'interroge sans cesse la science des exégètes, mais je récuse leur magistère."[34]

In the final analysis, of course, the argument in these chapters aims only at what David Tracy, in a suggestive phrase, calls the "relatively adequate."[35] This is true, first of all, of the scope of the book itself. It does not say everything relevant to the topic of Ratzinger on inspiration and truth. Book-length treatments exist of topics that will here receive only passing attention: his notion of truth;[36] his understanding of individual biblical themes, such as

---

34 Y. M. Congar, *Vraie et fausse réforme dans l'Église* (Paris: Cerf, 1950), 498–99. "I respect and investigate ceaselessly the science of the exegetes, but I refuse their magisterium."

35 *The Analogical Imagination: Christian Theology in a Culture of Pluralism* (New York: Crossroad, 1981), 249.

36 Dorothee Kaes, *Theologie im Anspruch von Geschichte und Wahrheit: Zur Hermeneutik Joseph Ratzingers* (St. Ottilien: EOS Verlag, 1997); Justinus Pech, *Paradox und Wahrheit: Henri de Lubac und Joseph Ratzinger im gnadentheologischen Gespräch*, Frankfurter Theologische Studien 77 (Münster: Aschendorff, 2020).

covenant history[37] or the role of women;[38] and his engagement with the more skeptical segments of historical criticism.[39] I can think of no book, however, that focuses on Ratzinger's way of discerning between Scripture's culturally conditioned periphery and its normative center, still less one that shows how Ratzinger's readerly assumptions follow consistently from his Bonaventurian metaphysics of Scripture.[40] From this angle, I consider this book more adequate than what has come before.

The same standard of relative adequacy applies to my claims on behalf of Ratzinger's thought. I do not insist that Ratzinger said the last word on the subject. Who can ever claim to exhaust the interpretation of Scripture? But I do propose that he said a seminal word, one that has introduced a new paradigm for the normative interpretation of Scripture. It exhibits an unrealized potential to span the division between historical and theological approaches to Scripture and to restore Scripture's centrality in theology, preaching, and devotion. Helping the seminal word to flower requires both sympathetic and critical engagement. This book is largely sympathetic to Ratzinger, but not entirely uncritical. I hope readers will engage it in the same spirit.

A final word is also in order about the verb tenses applied to Ratzinger's scholarly activity. In between the substantial completion of this book and its publication, Ratzinger passed from this life. Rather than correct all present-tense verbs to past, I decided to leave them as they are, inviting the reader to construe them in the "historical present."

---

37 See Scott Hahn, *Covenant and Communion: The Biblical Theology of Pope Benedict XVI* (Grand Rapids, MI: Brazos, 2009).

38 See Frances McKenna, *Innovation within Tradition: Joseph Ratzinger and Reading the Women of Scripture* (Philadelphia: Fortress, 2015).

39 See Matthew Ramage, *Jesus, Interpreted: Benedict XVI, Bart Ehrman, and the Historical Truth of the Gospels* (Washington, DC: The Catholic University of America Press, 2017).

40 Thomas Rausch dedicates only a chapter to Scripture in his *Pope Benedict XVI: An Introduction to His Theological Vision* (New York: Paulist, 2009). Matthew Ramage offers book-length study of Ratzinger's and Aquinas's hermeneutics of faith and reason, but gives less attention to the distinctively Bonaventurian model of revelation that underlies Ratzinger's interpretive habits in *Dark Passages of the Bible: Engaging Scripture with Benedict XVI and Thomas Aquinas* (Washington, DC: The Catholic University of America Press, 2013).

CHAPTER ONE

The Search for a New Paradigm of Biblical Inspiration and Truth

S howing the merits of Ratzinger's theology of Scripture requires us to begin by examining other Catholic theologies of Scripture influential since the advent of "historical consciousness." Toward that end, this chapter will retrace Catholic theology's search for a new paradigm of biblical inspiration in the era after Pope Leo XIII's *Providentissimus Deus* (1893), the encyclical widely perceived to have proscribed Newman's attempt to identify faith and morals as the inspired "drift" of Scripture. It will focus on the emergence of three salient models of biblical inspiration, along with their corresponding theories of inerrancy. The first, most ably defended by the French Dominican Pierre Benoit and largely assumed into the pre-Vatican II biblical encyclicals, can be broadly characterized as the Thomist-instrumental model. In the late 1950s, the German Jesuit Karl Rahner proposes a second account of inspiration that, for reasons to be shown below, I call the Molinist-predefinitive model. About twenty years later, the American diocesan priest David Tracy develops a third framework, advancing what I call a Heideggerian-disclosive model. Since each typology will receive fuller treatment below, it suffices for now to note that the first word in each hyphenated model designates a school of thought, the second word the way by which God becomes a true "author" of Scripture. This first chapter will survey these influential Catholic positions in the chronological order of their appearance, highlighting significant points of comparison and contrast along the way. All three models surveyed in this first chapter will offer instructive points of comparison with Ratzinger's own Bonaventurian-ecclesial approach to Scripture as revelation, the focus of the second chapter.

BENOIT'S THOMIST-INSTRUMENTAL
MODEL OF INSPIRATION

Because of the great influence it exercised, Pierre Benoit's Thomist-instrumental model of inspiration merits a place in any survey of Catholic theories of inspiration and inerrancy. Its decline from a position of unchallenged ascendancy in the 1940s and 1950s to one of relative obscurity today reflects in many ways the disappearance of the theological culture that had served as its plausibility structure. The encyclicals of Pope Leo XIII (r. 1878–1903) laid the groundwork for two salient features of this theological culture. First, *Aeterni Patris* (1879) made Thomism the norm for Catholic education, and thus increasingly the *lingua franca* of Catholic intellectual life.[1] Later, *Providentissimus Deus* (1893) prohibited Catholic exegetes from admitting any formal error in a divinely inspired document.[2] This set the tone for subsequent magisterial teaching on the subject, most notably for the *Responsa* of the Pontifical Biblical Commission, which forbade Catholic theologians publicly to credit certain exegetical hypotheses that seemed to undermine faith in Scripture's reliability. These touched on questions ranging from Mosaic authorship of the Pentateuch to the historicity of Genesis 1–3 to Paul's belief in an imminent end of history.[3] Such a theological climate favored the widespread acceptance of any theory of biblical inspiration that both preserved Scripture from formal error and pleaded its case in the idiom of Thomist metaphysics and rational psychology. Benoit's Thomist-instrumental model, having achieved just such a synthesis, gained a ready hearing. "By and large," observes James Burtchaell, "the Benoit position rises as the classic theory of the years immediately after *Divino afflante Spiritu*" (1943).[4] Because these years coincide with Ratzinger's theological formation, Benoit's theory remains an obligatory reference point for any study of Ratzinger's theology of Scripture.

---

1 *AP*, no. 31.

2 *PD*, no. 20–22.

3 For English translations of these Responses of the Pontifical Biblical Commission, dating from 1905 to 1933, see Dean P. Béchard, ed. *The Scripture Documents: An Anthology of Official Catholic Teachings*, trans. Dean P. Béchard (Collegeville, MN: Liturgical, 2002), 187–211.

4 James Tunstead Burtchaell, *Catholic Theories of Biblical Inspiration since 1810: A Review and Critique* (Cambridge: Cambridge University Press, 1969), 245.

Extending Thomistic Principles

What exactly was Benoit's theory? Finding in Aquinas no ready-made treatise on biblical inspiration in the modern sense—that is, the process by which God "authors" the biblical text—Benoit had to cobble one together from the analogous Thomistic notions of prophecy and instrumental causality. In Thomas's treatise on prophecy,[5] Benoit found a model for transposing divine truth into human language that required relatively little adjustment to the special case of textual production. Thomas, he observed, defined prophecy as the "knowledge, supernaturally given to man, of truths exceeding the present reach of his mind, which God teaches for the benefit of the community."[6] Biblical authors resembled prophets to the extent that their writing transmitted to a community a knowledge formulated under supernatural influence.

This significant similarity notwithstanding, Benoit had both to narrow and to broaden the notion of prophecy to make it into a serviceable model for inspiration. To distinguish inspiration from revelation more generally, he had to define it more narrowly as a divine impulse to write. At the same time, to ensure that inspiration applied to all the contents of Scripture, he had to broaden its scope to include more than just "truths exceeding the present reach of [the author's] mind." Scripture, unlike prophecy, contains not only mysteries in the strict sense, such as the Trinity, or events unforeseeable by human calculation, such as the coming of the Messiah. It also records historical events accessible to empirical observation and moral imperatives knowable by natural reason. Inspired biblical authors are like prophets in that they form judgments under the influence of supernatural light, but are unlike prophets in that they often form judgments about the meaning of naturally observable happenings and behaviors.[7] An important implication of the naturalness of the objects of the biblical authors' judgment is the fact

---

5 See especially ST II–II, q. 171–78.

6 Pierre Benoit, *Prophecy and Inspiration: A Commentary on the Summa Theologica II–II, Questions 171–178*, trans. Avery Dulles and Thomas L. Sheridan (New York: Desclée, 1961), 61.

7 Benoit notes how Thomas allows for the possibility that a "supernatural light may be given to the prophet simply to make him judge in a divine way about human matters." *Prophecy and Inspiration*, 66. When Aquinas in ST II–II, q. 174, a. 2, ad 3 describes the biblical authors "as writing under the inspiration of the Holy Spirit"—*sicut ex inspiratione Spiritus Sancti scribentes*—Benoit interprets this inspiration to mean "light without [supernatural] representations." *Prophecy and Inspiration*, 71.

that they may work under the influence of inspiration—for example, by selecting the motives and characters for a narrative of dynastic succession—without any awareness of being inspired.[8]

In the treatise on prophecy, Benoit also discovered Aquinas teaching that God not only endows his prophets with supernatural knowledge but employs them as living instruments.[9] Now the category of instrumental causality, as applied to biblical authors, had the potential to be developed in either minimizing or maximizing directions, depending on whether one placed the accent on the writers as *instrumental* efficient causes or as instrumental *efficient causes*. Aquinas himself set the precedent for the former, using the category of instrumental causality to explain why the prophets, being mere instruments, enjoyed only imperfect understanding of their own prophecies.[10] As Aidan Nichols points out, early-modern applications of Thomas's metaphysics of prophecy to biblical inspiration tended to follow suit, likening the biblical authors to unimaginative amanuenses.[11] Benoit, for his part, opted to develop the category of instrumental causality in the other direction, underscoring the hagiographers' title to be considered creative authors in their own right. By accentuating the proper agency of the human instruments, Benoit aimed to give a robust grounding to the traditional theological conviction that both God and human beings "authored" Scripture, each on their own level and in the mode proper to their natures.[12]

Casting God in the role of Scripture's principal author allowed Benoit to explain more easily the unique authority of Scripture, the traditional understanding of which Raymond Brown sums up as follows: "All other works, patristic, Thomistic, and ecclesiastic, are words about God; only the Bible is

---

8 Benoit, *Prophecy and Inspiration*, 72–74.

9 Benoit underscores that Thomas mentions instrumental causality in connection with prophecy only twice: ST II-II, q. 172, a. 4, ad 1; q. 173, a. 4.

10 Thomas Aquinas, ST II-II, q. 173, a. 4.

11 Aidan Nichols, OP, *The Shape of Catholic Theology: An Introduction to its Sources, Principles, and History* (Edinburgh: T&T Clark, 1991), 117–118.

12 Benoit's depiction of the authors as instruments could claim the broad support of the biblical encyclicals. *Providentissimus Deus* calls the hagiographers "inspired instruments" (*PD*, no. 41); *Spiritus Paraclitus* (1920) calls God the "principal cause of all that Scripture means and says" (*SP*, no. 3); and *Divino afflante Spiritu* (1943), without developing this idea along specifically Thomist lines, nevertheless calls each writer a "living and reasonable instrument (ὄργανον) of the Holy Spirit" (*DAS*, no. 19).

the word of God."[13] By limiting the dignity of instrumental cooperation to the biblical authors alone, Benoit's theory explains why only the Bible qualifies as God's word, to which all theological speculations and doctrinal definitions remain subservient.[14] In this respect, Scripture differs qualitatively from both academic theology and ecclesial dogma.

Anticipating the objection that the human writers cannot be at once both genuine authors and "instruments," since the latter implies a certain passivity, Benoit notes that Thomas speaks of instrumental causality in analogous ways. The instrument always contributes to the total effect according to its own proper nature. In the case of free and personal instruments, this means the instruments will contribute according to their own initiative and talent. "In the problem that we are at present considering," writes Benoit, "this implies that the sacred writer retains his own intellectual personality even when under the divine influence."[15] According to Thomas, moreover, when God as principal cause produces an effect, he does not operate on the same metaphysical level as his instruments. One cannot neatly parcel out divine and human contributions to Scripture, therefore, as if God supplied some words but not others, or even as if God instigated the thoughts but not the literary expression.[16] One should rather conceive the effect as if resulting "wholly from each according to their distinct mode, just as the same effect is attributed wholly to the instrument and also wholly to the principal agent."[17] One can thus expect human instruments to write a thoroughly human document, reflecting their own personalities and historical circumstances.

The Thomist-instrumental model, in sum, strikes a balance between the divinity and humanity of Scripture. Because God employed *human*

---

13 Raymond E. Brown, *The Critical Meaning of the Bible: How a Modern Reading of the Bible Challenges Christians, the Church, and the Churches* (New York: Paulist, 1981), 21.

14 *Dei Verbum* teaches the priority of Scripture over even magisterial teaching: "This teaching office is not above the Word of God but serves it by teaching only what has been handed on" (*DV*, no. 10).

15 Benoit, *Prophecy and Inspiration*, 95–96.

16 This latter division of labor is presupposed in the *res-et-sententia* theory of inspiration, to be revisited below in connection with Rahner, which was defended especially by nineteenth-century Jesuits of the Roman College. For a broader treatment, see the chapter on "Content Inspiration" in Burtchaell, *Catholic Theories of Biblical Inspiration since 1810*, 88–120.

17 Thomas Aquinas, *Summa contra gentiles*, III, 70, cited in Benoit, *Prophecy and Inspiration*, 95. My translation.

instruments, Scripture remained fully human. Yet because God employed human *instruments*, Scripture remained fully divine, the only text having God as its "author" in the fullest sense. Benoit's model arguably succeeded in patterning Scripture after the Incarnation.

INTERPRETIVE CONSEQUENCES

Building on this Thomist-instrumental model of inspiration, Benoit could draw out the implications for the thorny question of Scripture's veracity. On the one hand, this model predicts that Scripture, written by free human instruments, will betray its human origins in some respects. On the other, it predicts that Scripture, having God as its principal author, will transcend the limitations of its instrumental authors in other respects, displaying a "fuller sense" and immunity from certain kinds of error and prejudice.[18] We do well to look at both these limitations and privileges a bit more closely.

On the side of limitations, the Thomist-instrumental model supposes that the Holy Spirit inspires noncoercively and conformably to the individual genius of the human authors. It thus encourages exegetes to treat the literary intentions of the human authors as Scripture's primary and "literal sense," the foundation for all biblical interpretation.[19] Just as all human authors express their intentions in the language, institutions, and literary forms of their surrounding culture, so the biblical authors expressed themselves through these media. The fully human authorship of Scripture implies that one can, without irreverence, employ the full array of philological, historical, and literary tools to unearth the intentions of its human authors. The expression of these intentions will be limited by the intellectual style and level of the ancient world.[20]

On the side of privileges, Benoit points to two properties unique to Scripture. First, he argues that God's role as principal cause of Scripture authorizes the biblical interpreter to look for a "fuller sense"—that is, a meaning

---

18 Benoit, *Prophecy and Inspiration*, 98–99.

19 Benoit, *Prophecy and Inspiration*, 147. This again sums up a long magisterial tradition. Pius XII reminds Catholic exegetes that "their foremost and greatest endeavor should be to discern and define clearly that sense of the biblical words that is called 'literal'" (*DAS*, no. 15). Without linking authorial intention directly with the "literal" sense, Vatican II will later reaffirm that "the interpreter of Sacred Scripture ... should carefully search out what the sacred writers truly intended to express and what God thought well to manifest by their words" (*DV*, no. 12).

20 For comparable concessions in the magisterial tradition, see *DAS*, no. 20; *DV*, no. 12.

exceeding (but not contradicting) the "literal sense" consciously intended by the human author. In other words, though God's intention *includes* the human author's intention, the converse does not hold. Whereas the human author of Numbers 21 intended the story of the bronze serpent as an account of miraculous healing, God intended it as a "figure of Christ on the Cross."[21] Benoit admits that ascribing such a fuller sense to God alone stretches the category of instrumental causality as he has developed it.[22] For with the introduction of the fuller sense, the meaning of Scripture is no longer ascribable wholly to God and wholly to his instruments, but partly to God alone (*sensus plenior*) and partly to God with his instruments (*sensus literalis*).[23] These tensions notwithstanding, Benoit gives some account of the bimillennial Christian tradition of reading Scripture typologically or spiritually.[24]

Benoit goes on to note that Scripture's literal sense, besides serving as a foundation for a fuller sense, enjoys a second distinction. Since an omniscient God has employed human authors as prophetic instruments, it follows that the latter will never intend what is in error. Benoit reasons in the following way:

> With such a close and complete compenetration of divine and human causality, it is impossible that the writer express anything whatever contrary to the divine pleasure.... The divine influence will lead the author to teach only the message entrusted to him, and will keep him from giving the same guarantee to his personal views which have not been included in the message. *This, in brief, is what formally constitutes the privilege of inerrancy.*[25]

---

21 Benoit, *Prophecy and Inspiration*, 150–51.

22 Despite stretching the category of instrument in Benoit's sense, the responsibility of the human authors for the *sensus plenior* better approximates Aquinas's normal notions of divine-human instrumentality. The Angelic Doctor typically invokes the category for divine-human synergies whose effects are altogether disproportionate to human agency, such as the confection of sacraments or the working of miracles. See Benoit, *Prophecy and Inspiration*, 77. As J. T. Forestell, CSB, pointed out in the heyday of the Thomist-instrumental model, the effect of inspiration remains, at least in its literary qualities, proportionate to human capacities. "The Limitation of Inerrancy," *CBQ* 20, no. 1 (1958): 11.

23 See Benoit, *Prophecy and Inspiration*, 150n1.

24 The encyclical tradition continued to endorse cautiously this search for the fuller sense. See *PD*, no. 27; *SP*, no. 14; *DAS*, no. 16.

25 Benoit, *Prophecy and Inspiration*, 140–41. On this view, Benoit echoes the magisterium of the first half of the twentieth century. Leo XIII judged that if one attempted to "save" God's veracity by restricting responsibility for the Bible's problematic passages to defects in the human instruments, one could no longer say that God "was the Author of the entire

Whatever the biblical author, communicating in the idiom and literary forms of the ancient world, truly "teaches," this (and only this) does God also teach. And since God cannot err, neither can the biblical authors err in what they teach.

Construing human authors as personal and intelligent instruments of God made the guarantees of inerrancy at once more expansive and more restrictive. On the one hand, this arrangement expanded the guarantees of inerrancy to the whole of Scripture, regardless of the subject matter treated. It implied the accuracy not only of biblical statements regarding faith and morals, but of whatever the biblical authors intended to teach. At least in principle, this included historical, anthropological, and scientific truth.[26] On the other hand, Benoit's model restricted inerrancy by limiting its scope to those biblical ideas, whether religious or profane, that the authors truly taught. One need not give full credit even to all biblical ideas on faith and morals unless the biblical authors properly intended to affirm them.

Since inerrancy extends only as far as the author's intention to teach, exegetes subscribing to Benoit's model remained free to limit the scope of inerrancy by an analysis of authorial intention. They relied upon a sophisticated taxonomy of mental postures, which neo-Thomist rational psychology readily supplied. According to Thomas, one could teach formal error only to the extent that one judged erroneously. And the scope and force of any judgment could be qualified in various ways. The author might consider the matter presented only from a certain point of view—for instance, describing the motion of the heavenly bodies for the purpose of extolling God's wisdom, not for the purpose of illustrating the laws of physics.[27] The author might

---

Scripture." *PD*, no. 41. The Pontifical Biblical Commission, condemning certain interpretations of biblical eschatology in its *Responsa ad proposita dubia de parousia seu de secundo adventu D.N. Iesu Christi in epistolis S. Pauli Apostoli* (June 18, 1915), likewise invoked the "Catholic doctrine regarding the inspiration and inerrancy of Sacred Scripture, whereby everything the sacred writer asserts, expresses, and suggests must be held to be asserted, expressed and suggested by the Holy Spirit." Béchard, *Scripture Documents*, 207.

26 The encyclical tradition condemned no fewer than four times the attempt to restrict biblical inerrancy to matters of faith and morals. Leo XIII forbade theologians to teach that "divine inspiration regards the things of faith and morals and nothing beyond." *PD*, no. 40. For similar teachings, see *Pascendi*, no. 118; *SP*, no. 5; *DAS*, no. 1.

27 Benoit treats the consideration of the "point of view from which [the author] is treating his subject" as the determination of the author's "formal object." *Prophecy and Inspiration*, 137. Without using the technical language of *objectum formale*, the encyclical tradition endorses the qualification in substance. Leo XIII concedes that the sacred writers "did not

perhaps include threatening oracles or report common judgments without affirming them as certain outcomes or categorical truths.[28] The author may even reshape events according to the literary and historiographical conventions of the ancient world, signaling the kind of truth he intends to teach by his choice of literary genres.[29] Whereas inspiration remains coextensive with the whole of the author's writing, Benoit could point out, inerrancy covers only the region of the author's intentional affirmation.

Evaluation

In sum, the prophetic-instrumental model of inspiration and inerrancy—classically exposited by Benoit—preferred to speak not of inspired texts or traditions but of inspired authors. Despite certain problematic assumptions, it had several strengths: it was respectful of magisterial definitions, spoke in the Thomist idiom familiar to the international body of theologians, and used a nuanced rational psychology to avoid wooden literalism. It was not without reason that it enjoyed a period of unrivaled popularity in the Church.

These strengths notwithstanding, the Thomist model also reflected increasingly implausible assumptions about the origins and ends of Scripture. Having moored his theory of inspiration in Thomist rational psychology, Benoit tended to present the truth of Scripture as predominantly propositional in character. Describing the sort of truth that Scripture reliably conveys, for instance, he observes, "Truth is the 'adequatio rei et intellectus.' It exists only in the judgment. And by 'judgment' we obviously do not mean

---

seek to penetrate the secrets of nature, but rather described and dealt with things in more or less figurative language," allowing that the same principle can be applied analogously to "cognate sciences and especially to History" (*PD*, nos. 39–40). Vatican II would later give conciliar sanction to this approach when it observes that the evangelists selected and organized traditions about Jesus "with an eye to the situation of the churches" (*DV*, no. 19).

28 Benoit calls this limiting according to "degree of affirmation." *Prophecy and Inspiration*, 138–39. The Pontifical Biblical Commission's "On Implied Quotations Contained in Sacred Scripture" (February 13, 1905) frowned upon those who would too readily take refuge in "implicit citations," but admitted the possibility in principle. Béchard, *Scripture Documents*, 187. See also *Pascendi*, no. 64; *SP*, no. 7.

29 Benoit calls this restriction of judgment according to "communicative intention," observing that a biblical author "assumes a social responsibility only for what he voluntarily submits to another for assent." *Prophecy and Inspiration*, 135–36. The encyclical tradition embraced the generic limitation of authorial judgment with the hopes that it might resolve the remaining objections to inerrancy. See *DAS*, no. 21; cf. *DV*, no. 12.

every proposition made up of a subject, verb, and predicate, but the formal act by which the intellect (*intellectus*) affirms its conformity (*adequatio*) to the object of knowledge (*res*)."[30] The practical difficulties of isolating such formal acts of judgment within diverse narrative and poetic genres were numerous. In an age of anxiety over biblical inerrancy, of course, this only enhanced the appeal of the Thomist-instrumental model. Because Scripture contained few discrete propositions demonstrably endorsed with a formal act of judgment, this approach considerably lightened the burden of biblical apologetics. When the age of anxiety had passed, however, students of the Bible began to wonder whether it was wise to center biblical inspiration on a faculty so seldom engaged in the composition of Scripture—that is, the author's formal act of judgment regarding a propositional truth.

Even to speak of a single author's judgment points to the second assumption of Benoit's model that historical research rendered increasingly implausible—namely, that a single authorial intention stood behind each biblical passage.[31] Though Benoit, a practicing exegete, knew full well that Scripture was a "curated" text, receiving its final shape from numerous anonymous tradents, he could integrate this corporate responsibility for Scripture only with great difficulty into a model of inspiration whose point of departure was the rational psychology of the solitary prophet. Benoit did later begin to speak of "analogies of inspiration," by which he meant a proportionate share in the charism of inspiration enjoyed by those who contributed to the final biblical text in any way, whether by composing, redacting, copyediting, or even having performed the notable deeds later recorded.[32] By the language of "analogies," Benoit hoped to acknowledge a certain degree of communal responsibility for Scripture without endorsing "collective inspiration," which he thought too dependent on a dubious "philosophy of sociology which would

---

30 Benoit, *Prophecy and Inspiration*, 134.

31 For the article that first focused English-language Catholic scholarship on the problem of multiple authorship, see Roderick A. F. MacKenzie, "Some Problems in the Field of Inspiration," *CBQ* 20, no. 1 (1958): 1–8. To the historical problems introduced by redaction criticism, one could add the problems introduced by ongoing clarification of Aquinas's understanding of the literal sense, which was neither governed entirely by authorial intention nor univocal. See Stephen E. Fowl, "The Importance of a Multivoiced Literal Sense of Scripture: The Example of Thomas Aquinas," in *Reading Scripture with the Church: Toward a Hermeneutic for Theological Interpretation* (Grand Rapids, MI: Baker Academic, 2006), 40–41.

32 See Pierre Benoit, "Analogies of Inspiration," in *Aspects of Biblical Inspiration*, trans. J. Murphy-O'Connor and S. K. Ashe (Chicago: Priory, 1965), 13–35. He foreshadows this solution in Benoit, *Prophecy and Inspiration*, 124.

impart to a group an autonomous, overriding existence which submerges the individual."[33] The "number and anonymity of these Biblical workers," Benoit concluded, need not "gainsay the fact that that they were individuals, moved by the Spirit to carry their stone, big or small, and contribute it to the building up of the monument of revelation."[34] But the analogical solution, despite its metaphysical elegance, offered little guidance on how to interpret a text increasingly viewed as an arena for competing visions, whether the Priestly school or the Deuteronomistic. Whose analogously inspired authorial intention regulates the global meaning of the text? The nonwriting prophet's? The Priestly composer's? The Deuteronomistic redactor's?

For all its strengths, then, the explanatory power of the Thomist-instrumental model depended in part on a fading image of Scripture as a quilt of monographs, whose single authors displayed the charism of inspiration most fully when offering true propositional judgments. As this image of biblical intentionality and truth began to fade, theologians continued looking for more adequate models. Tracy would explore different models of truth, and Rahner, to whom we now turn, would explore models of corporate intentionality.

RAHNER'S MOLINIST-PREDEFINITIVE MODEL OF INSPIRATION

Sensing the inadequacies of Benoit's model of biblical inspiration to the new exegetical situation, Karl Rahner proposed reconceiving the divine-human authorship of Scripture not on the model of Thomist instrumental causality but on the model of predestinating grace developed by the Jesuit Luis de Molina (1535–1600). Although we will therefore call Rahner's model of inspiration "Molinist-predefinitive," this should not obscure the fact that Rahner adapts Molina much more than Benoit adapts Aquinas. Most significantly, the German Jesuit introduces an element of communal consciousness more indebted to German Romanticism than Iberian scholasticism. Perhaps wary of innovating too much at one time, Rahner limits his speculation to God's assistance on the composition of Scripture, leaving it largely to others to develop the implications for Scripture's veracity. In keeping with

33 Benoit, "Analogies of Inspiration," 16.
34 Benoit, "Analogies of Inspiration," 16.

the limited scope of his project, then, this section will focus on how Rahner repurposes Molina's predefinitive grace as a model for ecclesial inspiration, concluding with an evaluation of its strengths and weaknesses.

Repurposing Molina

Molina is best known for his way of harmonizing divine providence and human freedom. He taught that "efficacious grace infallibly led to human assent, not from its own internal nature, but from the free consent of the created will, which consent God foreknows."[35] God brings it about that free agents should do his will, in other words, not "from the inside" but "from the outside"—that is, not by moving the will itself to a determinate end, but by arranging circumstances external to the will in such a way that the agent freely yet unfailingly chooses what God desires. This contradicted "what was accepted as the Thomistic theory of God's physical predetermination of acts to a definite outcome," a theory defended vigorously by Domingo Bañez (1528–1604) and his Dominican confrères.[36] The ensuing *De auxiliis* controversy dominated seventeenth-century Catholic theology. Without entering into distracting detail, one can say that Molina and his Jesuit supporters tended to view human and divine responsibility more contrastively than Bañez and his Dominican followers, carving out distinct contributions for God and the human person in any joint project.

This contrastive sensibility regarding grace and free will gave rise to a full-fledged theology of inspiration in the nineteenth century. Jesuit theologians of the Roman School, beginning with Giovanni Perrone, began to partition divine and human responsibility for Scripture along the lines of substantial content and verbal expression. According to this model, God inspires the Bible's "substance and ideas" (*res et sententias*),[37] while in many cases leaving the human author responsible for the choice of words or literary form. Were a theory of inspiration to extend God's responsibility down to the Bible's "individual words, commas, and dots," Perrone reasons, it would imply "that the sacred writers were merely passive instruments in writing down those

---

35 John P. Doyle, "Hispanic Scholastic Philosophy," in *The Cambridge Companion to Renaissance Philosophy*, ed. James Hankins (Cambridge: Cambridge University Press, 2007), 250–269 at 260.

36 Doyle, "Hispanic Scholastic Philosophy," 260.

37 Perrone, *Praelectiones Theologicae* II, 2:63.

things divinely handed down to them."[38] By diversifying responsibility for Scripture's ideative content and its individual words, Perrone sought to vindicate the divine provenance of Scripture without enervating human authorship. Variations on this *res-et-sententiae* theory would dominate Catholic theology through the nineteenth and early twentieth centuries.[39]

Rahner's theory of inspiration continues this classically Jesuit strategy for reconciling divine providence and human freedom. The German Jesuit begins by emphasizing the interpretive freedom of the theologian vis-à-vis the teaching of Trent and Vatican I, both of which teach that the whole of Scripture has God as its "author" (*auctor*).[40] Although Rahner takes God's authorship of Scripture as a binding doctrine, he nevertheless observes that the Latin word *auctor* has a broad semantic range, designating a role sometimes as narrow as "literary author" (*Verfasser*) and at other times as broad as "originator" (*Urheber*).[41] Even those theologians aware of these interpretive possibilities have been too quick to conceive inspiration along the lines of literary authorship. One could satisfy doctrinal requirements simply by affirming God as Scripture's originator, provided of course that one can distinguish the way Scripture originates from God from the way creation in general does.[42]

Rahner opts for the broader construction of God as Scripture's *auctor* in order better to safeguard the agency of the human author under inspiration. Truly human authorship, he argues, remains irreconcilable with properly instrumental subordination. When Thomas asserts that the same effect may be ascribed wholly to the divine cause and wholly to the human instrument, Rahner argues, the context makes clear that Aquinas has in mind God's transcendental and ongoing act of creation, not his categorical work "within

---

38 Perrone, *Praelectiones Theologicae* II, 2:63.

39 Burtchaell, *Catholic Theories of Biblical Inspiration since 1810*, 92.

40 See DH 1501, 3005.

41 Karl Rahner, *Inspiration in the Bible*, trans. Charles Henkey, QD 1 (New York: Herder & Herder, 1961), 12n2.

42 Rahner mentions an influential article written in 1943 by his German Jesuit confrère Augustin Bea. For Bea, the patristic evidence suggests that, when calling God *auctor* in the first centuries, "man nicht bloss an eine Urheberschaft im allgemeinen, sondern an die eigentliche *Inspiration* dachte." Augustin Bea, "Deus auctor Sacrae Scripturae: Herrkunft und Bedeutung der Formel," *Angelicum* 20 (1943): 30. The contrast presumes, of course, that the only alternative to literary authorship is "Urheberschaft im allgemeinen." For the far-reaching influence of Bea's article, see Denis Farkasfalvy, *A Theology of the Christian Bible: Revelation, Inspiration, Canon* (Washington, DC: The Catholic University of America Press, 2018), 31–33.

the redemptive dimension of the world." To pattern inspiration after God's general concurrence with creation, on the one hand, would evacuate divine authorship of all meaning, since it makes every book written by creatures—indeed, every act performed by creatures—"inspired" in the same sense. On the other hand, to pattern inspiration after God's special providence—for example, miracles, prophetic inspiration, the incarnation—precludes attributing the whole effect to both principal cause and instrument. For such works of redemption, in contrast to those of creation, possess a "spatio-temporal determination" such that not only the effects but the causality itself unfolds in history. God's grace and healing go forth from Jesus' humanity, for instance, located in time and space. In such cases divine and human causality no longer operate as if on distinct planes. And since the "same work from the same angle can have but one cause," God must be the sole formal cause of any effect produced by human instruments of God's special providence. Therefore, if one wants to carve out a space for human literary authorship without thereby rendering "inspiration" indistinguishable from God's ongoing act of creation, one must identify two distinct authorial "angles."[43]

In light of these difficulties, Rahner reimagines inspiration not as a kind of instrumental causality but as a combination of grace and providential circumstance sufficient to dispose the will to move rightly. On the Molinist view, grace, to guide the will infallibly, need not have some special "mark" enabling it to move the will inwardly and immediately. Rahner observes,

> What is required for the sufficiency of grace (as distinct from merely sufficient grace) may depend on some extrinsic circumstances, which, according to the Molinists, has [sic] been foreseen by God ... foreseen and willed by him as material to man's decision. Why should we not assume this also to be the case in inspiration, both in regard to the divine influence on human reason and on the human will? For it is, in fact, this absolutely willed effi-

---

43 For Rahner's more extensive discussion of the inadequacies of instrumental causality, here summarized in a paragraph, see *Inspiration in the Bible*, 12–18. Benoit himself, aware of the shortcomings in the instrumental model, toggles between instrumentality in a "broad sense" (which accounts for true human authorship) and instrumentality in a strict sense (which accounts for the *sensus plenior* unsuspected by the human authors). See *Prophecy and Inspiration*, 150n1. Benoit would later insist that Scripture is "entirely the work both of God and of the human author, each in different respects" ("Inspiration and Revelation," *Concilium* 10 [1965]: 9), but does not elaborate on these different "respects."

ciency of the influence, that is, a predefining efficiency, that is required by
God to be the author of the Scriptures.[44]

Seen as a case of Molinist formal predefinition, then, God's inspiration of
Scripture becomes equivalent to his arrangement of "external" circumstances
in such fashion that the human authors write what God wants them to write,
freely and yet unfailingly. Rahner suggests, for instance, that God might
simply "accomplish the motioning of the writer's will by causing him to
be asked through other people to produce [biblical] writings."[45] Moved in
this occasional (as opposed to instrumental) way, the human authors now
contribute to the composition of Scripture under an "angle" different from
God's. Rahner allows, for instance, that, even if God "predefines" the Bible's
substantial message, the "literary form is not God's own work."[46] The echoes
of Perrone's *res-et-sententiae* theory are unmistakable. Though we will return
momentarily to the nature of God's contribution to Scripture, it suffices for
now to note that it differs formally from the human one, thus opening a space
for human literary authorship.

Despite the ostensible simplicity of the solution, Rahner acknowledges
that it raises new problems. Most notably, the Molinist-predefinitive model
has not yet shown how it qualifies Scripture uniquely as the Word of God
rather than mere words about God. For if God predestines the composition
of Scripture just as he predestines the performance of any other good deed,
how would Scripture differ from any other edifying writing penned in fidelity to the promptings of grace? Rahner answers this objection by arguing
that Scripture issues not just from any formal predefinition, but from the
same modality of predefinition that produced the Apostolic Church. It is in
linking inspiration to the Apostolic Church that Rahner arguably makes his
most original contribution.

To Rahner's thinking, God has miraculously demarcated the Apostolic Church from the normal run of history in at least two ways. First, the
Apostolic Church continues salvation history, that spatio-temporal sphere
where God has concentrated his historical action in the world. Beginning
especially with the election of Israel, God has assumed responsibility for the
works of redemption in a qualitatively higher way than the works of nature.

---

44 Rahner, *Inspiration in the Bible*, 22n12.

45 Rahner, *Inspiration in the Bible*, 23.

46 Rahner, *Inspiration in the Bible*, 77.

"In the latter, God deals with the (historical) world," Rahner concludes, "in the former, he enacts his own history in the world."[47] Second, the Apostolic Church brings salvation history to its eschatological depth. "This historical action of God once again attains its unique climax in Christ and the Church," asserts Rahner, in such a way that its final outcome no longer bears the "possibility of frustration or revocation." [48] In other words, there can be no fuller or more perfect revelation in human history than that given with Christ and the Church. And though God sustains the Church across her whole history, he "authors" the Church most intensely in the apostolic era, when it was still accruing to the whole deposit of revelation: "The Apostolic Church in a qualitatively unique manner is subject to divine intervention also as distinct from the Church in the course of history."[49] To sum up, God is, for Rahner, more *auctor* of the Apostolic Church than of either Israel or of the post-Apostolic Church.

Having established the preeminence of the Apostolic Church, Rahner can easily justify Scripture's preeminent claim to be "God's Word." For the New Testament, he reasons, is nothing other than the "written embodiment of what the primitive Church believed and what in faith she laid down for herself."[50] And inasmuch as God wills the Old Testament as the "definitive image of the pre-history of the Church," the Old Testament too constitutes an element of the Apostolic Church and has God as its author.[51] God thus "authored" both Old Testament and New Testament more than any other writing—whether council, creed, or encyclical—because he "authored" the Apostolic Church more than any other segment of salvation history.

Having identified Scripture as the literary sedimentation of the early Church's faith consciousness, Rahner can give a fuller account of the distinctive contributions of the divine and human authors. The human authors, as we saw above, contribute the literary form. But what does the divine author contribute? God, simply put, contributes the mind of the early Church, which he has predestined to conformity with his own mind. Rahner explains,

---

47 Rahner, *Inspiration in the Bible*, 41.

48 Rahner, *Inspiration in the Bible*, 41.

49 Rahner, *Inspiration in the Bible*, 42.

50 Rahner, *Inspiration in the Bible*, 48.

51 Rahner, *Inspiration in the Bible*, 54.

> God, for example, did not write a letter to Philemon, although he is author
> of the epistle. Why not? Because he is author by willing absolutely and
> effectively that the Church as a community of love should manifest for all
> ages "canonically" her nature, her faith and her love, even in such a letter.
> Because God wills this letter in this way . . . the literary form will not affect
> God's authorship in a specific manner.[52]

Paul may have authored the letter *qua* letter, in other words, but God authored
the letter *qua* ecclesial self-expression. Rahner here reprises Perrone's *res-et-
sententiae* theory of inspiration: God continues to supply Scripture's revealed
"content." But Rahner now understands this "content" as the faith consciousness of the Apostolic Church, no longer as a body of discrete propositions.
The human authors continue to be responsible for clothing this ecclesial
mind with literary vesture.

In this division of labor Rahner most clearly reveals his "Molinist
proclivities."[53] God and the human authors both cause Scripture, but they
do so from different angles or—to use Rahner's language—under different
"formalities." God stands as Scripture's originator, who supplies its revealed
ideas. Biblical authors, though guided by efficacious grace, nevertheless act
as true literary authors, assigning these ideas a creative literary shape. In
this way, Rahner can affirm that Scripture belongs to God's initiatives in the
redemptive order without reducing the hagiographers to passive copyists.

Interpretive Consequences

Rahner's Molinist-predefinitive model abounds, of course, in hermeneutical implications. Curiously, however, he does not appeal to the purely
human origin of Scripture's literary form, which he established so laboriously,
to develop a notion of inerrancy different from Benoit's. Indeed, like Benoit,
Rahner holds that God guarantees "whatever the human writer wishes to say
as true," identifying literary analysis as an indispensable tool for determining
this inerrant meaning.[54] Rahner proves instead more interested in unfolding the interpretive consequences of his view, not shared with Benoit, that
Scripture canonizes the consciousness of the primitive Church. Building on
this premise, Rahner can argue that the theologically sophisticated reader,

---

52 Rahner, *Inspiration in the Bible*, 77.

53 See Burtchaell, *Catholic Theories of Biblical Inspiration since 1810*, 224.

54 Rahner, *Inspiration in the Bible*, 77.

when determining the human writers' intentions, should consult not only ancient literary genres but also post-apostolic doctrines. This point deserves unpacking.

Rahner's argument for the interpretive relevance of ecclesial tradition vis-à-vis Scripture is straightforward. Since God, by an act of redemptive-historical predefinition, causes the Church's intentionality to supervene upon the intentions of the individual biblical authors, this implies a certain interpenetration of the individual and the Church. "If the author writes *a priori* as a member of the Church, then interpretation, if it is to be correct and adequate, has to observe two points, that he writes as a *member* of the Church, and that he writes as a member of the *Church*."[55] It follows that biblical exegesis will unfold as a sort of dialectic between individual and ecclesial intentionality.[56] Exegesis, in other words, should allow a given writing to "express itself in its theological individuality for itself."[57] At the same time, exegesis cannot entirely forget that "every author, as a member of the *Church*, was open to the whole of the Church, believed and taught within the Church and was in his own theology always integrated, even where he himself could not have surveyed it explicitly, into the universal theology of the one and whole Church of his times."[58] Still working within the horizon of individual authorial intention, Rahner implies that the biblical writers, by virtue of their membership in the Church, have implicit intentions—that is, intentions to integrate their theology into the whole, to round out what is partial and balance out what is extreme.

If the biblical writers composed within the horizon of the Apostolic Church's faith, this implies in turn that post-apostolic doctrine will tend to illuminate rather than obscure their authorial intentions, whether explicit or implicit. "Infallibility of the teaching authority of the later Church is, by definition, the inerrant interpretation of the Scripture, because it includes by definition the link with the teaching of the early Church, which necessarily teaches the later Church and has expressed her teaching in the Scripture."

---

55 Rahner, *Inspiration in the Bible*, 79.

56 According to Robert Gnuse, the German Jesuit *Alttestamentler* Norbert Lohfink elaborates Rahner's dialectic with an exegete's knowledge. *The Authority of the Bible* (New York: Paulist, 1985), 56. See Lohfink, "The Inerrancy of Scripture," in *The Christian Meaning of the Old Testament* (Milwaukee, WI: Bruce, 1968), 24–51.

57 Rahner, *Inspiration in the Bible*, 79.

58 Rahner, *Inspiration in the Bible*, 79–80.

[59] Because the faith-consciousness of the Apostolic Church informs both biblical and post-biblical writers, albeit to different degrees, exegesis and dogma turn out to be not conflictual but reciprocally interpretive. Rahner will develop this position later in his essay "Exegesis and Dogmatic Theology," where he argues that exegetes should take magisterial teaching not just as a negative limit on exegesis but as an "inner, positive principle of research for the work of exegesis itself."[60] Benoit too taught that the post-apostolic Church has a charism for surely and connaturally interpreting Scripture, which gift he would later call "ecclesial inspiration."[61] By folding ecclesial consciousness into authorial intention itself, however, Rahner arguably better explains why Church doctrine can claim to be exegetical rather than eisegetical vis-à-vis Scripture.

Evaluation

Despite having articulated the relevance of both literary and doctrinal criteria for interpreting Scripture, Rahner's Molinist-predefinitive paradigm did not escape criticism. I will note the two most persistent and add a third criticism that anticipates the difference between Rahner's and Ratzinger's notions of inspiration.

The earliest and perhaps most enduring criticisms of Rahner's Molinist-predefinitive model of inspiration find their origin in the Dominican Yves Congar's review article, "Inspiration des écritures canoniques et apostolicité de l'église" (1961). To Congar's thinking, Rahner's depiction of Scripture as the literary sedimentation of the Apostolic Church's consciousness, whatever its other merits, insufficiently explains the importance that the Apostolic Church attributed not only to possessing the Scriptures but to "having *received* them from men chosen by God, spiritually endowed [*dotés*] by God, and having received a mission and authority from God for this purpose."[62]

---

59 Rahner, *Inspiration in the Bible*, 72.

60 Rahner, "Exegesis and Dogmatic Theology," in *Theological Investigations*, vol. 5 (London: Darton, Longman & Todd, 1966), 70.

61 Paul Rogers, "Pierre Benoit's 'Ecclesial Inspiration': A Thomistic Notion at the Heart of Twentieth-Century Debates on Biblical Inspiration," *Thomist* 80, no. 4 (2016): 545–48. Benoit distinguishes the "ecclesial inspiration" he accepts from the "collective inspiration" he rejects, defining the latter as a charism to write given to an "anonymous mass."

62 Yves Congar, "Inspiration des écritures canoniques et apostolicité de l'Église," *Revue des sciences philosophiques et théologiques* 45 (1961): 41. For similar criticisms, see Helmut

Rahner would subsequently attempt to nuance this diffusiveness, but would never fundamentally overturn it. In an essay published the year after Congar's criticisms, Rahner acknowledges the protagonism of the apostles in a subordinate clause: "However much it is true that the Apostles (the Twelve, with Peter and Paul standing in a relationship difficult to define but one with which we are not concerned here) played a leading and unique role this period, we would prefer to call it 'the primitive Church' rather than the 'age of the Apostles.'"[63] Such an approach, he explains, better accounts for the fact that the charism of inspiration extends beyond the twelve (to Paul, Mark, Luke, the author of Hebrews) and perhaps even beyond the physical death of the last apostle.[64] For many, however, this way of declaring independence from the shifting exegetical landscape came at too high a price. Having subsumed the distinctive role of the prophet and apostle under an undifferentiated ecclesial consciousness, they concluded, Rahner empties inspiration of all meaningful content.[65] Even those who notice the role Rahner carves out for individual authorial agency have tended to agree that the German Jesuit attributes too much to inspiration's "collective" subject.[66]

A second objection raised by Congar concerned the difficulty of squaring Rahner's theory with the inspiration of the Old Testament. Does the fact that Jesus and the apostles were citing the Old Testament as an authority before the close of the apostolic age not suggest that they regarded these Scriptures as already inspired? Does Israel's status as the People of God, an

---

Gabel, "Inspiration und Wahrheit der Schrift (DV 11): Neue Ansätze und Probleme in Kontext der gegenwärtigen wissenschaftlichen Diskussion," *Theologie der Gegenwart* 45 (2002): 122–24.

63 Karl Rahner, "Reflection on the Concept of '*Ius Divinum*' in Catholic Thought," in *Theological Investigations*, vol. 5 (London: Darton, Longman & Todd, 1966), 231–32.

64 Rahner, "Reflection on the Concept of '*Ius Divinum*' in Catholic Thought," 232.

65 Dennis J. McCarthy echoed Congar's criticism in 1963, objecting that "to subsume all the various forms of inspired writing under an anonymous social form of production is to apply a univocity with its own dangers of distortion." "Personality, Society, and Inspiration," *Theological Studies* 24, no. 4 (1963): 554.

66 Brendan Blankenhorn, OP, faults Rahner for identifying the collective Church not as inspiration's only subject but as its "primary subject." "God Speaks: Divine Authorship of Scripture in Karl Rahner and Pierre Benoit," *Angelicum* 93, no. 3 (2016): 447. Luis Alonso Schökel, while acknowledging that Rahner's "activity of self-expression is accomplished in the Church by individual persons responding to specific occasions within her life," nevertheless agrees that Rahner's appeal to the consciousness of the early Church smacks too much of the *Volksgeist* of German Romanticism. *The Inspired Word*, trans. Francis Martin (New York: Herder & Herder, 1969), 221, 224.

election received even before the incarnation, not suggest the divine authorship of their holy books?[67] If the books of Old Testament become "inspired"
only as they are assumed into the Apostolic Church, does this not mean they
are inspired only because the Church "subsequently approved them by her
authority after they had been composed by unaided human skill"—a position condemned at Vatican I?[68] And does it not also undercut the biblical
basis for Christian-Jewish dialogue—a dialogue encouraged by Vatican II?[69]

We might add a final weakness in Rahner's proposal, less noted in the
secondary literature, but nevertheless instructive for later comparison with
Ratzinger's. Rahner provides little in the way of natural analogy for how collective and individual intentions might come to interpenetrate. By explaining
inspiration as a special case of predestination rather than as a supernaturally
elevated case of some more familiar anthropological process, Rahner risks
explaining the mysterious from the even more mysterious. Absent any such
natural foundation, inspiration comes to seem a matter of divine *fiat*, no
matter how much Rahner insists on the role that external circumstances play
in aligning personal and ecclesial consciousness. This is a point to which we
will return when treating Ratzinger.

In sum, Rahner tied up some loose ends in the theory of inspiration but
left others more frayed. In Rahner's scheme, God becomes Scripture's originator (*Urheber*) but not its literary author (*Verfasser*), a role more fittingly
ascribed to human agents. Rahner likewise manages to give a robust account
of the reciprocal dependence of Scripture and Church. Since Scripture and
the Apostolic Church emerged from the same divine milieu, the Church
must have something to say about Scripture's proper interpretation. The
Molinist-predefinitive theory of authorship struggled to explain, however,
the link between the biblical canon and the authority of charismatic individuals, the inspiration of the Old Testament, and the mechanism by which
individual and corporate intentions compenetrate. Rahner had not, in short,
said the last word on biblical inspiration.

---

67 Congar, "Inspiration des écritures," 38.

68 *DF*, cap. 2, p. 806. The citation of Vatican I is mine, not Congar's. Albert Cardinal Van-
hoye, SJ, lamented that Rahner's theory of formal predefinition said nothing of "the Old
Testament, or the salvation of the world." "The Reception in the Church of the Dogmatic
Constitution '*Dei Verbum*,'" in *Opening Up the Scriptures: Joseph Ratzinger and the Founda-
tions of Biblical Interpretation*, ed. J. Granados, C. Granados, and Luis Sánchez-Navarro
(Grand Rapids, MI: Eerdmans, 2008), 117.

69 Blankenhorn, "God Speaks," 449.

TRACY'S HEIDEGGERIAN-DISCLOSIVE
MODEL OF INSPIRATION

The third salient model of biblical inspiration, best represented by the American Catholic theologian David Tracy, sharpens Rahner's tendency to locate biblical meaning beyond the explicit intentions of the solitary author. Tracy does not, like Benoit and Rahner, dedicate an *ex professo* treatise to the question of inspiration, but *Blessed Rage for Order* (1975) and *The Analogical Imagination* (1981) nonetheless offer one of the more thoroughgoing and philosophically sophisticated remodelings of biblical authority. It may seem a bit backward to discuss Tracy, a largely postconciliar theologian, before a discussion of Vatican II itself. It should be kept in mind, however, that Tracy draws heavily on the "disclosure" model of truth proposed in the preconciliar era, starting with Martin Heidegger and continuing through H. G. Gadamer and Paul Ricoeur. Tracy's contribution is to have deeply assimilated this philosophical tradition and applied it unflinchingly to the traditional problems of biblical inspiration and truth. For the sake of parallelism with the other models, each of which refers to a single inspiring figure, I will call Tracy's model of inspiration "Heideggerian-disclosive."

Extending Heideggerian Insights

Before turning to Tracy's theological application of Heideggerian hermeneutics, however, we do well to review Heidegger's disclosure model of truth and its legacy. Heidegger's model of truth rests on the foundational insight that there are really two dimensions of truth. One dimension is truth as correctness, the accurate correspondence of my knowledge to the various items of reality, whether things "out there" or propositions. But exclusive attention to truth as correspondence overlooks the fact that the same object may be disclosed in various modalities, each revealing or concealing different aspects of the item known. As a rather homespun example, one can contrast the ways bucolic scenery discloses itself to a landscape painter, to a farmer, and to a real-estate developer. Because each brings a different kind of attention to bear on the scene, each will perceive it in a different modality, whether admiringly, collaboratively, or acquisitively. For Heidegger, the comportment determining whether and how the landscape will appear constitutes an even more fundamental dimension of truth: "What first makes correctness possible must with more original right be taken as the essence of truth."[70] It is the attention and priority given to the way things appear—to the Being of beings—that distinguishes Heidegger's "disclosure" model of truth.[71]

Heidegger's epistemology becomes a kind of ethical imperative by the addition of two other postulates. First, our comportment toward the world admits of degrees of authenticity. We approach reality with either more open or more manipulative postures, determining in advance which aspects of a thing come to light. This seems to be the meaning of Heidegger's observation that "*the essence of truth is freedom.*"[72] Second, the relationship between things and our comportment toward them runs in both directions. Yes, authenticity unconceals beings. But certain beings, especially works of art, may also engender authenticity. A genuine artwork, writes Heidegger, "opens up a *world* and keeps it abidingly in force."[73] By projecting a more generous "world," art transforms those who participate in it. Heideggerian ethics thus enjoins its adepts to grow in authenticity by making use of aesthetic works, which are in turn nothing other than active sites for the disclosure of this more primordial dimension of Being.

H.-G. Gadamer basically accepts Heidegger's disclosure model of truth, with its insistence that the *what* of perception is derivative of the *how*. For Gadamer, however, not only personal authenticity but a broader web of historical forces affects the modality of reality's appearance. Every event creates a historical ripple effect, and this "effective-history," or *Wirkungsgeschichte*, becomes a horizon conditioning the modality of the event's appearance. In his seminal *Truth and Method* (1960), Gadamer observes, "If we are trying to understand a historical phenomenon from the historical distance that is characteristic of our hermeneutical situation, we are always subject to the effects of effective-history. It determines in advance both what seems to us worth inquiring about and what will appear as an object of investigation, and

70 Martin Heidegger, *Basic Writings*, ed. David Farrell Krell, rev. and exp. ed. (San Francisco: HarperCollins, 1993), 122.

71 James J. DiCenso, *Hermeneutics and the Disclosure of Truth: A Study in the Work of Heidegger, Gadamer, and Ricoeur* (Charlottesville: University of Virginia Press, 1990), 56–65.

72 Heidegger, *Basic Writings*, 123. Emphasis original.

73 Martin Heidegger, *Poetry, Language, Thought*, trans. Albert Hofstadter (New York: Harper & Row, 1971), 44.

we more or less forget half of what is really there."[74] In other words, there simply is no perfectly innocent and presuppositionless understanding of historical phenomena. For historically situated knowers like ourselves, good interpretation consists not in eliminating all prejudices but in adopting the right prejudice.

The French Reformed philosopher Paul Ricoeur would carry the Heideggerian legacy a step further by presenting effective history not simply as an inescapable interpretive lens but as the medium in which the meaning of the text comes increasingly to light. If a text discloses a transformative "world" and keeps it permanently in force, this means that the meaning of the text transcends whatever its author consciously intended or its first addressees explicitly understood. Ricoeur calls this semantic transcendence "distance."[75] As new readers appropriate the text in new situations, they discover new dimensions of the "world" of the text, expanding its range of meaning. The first effect of ongoing appropriation, according to Ricoeur, is "to confer an autonomy, an independent existence on a text, which thereby opens it to subsequent developments and subsequent enrichments, all of which affect its meaning."[76] In this connection, Ricoeur approves St. Gregory the Great's observation, "Scripture grows with its readers."[77]

Tracy's contribution to theology is arguably to have pressed these post-Heideggerian hermeneutical insights into the service of a Catholic theology of Scripture. In keeping with the disclosure model of truth, Tracy proposes reconceiving Scripture not as a repository of ethical and dogmatic propositions but as something more like a Heideggerian work of art, a "classic" that opens up a more authentic world.[78] The task of the biblical interpreter

---

74 Hans-Georg Gadamer, *Truth and Method*, trans. Joel Weinsheimer and Donald G. Marshall, 2nd rev. ed. (New York: Crossroad, 1989), 300.

75 Paul Ricoeur, *Hermeneutics and the Human Sciences*, ed. and trans. John B. Thompson (Cambridge: Cambridge University Press, 1981), 131–44.

76 Paul Ricoeur and André LaCocque, *Thinking Biblically: Exegetical and Hermeneutical Studies*, trans. David Pellauer (Chicago: University of Chicago Press, 1998), xi.

77 The citation is more a paraphrase than a translation of Gregory's original saying, which runs, "Divina eloquia cum legente crescunt." Gregory the Great, *Homiliae in Hiezechielem prophetam*, ed. Marcus Adriaen, CCSL 142 (Turnhout: Brepols, 1971), 1.7.8; p. 87. Ratzinger will cite this same passage as pope in *VD*, no. 30.

78 David Tracy acknowledges his debt to Heidegger's disclosive model of truth: *The Analogical Imagination: Christian Theology in a Culture of Pluralism* (New York: Crossroad, 1981), 150n101.

approaching the Bible, therefore, is not to reconstruct the historical author's mind. It is rather to enter sympathetically, through something like the biblical text's "effective history," into the existential and aesthetic vision of its "implied author." One looks to the Bible not so much for particular judgments or pastoral solutions as for the "world" it discloses.

Tracy's contribution to the search for a new paradigm of biblical inspiration and inerrancy is to have reconceived biblical revelation along these Heideggerian lines. Though he wrote after Vatican II, he brings to a head certain interpretive ideas already influential before the Council. We can thus still read his Heideggerian-disclosive model as representative of currents of thought vying for recognition in the text of *Dei Verbum*. To give an ordered account of Tracy's thought, I will begin first with his notion of the Bible as "classic," unpacking the model of divine authorship implied therein, and then proceed to its interpretive implications.

The Bible as Christian "Classic"

What is a "classic" in Tracy's stipulative sense? As elaborated in the *Analogical Imagination*, a classic is a permanently active site of disclosure for the truth of human existence. Tracy takes the existence of such classics as a given of human experience: "We all find ourselves compelled both to recognize and on occasion to articulate our reasons for the recognition that certain expressions of the human spirit so disclose a compelling truth about our lives that we cannot deny them some kind of normative status. Thus do we name these expressions, and these alone, 'classics.' Thus do we recognize . . . a normative element in our cultural experience, experienced as a realized truth."[79] Such a classic will communicate its "truth" not simply on one occasion or for one individual but will retain an enduring and inexhaustible disclosive power for a whole culture.[80]

Applying this understanding of "classic" to texts, especially religious texts, implies a new understanding of authorship and the interpreter's task. Tracy spells out these amendments to traditional ideas of authorship perhaps most explicitly in *Blessed Rage for Order*. There Tracy agrees with the Heideggerian tradition that classic texts can serve as the site of disclosure for an inexhaustible reservoir of meaning only if they enjoy a certain autonomy

---

79 Tracy, *Analogical Imagination*, 108.
80 Tracy, *Analogical Imagination*, 116.

from the "world behind the text"—that is, from the intention of the text's literary author, from the historical circumstances of its production, from the likely effect on its intended audience. The true referent of any great text is rather the perspective disclosed by the text as such—that is, by the world "in front of the text."

> More exactly, we can determine both an object-referent of some existential import (viz. that way of perceiving reality, that mode of being-in-the-world which the text opens up for the intelligent reader) and a subject-referent (viz. the personal vision of the author implied by the text). In the latter case, one can establish the meanings present in the basic vision of the world of that "implied author" (for example, the vision of the "world" of Jesus as referred to by the parabolic texts).[81]

It is worth emphasizing that the "implied author" is not the historically identifiable composer of the text, the sort of author whose opinions and enthusiasms might be reconstructed by painstaking researching into unpublished diaries and personal biography. The "implied author" instead designates the personal vision that the world of the text evokes. In the passage above, Tracy applies the distinction between historical and implied author to the parables in such a way as to identify Jesus Christ—and, by implication, God—as their "implied author." This identification may hold true even if the parables do not reflect Jesus' *ipsissima verba* but what an evangelist thought Jesus would have said on a given occasion.

Because the God of Jesus Christ is the implied author of the Christian Scriptures, Tracy argues, the literary classic provides a useful but limited analogy to the status of the Bible in Christianity. While every classic will disclose the deeper truth of existence in a transformative way, it belongs to "religious" classics to disclose the world at its "limit-situation." "Unlike the experience of nonreligious classics, in the religious classics this common intensification process is itself intensified to the point of a transgression of the usual limits of participation and non-participation in the whole."[82] Religious encounter, in other words, includes an experience of simultaneous union with and distance from the power of the transcendent whole—what

---

81 David Tracy, *Blessed Rage for Order: The New Pluralism in Theology* (New York: Seabury, 1975), 78.

82 Tracy, *Analogical Imagination*, 173.

Rudolf Otto famously called the *mysterium tremendum et fascinans*.[83] Religious classics render this limit-experience in a poetic medium, establishing thereby a permanent site of disclosure for this most spacious "world" and this most transgressive "truth."

For the Christian, this commanding and sustaining whole finds classic expression at two levels. The only definitive and unsurpassable self-manifestation of God is Jesus Christ.[84] The books of the Hebrew Scriptures and the New Testament represent, by contrast, the always normative but only "relatively adequate" expressions of this same Christ event.[85] These texts remain normative because they embody the "original witness" to this event, but they qualify as only relatively adequate because, in choosing a particular set of symbols and narrative techniques to render the limit experience, they inevitably leave concealed some aspect of the whole.[86] For Tracy, the fact that Christians have accepted a canon with so many inner tensions—between the Jesus-kerygma of the Synoptics and the Christ-kerygma of John and Paul, between James' moralizing and Paul's explosive logic of grace, between the imminent and delayed expectations of the *parousia*—demonstrates their recognition of the merely relative adequacy of any rendering of the Christ event.[87] No canonical book, in sum, either fundamentally falsifies or renders without remainder the God manifest in Jesus Christ.

For Tracy, then, God remains Scripture's "implied author," the one whose vision of the world becomes uniquely accessible through the biblical text. Human authors contribute too, of course, insofar as they encounter God in the particularity of their own lives and render the experience in the concreteness of a literary text. Any major "classic," inasmuch as it successfully projects a world saturated with meaning, furnishes at least an analogy to the way Scripture signifies. But Scripture stands alone even among the "classics" by referring to the world at its paradoxical "limit situation"—that is, by manifesting the transcendent whole in the humanity of Jesus Christ.

83 Tracy, *Analogical Imagination*, 174. See Rudolf Otto, *The Idea of the Holy: An Inquiry into the Non-rational Factor in the Idea of the Divine and Its Relation to the Rational*, trans. John W. Harvey, 2nd ed. (London: Oxford University Press, 1958), esp. 31–34.

84 Tracy, *Analogical Imagination*, 248.

85 Tracy, *Analogical Imagination*, 249.

86 Tracy, *Analogical Imagination*, 199–200.

87 Tracy, *Analogical Imagination*, 250.

Interpretive Consequences

The hermeneutical consequences of Tracy's recasting of Scripture as Christian "classic" are manifold. We will nevertheless confine ourselves to the points most germane for comparing him with Benoit, Rahner, and (later) Ratzinger on our main interpretive question: How is Scripture normative and true? This will require us to examine Tracy's hermeneutical model of "truth" and his openness to both internal and external correction of the Bible.

As the language of "existential truth" and "truth of human life" suggests, Tracy does not locate the truth of Scripture primarily in the reliability of its propositional judgments, whether scientific, ethical, or historical. In recognizably Heideggerian fashion, he envisions truth instead as an "event," roughly analogous to the deeper recognition of reality compelled by a profound work of art.[88] "As we argued in the case of all artistic classics," Tracy elaborates, "the classic by definition incarnates a notion of truth that is neither mere adequation nor correspondence, neither verification nor falsification. Rather truth here becomes a manifestation that lets whatever shows itself to be in its showing and in its hiddenness."[89] In this respect, Scripture is just like any other major "classic." Just as we do not adequately evaluate the truth of the world disclosed by Dante's *Commedia* by comparing the sophistication of its metaphysics to that of contemporary modal logic, so we do not evaluate the world disclosed by Scripture by comparing its historical accuracy and moral legislation to contemporary standards. We instead judge classics according to their power to make their readers live in the truth. For Tracy, Scripture is true not so much because its propositional judgments are always true but because it makes truth appear and human authenticity possible.

This "disclosure" model of truth inevitably relativizes the regulative role of the "world behind the text"—that is, the circumstances of a text's production—for determining the range of its legitimate interpretations. Both Benoit and Rahner, as we saw, circumscribe the scope of Scripture's binding teachings to what the human authors intend to affirm. This means studying the historical situation the biblical authors addressed and the literary genres they employed, "getting inside" the original authors' minds so as to gauge the force and reach of their affirmations. For Tracy, by contrast, the very act of writing "codifies" an experience in a public medium and thereby

---

88 Tracy, *Analogical Imagination*, 111–12.

89 Tracy, *Analogical Imagination*, 195. See also 130.

"allows that meaning to escape the confines of the author's intention, the original addressee's reception or the original sociohistorical locus of the text."[90] Restricting a text's meaning to interpretations probable within its original *Sitz im Leben* would imply that the Bible could function as a "classic" only for its contemporaries. Yet the Bible manifestly signifies beyond the life and times of its authors.

Tracy, borrowing a phrase from Ricoeur, refers to the many possible ways of being in the world that the text discloses as the world "in front of the text."[91] And it is chiefly to this ever-expanding referent that he would direct the theologian's gaze. Consider, for example, the Markan Jesus' counsel to the Rich Man to sell all, give to the poor, and follow (Mk 10:21). One could reconstruct the world *behind* the text by attempting to get inside the mind of the historical author and addressees. Or one could follow the world in front of the text, the history of its appropriations by Anthony of the Desert, Augustine, Francis of Assisi, and countless other exemplary disciples. If one took the latter approach, one might take the scene not as an unrepeatable invitation directed to one man in one setting, but as an adaptable charter for what Catholics today call religious life. For Tracy, reading the Rich Man in this second way would not be a naive distortion of Mark, but an acknowledgment that the effective history of a classic forms part of its total meaning.

If the Bible accrues meaning through reception, it follows that we depend upon tradition for access to the total meaning of Jesus Christ. "Jesus is none other," Tracy reasons, "than the one remembered by the church from the earliest apostolic tradition to the present."[92] It is neither factually possible nor hermeneutically responsible to approach so "classic" a figure as Jesus except through the medium of his *Wirkungsgeschichte*. Through his Heideggerian-disclosive framework, then, Tracy arrives at the same conclusion Rahner reached through his Molinist-predefinitive framework: "The scriptures themselves are the church's book."[93] Tracy explains the nonredundancy of church and canon, however, not as the preestablished harmony of the individual and ecclesial consciousnesses, but as the symbiosis between a religious classic and its transhistorical community of readers.

90 Tracy, *Analogical Imagination*, 128.

91 Tracy, *Analogical Imagination*, 122.

92 Tracy, *Analogical Imagination*, 236.

93 Tracy, *Analogical Imagination*, 249.

With such an open-ended vision of biblical meaning proposed, one may well wonder whether benchmarks exist for distinguishing good interpretations from bad ones. Tracy proposes only "criteria of relative adequacy"[94]—that is, criteria for identifying expressions as more or less appropriate to the inexhaustible Christ event. A theology faithful to the biblical witness should, first of all, comprehend the plurality of perspectives and emphases present in the apostolic canon itself, according the same relative prominence to each. For Tracy this means assigning a regulative role to the New Testament genre of narrative proclamation, with its key Christological moments of incarnation, cross, resurrection.[95] Other genres, however, may play a subordinate and corrective role in New Testament. The apocalyptic genre serves as the constant corrective to any "slackening of eschatological intensity," while the doctrinal confessions of what Tracy calls "early Catholicism" counteract temptations to "shirk the ordinary," especially the ordinary business of clarifying shared beliefs and church order.[96] A relatively adequate interpretation of Scripture should represent, in short, a weighted synthesis of the many mutually corrective voices in Scripture. Accountability to the whole canonical witness thus provides the "internal corrective" to idiosyncratic interpretations.[97]

If the "internal corrective" means reading Scripture within the whole, the "external corrective" means applying historical-critical, literary-critical, and social-scientific methods to the text with a view to exposing arbitrary interpretations.[98] The historical-critical method will be used to reconstruct the original apostolic witness. Literary-critical methods can show the expressive fittingness of various genres and narratives in Scripture. Social-critical methods can provide ideology critique, deploying all the resources of critical reason—even the "secular hermeneutic of suspicion" customary in liberationist and feminist thought[99]—to show where unconscious bias generated distortions in the tradition.

94 Tracy, *Analogical Imagination*, 320.

95 Tracy, *Analogical Imagination*, 281.

96 Tracy, *Analogical Imagination*, 268.

97 Tracy, *Analogical Imagination*, 236.

98 Tracy, *Analogical Imagination*, 238–40.

99 Tracy, *Analogical Imagination*, 381, 240n26.

As Tracy's twin requirements of both fidelity to the apostolic norm and vigilance against self-serving rationalizations suggest, tradition in the Heideggerian-disclosive model remains something ultimately ambiguous. Tradition is "fundamentally to be trusted yet ever in need of self-reform, self-correction, self-clarification."[100] Only the whole community can, therefore, determine the relative adequacy of proposed amendments to the tradition. "The whole church community decides in the long run whether these new interpretations and proposed correctives are faithful to the tradition's own call to constant self-reformation in its fidelity to its witness."[101] Scripture and Church constitute a sort of hermeneutical circle, each serving as a standard for the other.

The interpretive strategies corresponding to Tracy's Heideggerian-disclosive paradigm depart even further from Benoit's Thomist-instrumental model than Rahner's Molinist-predefinitive model. Whereas Rahner retained the basic framework of authorial intention and propositional judgment, merely adding a layer of ecclesial consciousness to each, Tracy abandons both. The Bible is finally true because the overall world that it projects is most true to life—that is, least inadequate to Jesus Christ's vision of reality. The historical authors' intentions do not govern the ever-expanding meaning of the text, nor are their judgments, even if solemnly proposed, always true. Rahner and Tracy agree, however, on the basic interdependence of text and interpretive community.

Evaluation

Tracy's recasting of "inspired Scripture" as a "Christian classic" naturally has its own share of strengths and liabilities. Here we will comment on a couple of themes where situating Tracy vis-à-vis Benoit, Rahner, and (eventually) Ratzinger proves illuminating.

On the side of explanatory strengths, Tracy's Heideggerian-disclosive model of biblical authority explains the nonredundancy of the canon and church at least as well as Rahner's Molinist-predefinitive model. Tracy's observation (drawn especially from Paul Ricoeur) that the public act of writing "distances" the meaning of a text from its literary author's private intentions explains more elegantly than Benoit's model the emergence of a *sensus*

100 Tracy, *Analogical Imagination*, 236.
101 Tracy, *Analogical Imagination*, 237.

plenior. Benoit, it will be remembered, toggled between instrumentality in proper and improper senses to show how the effect of Scripture was both proportionate to its human instruments (because expressed in human language and artistry) and disproportionate to these same instruments (because carrying "fuller senses" unsuspected by its historical authors). Drawing an analogy to all great "classics," Tracy suggests how Scripture develops its *sensus plenior* organically and incrementally, yet in virtue of its divine provenance. For if God's authorship of Scripture means that Scripture projects Jesus' personal vision, and if this vision remains in principle inexhaustible, then the history of its appropriations will continue to reveal the text's latent possibilities, its "fuller sense." Tracy thus legitimizes the figural playfulness of premodern interpreters toward the biblical text.

At the same, Tracy's adoption of a "disclosure" model of truth brings its own difficulties in tow. By recasting Scripture's "inerrancy" as unfailing trueness to life rather than unfailing trueness in propositional judgment, Tracy admittedly relieves exegetes of the burden of explaining away the many ostensibly inaccurate historical, scientific, and even ethico-religious ideas found in the Bible. But does this existential recasting of inerrancy do justice to the historical dimension of Christianity? Does it matter, for instance, whether the stories really happened? Or would a narrative having what Hans Frei calls a "'history-like' force"[102] project a world just as transformative and, therefore, just as true?

Another possible objection to Tracy's Heideggerian-disclosive model is the inherent difficulty of resolving existential truth into concrete directives and doctrines. Tracy might answer that the readers of Scripture bridge the spheres of existential and propositional truth imaginatively, not by following every biblical norm literally but by bringing minds renewed by the biblical "world" to the questions of everyday ethics or communal order. But this leaves unparsed the authority of the many nonnarrative obligations for thought and action imposed by Scripture. Do we need to take any of these as expressing transcendent truth or enduring obligation? Do we need to accept, for instance, Jesus' demonic diagnosis of epilepsy-like afflictions (Mark 9:25)? Or his claim that those who divorce and remarry commit adultery (Mark 10:11–12; Matt 5:31–32; Luke 16:18)? Must we honor even now the prohibition, found in both Old and New Testaments, against consuming the meat of

---

102 Hans Frei, *The Eclipse of Biblical Narrative* (New Haven: Yale University Press, 1974), 16. Tracy seems to approve Frei's characterization of biblical narrative as "history-like." *Analogical Imagination*, 263; see also 251.

strangled animals and blood (Gen 9; Acts 15:20)?[103] If the Gospel is to serve as a charter for Christian culture and morality, then there must be some way of adjudicating how and to what extent these discrete propositions claim our observance and assent.

Tracy's Heideggerian-disclosive model does not, however, seem likely to resolve interpretive disputes on such points. Leaving the interpretive community confessionally pluralistic, he defines "church" as "all that are grounded in the confession that Jesus Christ is Lord."[104] The regulative role he assigns to narrative proclamation, moreover, suggests that many biblical norms for doctrine, ethics, and polity would not be valid in their own right: "The doctrines of early Catholicism . . . may best serve their roles in a contemporary interpretation of the actual diversity of the New Testament not as *the* truth but as the truth of important correctives."[105] The household codes, in other words, may no longer bind in their particular mandates—for example, the obedience of slaves and wives to masters and husbands—but they may continue to communicate, against every eschatological fanaticism, the formal truth that the Church must always translate the extraordinary into everyday order:

> The confessions and doctrines remind us as well that sheer intensity without any principles of ordering can lead eventually to a self-destructive chaos, that all immediacy must eventually find some mediation, that the witness of the symbol does give rise to the clarifying thought of doctrines, that the extraordinary, if it is to live, must return to the ordinary and, in that very return, disclose the extraordinariness of the ordinary itself.[106]

Indeed, Tracy goes so far as to apply analogously to the Bible the Swiss theologian Hans Küng's notion of the "indefectibility of the Church in spite of errors."[107] This operative distinction between formal truth and material

---

103 In the Decree for the Jacobites (February 4, 1442), the Council of Florence ruled that prohibition of Acts ceased "as soon as the Christian religion was promulgated to the point that no Jew according to the flesh appeared within it." DH 1350.

104 Tracy, *Analogical Imagination*, 251.

105 Tracy, *Analogical Imagination*, 268.

106 Tracy, *Analogical Imagination*, 268.

107 Hans Küng, *Infallible? An Inquiry* [I, no. 96], 81–124. Cited in *Analogical Imagination*, 236n15. Tracy also implies his agreement with Küng on the "intrinsic inadequacy of any propositions to express 'reality' with finality." "Hans Küng: Loving Critic of His Church," *The Christian Century* 88, no. 20 (May 19, 1971): 632. Tracy elsewhere suggests that one possible theological vocation is to constitute "'loyal opposition' to present church self-understanding and practice." *Analogical Imagination*, 25.

truths allows Tracy to counsel simultaneously fundamental trust in the world that Scripture projects and suspicion of its individual judgments. One may be forgiven for doubting whether faith can long endure such ambivalence.

With the inerrancy of biblical teachings now exchanged for the indefectibility of a biblical world, most of Benoit's and Rahner's careful qualifications of inerrancy become superfluous. One need no longer, like Benoit, carefully parse authorial judgment with a view to determining its exact scope and force. Nor need one any longer, like Rahner, invoke compenetrating authorial and ecclesial faith-consciousness to conciliate ostensibly conflicting biblical judgments. For one may simply accept that such certain biblical judgments are untrue in themselves, provided they contribute correctively to the truth of the biblical "world." For those convinced that it strains credibility to insist that the biblical authors so seldom asserted what they in fact wrote, Tracy's proposal will come as a relief. For those who feel Scripture discloses not only an existential landscape but also, at least on some occasions, concrete and abiding norms for belief and action, Tracy will have painted with too broad a brush.

CONCLUDING REFLECTIONS IN LIGHT OF *DEI VERBUM*

This survey of the influential twentieth-century models of inspiration reveals, perhaps unsurprisingly, that none accounts for everything that the Church's faith would want to affirm about God's authorship of Scripture and its interpretive consequences. But this same survey, it must be admitted, referenced the doctrinal tradition only obliquely and in broad strokes. With a view both to consolidating the gains of the present chapter and to preparing for Ratzinger's own theology, then, it behooves us to review our theologies of Scripture in light of *Dei Verbum*, the Second Vatican Council's Dogmatic Constitution on Divine Revelation, the Catholic Church's most authoritative teaching on Scripture since Vatican I. There one finds not so much a theory of Scripture's divine and human origins as a catalogue of various elements to be affirmed in faith. The council lays down the doctrinal "pegs," in other words, leaving it to theological ingenuity to stretch a theoretical fabric over them. Each of the models of inspiration surveyed covers some pegs better than others.

The first "peg" is the mediation of Scripture by ecclesial tradition. Rahner and Tracy arguably cover this more adequately than Benoit. Rahner's idea that God inspires Scripture in the course of inspiring the mind of the Apostolic Church did not go unnoticed by the council fathers, but it remained too adventurous and too recent for wholesale reception.[108] The final version of *Dei Verbum* nevertheless affirms the organic interpenetration of Scripture and the Church's life and teaching office: "Sacred tradition and Sacred Scripture form one sacred deposit of the word of God, committed to the Church."[109] Because Scripture must be read in the sacred Spirit in which it was written, moreover, "no less serious attention must be given to the content and unity of the whole of Scripture if the meaning of the sacred texts is to be correctly worked out. The living tradition of the whole Church must be taken into account along with the harmony which exists between elements of the faith."[110] In insisting that the living tradition of the Church mediates the meaning of Scripture, *Dei Verbum* echoes Rahner's teaching on the interdependence of Scripture and magisterium and anticipates Tracy's observation that the Bible is the ultimately "the church's book."[111]

Reflecting more Benoit's emphasis, however, *Dei Verbum* still prefers to speak, albeit in a rather loose sense, of God's guiding individual human instruments. "In composing the sacred Books, God chose and employed [*adhibuit*] certain men, who, while engaged in this task, made full use of their faculties and powers, so that, with God himself acting in them and through them, they as true authors committed to writing everything and only those things that he wanted written."[112] While Rahner might object that his Molinist-predefinitive model better maintains humans as "true authors,"

---

108 For instance, Bishop Joseph Schoiswohl of Seckau, Austria, the country where Rahner lived and taught, suggested in the council's antepreparatory phase that the Church define the notion of inspiration more ecclesially: "Momentum decisivum tunc non esset inspiratio singulae personae sed definitio ab Ecclesia prolata," *ADA* 2:67. A quick glance at the broader pool of postulates, however, suggests that this need was not widely felt. See *ADA, Appendix Voluminis II: Analyticus conspectus consiliorum et votorum quae ab episcopis datae sunt, pars 1,* 16–18. I owe these references to Msgr. Michael Magee.

109 *DV*, no. 10.

110 *DV*, no. 12. Translation slightly modified.

111 Tracy, *Analogical Imagination*, 249.

112 *DV*, no. 11. Commentators, however, note that the absence of language such as *auctor principalis* may represent a slight retreat from the specifically Thomistic prophetic-instrumental model. See Alois Grillmeier, "The Divine Inspiration and the Interpretation of Sacred Scripture," in *Commentary on the Documents of Vatican II*, ed. Herbert Vorgrimler, trans. William Glen-Doepl, vol. 3 (New York: Herder & Herder, 1967), 203; Denis Farkasfalvy, "Inspiration and Interpretation," in *Vatican II: Renewal within Tradition*, ed. Matthew Levering and Matthew L. Lamb (Oxford: Oxford University Press, 2008), 84.

the emphasis on God's moving individuals to write "only those things that he wanted written" savors more of Benoit's Thomist-instrumental model, with its supposition that God takes responsibility not only for Scripture's ideas but for its very words. Tracy's distinction between the human author's presence in the literary form of the text and the divine author's presence in the "world of the text" reflects a hermeneutical philosophy too lately developed to find any echo at Vatican II.

In the hermeneutical implications, especially with respect to inerrancy and the "fuller sense," we again find no single author coinciding with all the conciliar *desiderata*. With regard to inerrancy, *Dei Verbum* teaches, "Therefore, since everything asserted by the inspired authors or sacred writers must be held to be asserted by the Holy Spirit, it follows that the books of Scripture must be acknowledged as teaching solidly, faithfully and without error that truth which God wanted put into sacred writings for the sake of salvation."[113] In taking the "assertions" of the sacred writers as its point of departure, *Dei Verbum* follows Benoit and Rahner in concluding that any error found in the human author's intended teaching must ultimately be imputable to God. In some respects, the council seems content to maintain the status quo.[114]

The passage cited above shows signs nevertheless of openness to the complementary insights of hermeneutical phenomenology and salvation-historical theology. Grammatically speaking, after all, it is not the individual authors but the "books of Scripture" that "must be acknowledged as teaching . . . without error." Here we see perhaps a subtle shift away from Benoit's authorial intentionality to Tracy's "autonomy of the text." Second, the same passage specifies the purpose for God's consigning truth to writing—namely, "for the sake of our salvation" (*nostrae salutis causa*). We will return to the interpretation of this contested phrase later. For now it suffices to note that, according to a consensus of interpreters, it excludes neither the relevance of God's saving purpose for discerning what the books of Scripture authentically

---

113 *DV*, no. 11.

114 It is commonly reported that the council fathers, to achieve near unanimity, agreed not to decide anything "new" relative to the biblical encyclicals. Grillmeier notes, for instance, that Paul VI expressed his *perplessità* over the penultimate draft of *Dei Verbum* because it seemed to offer a looser view of inerrancy, a "doctrine not yet general in the scriptural and theological instruction of the Church." Grillmeier, "Divine Inspiration and Interpretation of Sacred Scripture," 213. Farkasfalvy observes, "Despite more than a century of bickering over the Bible's antiquated notions about the physical world and events of history as errors, the experts of the Council did not manage to reformulate the issue of inerrancy." Farkasfalvy, "Inspiration and Interpretation," 87.

teach, nor the possibility that Scripture teaches some scientific and historical truths inerrantly, by virtue of their intrinsic connection to God's saving
purpose.[115] *Dei Verbum* also insists, for instance, on the "historical character"
(*historicitatem*) of the four canonical Gospels, adding that the evangelists'
"intention in writing" was to present a true picture of Jesus rooted in personal memory and eyewitness testimony.[116] One might say, then, that *Dei
Verbum* did not so much repudiate earlier models of authorial inerrancy as
yoke them to hermeneutical and salvation-historical perspectives, leaving it
to theologians to fit a theory to the various doctrinal *desiderata*.

Though *Dei Verbum* has more to say about inerrancy than Scripture's
"fuller sense," it does suggest that the biblical texts signify more than even
their human authors suspected. Its explanation of this surplus of meaning, moreover, shows a certain affinity for Tracy's notion of a trajectory of
meaning. Far from presenting the meaning of Scripture as "fixed" by the
circumstances of its production, the Dogmatic Constitution describes how
the words of Scripture accrue new layers of meaning:

> For there is a growth in the understanding of the realities and the words
> which have been handed down. This happens through the contemplation
> and study made by believers, who treasure these things in their hearts
> (see Luke, 2:19, 51) through a penetrating understanding of the spiritual
> realities which they experience, and through the preaching of those who
> have received through Episcopal succession the sure gift of truth. For as
> the centuries succeed one another, the Church constantly moves forward
> toward the fullness of divine truth until the words of God reach their
> complete fulfillment in her.[117]

---

115 For a linguistic analysis of this and other passages, see Brian W. Harrison, "Restricted
Inerrancy and the 'Hermeneutic of Discontinuity,'" *Letter and Spirit* 6 (2010): 233–36. For
the conclusion that *Dei Verbum* did not mean to restrict the scope of inerrancy to matters
of faith and morals, see Grillmeier, "Divine Inspiration and Interpretation of Scripture," 211;
Farkasfalvy, "Inspiration and Interpretation," 87. The Pontifical Biblical Commission's *Inspiration and Truth of Sacred Scripture* (2014) has more recently corroborated these interpretations
(*IVSS*, no. 63).

116 *DV*, no. 19.

117 *DV*, no. 8. In his commentary on *Dei Verbum*, Ratzinger notes that the Constitution
refused to decide whether the Tradition had an exclusively interpretive function (Rahner's
position) or whether it also contained propositional content not found in Scripture. "Dogmatic Constitution on Divine Revelation," in *Commentary on the Documents of Vatican
II*, ed. Herbert Vorgrimler; trans. William Glen-Doepl, vol. 3 (New York: Herder & Herder,
1967), 194.

The Dogmatic Constitution ascribes something similar to the Old Testament: "The books of the Old Testament with all their parts, caught up into the proclamation of the Gospel, acquire and show forth their full meaning [*significationem suam completam*] in the New Testament and in turn shed light on it and explain it."[118] Tracy's Heideggerian-disclosive model, according to which Scripture's meaning expands with its readership, most easily explains how the Old Testament—and, indeed, any layer of tradition—gains meaning through its effective history.

Summing up, one can say that neither Benoit nor Rahner nor Tracy accommodates with equal elegance everything that *Dei Verbum* wants to affirm about the reality of Scripture. Admitting that all models remain only "relatively adequate" remains perfectly compatible, however, with holding that some models are more relatively adequate than others. In the chapters that follow, I will argue that Joseph Ratzinger, by incorporating the strengths of various models, offers a more relatively adequate theology of Scripture as the Word of God.

---

118 *DV*, no. 16.

CHAPTER TWO

Ratzinger on
Scripture as God's Word

The previous chapter surveyed the most influential and representative non-Ratzingerian models of biblical authorship and truth: Benoit's Thomist-instrumental model, Rahner's Molinist-predefinitive model, and Tracy's Heideggerian-disclosive model. The hyphenated descriptions attempted to provide convenient handles by which to evoke the distinctives of each thinker, with the first term designating a guiding philosophical sensibility and the second term recalling the mechanism by which God transposes his word into human words. The survey of positions concluded, no doubt unsurprisingly, that none of these models had pronounced the final word on the subject on biblical inspiration. Each excels in explaining some aspects of Scripture's authority and function in the Church while struggling to explain others.

Building on this background, the present chapter argues that Ratzinger has a distinctive theology of biblical inspiration, which, if likewise reduced to a hyphenated handle, would aptly be called a "Bonaventurian-ecclesial" model. Bonaventure's understanding of revelation provides its underlying intuition, and the Church provides the governing medium of divine-human interaction. This "Bonaventurian-ecclesial" model turns out, moreover, to labor under lesser difficulties than the other models.

With a view to showing the greater relative adequacy of Ratzinger's model, the argument will unfold along the following lines. It will begin with an account of Ratzinger's attempt to retrieve Bonaventure's theology of history as a resource for reframing preconciliar debates on biblical revelation and inspiration. Transposing Bonaventure's thought, Ratzinger begins to advance a model of biblical inspiration that is mystical, historically progressive, subject-inclusive, and rationally corrective. The second part of the chapter will turn to the question of relative adequacy, comparing Ratzinger's model to those of Benoit, Rahner, and Tracy on their capacities to reconcile both dogmatic and exegetical data. It aims to show that Ratzinger's model, though not altogether free from internal tensions, has much to recommend it.

RATZINGER'S BONAVENTURIAN-ECCLESIAL MODEL OF INSPIRATION

Though the influence has not yet received the attention it deserves, there are good reasons for considering Ratzinger's theology of Scripture distinctively Bonaventurian.[1] After Ratzinger studied Augustine on the Church, winning an academic prize for his dissertation *Volk und Haus Gottes in Augustins Lehre von der Kirche* (1951),[2] he went on to study Bonaventure on revelation in history. According to Ratzinger's own recollections, his mentor Gottlieb Söhngen had good reasons for suggesting this line of research to him. It would allow Ratzinger to continue tracing the development of Augustinian thought, broadly conceived, into the Middle Ages. It would also allow him to take up the relationship between revelation and history, one of the day's most burning issues.[3] Influenced by the Lutheran exegete Oscar Cullman's *Christus und die Zeit* (1946), Catholic theologians of the 1950s proposed replacing neo-scholastic models of revelation with "salvation-historical" (*heilsgeschichtlich*) models, so that revelation would appear "no longer simply as a communication of truths to the intellect but as a historical action of God in which truth gradually becomes unveiled."[4] Ratzinger made waves when he argued that Bonaventure, a doctor of the Church, embraced such a salvation-historical approach *avant la lettre*.

---

1 In 2007, Aaron Canty noted the lack of studies on the influence of Bonaventure's theology of Revelation on Ratzinger. "Bonaventurian Resonances in Benedict XVI's Theology of Revelation," *Nova et Vetera* 5, no. 2 (2007), 249. Hansjürgen Verweyen titled his 2010 study of Ratzinger's *Habilitation* "An Unknown Ratzinger." *Ein unbekannter Ratzinger: Die Habilitationschrift von 1955 als Schlüssel zu seiner Theologie* (Regensburg: Friedrich Pustet, 2010).

2 Joseph Ratzinger, *Milestones: Memoirs, 1927–1977* (San Francisco: Ignatius, 1998), 97. The dissertation itself can be found in JRGS 1.

3 Ratzinger, *Milestones*, 104; JRGS 2:6–7; *Salt of the Earth: The Church at the End of the Millennium—An Interview with Peter Seewald* (San Francisco: Ignatius, 1997), 62–63.

4 Ratzinger, *Milestones*, 104. Ratzinger mentions the influence of Cullman's work in JRGS 2:6.

The controversial nature of his findings, in fact, long prevented their unabridged publication. One of his examiners found Ratzinger's interpretation of Bonaventure suspiciously "modernist," which led Ratzinger to submit officially only the part of his research treating Bonaventure's theology of history.[5] This would appear in German in 1959 as a landmark monograph, later translated into English as *The Theology of History in St. Bonaventure* (1971).[6] He then turned some of his research treating Bonaventure's theology of revelation into a series of articles.[7] Only with the publication of the second volume of his *Gesammelte Schriften* (2008) did Ratzinger's *Offenbarung und Heilsgeschichte nach der Lehre des heiligen Bonaventura* (1955) appear in its original integrity.[8]

Though Ratzinger's findings regarding Bonaventure's theology of revelation long remained unpublished, they continued to exercise a strong influence on his thought.[9] He would bring them to bear on debates about biblical revelation at Vatican II. And he would later develop them through his own writings—in conversation with philosophical hermeneutics, personalism, and critical exegesis—into one of the more sophisticated models of divine authorship on offer. We find traces of Bonaventure's influence particularly in what I call the mystical, subjective-inclusive, historically progressive, and rationally corrective aspects of Ratzinger's theology of inspiration.

---

5 For what Ratzinger calls the "drama of *Habilitation*," including Michael Schmaus's opposition to its allegedly modernist doctrine of Revelation, see *Milestones*, 103–14.

6 The Bonaventure scholar Oktavian Schmucki calls Ratzinger's book a "turning point [*Wendepunkt*] in the scholarship on Bonaventure and his environment." "Joseph Ratzingers 'Die Geschichtstheologie des hl. Bonaventura: Nachwirken in der Forschung und der Folgezeit," in *Gegenwart der Offenbarung: Zu den Bonaventura Forschungen Joseph Ratzingers*, ed. Marianne Schlosser and Franz-Xaver Heibl, Ratzinger-Studien 2 (Regensburg: Friedrich Pustet, 2010), 357.

7 See JRGS 2:663–786.

8 For the *Habilitationsschrift* in its entirety (with the 1955 chapters on Bonaventure's *Offenbarungsverstandnis* and 1959 chapters on Bonaventure's *Geschichtstheologie*), see JRGS 2:53–659.

9 For a wide-ranging consideration of Bonaventure's influence on Ratzinger, focusing mostly on Ratzinger's Christocentrism and anti-utopianism, see Kurt Koch, "Benedict XVI. und Bonaventura," in *Das Geheimnis des Senfkorns: Grundzüge des theologischen Denkens von Papst Benedict XVI* (Regensburg: Friedrich Pustet, 2010), 45–68. For similar reflections, see Marianne Schlosser, "Zu den Bonaventura-Studien Joseph Ratzingers," in JRGS 2:29–37.

Mystical Revelation

Among the chief discoveries of Ratzinger's *Habilitationsschrift* is the fact that Bonaventure's use of words like "inspiration" and "revelation" do not correspond exactly to the narrower meanings they acquired by the mid-twentieth century. For by then, as the writings of Benoit and Rahner demonstrate, *inspiratio* had come to designate divine assistance in composing canonical writings, an assistance that ceased with the closure of the canon. *Revelatio*, by contrast, came to designate the objectified results of God's self-communication—namely, the sum total of those propositions contained in the biblical text or oral tradition that lie beyond the ken of unaided human reason. But this lexical precision, long taken for granted, did not govern Bonaventure's theological idiom. The Seraphic Doctor uses *inspiratio* and *revelatio* not only interchangeably but according to their resonances in Christian mystical theology.[10]

In their mystical acceptation, Ratzinger suggests, *inspiratio* and *revelatio* belong exclusively neither to the domain of subjective assistance nor to that of objectified product. These concepts seem to straddle the subject-object divide because they presuppose a "subject-relatedness" (*Subjektbezogenheit*) that allows an "immediate transition from salvation history to mysticism."[11] All outwardly perceptible historical events remain brute facts unless accompanied by an "interior self-disclosure of the divinity, which alone is revelation in the true sense and is indicated by the names 'revelatio,' 'inspiratio,' 'illuminatio.'"[12] The fact that such a mystical disclosure proves necessary to perceive God at work in history means this same disclosure will prove necessary for the composition of biblical books—that is, for "inspiration" in the modern sense. "The process of inspiration includes a penetration through the *mundus sensibilis* to the *mundus intelligibilis*."[13] And because such an illumination guides the biblical author, or hagiographer, a similar illumination must guide the biblical interpreter: "The inspired writer cannot relate his *visio intellectualis* in its naked spirituality; he must wrap it in the swaddling clothes of the written word. This means that that which truly consti-

---

10 Joseph Ratzinger, *The Theology of History in St. Bonaventure* (Chicago: Franciscan Herald, 1989), 64.

11 JRGS 2:117. For the "mystical status" of Bonaventure's understanding of revelation, see also Ratzinger, *Theology of History in St. Bonaventure*, 65.

12 JRGS 2:106.

13 Ratzinger, *Theology of History in St. Bonaventure*, 66.

tutes revelation is accessible in the word written by the hagiographer, but that it remains to a degree hidden behind the words and must be unveiled anew."[14] Hence, illuminating *revelatio* and *inspiratio* prove necessary not only for composing Scripture but for interpreting it—that is, for unlocking its properly revelatory meaning. Ratzinger thus concluded that Bonaventure departs from later usages of *revelatio* and *inspiratio* by using the terms both interchangeably and less narrowly. Both terms designate the process by which God, through mystical self-disclosure, guides Scripture's composition as well as its reception in faith.

Having retrieved Bonaventure's more mystical and relational understanding of *revelatio-inspiratio*, Ratzinger would waste little time applying it to the theological ferment of the preconciliar era. On the eve of the opening of the Second Vatican Council, Cardinal Josef Frings invited Ratzinger to appraise *De fontibus revelationis*, the draft schema on divine revelation, before nearly fifty German-speaking bishops.[15] The Bonn professor, though not yet granted the status of official *peritus*,[16] made bold enough to level a recognizably Bonaventurian criticism of the schema. It is not truly traditional, he argued, to describe Scripture and tradition as two *fontes revelationis*. For the great doctors have always understood revelation not as a verbal artifact but as God's self-manifestation, and thus as the "*unus fons* [one source], from which then the two streams of Scripture and tradition flow out."[17] The formulation found in the draft schema reflects a narrowing of perspective rooted in the Church's reactionary posture against historicism: "If revelation comes first, with Scripture and tradition proceeding from it and only being understood from it, then one cannot simply begin a presentation of revelation with Scripture and tradition. The latter order fits with historicism, but not with faith. Before speaking of the documents, one has to say something about God's action from which the documents come; otherwise,

---

14 Ratzinger, *Theology of History in St. Bonaventure*, 66.

15 For the circumstances of this address, see Jared Wicks, "Six Texts by Prof. Joseph Ratzinger as *Peritus* before and during Vatican Council II," *Greg* 89, no. 2 (2008): 241–43; Manuel Schlögl, *Am Anfang eines großen Weges: Joseph Ratzinger in Bonn und Köln*, MMIPB 1 (Regensburg: Schnell & Steiner, 2014), 80.

16 Ratzinger was sworn in as personal advisor to Cardinal Frings on April 4, 1962, but was appointed *peritus* on November 30 of the same year. Schlögl, *Am Anfang eines großen Weges*, 78, 81. See also Ratzinger, *Milestones*, 121.

17 I use the English translation of this address found in Wicks, "Six Texts," 270. The German original can be found in JRGS 7, 1:157–74.

while they may be tools of historians, they will not be wellsprings of faith and of life welling up to eternal life."[18] When Ratzinger presents *revelatio* as a wellspring of divine self-manifestation, with Scripture "proceeding from it and being understood only from it," he advocates for the model of revelation he discovered in Bonaventure. Through the mediation of Cardinal Frings, who championed Ratzinger's single-source view of revelation, Bonaventure's theory of revelation had a significant influence at Vatican II.[19]

In retrieving the Bonaventurian sense of *inspiratio-revelatio*, Ratzinger was doing more than just adducing a weighty authority by which to unsettle manualist theology. He was also recovering a positive orientation on the question of biblical inspiration. One sees this in his willingness to ascribe the functional equivalent of Bonaventurian inspiration—a mystical perception enabling the visionary both to formulate and interpret canonical writings—to founding religious figures. He describes Abraham, for instance, as a man who "enjoyed some kind of mystical experience, a direct eruption of the divine, which . . . enlarged his perception beyond the bounds of what is accessible to our normal senses."[20] And he goes on to present the whole religious tradition of Israel, presumably including its sacred writings, as nothing other than a participation in the "broadening of the horizon that was granted to him."[21] Here the vertical dialogue between Abraham and God continues through the horizontal dialogue among the generations of Abraham's descendants. "God's dialogue with men," he says in *Introduction to Christianity*, "operates only through men's dialogue with each other."[22] Abraham thus counts as a kind of "inspired" author in the Bonaventurian sense. His mystical encounter has inscribed itself into a sacred literature that continues, in turn, to occasion new mystical encounters for "inspired" readers.

As a nonwriting "author" of the Bible, Abraham provides a model for thinking of Christ as an "inspired" author as well. Though Jesus arrives on

18 Wicks, "Six Texts," 271.

19 For Frings's intervention criticizing the language of two sources, see AS I, 3:35. For further references, see Rudolf Voderholzer, "Joseph Ratzinger und das Zweite Vatikanische Konzil," in *Erneuerung in Christus. Das Zweite Vatikanische Konzil (1962-1965) im Spiegel Münchener Kirchenarchiv*, ed. Peter Pfister, Schriften des Archivs des Erzbistums München und Freising 16 (Regensburg: Schnell & Stein, 2012), 99.

20 Joseph Ratzinger, *Faith and the Future* (Chicago: Franciscan Herald, 1971), 33.

21 Ratzinger, *Faith and the Future*, 34.

22 Joseph Ratzinger, *Introduction to Christianity* (San Francisco: Ignatius, 1990), 60.

the scene after the Old Testament was textually complete, his unsurpassably intimate dialogue with the Father allows him to imbue it with new meaning. In an essay from the early 1970s, Ratzinger writes, "Both [Jesus'] freedom and his strictness proceed from a common source: from his prayerful inter-course with the Father, from his personal knowledge of God, on the basis of which he draws the dividing line between center and periphery, between the will of God and the work of man. Jesus has spiritualized the letter . . . in terms of his relationship with God."[23] Again in the 1980s Ratzinger portrays Jesus as one who "spiritualizes" the Abrahamic tradition by virtue of the dialogue with the Father that constitutes the core of his identity: "In this dialogue he passed beyond the letter of the Old Testament and laid bare its spirit in order to reveal the Father 'in the Spirit.'"[24] Though Ratzinger here uses the language of "spiritualizing the letter" or "laying bare its spirit . . . 'in the Spirit'" rather than the technical term "inspiration," one nevertheless detects echoes of Bonaventure's mystical idea of *inspiratio*. By penetrating to the inner meaning of the Old Testament "in the Spirit," Jesus "inspires" it, making such a spiritual reading accessible to others in turn. We will return to the idea of *relecture* as an act of "inspired" authorship below, when we turn to Ratzinger on the inspiration of Old Testament.

If Jesus can imbue even closed texts with new meaning, it stands to reason that he can also "inspire" writings yet to appear, such as the New Testa-ment. In the first volume of *Jesus of Nazareth*, Ratzinger observes that there is a kind of remembering of Jesus' words and deeds, exemplified by Mary and the author of John's Gospel, that "penetrates into the interior dimen-sion" and becomes a "pneumatic event."[25] He continues, "This also has some fundamental implications for the concept of inspiration. . . . Because the author thinks and writes with the memory of the Church, the 'we' to which he belongs opens beyond the personal and is guided in its depths by the Spirit of God, who is the Spirit of truth."[26] Though we will have more to say about the ecclesial dimensions of inspiration in the next section, it is worth noting the continuing influence of Bonaventure's "mystical" model of *inspiratio* in

23 Joseph Ratzinger, *Principles of Catholic Theology: Building Stones for a Fundamental The-ology* (San Francisco: Ignatius, 1987), 98.

24 Joseph Ratzinger, *Behold the Pierced One: An Approach to a Spiritual Christology* (San Francisco: Ignatius, 1986), 29.

25 JN 1:234.

26 JN 1:234.

one of Ratzinger's later works. The Church's memory has implications for inspiration because it constitutes a horizon of enlarged perception, a place where one "penetrates into the interior dimension" of events and receives the experiences to be later consigned to writing. Though not every mystical perception generates canonical Scripture, all canonical Scripture seems to lie downstream from such an enlarged perception.

In identifying mystical perception as the medium of divine-human interaction, Ratzinger stakes out a distinctive position on inspiration. He defines inspiration less narrowly, making it hard to distinguish cleanly from the general current of historical revelation. If there were any rationale in Ratzinger's scheme for employing the word "inspiration" in contradistinction to revelation or tradition, it would be not to pick out a different kind of causal influence but to draw attention to one of the many effects of this enhanced perception: textual production. Ratzinger does not, like Benoit, attempt to distinguish Scripture from all other theological discourse by invoking the category of instrumental causality. Nor does he, like Rahner, appeal to a formally predefinitive grace to consign the Church's mind to writing. Indeed, it is perhaps because Ratzinger knows he risks confusion with the standard definition that he uses the term "inspiration" sparingly in later writings. And while Ratzinger might, with Benoit, grant that literary authors share "analogously" in the charism of inspiration, he nevertheless presents the religious visionary as the prime analogate. Perhaps surprisingly, given their respective reputations in the world of ecclesiastical politics, Ratzinger's mystical emphasis comes close to Tracy's "disclosive" model. Both identify inspiration with the manifestation-to-subjectivity of primordial reality, whether the deepest existential horizon or the memory of the Church. As we shall soon see, however, Ratzinger and Tracy differ on the nature of both the truth being disclosed and the subjectivity receiving the disclosure.

Subject-Inclusive Word of God

From Bonaventure's "mystical" model of inspiration Ratzinger draws forth another seminal insight: the believing subject belongs to the very concept of inspired Scripture. After all, if Scripture remains a dead letter until its meaning has been mystically perceived, Scripture *qua* revelation (as opposed to Scripture *qua* verbal artifact) must represent a complex whole, comprising both text and understanding subject. This holistic vision of Scripture underlies his opposition to certain formulations in the preconciliar draft schema *De fontibus revelationis* and forms the basis for his understanding of the Church as the chief animating subject of Scripture. Having shown that for Bonaventure revelation exists, in a certain sense, only in act, Ratzinger must confront a problem. Does the "subject-relatedness" of Scripture as revelation, mentioned above, not "destroy the objectivity of revelation in favor of a subjective actualism?"[27] Ratzinger is well aware that the influential Reformed theologian Karl Barth conceived the Word of God in proper sense as "pure act"—that is, as a free "event of personal address" untethered from the "constantly available connexion" of dogma and sacrament.[28] Yet nothing could be farther from Bonaventure's mind, Ratzinger answers, than to leave the content of faith up to individual whim.

> Bonaventure's writings take for granted that the mystical perception called *inspiratio* has already been objectified in part in the teachings of the Fathers and in theology so that the basic lines are accessible simply by the acceptance of the Catholic faith,[29] which—as it is summarized in the *Symbolum*—is a principle of exegesis.[30] ... The understanding which elevates Scripture to the status of "revelation" is not to be taken as an affair of the individual reader; but is realized only in the living understanding of Scripture in the Church.[31]

The mystical penetration from which Scripture lives clearly admits of degrees, the lowest and broadest of which is simply the Church's faith. As long as the individual reader adheres to this perduring communal faith, faith's objectivity remains intact. This explains both how Bonaventure's "subject-relatedness" differs from Barth's "subjective actualism," and how even authors not themselves given to be mystic transports may nevertheless be "inspired." It sometimes suffices for them to share in the common mysticism of the faith of the People of God.

Bonaventure's subjective-inclusive understanding of the Word of God sets him apart not only from Barth but from the theology typical of the

---

27 Ratzinger, *Theology of History in St. Bonaventure*, 66–67.

28 Karl Barth, CD I, 1:41. For Ratzinger's use of "subjective actualism" in connection with Barth's doctrine of Revelation, see JRGS 2:61, 69.

29 Here Ratzinger cites *De donis Spiritus Sancti*, coll IV, 13f. and III *Sent*. d. 25, a. 1, q. 1, where Bonaventure explains that Scripture is founded on faith and has the articles of faith for its first interpretive principles.

30 Here Ratzinger refers the reader to the prologue of Bonaventure's *Breviloquium*.

31 Ratzinger, *Theology of History in St. Bonaventure*, 66–67.

mid-twentieth-century neo-scholastic manuals. If Barth neglected the objective aspect of what Bonaventure calls *revelatio*, the neo-scholastics tended to neglect the subjective aspect. The latter group became so habituated to thinking of *revelatio* as propositional objects, Ratzinger implies, that they unwittingly read the tradition anachronistically. When they encountered Trent's teaching that the "truth and rule [of the Gospel] are contained in the written books and unwritten traditions" (*veritatem et disciplinam contineri in libris scriptis et sine scripto traditionibus*),[32] for instance, they could imagine this evangelical truth and rule only as a kind of collection of formulas, distributed partly into Scripture and partly into oral tradition. This became known as the *partim-partim* theory. Conceiving tradition as an extrabiblical "sayings source," theologians tended to invoke it only in cases of extreme need, when they found biblical material alone insufficient to justify evolving Catholic beliefs, such as the Marian dogmas.[33] Whatever its merits, Ratzinger concluded, the *partim-partim* theory was obviously not Bonaventure's. Though both models agree that Scripture *qua* text cannot be the whole of revelation, they supplement Scripture in different ways. The *partim-partim* theory adds unwritten sayings, a complementary material principle, whereas Bonaventure adds the subjectivity of the Church, a complementary formal principle.[34]

Given the opportunity, Ratzinger did not hesitate to use these Bonaventurian insights to criticize *De fontibus revelationis*. During the address delivered to the German bishops on the eve of the opening of Vatican II, already mentioned above, Ratzinger noted the presence of the *partim-partim* formula in the document, criticizing it on historical grounds. There was little evidence, he observed, that orthodox theologians of the pre-Tridentine era ever invoked an esoteric "sayings source" to defend those beliefs lacking obvious foundation in Scripture. After adducing a catena of texts from Tertullian, Aquinas, and Bonaventure, all roundly denying that revelation has a second "material principle" (*Materialprinzip*) alongside Scripture, Ratzinger draws the obvious conclusion: "One cannot in the name of tradition condemn

---

32 DH 1501.

33 Ratzinger notes that those who understood tradition as the "handing down of fixed formulas" tended to oppose dogmatically defining the Assumption, which finds explicit mention no earlier than the fifth century. *Milestones*, 59.

34 For Ratzinger's contrastive comparison of Bonaventure and the *partim-partim* theory in the introduction to his *Habilitationsschrift*, see JRGS 2:66.

as wrong the largest and most venerable part of the tradition."[35] The best way of foreclosing the complete identification of revelation with Scripture as text, accordingly, is not to treat Scripture, tradition, and magisterium as "static entities placed beside each other," but to see them instead as "one living organism of the word of God, which from Christ lives on in the Church."[36] One does better to understand tradition, in other words, not as the prosthesis added to the truncated corpus of Scripture, but as the soul animating the whole body.

Ratzinger, for his part, remains permanently committed to this understanding of the "living organism of the Word of God," whereby revelation comprises both text and ecclesial subject, both material and formal principles. Speaking in his own voice in the early 1970s, Ratzinger observes, "The human subject of the Bible is the Church; she is at the same time the place of transition from human spirit to *Pneuma*, to the Spirit of the common Body of Jesus Christ and, thus, generally the place in which inspiration is possible."[37] Again in the late 1990s, recollecting the chief lessons he took from Bonaventure, Ratzinger explains, "There can be no such thing as *sola scriptura* ('by Scripture alone'), because an essential element of Scripture is the Church as understanding subject, and with this the fundamental sense of Tradition is already given."[38] Perhaps sensing that his wonted emphasis on the ecclesial subject of Scripture threatened to eclipse the contributions

---

35 Wicks, "Six Texts," 275–77. Ratzinger had already elaborated this point in his 1961 essay "Primacy, Episcopacy, and *Successio Apostolica*," in *God's Word: Scripture—Tradition—Office*, ed. Peter Hünermann and Thomas Söding, trans. Henry Taylor (San Francisco: Ignatius, 2005), 26–27.

36 Wicks, "Six Texts," 277.

37 Joseph Ratzinger, *Dogma and Preaching*, ed. Michael J. Miller, trans. Michael J. Miller and Matthew J. O'Connell (San Francisco: Ignatius, 2011), 23.

38 Ratzinger, *Milestones*, 109. He expands on his position elsewhere, "Revelation is always greater than what can be contained in human words, greater even than the words of Scripture. As I have already said in connection with my work on Bonaventure, both in the Middle Ages and at Trent it would have been impossible to refer to Scripture simply as 'revelation,' as is the normal linguistic usage today. Scripture is the essential witness of revelation, but revelation is something alive, something greater and *more*: proper to it is the fact that it *arrives* and *is perceived*—otherwise it could not become revelation.... Revelation has instruments; but it is not separable from the living God, and it always requires a living person to whom it is communicated. Its goal is always to gather and to unite men, and this is why the Church is a necessary aspect of revelation.... And what we call 'tradition' is precisely that part of revelation that goes above and beyond Scripture and cannot be comprehended with a code of formulas" (127).

of individual authors, Ratzinger clarifies just ten years later that Scripture actually emerges from "three interacting subjects":

> First of all, there is the individual author or group of authors to whom we owe a particular scriptural text. But these authors are not autonomous writers in the modern sense; they form part of a collective subject, the "People of God," from within whose heart and to whom they speak. Hence this subject is actually the deeper "author" of the Scriptures. And yet likewise, this people does not exist alone; rather, it knows that it is led, and spoken to, by God himself, who—through men and their humanity—is at the deepest level the one who is speaking.[39]

Perhaps because *inspiratio* involves both producing and receiving texts *qua* revelatory, Ratzinger prefers to speak of Scripture's "subjects," putting "author" in scare quotes. At any event, his most considered statements on divine-human authorship structure the Word of God like a set of Russian dolls. God enfolds the faith of the Church, which enfolds the individual author or interpreter, which enfolds the otherwise inert text.

Ratzinger's mature conclusion that Scripture's meaning reflects a three-fold subjectivity sets him apart, to differing degrees, from Benoit, Rahner, and Tracy. It aligns Ratzinger perhaps most closely with Rahner's Molinist-predefinitive model, according to which God makes the Church's faith-consciousness supervene upon individual authorial intentions. The explanatory mechanism for such an intersubjectivity nevertheless remains rather different—a point to be explored below. The triadic model of authorship distinguishes Ratzinger perhaps most clearly from Benoit, who offers a dyadic model. Benoit's later appeal to "ecclesial inspiration" seems to refer to the Church's charism for getting the original authorial intention correct, not the Church's charism for bearing its own authorial intention. This same point also distinguishes Ratzinger subtly from Tracy. For Tracy, there is a sense in which the Bible, once written down and "distanciated" from the original circumstances of its production, ceases to bear the intention of any historically

---

39 JN 1:xx–xxi. One finds the same threefold nesting of individual authors-People-God in Joseph Ratzinger, "Exegesis and the Magisterium of the Church," in *Opening Up the Scriptures: Joseph Ratzinger and the Foundations of Biblical Interpretation*, ed. J. Granados, C. Granados, and Luis Sánchez Navarro (Grand Rapids, MI: Eerdmans, 2008), 130; "Is the *Catechism of the Catholic Church* Up-to-Date? Reflections Ten Years after Its Publication," in *On the Way to Jesus Christ*, trans. Michael J. Miller (San Francisco: Ignatius, 2005), 148; JN 1:234.

located author. Ratzinger, by contrast, continues to moor the meaning of Scripture in the intentions of historically identifiable authors. The foremost of these historical authors just happens to be corporate and transhistorical: the People of God. Ratzinger thus renders biblical interpretation not so much acontextual as transcontextual, legitimating historically oriented research into both the world behind the text and the world before it.

Historically Progressive Inspiration

Having identified the Church as the principal created subject of Scripture, without whose faith-filled understanding the Bible would not be divine revelation, Ratzinger draws a rather ineluctable conclusion. *Inspiratio* must be ongoing, at least in its receptive sense. After all, if the Church's memory is the site of inspiration, and if the Church marches forward in history, then the charism of inspiration must also perdure in some way. Here again, Ratzinger finds the precedent for such a historically progressive model of inspiration in Bonaventure, whose insights he develops in his own way.

While engaged in his *Habilitation*, Ratzinger noticed that Bonaventure uses the biblical narrative to periodize world history and, indeed, to predict its future course. Departing from Augustine, Bonaventure "schematizes" history in such a way that each event of the Old Testament prophesies an analogous event in the age of the Church. In Bonaventure's own idiom, each Old Testament event contains a "seed" that flowers in the course of history.[40] By Bonaventure's reckoning, some of these event-prophecies had already found fulfillment: Ezekiel corresponded to Charlemagne, for instance,[41] and the division between the Northern and Southern tribes of Israel adumbrated the schism between Eastern and Western Churches.[42] Bonaventure became convinced, however, that some Old Testament episodes adumbrated events still to come. History still awaited a great Christian king corresponding to

---

40 Bonaventure, *Collationes in Hexaemeron*, XIII, 2. Cited in Ratzinger, *Theology of History in St. Bonaventure*, 7–8; for the language of "schema," see 17. In his *Promotionsschrift*, Ratzinger notes that what Augustine sees prefigured in the Old Testament is not the "articulation [*Vereinzelung*] of the historical course" of the Church but "the whole Christ, head and body." JRGS 1:396.

41 Ratzinger, *Theology of History in St. Bonaventure*, 30. With respect to Bonaventure's specific predictions, Ratzinger relies heavily on *Collationes in Hexaemeron* XVI, 29.

42 Joseph Ratzinger, "Offenbarung—Schrift—Überlieferung," *Trierer Theologische Zeitschrift* 67 (1958): 18.

Josiah, for example, as well as a period of great tribulation corresponding to the Babylonian exile.[43] By ascribing such a patterned intelligibility to history, Bonaventure implied that postcanonical historical events could cast a backward light on Scripture, progressively unveiling its meaning.

Ratzinger found this open-ended hermeneutic integrated into the Seraphic Doctor's broader cosmology. Breaking with Aristotelian physics, which treated time as a mere accident of movement, and thus history as a concatenation of unintelligible particulars, Bonaventure recasts temporality as a structural element of the cosmos and the measure of creation's return to God.[44] Christ gives the temporal process its orientation and inner logic,[45] such that cosmos, history, and revelation—without ever progressing beyond Christ—can nevertheless be said to exhibit a forward movement.[46] Ratzinger's conclusion: for Bonaventure, the meaning of Scripture grows as the People of God progresses along its historical journey.[47]

Though Ratzinger advocates for ongoing inspiration only in rather general terms during his activity as *peritus* at Vatican II, Bonaventure's influence remains unmistakable. One hears echoes of Bonaventure's dynamic view of history in Ratzinger's brief statement *De voluntate Dei erga hominem*,[48] for

---

43 Ratzinger, *Theology of History in St. Bonaventure*, 30.

44 Ratzinger, *Theology of History in St. Bonaventure*, 138–43. Ratzinger notes that Bonaventure lies between Aristotle and Augustine in terms of his understanding of time. With Aristotle, he makes time a function of the movement of the heavenly spheres rather than a purely psychological *distentio animi*. However, with Augustine, Bonaventure makes time anthropocentric by envisioning that the heavenly spheres will continue to move only until the full number of God's elect have been gathered. See Joseph Ratzinger, "Der Mensch und die Zeit im Denken des heiligen Bonaventura," in *L'Homme et son destin d'après les penseurs du moyen âge* (Louvain and Paris: Neuwelaerts, 1960), 481. Subsequent scholarship has criticized Ratzinger's *Habilitation* for exaggerating Bonaventure's anti-Aristotelianism and implying Bonaventure's direct dependence on Joachim of Fiore. Schmucki, after reviewing this critical reception, concludes that Ratzinger's interpretation has been nuanced rather than overturned. "Joseph Ratzingers 'Die Geschichtstheologie des hl. Bonaventura,'" 359.

45 "Here [with Bonaventure] something novel occurs: history itself becomes logicized [*logisiert*], becomes understood as a process of the Logos." JRGS 2:245.

46 Ratzinger, *Theology of History in St. Bonaventure*, 117–18.

47 Having identified the Church as the site of Spirit's interpretation of Scripture, Ratzinger adds, "New *contents* can come into view through such an ecclesial interpretation.... But the new content comes into view above all only through a new interpretation of *Scripture*." JRGS 2:67.

48 For a Latin-English version of this document, see Jared Wicks, "Another Text by Joseph Ratzinger as *Peritus* at Vatican II," *Greg* 101, no. 2 (2020), 237–40. A Latin-German version can be found in JRGS 7, no. 1:177–82.

instance, which circulated as an alternative to certain parts of *De fontibus revelationis*[49] and was later incorporated into the so-called Rahner-Ratzinger schema.[50] There Ratzinger speaks of truth's historical pilgrimage: "In this man, Christ Jesus, the end toward which human history tends has already begun. . . . Therefore, all divine discourse, traversing this history [*hanc historiam transcurrens*], arises in a hidden way from what is Christ's (see John 16:14), it regards him, tends toward him, and is fulfilled in him."[51] Divine discourse not only enters history but has a history.

Just how directly Ratzinger's literary efforts influenced the final shape of *Dei Verbum* remains hard to determine. The more distinctively Bonaventurian passages do not seem to have entered the Ratzinger-Rahner schema, which, though widely circulated, itself never managed to become the Council's working document.[52] Still, some of the affirmations of *Dei Verbum*, no. 8, already cited last chapter, bear a striking resemblance. There the Dogmatic Constitution teaches, for instance, that "there is a growth in the understanding of the realities and the words which have been handed down," and that the "Church constantly moves forward toward the fullness of divine truth until the words of God reach their complete fulfillment in her." The Christological *telos* of this forward movement becomes for Ratzinger, as we will see in the next chapter, an important criterion for identifying which ideas Scripture truly intends to affirm.

In the postconciliar period Ratzinger will continue developing in his own voice some of the more adventurous implications of "ongoing" inspiration. Though he never espouses Bonaventure's belief in the historical isomorphism of Israel and Church, he insists often that the Scriptures disclose their full meaning only in the course of history. In an essay dating to 1972, he continues to invoke Bonaventure as an authority for the possibility of the progress of revelation: "Bonaventure . . . coins a striking phrase: *Christi opera*

49 For the influence of this text, see Wicks, "Another Text by Joseph Ratzinger," 233–34; "Joseph Ratzinger Warming the Christic Imagination, October 1962," in *The Center Is JESUS CHRIST Himself: Essays on Revelation, Salvation, and Evangelization in Honor of Robert P. Imbelli*, ed. Andrew Meszaros (Washington, DC, The Catholic University of America Press, 2021), 30–35.

50 For the German-Latin version of the Ratzinger-Rahner collaboration, *De revelatione Dei et hominis in Jesu Christo facta*, see JRGS 1:183–209.

51 Wicks, "Another Text by Joseph Ratzinger," 239. English translation slightly modified.

52 Wicks, "Another Text by Joseph Ratzinger," 235–36. See also John O'Malley, *What Ever Happened at Vatican II?* (Cambridge, MA: Belknap, 2008), 145.

non deficiunt, sed proficiunt ... the seed of apostolicity waxes through the ages unto the fullness of Christ."[53] In the first volume of *Jesus of Nazareth* Ratzinger connects this progressive unfolding of meaning to a rather Bonaventurian notion of *inspiratio*: "The process of continually rereading and drawing out new meanings from words would not have been possible unless the words themselves were already open to it from within. At this point we get a glimmer, even on the historical level of what inspiration means."[54] In the same foreword, Ratzinger also returns to the Bonaventurian image of the "seed" of Scripture, observing how older texts are incorporated into Scripture through a "process in which the word gradually unfolds its inner potentialities, already somehow present like seeds, but needing the challenge of new situations, new experiences and new sufferings in order to open up."[55] His midcareer work *Eschatology* likewise refers to the biblical text as a "schema" that gains its full meaning from the "harvest of historical experience," filling itself with the "reality of subsequent history."[56] The late-career echoes of Bonaventure's *Habilitation* are unmistakable.[57]

This reference to the "reality" of subsequent history points to yet another transposition. Ratzinger's familiarity with Bonaventure's theology of history seems to have prepared him to embrace certain aspects of the Jesuit Pierre Teilhard de Chardin's process-Christology, which conceives history, cosmos, and humanity evolving together toward the "omega" of Christ.[58] "In

---

53 Ratzinger, *Principles of Catholic Theology*, 63–64. Ratzinger cites Bonaventure, *Opusculum* 12, "Epistola de Tribus Quaestionibus," s. 13.

54 JN 1:xx.

55 JN 1:xix.

56 Joseph Ratzinger, *Eschatology: Death and Eternal Life*, trans. Michael Waldstein and Aidan Nichols (Washington, DC: The Catholic University of America Press, 1988), 43.

57 One need only compare this later language to Ratzinger's early comments in his *Habilitationsschrift*: "Certainly Scripture is closed objectively. But its meaning is advancing in a steady growth through history; and this growth is not yet closed. As the physical world contains seeds, so also Scripture contains "seeds"; that is, seeds of meaning. And this meaning develops in a constant process of growth in time." Ratzinger, *Theology of History in St. Bonaventure*, 9. For further observations on the influence of Bonaventure's biblical *semina* on Ratzinger's notion of tradition and dialogical revelation, see, respectively, Joshua Brotherton, "Revisiting the *Sola Scriptura* Debate: Yves Congar and Joseph Ratzinger on Tradition," *Pro Ecclesia* 24, no. 1 (2015), 98–101; Christopher Collins, *Word Made Love: The Dialogical Theology of Joseph Ratzinger/Benedict XVI* (Collegeville, MN: Liturgical, 2013), 28–31.

58 For the unity of these elements: "We said just now that the cosmos was not just an outer framework of human history, not a static mould—a kind of container holding all kinds of living creatures which could just as well be poured into another container. This means, on

a sense," Ratzinger affirms, "creation *is* history."[59] Whether citing Bonaventure or Teilhard, Ratzinger can hold that Scripture, even though its canon remains closed, accrues "reality" over time. For the "reality" that Scripture chiefly intends, namely Christ, gradually gathers all things into himself through his body, the Church.

The historically progressive aspect of Ratzinger's Bonaventurian-ecclesial model of inspiration again distinguishes it to varying degrees from the alternative models. Whereas Benoit's "ecclesial inspiration" understands the ongoing current of inspiration more negatively, as the assistance by which the Spirit prevents the Church from definitively erring in biblical interpretation, Ratzinger conceives it more positively, as the unfolding of Scripture's meaning through the experiences of its ecclesial subject. Rahner has even less to say than Benoit about Scripture's historical growth in meaning. Tracy's notion of Scripture as a religious "classic" generating a "world in front of the text" offers the clearest parallel to Ratzinger's model of ongoing inspiration. Even here, though, differences remain. Whereas Tracy's "classic" floats in some sense above history, "distanced" from its sociohistorical locus, Ratzinger's Bible remains embedded within history, but a history that is itself in motion.

Rationally Corrective Inspiration

Ratzinger's attention to salvation history as a medium of understanding points to a final, recognizably Bonaventurian emphasis of Ratzinger's theology of inspiration—namely, that reason depends greatly on revealed tradition for its right functioning. Ratzinger discovers that Bonaventure focuses on reason in its concrete historical condition, darkened by original sin and

---

the positive side, that the cosmos is movement; that it is not just another case of history *existing in it*, that cosmos itself *is* history. . . . Finally, there is only one single all-embracing world-history, which for all the ups and downs, all the forwards and backwards that it exhibits, nonetheless has a general direction and goes 'forward.'" Ratzinger, *Introduction to Christianity*, 245. For their consummation in Christ: "Faith in Christ will see the beginning of a movement in which dismembered humanity is gathered together more and more into the being of one single Adam, one single body—the man to come. It will see in him the movement to that future of man in which he is completely 'socialized', incorporated into one single being" (179).

59 Joseph Ratzinger, *The Spirit of the Liturgy*, trans. John Saward (San Francisco: Ignatius, 2000), 28. Ratzinger proceeds to connect this idea of a cosmos in movement to both the Teilhard's "modern evolutionary world view" and the Bonaventurian paradigm of creation's *"exitus* and *reditus"* (28–31).

therefore highly dependent on the light of faith for its proper exercise. Combining this basic faith-and-reason sensibility with the corporate model of faith, Ratzinger eventually develops a rather communally and historically "situated" model of human reason. Drawing out the implications of this theory, he concludes to the impossibility of a "view from nowhere"—that is, of a perfectly neutral alternative to the Church's own faith-based tradition of rational inquiry.

Ratzinger reports discovering in Bonaventure a "very different concept of human reason" from that presupposed by Thomas Aquinas.[60] As Ratzinger reads him, Aquinas, when articulating the relationship between faith and reason, takes his point of departure from the abstract order of nature as such, thus emphasizing the integrity of reason.[61] Bonaventure, by contrast, takes his point of departure from the historical order of nature, where reason has been darkened by original sin and remains thrall to various unruly affections.[62] This leads to a different conception of the relation between faith and reason. Whereas the Thomist school, at least in its neo-scholastic iteration, tends be equally comfortable speaking of reason seeking faith and vice versa, Bonaventure admits only the vice versa. In the Bonaventurian journey toward wisdom, reason occupies the middle position in an irreversible sequence: *a fide–per rationem–ad contemplationem*.[63] In the Bonaventurian scheme, reason is "strictly 'natural' according to its origin and inner form, but in the present salvation-historical situation can exercise its function meaningfully only if it subordinates itself to faith, following it and not going ahead

---

60 Ratzinger, *Principles of Catholic Theology*, 320.

61 For exposition of this position and citations, see JRGS 2:342–45.

62 JRGS 2:346–349. Ratzinger says elsewhere, "Bonaventure knows a *violentia rationis*—a violence of reason—that is not to be measured by personal reality." *Principles of Catholic Theology*, 320. He refers to a passage from Bonaventure's *Sentence Commentary*, proemium, quaestio 2, ad 6. There, to the objection that a method "inquisitive of secrets" (*inquisitivus secretorum*) does not befit the end of theology, since it tends to enervate faith, Bonaventure replies: "Quando assentitur propter se rationi, tunc aufertur locus fidei, quia in anima hominis dominatur violentia rationis. Sed quando fides non assentit propter rationem, sed propter amorem eius cui assentit, desiderat habere rationes; tunc non evacuat ratio humana meritum, sed auget solatium." *Sent.* I:11.

63 JRGS 2:403. Ratzinger points to the following passage from Bonaventure's homily "Christ the One Teacher of All": "Ex praedictis ergo apparet, *quo ordine* et *quo acutore* pervenitur ad sapientiam.—Ordo enim est, ut inchoetur a stabilitate *fidei* et procedatur per serenitatem *rationis*, ut perveniatur ad suavitatem *contemplationis*." *Chr mag* 15, p. 571.

of it."[64] Though reason represents an autonomous principle, in other words, it can advance to contemplative insight only under the tutelage of ecclesial faith. For Ratzinger's Bonaventure, reason represents something of a wax nose that the passions are forever pulling out of joint.

In his theological advocacy at the Second Vatican Council, Ratzinger will make Bonaventure's wax-nose model of reason his own, while transposing it into the more contemporary conceptuality of historical conditioning.[65] In a lecture on the cultural moment to be addressed by Vatican II, which Ratzinger composed for delivery by Cardinal Frings in November 1961, Ratzinger encourages the Council to embrace a certain kind of cultural "relativism."[66] "It would be a mistake to think that relativism is completely bad. . . . If it helps us recognize the relativity and mutability of merely human forms and institutions, then it can contribute to setting free what is really absolute from its only apparently absolute casing and so let us see this really absolute more clearly in its true purity. Only when relativism denies all absolutes and admits only relativities is it then certainly a denial of faith."[67] Despite denying the absoluteness of European Christianity, Ratzinger does not pretend that all cultural forms are equally suited to the Church's mission. A certain "technological civilization" has replaced Hellenism as the world's new *koinē*. And this technological paradigm has in turn rendered the natural world religiously mute and opaque, precipitating a decline of faith and calling for a new evangelizing strategy, one centered in the heart.[68] Significantly, Ratzinger's remarks imply that an era's intellectual categories and passions not only reflect human reason but shape it, leaving it more sensitive to some values and realities than others.

By the mid-1970s Ratzinger would develop this neo-Bonaventurian insight into a full-blown anthropology accentuating the inescapable mutual conditioning of private reason and historical tradition. Ratzinger argues for this interdependence most strikingly in an essay originally entitled "Tradition und Fortschritt" (1974), later retitled "Scripture and Tradition" and

---

64 JRGS 2:403. See also Ratzinger's 1962 essay *"Gratia Praesupponit Naturam,"* in *Dogma and Preaching,* 143–61.

65 For Ratzinger's attentiveness to reason in its salvation historical condition, albeit with more reference to its Augustinian precedents, see Pech, *Paradox und Wahrheit,* 150–52.

66 For the historical background to this address, see Wicks, "Six Texts," 234–35.

67 Wicks, "Six Texts," 256–57.

68 Wicks, "Six Texts," 257–58.

incorporated into *Principles of Catholic Theology*.[69] The essay contends that "humanity and historicity, intellect and history, are inextricably related," not only for the case of Christian revelation, but for all of human existence.[70] There Ratzinger takes the everyday experience of speech as a sort of paradigm case for the embeddedness of individual creativity within communal tradition. "As for speech, it is essentially as something bestowed, something received, that it fulfills its function of conferring unity."[71] As anyone who studies a foreign language soon discovers, a certain arbitrariness governs the grammar and vocabulary of any language. Lacking necessary reasons for inevitable decisions regarding genders, tenses, and phonemes, a mother tongue must be accepted on naked authority if it is to serve its purpose of uniting communities.

The idea that language itself represents an authoritative, communal tradition has important anthropological consequences. It means, first of all, that everyone who uses language for self-expression, no matter how original or idiosyncratic, nevertheless stands embedded within a kind of corporate subjectivity. "Tradition," observes Ratzinger, "requires a subject in whom to adhere, a bearer, whom it finds (not only, but basically) in a linguistic community. The matter of tradition relates to both history and community. It is possible only because many subjects become, as it were, one subject in the context of a common heritage."[72] All language users, therefore, find themselves "incorporated" into a collective personality, heir to the blessings and curses of a "particular history."[73]

Here Ratzinger works out the deeper anthropological foundations for his proposal, explored above, to treat biblical inspiration as a dimension of mystical tradition. Any attempt to pass on an unrepeatable religious encounter by symbolic communication requires a transgenerational communal authority analogous to that of a linguistic community. "To that extent, even the awareness that religion must rest on a higher authority than that of one's own reason, and that it needs a community as a 'carrier,' is part of mankind's

---

69 See Ratzinger, *Principles of Catholic Theology*, 87–94. Ratzinger cites as the source for his chapter: "Tradition und Fortschritt," *ibw-Journal* 12 (1974): 1–7.

70 Ratzinger, *Principles of Catholic Theology*, 87.

71 Ratzinger, *Principles of Catholic Theology*, 88.

72 Ratzinger, *Principles of Catholic Theology*, 88.

73 Ratzinger, *Principles of Catholic Theology*, 89.

basic knowledge, though found in manifold forms and even distortions."[74] It is the common experience of all humanity, then, that both reason and religion live within a collective subjective.[75] This subject not only reflects the rational and religious nature of its constituents, but determines in part what they will find both rationally and religiously plausible. Since reason cannot develop outside a linguistic community, it cannot escape such historical conditioning. At most, reason can hope to be particularized by an "inspired" tradition, one purified by the constant pressure of revelation and pregnant with the thoughts of a transcendent mind.

Ratzinger's ecclesial model of inspiration, with its mystical, subject-inclusive, historically progressive, and rationally corrective dimensions, shows the unmistakable influence of the Seraphic Doctor. As a theological expert at the Second Vatican Council, Ratzinger brought these Bonaventurian principles to bear on the debates over *De fontibus revelationis* and the nature of the Council itself. Later, as a theologian speaking in private capacity, he would carry these Bonaventurian principles forward in his own distinctive style. He transposes the Bonaventurian language of mystical *revelatio* into personalist language of prayerful "dialogue" and "understanding subject." He likewise recasts Bonaventure's cosmology of progressive return to Christ into a modified Teilhardian process-Christology, drawing interpretive implications from it not unlike the those theorized in post-Heideggerian hermeneutics. He translates Bonaventure's attention to the affective preconditions for reason's right exercise into a frank admission of the historical situatedness of all human reason. In all these ways, Ratzinger appropriates elements of Bonaventure's *Offenbarungsverständnis*, transposing them into a contemporary idiom. It still remains, however, to test the relative adequacy of this transposition.

THE GREATER RELATIVE ADEQUACY OF THE BONAVENTURIAN-ECCLESIAL MODEL OF INSPIRATION

The previous chapter concluded by considering a few of the doctrinal "pegs" that *Dei Verbum* staked out but then entrusted to theologians for

---

74 Ratzinger, *Behold the Pierced One*, 29.

75 For further reflections on the interdependence of individual religious genius and communal religious traditions, see also Ratzinger, *Introduction to Christianity*, 59–60.

theoretical reconciliation. These concerned principally the nature of the relationship between Scripture's divine and human authors and the implications of this synergy for the truth of Scripture. Deferring the discussion of biblical veracity to the next chapter, I would like to focus here on the doctrinal "pegs" more closely related to the question of authorship. Chief among the *desiderata* expressed by *Dei Verbum* is a theory of inspiration that accounts for the interdependence of Scripture and the Church. The more adequate the theory, however, the more it will offer such an account without loosening the other doctrinal "pegs," such as the authority of Scripture over the Church's teaching, or the "analogous" inspiration of Old and New Testaments.

The reflections that follow attempt to deepen the systematic reflection broached in the last chapter. They examine more closely the doctrine of Vatican II, making some allusion to Trent and Vatican I in passing. But they also consider the respective capacities of Ratzinger, Benoit, Rahner, and Tracy to harmonize the doctrinal data. I argue that Ratzinger attains a better relative adequacy overall. This remains true even though other authors excel at securing one or another doctrinal *desideratum*, and even though Ratzinger leaves certain premises speculatively underdeveloped.

Organic Unity of Scripture and Church

Over and against the Reformers' *cri de coeur* of "Scripture alone" (*sola scriptura*), the Catholic tradition affirms in many ways that Scripture lives essentially as the "Church's book." Trent teaches that the truth of the Gospel inheres in "written books and unwritten traditions." With even more explicit reference to the Church, Vatican II states that "sacred tradition, Sacred Scripture and the teaching authority of the Church, in accord with God's most wise design, are so linked and joined together that one cannot stand without the others."[76] None of the Catholic authors surveyed fails to affirm such a fundamental Catholic doctrine. But this does not mean that all explain the reciprocal dependence of Scripture and ecclesial tradition with equal elegance. Ratzinger arguably excels on this point both by introducing the People of God as a third level of authorship and by developing an anthropological foundation for it.

Before discussing the advantages of Ratzinger's social theory of inspiration, however, we do well to consider its compatibility with the picture of

76 *DV*, no. 10.

authorship taught by Vatican II. By its silence on the matter of communal authorship, one might easily conclude that *Dei Verbum* excludes it: "In composing the sacred Books, God chose and employed certain men, who, while engaged in this task, made full use of their faculties and powers, so that, with God himself acting in them and through them, they as true authors committed to writing everything and only those things that he wanted written."[77] Here, as elsewhere, the only agents mentioned are God and individual human authors. But a look at the drafting history suggests that, once again, the Council opted to leave the question of social inspiration open. It quietly dropped the first draft schema's statement that the "charism of sacred inspiration was proper and personal to the sacred authors chosen and guided by God, not a charism common and communicated to the assembly [*coetui*] of the faithful."[78] At the same time, however, it also avoided any language that positively distinguished the community as an agent in its own right. When various council fathers proposed that the Dogmatic Constitution describe God using human authors "individually or collectively" (*singillatim vel collective*), the drafting committee rejected it. "Our text," explains the *relator* Alois Grillmeier, "leaves the matter open."[79] This openness seems to characterize the text in its final state as well.[80]

As we have already seen, Ratzinger's Bonaventurian-ecclesial model takes advantage of this openness, blending individual and corporate authorship of Scripture. As we have also already seen, he additionally argues that embeddedness in a kind of "collective subject" is the normal condition of all language users. Combining these two insights, Ratzinger more easily presents his Bonaventurian social inspiration not as a *sui generis* phenomenon but as the supernatural elevation of the traditionary process basic to human nature. He makes this point especially clear in his essay "What in Fact Is

---

77 *DV*, no. 11.

78 *AS* I, 3:18.

79 AS IV, 1:360. This arguably reflects Ratzinger's own 1962 proposal that the draft schema's treatment of individual authorship "be developed so as to show that the human writer really is an *auctor* [author] and is inserted into the people of God. That can be done with light touches so that it does not lead to dogmatically defining a new theory in place of the old." Wicks, "Six Texts," 279.

80 For a brief history of the debate on this topic, see Helmut Gabel, *Inspirationsverständnis im Wandel: Theologische Neuorientierung im Umfeld des Zweiten Vatikanischen Konzils* (Mainz: Matthias Grünewald, 1991), 101–3.

Theology?" (2000).[81] There, taking up the "nature of inspiration," he remarks that

> scripture is not a meteorite fallen from the sky, so that it would . . . stand in contrast to all human words. Certainly, Scripture carries **God's thoughts** within it: that makes it unique and constitutes it an "authority." Yet it is **transmitted by a human history**. It carries within it the life and thought of a historical society that we call the "People of God," because they are brought together, and held together, by the coming of the divine word.[82]

God has not only enlightened the minds of desultory individuals, in other words, but has elected and elevated a corporate personality, the People of God, endowing it with revelation and a more-than-sociological unity.[83] Because Scripture took shape in a rhythmic exchange between individual, community, and Word, it enjoys an organic relationship to the Church.

This reprised Bonaventurian-ecclesial model enjoys certain advantages in explaining the nonredundancy of the Church. Both Benoit and Tracy remain hampered in their ability to yoke Scripture to ecclesial tradition by their rather privatized notions of inspiration. Benoit defines inspiration as God's instrumentalization of an individual's faculties, effectively leaving the People of God outside the process. Tracy, for all his insistence on the Bible as the "church's book," defines "church" rather loosely. For him, "church" designates "all that are grounded in the confession that Jesus Christ is Lord."[84] There is little appeal to sacramental character, theological virtues, or anything else that might characterize the Church as a true corporate personality

---

81 This address to the theological faculty at the University of Navarre was republished in Ratzinger, *Pilgrim Fellowship of Faith: The Church as Communion*, ed. Stephan Otto Horn and Vinzenz Pfnür, trans. Henry Taylor (San Francisco: Ignatius, 2005), 29–37.

82 Ratzinger, "What in Fact Is Theology?," *Pilgrim Fellowship of Faith*, 33. Boldface original.

83 For Ratzinger's belief that the Church, as Christ's body, enjoys a more than a "purely sociological" unity, see his *The Nature and Mission of Theology: Essays to Orient Theology in Today's Debates* (San Francisco: Ignatius, 1995), 53–54, 94–95.

84 David Tracy, *The Analogical Imagination: Christian Theology in a Culture of Pluralism* (New York: Crossroad, 1981), 251. Protestant exegesis concerned with effective-historical interpretation often presupposes a similarly diffuse model of ecclesiality. For the Swiss theologian Ulrich Luz, for instance, Scripture lives from the church understood as an "unbounded community of dialogue among confessions and persons, who hear the Bible and interpret it, who are on the way to reciprocal understanding, consensus, and love." *Theologische Hermeneutik des Neuen Testaments* (Neukirchen-Vluyn: Neukirchener Verlag, 2014), 556.

rather than a voluntary aggregate of sincere individuals.[85] For neither Benoit nor Tracy, then, does the selfsame People of God stand on both sides of the traditioning process, as both shaper and receiver of texts. This implies a weaker bond between Scripture and Church.

As the previous chapter made clear, however, things stand rather differently with Rahner. For him inspiration designates the process by which God predestines individual authors to represent the mind of the Church, in which they participate as members, and to assign the contents of this mind a literary form. Ecclesial consciousness, therefore, means more for the German Jesuit than simply the aggregate of individual interpretations. Indeed, it closely resembles Ratzinger's idea of the Church as "understanding subject." This allows Rahner to claim that the same mind that produced Scripture also produced the Church's dogmatic tradition, which can thus hardly be irrelevant to sound exegesis. Though Rahner anticipates Ratzinger's own position to a great extent, his reliance on certain aspects of Molinist anthropology ultimately gives the coincidence of individual and ecclesial consciousness a rather adventitious quality.

The anthropological difference can be glimpsed in the respective attitudes toward language. Rahner's global framework remains a *res-et-sententiae* theory. God ensures the revealed contents, now reconceived as the mind of the inspired Church, and the human author assigns these contents a literary form, assuming sole responsibility for language, genre, and so on. Rahner's replacement of prelinguistic divine content with ecclesial consciousness goes a long way toward justifying the organic interdependence of Scripture and Church. But it nevertheless remains vulnerable to a couple of the objections also leveled against its nineteenth-century precursors.

First, it continues to presuppose a rather extrinsic relationship between thought and language. Among the most frequent criticisms of nineteenth-century versions of the *res-et-sententiae* theory was its reliance on a "psychological vivisection," a parting of thought and expression that left no organically unified account of authorship.[86] This anticipated Wittgenstein's famous

---

85 In his foreword to the German Edition of *Biblical Interpretation in Crisis*, Ratzinger insists that the People of God constitutes a subject distinct from either the individual scholar or even the whole "Republic of the Learned." JRGS 9, 2:784.

86 Derek Holmes and Robert Murray, introduction to *On the Inspiration of Scripture: John Henry Newman*, ed. Derek Holmes and Robert Murray (Washington, DC: Corpus Books, 1967), 54. James Tunstead Burtchaell lists several complaints against Franzelin's model

objection to Augustine's *Confessions* on thought and language: "Augustine describes the learning of human language as if the child came into a strange country; that is, as if it already had a language, only not this one. Or again: as if the child could already *think*, only not yet speak. And 'think' would here mean something like 'talk to itself.'"[87] Wittgenstein's insight that language shapes thought as much as reflects it lies at the root of the so-called linguistic turn in philosophy. But Rahner remains reluctant to take this turn. Even in "Theology in the New Testament," a 1962 essay originally contributed to a Ratzinger-edited *Festschrift* for Gottlieb Söhngen, and evidently intended to address certain criticisms of his theory of inspiration, he continues to distinguish rather sharply between the biblical author's original experience of revelation (*kerygma*) and its linguistic expression. "The kerygma, properly understood, is not an additional discourse about something, but is the reality itself."[88] Here the contrast between the "reality itself" and "additional discourse" hearkens back to the Jesuit *res-et-sententiae* theory. But Rahner speaks increasingly of "reality itself" as something so ineffable as to be addressable only to the human person's prelinguistic and preconceptual core: "No doubt, the actual event of revelation in man begins also so 'profoundly' in his innermost center . . . that every conceptual objectification of what is thus communicated is secondary in comparison, even though this objectification is also utterly willed in itself by God and guaranteed in its rightness."[89] Such statements led Avery Dulles to group Rahner with thinkers like David Tracy, who locate biblical authority not in what the words teach but in some existential experience standing behind it.[90] They likewise won Rahner a place among George Lindbeck's "experiential-expressivists," those theologians who imagine a universal religious experience "prior to all conceptualization" and unstructured by cultural-linguistic frameworks.[91] A

---

along these lines. See Burtchaell, *Catholic Theories of Biblical Inspiration since 1810: A Review and Critique* (London: Cambridge University Press, 1969), 150–63.

87 Ludwig Wittgenstein, *Philosophical Investigations* (Oxford: Blackwell, 1997), 32.

88 Karl Rahner, "Theology in the New Testament," in *Theological Investigations*, vol. 5 (London: Darton, Longman & Todd, 1966), 36.

89 Rahner, "Theology in the New Testament," 39.

90 Avery Dulles, *The Craft of Theology: From Symbol to System*, new exp. ed. (New York: Crossroad, 1992), 77–78.

91 George A. Lindbeck, *The Nature of Doctrine: Religion and Theology in a Postliberal Age* (Philadelphia: Westminster, 1984), 32.

more organic and reciprocal relationship between the "private language" of revelation and its public literary expression seems desirable.

The second difficulty, following closely on the first, has to do with a lack of natural analogies for the ecclesial dimension of inspiration. Rahnerian "formal predefinition" presupposes that God infallibly guides the author toward producing writings expressive of the Church's mind by the providential arrangement of external circumstances, such as a request for a clarifying letter. But this does not exactly explain how the author's mind comes to contain at least implicitly the mind of the Church, possessing intentions that it itself cannot comprehensively survey. The process by which God inspires the individual author with the mind of the Church remains a sort of "black box," veiled behind the opacity of divine predestination. Ratzinger's appeal to the notion of the corporate personality, by contrast, tends to demystify this divinely ordained harmony. Since individual thinking develops in the medium of common language, according to Ratzinger, the linguistic community naturally inscribes itself in individual thought. In an even more profound way, then, the mind of the Church would inscribe itself on those who share both the supernatural virtue of faith and common cultural-linguistic framework of the Church's life. Ratzinger thus more easily presents his theory of communal inspiration as the elevation of a natural process than as a replacement for one.

It should not surprise, then, if Ratzinger shows a steadily growing ambivalence toward Rahner's thinking. When Ratzinger reviews the German edition of *Inspiration in the Bible* in 1958, he hails it as a "brilliant example of theological thinking that firmly grasps and gets at the heart of the matter."[92] He adds nothing in criticism. By the time he reviews the second edition of Rahner's *Visions and Prophecies* two years later, however, he shows more reserve. This is especially true of Rahner's tendency to place prophetic and individual mysticism on a common level: "It is clear that in the latter case overlooking an imaginative vision does not reject or hinder what has genuinely been worked by God; but can we also apply that without qualification to the prophetic vision, or must not say that … precisely here the communicable

---

92 Joseph Ratzinger, "Theologie im Präsens" (review of *Über die Schriftinspiration*, by Karl Rahner, *Zur Theologie des Todes*, by Karl Rahner, and *Mächte und Gewalten im Neuen Testament*, by Heinrich Schlier), *Wort und Wahrheit* 13 (1958): 645.

and expressible represent the genuine element?"[93] Here Ratzinger resists treating prophetic visions, the kind from which Scripture originates, as a purely private language, indifferently translatable into any number of public literary forms.

This basic difference from Rahner would become more apparent to Ratzinger during and after the Council. Reflecting in *Milestones* on his experience collaborating with Rahner to improve *De fontibus revelationis*, Ratzinger recalls, "It became clear to me that, despite our agreement in many desires and conclusions, Rahner and I lived on two different theological planets.... Despite his early reading of the Fathers, his theology was totally conditioned by the tradition of Suarezian scholasticism and its new reception in light of Heidegger. His was a speculative and philosophical theology in which Scripture and the Fathers in the end did not play an important role and in which the historical dimension was really of little significance."[94] Though they often found themselves agreed on the inadequacy of neo-scholastic solutions, in other words, Ratzinger found himself more concerned with the "historical dimension" of both human nature and inspiration than Rahner's formation in Jesuit scholasticism had prepared him to be. Ratzinger would manifest this difference of sensibility after the Council in criticizing, *inter alia*, Rahner's proposal to substitute the traditional creeds with various "short formulas of faith." For Ratzinger, such a position naively assumes the "fiction of a commonly understood universal language," failing to see the Church as an "independent linguistic subject."[95] Whereas Ratzinger relates thought and historically transmitted language in a roughly hylemorphic way, emphasizing their inseparability and reciprocal influence, Rahner inclines toward a more Platonic dualism, whereby language functions as thought's detachable vehicle.

Scripture's Unique Authority as God's Word

Given Ratzinger's accent on the Church as Scripture's animating subject, without which the text fails to reveal properly, one might naturally wonder whether he does justice to Scripture's unique authority vis-à-vis the Church.

---

93 Joseph Ratzinger, review of Karl Rahner, *Visionen und Prophezeiungen*, 2nd ed., TRev 56, no. 6 (1960): 250.

94 Ratzinger, *Milestones*, 128.

95 Ratzinger, *Principles of Catholic Theology*, 127, 125.

If God is more *auctor* of Scripture than of any other religious document, it follows that Scripture should enjoy more *auctoritas* than any other statements, including doctrinal decrees. *Dei Verbum* teaches as much when it observes, "This teaching office is not above the word of God, but serves it, teaching only what has been handed on, listening to it devoutly, guarding it scrupulously and explaining it faithfully in accord with a divine commission and with the help of the Holy Spirit."[96] How well does Ratzinger's Bonaventurian-ecclesial inspiration preserve the unique authority of the Bible and the serving and preserving character of the teaching office? A careful consideration shows that Ratzinger accounts for the ongoing normativity of Scripture as elegantly as any save perhaps Benoit.

By way of assessment, it must first be noted that Ratzinger does affirm Scripture's preeminence. Ratzinger reports approvingly, for instance, how the later Bonaventure, as soon as he comes to define *theologia* more narrowly as divine discourse (as opposed to human efforts to articulate the divine), begins to reserve the designation *theologia* for the Bible alone.[97] Ratzinger sees in these linguistic decisions a sign of Bonaventure's reverence for the Bible's unique authority: "The writers of Holy Scripture speak as themselves, as men, and yet, precisely in doing so, they are 'theologoi,' those through whom God as subject, as the word that speaks itself, enters into history. What distinguishes Holy Scripture from all later theology is thus completely safeguarded."[98] But is Bonaventure's solution Ratzinger's solution? Does Scripture stand above all other teaching because God became its "subject" through the mystical elevation of its authors? To my knowledge, Ratzinger nowhere tackles this question head on. His various accounts of the preeminence of Scripture, however, seem to require the mystical preeminence of Christ and the apostles.

Ratzinger sometimes offers a functional account of biblical authority, ranking Scripture above dogma because of the natural hierarchy of their respective tasks. According to *Dogma and Preaching*, for instance, it

---

96 *DV*, no. 10. It was customary among neo-scholastic manuals to distinguish the positive inspiration characterizing the Bible and the merely negative assistance of the Holy Spirit preserving magisterial statements from error. See, for instance, Sebastian Tromp, *De Sacrae Scripturae inspiratione*, 6th ed. (Rome: Gregorian University Press, 1962), 111.

97 Ratzinger, *Principles of Catholic Theology*, 321. For the Pseudo-Dionysian background to this use of *theologia*, Ratzinger refers the reader to *The Theology of History in St. Bonaventure*, 89n18. But see also JRGS 2:395–96.

98 Ratzinger, *Principles of Catholic Theology*, 321.

is dogma's job to interpret Scripture. Hence, "There is a necessary mutual relationship and a priority between Scripture and dogma. The interpreter ranks not higher but lower than what is interpreted."[99] The simplicity of this explanation is deceptive, however, since Ratzinger just a few years earlier admits that the interpretive function runs both ways. *Das Problem der Dogmengeschichte in der Sicht der katholischen Theologie* (1966) agrees that Scripture's narrative mode requires a dogmatic interpretation whereby the "multivalent image-language of Scripture is translated into the univocity [*Eindeutigkeit*] of the concept."[100] But it also adds that the "supra-historical constancy of images (at least of the great *Ursymbole* of humanity) is greater than that of concepts," with the result that "dogma as interpretation must be constantly read backwards with reference to what is interpreted and must be understood on that basis."[101] When the conceptual background presupposed in any dogmatic clarification fades, Scripture must eventually play some role in interpreting dogma. Ratzinger's Commentary on *Dei Verbum* argues, in fact, that proceeding as if all clarity lay on the side of dogma and all obscurity on the side of Scripture would "ultimately destroy the serving character of the teaching office."[102] Ratzinger would reaffirm this position twenty years later when, in response to Orthodox exegete Thomas Hopko's

---

99 Ratzinger, *Dogma and Preaching*, 51. Again, "The Church never coincides with the Word. It is in her and above her" (23). Elsewhere he proposes that Scripture and the Fathers of the Church belong together as "word and answer": "The two are not identical, are not of equal importance, do not possess the same normative power." *Principles of Catholic Theology*, 147. Ratzinger elsewhere notes that "office" has a lower rank than word and sacrament because it is not the "cause" of unity but the "condition" for it. "Ministerial Office and the Unity of the Church," 56.

100 Joseph Ratzinger, *Das Problem der Dogmengeschichte in der Sicht der katholischen Theologie*, Arbeitsgemeinschaft für Forschung des Landes Nordrhein–Westfalen 139 (Köln: Westdeutscher Verlag, 1966), 26. He remarks similarly elsewhere that "magisterial pronouncements have their own historicity and their own need of interpretation [*Auslegungsbedürftigkeit*] in light of their historical totality as well as their essential ordination to their sources." "Das Problem der Mariologie," *TRev* 61, no. 2 (1965), 82. In later writings, however, Ratzinger tends to emphasize the clarification of dogma by Scripture less, observing simply that "apostolic authority ... interprets the word which is handed down and gives it unequivocal clarity of meaning." *Nature and Mission of Theology*, 60.

101 Ratzinger, *Das Problem der Dogmengeschichte*, 27.

102 Joseph Ratzinger, "The Transmission of Divine Revelation," in *Commentary on the Documents of Vatican II*, ed. Herbert Vorgrimler; trans. William Glen–Doepl, vol. 3 (New York: Herder & Herder, 1967), 187. Eckart Schmidt notes that Ratzinger is nowhere more optimistic about the possibilities of historical criticism to clarify the meaning of Scripture than in this essay. Eckart D. Schmidt, *"... das Wort Gottes immer mehr zu lieben:" Joseph Ratzingers*

plea for a more liturgical and dogmatic hermeneutic, he proposed a two-way street: "The Bible interprets the church, and the church interprets the Bible. . . . We cannot seek refuge in an ecclesiastical positivism. Finally, the last word belongs to the church, but the church must give the last word to the Bible."[103] Scripture thus ranks highest both because (in the short run) dogma interprets it and because (in the long run) it interprets dogma. Hence, even though Ratzinger always subordinates the magisterium and its dogmas to Scripture, the functional rationale does not always support this conclusion.

Perhaps sensing this inadequacy, Ratzinger elsewhere supplements the functional explanation with a more Christological one. That is to say, he sometimes suggests that the functional distinction between Scripture (the interpreted) and dogma (the interpreter) reflects two intensities of revelation, the peak intensity of the "once only," and the lesser intensity of the "forever."[104] The "once only" refers to the unrepeatability of the Incarnate Word, while the open-endedness of dogmatic interpretation corresponds to the limitless diffusion of Christ's presence through the Spirit to the Church.[105] In a letter to Karl Rahner dating from the time of their collaboration as conciliar *periti*, Ratzinger further clarifies that the Christ-event constitutes a "once only" not simply because it stands first in time but because it represents an unsurpassable fullness. It is therefore better, he concludes, to speak not of a "last public revelation" (*ultima revelatio publica*) but of the "complete revelation" (*completa revelatio*).[106] Though Ratzinger obviously believes that this unsurpass-

---

Bibelhermeneutik im Kontext der Exegesegeschichte der römischkatholischen Kirche, SBS 233 (Stuttgart: Katholisches Bibelwerk, 2015), 79, 167.

103 Paul T. Stallsworth, "The Story of an Encounter," in *Biblical Interpretation in Crisis. The Ratzinger Conference on Bible and Church*, ed. Richard John Neuhaus, Encounter Series 9, (Grand Rapids, MI: Eerdmans, 1989), 118.

104 Joseph Ratzinger, "The Question of the Concept of Tradition: A Provisional Response," in *God's Word: Scripture, Tradition, Office*, ed. Peter Hünermann and Thomas Söding, trans. Henry Taylor (San Francisco: Ignatius, 2008), 65.

105 Ratzinger explains, "Incorporated into the Church's authoritative office of witness, which derives its rights and power from the presence of the Spirit, from Christ's contemporaneity with all our days, in which he is ever the Christ today, the office of witness that belongs to the unique word of Scripture set down once and for all will have to be restored to rights and power; that office of witness of the Scriptural word derives its enduring validity from the uniqueness of the historical act of salvation of Jesus Christ, who once gave up his crucified body." "Question of the Concept of Tradition," 67.

106 "Wenn hier (sachlich mit Recht) die Christus-Offenbarung als die ultima revelatio publica bezeichnet wird, wird sehr stark der Eindruck einer stückweisen Reihe von einzelnen nacheinander gesagten Offenbarungen erwähnt, während es doch in Wirklichkeit so ist,

able fullness of revelation has a metaphysical root—namely, the "hypostatic union"—he prefers to transpose this union into the personalist-mystical key of relational depth. It is Jesus' inner dialogue with the Father that teaches him to "know Scripture more deeply than anyone else—to know it from God himself."[107] Christ is the fullness of revelation, in other words, because in him God became a subject of human reading, knowing, and speaking.

For Ratzinger, both the apostles and Scripture seem to fall within the penumbra of the unrepeatable Christ-event and share in its revelatory pre-eminence. That Ratzinger reckons the apostles among the constitutive elements of the "once only" becomes clear in other writings. "By restricting the term apostle to the Twelve," Ratzinger observes in *Called to Communion*, "[Luke] distinguishes what happened once only at the origin from what remains in perpetuity through succession. . . . The presbyter-bishops are successors but are not themselves apostles. The 'once only' as well as the 'forever' belong to the structure of revelation and of the Church." [108] And just as the apostles share in Christ's unsurpassably intimate dialogue with God, so does Scripture participate in the apostle's dialogue. This, at any rate, is the impression that Ratzinger gives in his commentary on *Dei Verbum*, where he connects the authority of Scripture to the enlarged perception of the apostles and prophets: "The resonance of the voice of the apostles and prophets throughout Scripture is important to it because the voice itself resounds with the Holy Spirit, because in them we encounter the dialogue of God with men."[109] The general structure of Ratzinger's thought seems to imply that the apostles enjoyed a charismatic plenitude unrivalled in future

---

dass in Christus die eine Bewegung der Selbsterschließung Gottes zu ihrer Fülle kommt und insofern nichts mehr darüber hinaus zu sagen ist, weswegen man vielleicht statt 'ultima' sagen könnte: revelatio completa est, der in Christo plenitudo revelationis venit, supra quam nihil adhuc addendum est oder dergleichen." Joseph Ratzinger, "Brief von Joseph Ratzinger an P. Karl Rahner vom 19. Juni 1963," *MIPB* 5 (2012): 13–14.

107 Ratzinger, *Principles of Catholic Theology*, 32.

108 Joseph Ratzinger, *Called to Communion*, trans. Adrian Walker (San Francisco: Ignatius, 1996), 123.

109 "Sacred Scripture in the Life of the Church," in *Commentary on the Documents of Vatican II*, ed. Herbert Vorgrimler; trans. William Glen–Doepl, vol. 3 (New York: Herder & Herder, 1967), 263. See Ratzinger's later reformulation of this principle: "The normative theologians are the authors of Holy Scripture. This statement is valid not only with reference to the objective written document they left behind but also with reference to their manner of speaking, in which it is God himself who speaks." *Principles of Catholic Theology*, 321.

ages. Aquinas holds such a position explicitly.[110] Ratzinger leaves it implicit, perhaps reflecting certain ambiguities in Bonaventure's own position.[111]

These ambiguities notwithstanding, the general picture remains clear. Because God himself was the subject of Jesus' words and deeds, God has become—through the mediation of apostolic witnesses—the subject of Scripture as well. The fact that the hypostatic union of God and humanity occurred only once, in Christ, ultimately grounds the preeminence of Scripture over doctrinal statements.[112] The writings of the Apostolic Church outrank those of the post-Apostolic Church not because God authored the whole early Church more intensely, but because Christ gave the apostles themselves a share in his dialogue with the Father that was never subsequently equaled.[113]

How does Ratzinger's Christological account of the Bible's unique status as God's word compare with its alternatives? Tracy and Rahner do not obviously outperform Ratzinger even on this more limited question. Though Tracy often presents Scripture as Christianity's most "disclosive" text, the

110 Thomas Aquinas writes: "We should not look forward to some future state in which the grace of the Holy Spirit will be received more perfectly than it has been up until now, especially [*maxime*] by the Apostles, who received the *firstfruits of the Spirit*, that is to say, received it *prior in time and more abundantly* [*abundantius*] *too*, as a gloss on this text puts it." ST I-II q. 106, a. 4. Again: "The *Gloss* says that the first Christians received the Spirit more abundantly [*abundantius*] than we who have come later. Just as no other woman can be compared to the Blessed Virgin, so no other saint can be compared to the apostles." *Super Psalmos* 44n11.

111 In his essay "Wesen und Weisen der auctoritas im Werk des hl. Bonaventura," Ratzinger observes how the insolubility of the medieval mendicant controversy by textual authorities moved Bonaventure to emphasize the "viva vox of the Church," which could licitly add even to the creed of the Apostles. JRGS 2:752–53.

112 For other references to Ratzinger on the servant character of the teaching office, see Verweyen, *Unbekannter Ratzinger*, 99.

113 In construing inspiration as a charism of perception, possessed paradigmatically by Christ and the apostles, rather than as charism of writing, Ratzinger recalls the near equation of apostolic tradition and inspiration envisioned by such Tübingen theologians as J.-S. Drey and J.-A. Möhler. Möhler would observe, "If Christianity first lived in the mind of our Lord and in the minds of his apostles who were filled by the Holy Spirit before it was a concept, speech, or letter, we must assert: the Spirit was before the letter." Möhler, *Unity in the Church or The Principle of Catholicism: Presented in the Spirit of the Church Fathers of the First Three Centuries*, ed. and trans. Peter C. Erb (Washington, DC: The Catholic University of America Press, 1996), 97. Drey had remarked a generation earlier, "Word of God it remained in the mouth of Christ, and it does not cease to be word of God in the mouth of the apostles or in their writings." Drey, "Gründsätze zu einer genaurn Bestimmung des Begriffs der Inspiration," *TQ* 3 (1821): 652–53. Cited in Burtchaell, *Catholic Theories of Inspiration*, 12–13.

greatest of religious "classics," he tends to reason from this position rather than to it. He does not explain why Scripture discloses the "limit situation" of human existence better than, say, the poetry of Dante or John of the Cross. Rahner, by contrast, leans heavily on the distinction between post-Apostolic and Apostolic Church, holding that God more fully authored the Apostolic Church, whose self-understanding the Scriptures canonize. At first glance, Rahner's strategy appears indistinguishable from Ratzinger's, who likewise appeals to collective authorship and distinguishes the "once only" of Christ and the Twelve from the "forever" of the post-apostolic Church. But Ratzinger, it will be remembered, ties the preeminence of the Apostolic Church to the preeminence of Christ and his apostles rather than to a decree of formal predefinition regarding the whole Church. Hence, he subtly reverses the vector of causality. Whereas Rahner tends to ascribe preeminence to apostles because they belonged to the Apostolic Church, Ratzinger tends to ascribe preeminence to the Apostolic Church because it still had apostles. In foregrounding what he calls the "structure of personal responsibility" for the word,[114] Ratzinger perhaps better avoids the charge of indiscriminate "collectivism" leveled against Rahner.[115]

Benoit's Thomist-instrumental model, it must be admitted, enjoys clear advantages when it comes to accounting for Scripture's unique standing as God's Word. If one accepts that God employed the biblical hagiographers alone as instrumental causes in the strict sense, one immediately sees why God has made their writings his own in some qualitatively higher sense. Every extrabiblical statement, by comparison, even that of the most solemn magisterial definition, remains a mere word *about* God, effectively subordinated to the Word *of* God. Though Ratzinger has an incipient Christological account of the preeminence of Scripture, the field of mystical perception knows no distinctions so clean as that of Thomistic causality. If Ratzinger is to be preferred to Benoit, it is not because Benoit's solution fails to account

---

114 Opposing "personal responsibility" to "anonymous" or "collective responsibility," Ratzinger uses the principle to explain the personal witness of Peter and the ongoing function of papal primacy. See Joseph Ratzinger, *Church, Ecumenism, Politics: New Essays in Ecclesiology*, trans. Robert Nowell (New York: Crossroad, 1988), 33.

115 Robert L. Fastiggi criticizes Rahner both for dissociating the charism of inspiration from distinct individuals and for blurring the distinction between inspiration and the Spirit's assistance to the magisterium. "Communal or Social Inspiration: A Catholic Critique," *Letter and Spirit* 6 (2010): 260–61. He overlooks, however, Rahner's distinction between Apostolic and post-Apostolic Church.

elegantly for the ascendancy of Scripture, but because it brings other difficulties in its train. For the present I note simply that Ratzinger has a way of accounting for the serving character of the teaching office, and that this way remains at least "competitive" with the alternatives.

Inspiration of the Old Testament

Ratzinger's model shows itself similarly competitive at resolving the ticklish question of the analogous inspiration of the Old Testament. When I call the doctrinally indicated account of Old Testament inspiration "analogous," I mean that it should be "proportionate" and "relative" to the inspiration of the New Testament, falling between two extremes. Vatican I rules out one extreme position when it teaches that Old Testament inspiration cannot be reduced to a purely retrospective approval by the authority of the Church.[116] Vatican II states the same teaching positively when it observes, "God, the inspirer and author of both Testaments, wisely arranged that the New Testament be hidden in the Old and the Old be made manifest in the New."[117] The Old Testament and New Testament are thus both "prospectively" inspired and are mutually interpretive. This means, minimally, that the Old Testament is more God's word than other ancient religious "classics," and that Israel's narrative history enjoys a kind of continuity with revelation in Christ unequalled by other national literatures and mythologies.

Despite affirming the common inspiration of both Old and New Testament, *Dei Verbum* elsewhere seems to attribute a more intense or direct modality of inspiration to the New Testament. Just after affirming the enduring value of the Old Testament, the Dogmatic Constitution goes on to teach,

> The word of God, which is the power of God for the salvation of all who believe (see Rom. 1:16), is set forth and shows its power in a most excellent way [*praecellenti modo praesentetur et vim suam exhibet*] in the writings of the New Testament. For when the fullness of time arrived (see Gal. 4:4), the Word was made flesh and dwelt among us in His fullness of graces and truth (see John 1:14).... This mystery had not been manifested to other generations as it was now revealed to His holy Apostles and prophets in the Holy Spirit (see Eph. 3:4–6, Greek text), so that they might preach the Gospel, stir up faith in Jesus, Christ and Lord, and gather together the

116 *DF* cap. 2, p. 806.
117 *DV*, no. 16.

Church. Now the writings of the New Testament stand as a perpetual and divine witness to these realities.[118]

Here the Council makes clear that the "word of God" comprises both Old and New Testaments but is present in the New "in a most excellent way" (*praecellenti modo*), since the New Testament stands as a witness to more definitive "realities" manifested only in the "fullness of time." But how does one explain the greater or lesser "excellence" or "fullness" of God's word? Is it simply a function of clearer interpretation, or does it also reflect an analogous intensification of inspiration itself? Ratzinger's Bonaventurian-ecclesial model of inspiration will opt for the latter. In doing so, I would argue, it accounts more elegantly for the unity-in-difference between Old and New Testament, an element of what Vatican II calls the *analogia fidei* ("analogy of faith").[119]

Ratzinger's mature understanding of Old Testament inspiration, as of many other subtopics in the field in inspiration, represents not so much a parroting of Bonaventure as a transposition in light of contemporary concerns. Though Gottlieb Söhngen had commended Bonaventure to Ratzinger as a "classic thinker of the analogia fidei,"[120] Ratzinger doubtlessly found the Seraphic Doctor's version of this doctrine, especially the presumption of one-to-one correspondence between the historical schemata of Israel and Church, too idiosyncratic for wholesale appropriation. However, other features of Bonaventure's understanding of inspiration—especially its mystical, subjective-inclusive, and historically progressive dimensions—opened a path for Ratzinger to reconceive inspiration as a charism varying in intensity and manner according to salvation-historical stage. This kind of salvation-historical thinking was very much in the air as Ratzinger was finishing his Bonaventure studies. In 1958 the French Dominican Yves Congar published *The Mystery of the Temple*, arguing that Scripture should be taken seriously

---

118 *DV*, no. 17.

119 This is often translated periphrastically into English as the "harmony which exists between the elements of faith" (*DV*, no. 12). See also the earlier mentions of the *analogia fidei* in the encyclical tradition, where the accent lies on the continuity between elements of faith: *PD*, no. 12; *DAS*, no. 24. The so-called Oath Against Modernism (1910) required candidates for orders to assent to the following proposition: "Reprobo pariter eam Scripturae Sanctae diiudicandae atque interpretandae rationem, quae, Ecclesiae traditione, analogia Fidei, et Apostolicae Sedis normis posthabitis, *rationalistarum* commentis inhaeret, et criticem textus velut unicam supremamque regulam, haud minus licenter quam temere amplectitur." See *SA*.

120 *JRGS* 2:58. Ratzinger refers to Söhngen's "Bonaventura als Klassiker der analogia fidei." *Wissenschaft und Weisheit* 2, no. 2 (1935): 97–111.

when it describes the "Missions of the Son and of the Holy Spirit as facts which took place at a given point in the history of salvation and, *from that moment onward*, established a new dispensation governing God's gifts and Presence."[121] For his part, Ratzinger, extending Bonaventure's insights, will proceed as if a great inflection point in the divine economy governs the "gift" of inspiration as well. After all, if the People of God is Scripture's "understanding subject," itself subsisting in the diverse historical modalities of Israel and Church, it follows that the charism of inspiration, too, may know various intensities. And if *inspiratio* is as much about receiving texts as composing them, it follows that a *relecture* in the Spirit may further "inspire" an already-inspired Old Testament.

Ratzinger seems to have found unlooked-for encouragement to embrace an incremental and salvation-historical model of inspiration in *Alter und Neuer Bund* (1956), a theology of the Bible by the reclusive Jesuit philosopher and theologian Erich Przywara.[122] Ratzinger, reviewing Przywara's book at around the same time he was preparing to publish *The Theology of the History in St. Bonaventure*, found several elements of Przywara's biblical theology congenial. His review singles out for special praise Przywara's understanding of the "'analogia fidei' as the analogous unity of Old and New Covenant," adding that "in recent Catholic literature there are scarcely expositions on this theme at the same level."[123] Here Ratzinger correctly notes

---

121 Yves Congar, *The Mystery of the Temple: Or the Manner of God's Presence to His Creatures from Genesis to Apocalypse*, trans. Reginald Trevett (London: Burns & Oates, 1962), 264. In later writings, Congar would note that Scripture itself teaches both the unity and diversity of salvation history. On the side of unity: "All ate the same spiritual food, and all drank the same spiritual drink, for they drank from a spiritual rock that followed them, and the rock was the Christ" (1 Cor 10:3–4). On the side of diversity: "There was, of course, no Spirit yet, because Jesus had not yet been glorified" (John 7:39). *I Believe in the Holy Spirit*, trans. David Smith, 3 vols. (New York: Crossroad Herder, 1997), 2:74, 77.

122 Przywara intended the book both as a complement to his own philosophy of the *analogia entis* and as an alternative to Gottlieb Söhngen's and Karl Barth's versions of the *analogia fidei*. For more on the influence of the debate between Gottlieb Söhngen, Karl Barth, and Erich Przywara over the nature of the *analogia fidei*, see Richard Schenk, "Bonaventura als Klassiker der analogia fidei: Zur Rezeption der theologischen Programmatik Gottlieb Söhngens im Frühwerk Joseph Ratzingers," in *Gegenwart der Offenbarung: Zu den Bonaventura-Forschungen Joseph Ratzingers*, ed. Marianne Schlosser and Franz-Xaver Heibl, Ratzinger-Studien 2 (Regensburg: Friedrich Pustet, 2010), 28–49; Bernhard Gertz, "Was ist Analogia Fidei: Klarstellungen zu einem Kontrovers-Thema," *Catholica* 26 (1972): 309–24.

123 Ratzinger, "Erich Przywaras Alterswerk" (review of *Alter und Neuer Bund* and *Gespräch Zwischen den Kirchen*), *Wort und Wahrheit* 13 (1958): 220.

that, for Przywara, it is the covenants themselves, not just our interpretive approaches to their respective literatures, that subsist in analogous unity.[124] But Ratzinger finds that Przywara's metaphysically thick description of the *analogia fidei* has important interpretive implications. More specifically, it appropriately discourages two kinds of "false directness" (*falsche Direktheit*) toward the Old Testament. On the one hand, it forbids the directness of post-Christian, "Judaizing" exegesis, which would admit only the Old Testament's "immanent-historical" meaning and would thereby stunt its "self-transcending dynamic" (*Selbsttranszendierung*). On the other hand, it also rejects any "naively Christian directness" that would overlook the otherness and integrity of the Old Testament witness. For such a directness denatures Christianity, "which is itself only in the originating movement [*als Von-her*] from the revelation of the Old Testament."[125] Przywara's understanding of the *analogia fidei* perhaps stimulates Ratzinger to insist that the Bible constitutes God's revelation not directly but in the play of intertestamental reference, in the continual movement of self-transcendence between Old Covenant and New.[126]

Ratzinger's appreciation for something like Przywara's version of the *analogia fidei* comes into view in the 1960s. In his address to the German Bishops on October 10, 1962, for instance, Ratzinger criticizes *De fontibus revelationis* for the "unhistorical nature of the inspiration-process" presupposed

---

124 In the first sentence of Przywara's "Nachwort" to *Alter und Neuer Bund*, on which Ratzinger heaps special praise, Przywara affirms a "*relationship* between Old and New Covenant *at the level of both being and consciousness*" (*das* seinshafte wie Bewußtseinshafte Verhältnis *zwischen Altem und Neuem Bund*). *Alter und Neuer Bund: Theologie der Stunde* (Vienna: Herold, 1956), 521.

125 Ratzinger, "Erich Przywaras Alterswerk," 220.

126 "Without the historical path of the [Old Testament], the New Testament message remains inexplicable." Ratzinger, *Dogma and Preaching*, 15. Ratzinger several times acknowledges his debt to Przywara's understanding of the "analogical unity" of Scripture. See Ratzinger, "Question of the Concept of Tradition," 60; *Dogma and Preaching*, 26; *Daughter Zion: Meditations in the Church's Marian Belief*, trans. John M. McDermott (San Francisco: Ignatius, 1983), 29. Przywara is, of course, far from Ratzinger's only influence. See also his appreciation for Henri de Lubac on the "concordia testamentorum" and Johann Sebastian Drey on the "leap of meaning" (*Sinnüberschritt*) that the Old Testament makes at the coming of Christ: JRGS 1:52; "Anmerkungen zur Aktualität von Johann Sebastian Dreys *Kurze Einleitung in das Studium der Theologie*," in *Theologie, Kirche, Katholizismus: Beiträge zur Programmatik der Katholischen Tübinger Schule*, ed. Michael Kessler and Max Seckler (Tübingen: Francke, 2003), 5.

therein:[127] "What is specific to biblical revelation is that it expresses a history God carries out with humans. . . . [The biblical writer] is certainly God's 'organ,' but he is this at quite a definite place in history, that is, only by being at the same time 'organ' of the Body of Christ and of the people of God in their covenant with God."[128] Because the inspired writers participate in an internally differentiated covenantal history, "inspiration" may itself be an internally differentiated phenomenon. Failure to attend to this covenantal unity-in-diversity, Ratzinger warns in an appendix to the same intervention, leads the draft schema to oscillate between the same two kinds of "false directness" criticized in his review of Przywara. That is to say, sometimes the draft schema speaks as if some parts of the Old Testament bear no relation to Christianity at all, while other parts are "at the same time already directly Christian and as such continue in force."[129] To Ratzinger's thinking, it would be better to say that the whole Old Testament is already inchoately Christian, even if every part of it also "has to pass through a Christological transformation."[130] Here Ratzinger crosses his notion of the covenantal people as inspired subject of Scripture with Przywara's notion of analogous covenants to formulate something like an analogous model of inspiration.

Just a few years later, in "The Question of the Concept of Tradition" (1965), Ratzinger will paint a similar, multilayered picture of the *analogia fidei*. There he states, "Just as the two covenants differ in their nature, as covenant, so also the fact of Scripture is not given the same way each time."[131] The way the first Christians referred to the Old Testament suggests both the unity and diversity internal to the field of Scripture. Ratzinger points out how Paul contrasts Old and New Covenants "as *gramma* and *pneuma*—that is, as Scripture and Spirit (2 Cor 3:6-18)—and calls the Lord the Pneuma who . . . is its true meaning."[132] This implies, on the one hand, that the Old Testa-

---

127 Wicks, "Six Texts," 278.

128 Wicks, "Six Texts," 278–79.

129 Wicks, "Six Texts," 282–83. Ratzinger alludes to *De fontibus revelationis*, no. 15, entitled *De auctoritate Veteris Testamenti in Ecclesia*, which taught as follows: "Itaque in iis praesertim quae ad Christianae religionis fundamenta sive in verbis sive in historiae rebus, ad finem usque temporis spectant, Veteris Testamenti vis, auctoritas et emolumentum minime enervata sunt." *AS* I, 3:20.

130 Wicks, "Six Texts," 283.

131 Ratzinger, "Question of the Concept of Tradition," 53–54.

132 Ratzinger, "Question of the Concept of Tradition," 54.

ment was not "inspired" in its definitive sense until it entered the pneumatic sphere of Christ.[133] On the other hand, the fact that the first Christians did not immediately establish a new body of writings, but remained initially content to reread the Old Testament in the Spirit, suggests the Old Testament's intrinsic aptness for a Christian rereading—or its already "inspired" nature. It is on the grounds of this intrinsic aptness that Ratzinger defends the legitimacy of a "New Testament theology of the Old Testament" differing from the historically discernible meaning of the Old Testament. "By effecting such a change in interpretation, [the New Testament] is not however doing anything completely foreign to the nature of the Old Testament ... it is continuing the inner structure of the Old Testament, which itself lives and grows through such reinterpretations."[134] Ratzinger goes on to suggest that the imperfect coincidence between Old and New Testament theologies of the Old Testament permits one to "say in a new way what the *analogia fidei* between the two testaments means."[135] Here Ratzinger references Przywara's *Alter und Neuer Bund*.[136] On this version of the *analogia fidei* there can be no question of reducing the inspiration of the Old Testament to the subsequent approval of the Church, since the latter continues the Old Testament's "inner structure." At the same time, this version of the *analogia fidei* strongly implies that the Church further "inspires" the Old Testament by rereading it in Christ's Spirit.

Having asserted the analogical unity of Scripture in the 1960s, Ratzinger turns in the next decade to justifying his analogical hermeneutics through a kind of personalist metaphysics of history. The *analogia fidei* comes to rest ever more decisively in the analogical unity of the faith of the People of God, understood as both Israel and Church. Ratzinger adopts this line

---

133 "In the New Testament conception, the Old Testament appears as 'Scripture' in the proper sense, which has attained its true significance through the Christ-event by being drawn into the living sphere of the reality of Christ." Ratzinger, "Question of the Concept of Tradition," 55.

134 Ratzinger, "Question of the Concept of Tradition," 61.

135 Ratzinger, "Question of the Concept of Tradition," 60.

136 Thomas Marschler notes that Ratzinger's narrower association of *analogia fidei* with intertestamental unity is distinctive, perhaps because he is unaware of Przywara's influence. "Analogia Fidei: Anmerkungen zu einem Grundprinzip theologischer Schrifthermeneutik," *Theologie und Philosophie* 87 (2012): 217. In later writings, Ratzinger will use *analogia fidei* more broadly, designating intertestamental unity as the *analogia scripturae*. "Biblical Interpretation in Conflict," in *God's Word: Scripture—Tradition—Office*, ed. Peter Hünermann and Thomas Söding, trans. Henry Taylor (San Francisco: Ignatius, 2005), 121.

of thinking clearly in *Dogma and Preaching*, where he expands on his now-familiar identification of the Church as the "acting subject of the Word"[137] and as the general "place in which inspiration is possible."[138] He clarifies that the history of this ecclesial subject really begins with the faith history of Israel: "Only in the shared process . . . of entering by faith into the faith history of Israel and into the turning point that occurs with Jesus does the tradition which is recorded in the Bible come about." [139] Here we do well to recall Ratzinger's earlier conclusion that, for Bonaventure, the Church's faith constitutes the lowest level of that mystical perception called *inspiratio-revelatio*. And it is this "faith of the simple people," according to Ratzinger, that supplies the strongest basis for continuity between Israel and Church: "In their basic intuition of the faith, they lived in terms of the core promise and teaching and thereby became the place in which Old Testament could be transformed into New Testament: Zechariah, Elizabeth, Mary, Joseph, Jesus himself."[140] Israel and Church constitute one subject because one faith animates them both.

Ratzinger will continue to underscore this continuity of faith in subsequent writings. His Christological meditation *Behold the Pierced One*, first published in German in 1984, recalls that Jesus did not simply abolish the faith of the Old Covenant but "entered into the already existing subject of tradition, God's People of Israel."[141] Again, in the 1990s, *The Nature and Mission of Theology* argues that the indissoluble tension between Old Testament and New Testament depends on the "continuity of a subject which organically traverses the whole of history and which remains one with itself throughout its own transformations."[142] Ratzinger is evidently developing in his own idiom the patristic theme of the *ecclesia ab Abel*, according to which the Church somehow embraces all the just who looked forward to the coming of Christ.[143] And because the common-yet-differentiated faith of this

---

137 Ratzinger, *Dogma and Preaching*, 22.

138 Ratzinger, *Dogma and Preaching*, 23.

139 Ratzinger, *Dogma and Preaching*, 23.

140 Ratzinger, *Dogma and Preaching*, 33–34.

141 Ratzinger, *Behold the Pierced One*, 30.

142 Ratzinger, *Nature and Mission of Theology*, 95.

143 For Ratzinger's mention of this theme in connection with the unity of salvation history, see Wicks, "Six Texts," 283. For a classic treatment of this theme dating from 1952, doubtlessly familiar to Ratzinger, see Yves Congar, "Ecclesia ab Abel," in *Abhandlungen über*

ecclesia ab Abel is the place where inspiration is possible, it seems to follow that inspiration itself may represent a common-yet-differentiated charism.

Having reviewed Ratzinger's position on the analogous inspiration of Old Testament as well as its justification, one can now ask how well it stacks up against the positions of Benoit, Rahner, and Tracy. Benoit and Tracy, each for different reasons, tend to construe the inspiration of the Old Testament with the aforementioned "false directness." For Tracy, a text has God as its author because it lays bare not propositional truth but existential truth at its limit situation. It must enjoy nearly complete autonomy vis-à-vis its historical setting to serve as a permanent site of such disclosure. On these presuppositions, however, one wonders why an Old Testament text of great poetic power would not already be "directly" inspired in the same sense that a Gospel would be. Benoit has a similar difficulty avoiding a univocal construal of inspiration. If Scripture qualifies as God's Word because God has employed the hagiographers as instrumental causes, then all Scripture produced by human instruments should be reckoned inspired with equal directness. By focusing inspiration narrowly on God's instrumental appropriation of isolated mental faculties, Benoit makes the developmental stage of the People of God, in whom and for whom individual authors write, largely irrelevant to the way the text is inspired. For both Tracy and Benoit, then, both Old and New Testament stand as univocally inspired, since God exercises a univocal mode of authorship for each.

Rahner's model runs up against the opposite difficulty, tending toward an excessively equivocal understanding of Old and New Testament inspiration. For if one takes inspiration to be the act of formal predefinition by which God harmonizes the intentions of individual authors with those of the Apostolic Church, one struggles to see how texts antedating the Apostolic Church can claim inspiration by virtue of anything other than this Church's "subsequent approval"—a position excluded by Vatican I. Rahner at least invites such an interpretation when he sums up his argument in the following way: "Because the Old Testament belongs *a priori* to the formation of the Church and not only the Synagogue, as part of her prehistory and as such remains actual for ever [*sic*], it can claim the same validity as the New

---

Theologie und Kirche. Festschrift für Karl Adam, ed. Marcel Reding (Düsseldorf: Patmos, 1952), 79–108. Ratzinger observes that his biblical theology converges with South American theology in privileging the perspective of the People of God, but differs in considering not just one social class or historical moment but the "*whole* 'People of God' in its synchronic and diachronic extension." JRGS 9, 2:785.

Testament."[144] Perhaps sensing the inadequacy of a strictly retroactive inspiration, however, Rahner also adds that the Old Testament is not just a "*de facto* account of the prehistory of the Church," but is "thus designed, for its own essence could not otherwise be completed in the New Testament."[145] By thus appealing to superintending design and essential completion, Rahner comes closer to Ratzinger's "germinal" or "analogous" notion of inspiration for the Old Testament. But tellingly even here, and in contrast to Ratzinger, Rahner gives little attention either to Israel as bearer of this design in the pre-Christian era or to Christ's role in "spiritualizing" the Old Testament.[146] These lacunae in Rahner make it easier for Ratzinger to explain the particular way the New Testament receives the Old, succinctly summed up by Christopher Seitz: "The church does not give birth to the Scriptures of Israel but instead receives them from Christ, and hears in their prior word given to Israel a present testimony for all time."[147]

Ratzinger's emphasis on the analogy of faith between Israel and Church naturally also gives him a firmer basis than Rahner for Jewish-Christian dialogue. Ratzinger can thus affirm that "Christ is the end [τέλος] of the law" (Rom 10:4) without claiming that the Church simply "substitutes" for Israel. In what turns out to be his last reflections on this theme, "Grace and Vocation with Remorse" (2018), Ratzinger observes that crass substitution theories inevitably presuppose a static vision of the Old Testament, according to which Old Testament institutions, such as the temple cult, must be either accepted or rejected *tout court*. But the Old Testament itself records a continuous development in the theology of the Temple, a growing refinement of the sacrificial ideal into an act both inwardly purified and outwardly visible. Seen from the point of view of the Christian Eucharist, then, the temple sacrifice assumes the aspect of a "journey [*Unterwegssein*] that eventually

---

144 Karl Rahner, *Inspiration in the Bible*, trans. Charles Henkey, QD 1 (New York: Herder & Herder, 1961), 54.

145 Rahner speaks of Synagogue and Church, not Israel and Church. *Inspiration in the Bible*, 54.

146 Already in the 1960s the American Jesuit John McKenzie proposed emending Rahner by making a "corporate personality" the real bearer of inspiration—a notion flexible enough to include both Israel and the Church and, therefore, both Old and New Testaments. "The Social Character of Inspiration," *CBQ* 24, no. 2 (1962), 115. Ratzinger had already independently arrived at the same conclusion.

147 Christopher Seitz, *Convergences: Canon and Canonicity* (Waco, TX: Baylor University Press, 2020), 106.

becomes one reality." "Instead of a static view of substitution or nonsubstitu-
tion," Ratzinger continues, "there is a dynamic consideration of the whole of
salvation history, which finds its ἀνακεφαλαίωσις [recapitulation] in Christ
(see Eph 1:10)."[148] Between the "Old Testament Theology of the Old Testament" and the "New Testament Theology of the Old Testament," there stands,
in short, enough discontinuity to make Jewish-Christian dialogue necessary,
as well as enough inner continuity to make it possible.[149]

Ratzinger's paradigm of Old Testament inspiration thus offers certain
advantages. God truly "authors" both Testaments, albeit in distinct modalities, because he gives to Israel and the Church a common yet gradated gift of
faith. This helps explain how Ratzinger, despite accusations to the contrary,[150]
can hold that Christianity "fulfills" Judaism without thereby endorsing supersessionism. Christianity represents an intensification, not an abrogation,
of Israel's faith. The developmental nature of this faith journey becomes
inscribed into Scripture as the analogical unity of its Testaments, just as
the succession of geological ages inscribes itself into a landscape as diverse
layers of sedimentation. Ratzinger's Bonaventurian-ecclesial model can thus
stake a strong claim to represent the more relatively adequate account of Old
Testament inspiration.

CONCLUSION

With Ratzinger's account of Old Testament inspiration described and
assessed, it perhaps behooves us to review the results of our investigation.
This second chapter attempted to profile Ratzinger's understanding of the

---

148 Ratzinger, "Grace and Vocation without Remorse: Comments on the Treatise *De
Iudeais*," *Communio* 45, no. 2 (2018): 171.

149 Ratzinger takes pains to emphasize that this Christological reading does not impose a
schema "foreign to the nature of the Old Testament, approaching it only from the outside;
rather, it is continuing the inner structure of the Old Testament, which itself lives and
grows through such interpretation." "Question of the Concept of Tradition," 61.

150 Steven Aguzzi argues that *Dominus Iesus* (2000) reflects Ratzinger's supersessionist
commitments when it claims that "Christianity enlightens Judaism with a 'fulfilment of
salvation that went beyond the Law,' ... as if the law itself was and is some cold, callous
conception, having nothing to do with God's grace." "One Step Forward, Two Steps Back:
Supersessionism and Pope Benedict XVI's Eschatological Ecclesiology Concerning Israel
and the Jewish People," *JES* 49, no. 4 (2014): 602. Ratzinger's covenantal model of analogous
intensification, however, permits him to affirm a dynamic of "fulfilment" without denying a
prior share of grace to what is being fulfilled.

inspiration of Scripture. How does God become the author of Scripture, transposing divine discourse into human words? And how well does Ratzinger's attempt to harmonize the Catholic tradition's various *desiderata* regarding inspiration stack up against other leading theologians?

Ratzinger's model of inspiration, as was shown above, can be justly characterized as Bonaventurian-ecclesial. Ratzinger takes from Bonaventure the idea that *inspiratio* constitutes a kind of mystical perception, necessary for both consigning *revelatio* to writing and for interpreting biblical writings in their revelatory sense. The basic form of such mystical perception is none other than the faith of the Church. This means that Scripture does not already constitute revelation in its naked verbalness, but only in conjunction with an "understanding subject"—the People of God. And as this understanding subject gains experience throughout its historical journey—a journey that includes epochal transitions from Israel to Church and from Apostolic Church to post-Apostolic Church—Scripture gradually accrues new layers of text (in the canonical period) and unfolds new layers of meaning (in the periods after the closure of each canon). Ratzinger thus presents the Word of God as a living and active "organism," accruing meaning until the eschaton, animated by the Spirit that indwells the Church and illuminates mystic souls.

Ratzinger's Bonaventurian-ecclesial model of inspiration shows points of contact with Benoit's Thomist-instrumental, Rahner's Molinist-predefinitive, and Tracy's Heideggerian-disclosive models, but coincides completely with none of them. It takes over Benoit's emphasis on authorial intentionality, but leaves behind the apparatus of instrumental causality in the strict sense. It adds Rahner's notion of the Church as a collective subject of inspiration, albeit in a more differentiated way, and without appeal to the conceptuality of formal predefinition. It anticipates Tracy's idea that Scripture's "effective history" belongs to its total meaning, but grounds this dynamic in the movement of the People of God *within* history rather in the text's aboriginal "distance" *from* its historical setting.

By making these adjustments, Ratzinger's model achieves not only a certain originality but, I would argue, a greater relative adequacy to the doctrinal givens. It better accounts for the organic interpenetration of Scripture and ecclesial tradition by recalling that every linguistic community constitutes something of a collective personality, whose authority must be accepted for the sake of initiation into thought and communion. The interdependence of Scripture and Church represents, therefore, only the supernatural elevation of a natural dynamic everywhere evident.

Despite his very ecclesial account of inspiration, Ratzinger also manages to offer a superior account of the inspiration of the Old Testament.
This he does by presenting the Old Testament as "analogously" inspired,
neither possessing its full measure of "inspiration" before Christ nor lacking
all such "inspired" status until "subsequently approved" by the Church. Here
Ratzinger's recourse to the one faith of the People of God, realized with different degrees of explicitness in Israel and Church, allows him to avoid both
excessively univocal understandings of Old Testament inspiration (Benoit,
Tracy) and excessively equivocal understandings (Rahner). He maintains
the inspiration of the Old Testament, in short, without countenancing "false
directness."

Finally, Ratzinger also manages to give a passable account of the Bible's
unique authority vis-à-vis the Church. Admittedly, his mystical model inspiration cannot distinguish the biblical Word *of* God from all other theological
words *about* God as cleanly as Benoit's notion of instrumental authorship
can. Ratzinger nevertheless offers an implicitly Christological account of the
same, tying Scripture's unique authority to its proximity to the Incarnation,
as well as to the witnesses personally authorized by the Incarnate Word. At
the same time, he manages to avoid some of the liabilities inherent in the
deployment of instrumental causality *stricto sensu*.

Despite the explanatory advantages of Ratzinger's position, it is perhaps
worth drawing attention to a point of underdevelopment. As we have seen,
Ratzinger relies heavily on the corporate agency of a historically differentiated People of God to span many of the doctrinal pegs traditionally associated with a theology of inspiration. Yet he himself does little to clarify just
how the Church's personality enjoys a capacity for unitary action superior
to that of any other juridical person, from nation-state down to family business. In Ratzinger's eyes the theological virtue of faith clearly constitutes the
principle of the People of God's identity across all its phase changes. And
there is good theological precedent for ascribing agency to this corporately
embodied faith. Ever since Augustine, for instance, Catholic theology has
held that the "faith of the Church" can supply for lack of conscious intention
on the part of baptized infants.[151] Even now the eucharistic liturgy appeals
to same corporate belief, praying to God, "Look not on our sins but on the
faith of your Church." But such tropes as the "faith of the Church" and the

---

151 For references, see Charles Journet, *La volonté divine salvifique sur les petits enfants*
(Paris: Desclée de Brouwer, 1958), 71–74.

"Church from Abel" are as much *explanandum* as *explanans*. And Ratzinger argues from these themes, as self-evident givens, rather than to them, as arduous conclusions.

The most serious attempts to clarify the nature of the personality of the People of God in recent time have doubtlessly emerged from French-language Thomism. Elaborating the analogy between human and ecclesial persons, Charles Journet identifies the theological virtue of faith as the "soul" of the Church.[152] Extending Journet's work, Benoît-Dominique de la Soujeole painstakingly distinguishes between the "physical" personality of the human person, the "moral" personality of the political community, and the "mystical" personality of the People of God, which shares traits of each of the previous.[153] Apart from the aforementioned analogy between the personality of the People of God and that of the linguistic community, however, there is no comparable effort on Ratzinger's part to spell out just how the People of God constitutes a single continuous person and thus "authors" Scripture in a more-than-metaphorical sense. A highly desirable complement to Ratzinger's social theory of inspiration would therefore be a "second-wave" Thomist theology of inspiration, one that takes its speculative point of departure not from the category of instrumental-prophetic agency but from that of ecclesial personality.

But a comprehensive evaluation of Ratzinger's achievement requires us to press on, to consider not only lacunae in Ratzinger's Bonaventurian-ecclesial theory of inspiration but also its implications for the question of the truth of Scripture. In an age of historical consciousness and scientific rationality, this doctrinal affirmation strains credibility more than any other. The next chapter will show how Ratzinger seeks to meet this challenge by building a model of authorial intention consonant with the threefold authorship of Scripture: divine, ecclesial, and literary.

---

152 With a Thomist's gift for subtle distinctions, the great ecclesiologist Charles Journet speaks of faith and hope as the "animal animation" of the Body of Christ, and charity as its "rational animation." See *L'Église du Verbe incarnée*, 2 vols. (Paris: Desclée de Brouwer, 1951–55), 2:1069.

153 For a chapter-length treatment of the theme of the People of God *ad mentem sancti Thomae*, beginning with the theme of the *ecclesia ab Abel* and ending with a survey of recent magisterial statements on salvation outside the Church, see Benoît-Dominique de la Soujeole, *Introduction to the Mystery of the Church*, trans. Michael J. Miller, Thomistic Ressourcement Series 3 (Washington, DC: The Catholic University of America Press, 2014), 199–289.

CHAPTER THREE

Ratzinger on the Truth of Scripture

B uilding on last chapter's conclusions regarding Ratzinger's Bonaventurian-ecclesial notion of inspiration, this chapter turns to its interpretive consequences. Christians have always associated the fact of
biblical inspiration with Scripture's preeminence in truth. The expectation
of superior veracity appears already in the New Testament itself, and in both
privative and positive aspects. Privatively, the New Testament attests a presumed immunity from error, which theologians would later call inerrancy.
Paul's exhortation to Timothy certainly lends itself to such an interpretation: "*All scripture* is inspired by God and is useful for teaching, for refuta-
tion, for correction, and for training in righteousness" (2 Tim 3:16). In John's
Gospel, Jesus himself, when defending his use of the title "Son of God," takes
as a premise of his argument the fact that "Scripture cannot be set aside
[λυθῆναι]" (John 10:35). From a Christian point of view, the authority thereby
claimed for the Old Testament would seem to apply *a fortiori* to the New.
And if both Old and New Testament are entirely suitable for teaching, and
neither can be "set aside" by human authority, this amounts to something
like a claim for Scripture's inerrancy.

Positively, Scripture attests to its own mysterious depth of meaning. This
self-understanding finds expression *inter alia* in the book of Revelation,
where John sees a vision of a sealed scroll, which only the Lamb can open,
"written both inside and on the back" (γεγραμμένον ἔσωθεν καὶ ὄπισθεν).
(Rev 5:1). The image of Scripture as a closed book, containing both esoteric and exoteric dimensions, proved richly suggestive to later interpreters.
According to Origen (b. ca. 184), the whole Church believed "that the Scriptures were written by the Spirit of God, and that they have not only the meaning [*sensum*] which is obvious, but also another which escapes the notice
of most. For the things that are described [therein] are the forms of certain

mysteries and images of divine things. There is one mind throughout the entire church about this, that *the* whole *law is* indeed *spiritual* [*spiritalem*]."[1] This idea that the Spirit's action imbued Scripture not only with immunity from error but with an inexhaustible multivalence would exercise a lasting influence on premodern exegesis in both Eastern and Western Christianity. J. H. Newman summed up the entire premodern tradition when he observed, "Scripture is full of mysteries."[2] Vatican I would enshrine a thin version of this conviction in doctrine, recalling that the Catholic Church holds the books of the Bible to be sacred and canonical "not simply because they contain revelation without error, but because, being written under the inspiration of the Holy Spirit, they have God as their author, and were as such committed to the Church."[3] Though inspiration entails "truth without error," in short, it implies more than that minimum.

Ratzinger is well aware, of course, of both the preeminent truthfulness traditionally ascribed to Scripture and of the challenges that the findings of modern exegesis pose to this claim. This chapter aims to examine, therefore, how well Ratzinger succeeds in making Scripture's claim to transcendent veracity, in both its privative and positive aspects, plausible in the new exegetical and hermeneutical situation. Here again the goal is to expound Ratzinger's thought with a view to evaluating it against two different standards. The first standard is the "uncurved grade"—that is, Ratzinger's ability to reconcile the Catholic tradition's core doctrinal affirmations with the new picture of the Bible painted by historical critical exegesis and contemporary hermeneutics. The second standard is the "curved grade," an assessment of Ratzinger against the theological field. Though Ratzinger surely did not speak the last word on the truth of Scripture, he spoke perhaps the least inadequate word lately.

With a view to achieving its aims efficiently, the chapter will proceed along the following lines. First, it will explore Ratzinger's proposal for squaring the doctrine of inerrancy, especially as formulated in *Dei Verbum* 11, with the ostensible "errancy" of Scripture in historical, scientific, and religious

---

1 Origen, *De Principiis*, Praef. 8; 1:19. Italics original, highlighting the indirect citation of Rom 7:14.

2 Newman, "Essay on the Inspiration of Scripture (1861–1863)," in *Newman's Doctrine on Holy Scripture: According to His Published Works and Previously Unpublished Manuscripts*, ed. Jaak Seynaeve, WF (Louvain: Publications Universitaires de Louvain, 1953), 100.

3 *DF* 806.

matters. Ratzinger's key contribution to this theological problem lies in his having devised a battery of tests for discerning the intention of Scripture's corporate "author," the People of God. The chapter will then turn to Ratzinger's attempts to do justice to Scripture's mysterious multivalence, especially as this finds expression in the hermeneutical guidelines of *Dei Verbum* 12. The mature Ratzinger, as we will see, will present a retooled version of the medieval doctrine of the fourfold sense as a model responsive both to *Dei Verbum* and to contemporary biblical exegesis. To avoid redundancy, comparisons with Benoit, Rahner, and Tracy will take place at the end of the chapter rather than after each section.

RATZINGER ON SCRIPTURE'S "TRUTH WITHOUT ERROR"

As is well known, various distinctively modern cultural developments—the scientific revolution, the establishment of critical historiography, the rise of the sociology of knowledge—have exerted a kind of intellectual "pressure" on the traditional Christian conviction that Scripture enjoys immunity from error. The Catholic Church, however, for a long time staunchly resisted opening most of the valves proposed for releasing this pressure. Pope Leo XIII's encyclical *Providentissimus Deus* (1893) set the tone for what was to follow by condemning any attempts to narrow the scope of inerrancy either to a canon within a canon or simply to matters of faith and morals, trusting that exegetes, historians, and scientists loyal to the Church would eventually vindicate Scripture from its ostensible errors.[4] Subsequent encyclicals down to Pius XII's *Divino afflante Spiritu* (1943) echo this teaching.[5] Over this same period, the Pontifical Biblical Commission, established by Leo XIII in 1902 to implement the vision of *Providentissimus Deus*, began regulating which new exegetical opinions Catholic exegetes could "safely" teach. The upshot

---

4 See, for instance, *PD*, no. 20–22.

5 In 1907 Pius X upbraided modernists for holding that "in the sacred Books there are many passages referring to science and history where manifest errors are to be found" (*Pascendi*, no. 36). In 1920 Benedict XV closed yet another loophole by condemning the position that the "effects of inspiration—namely, absolute truth and immunity from error—are to be restricted to the primary or religious element" (*SP*, no. 19) *Divino afflante Spiritu* (1943) censures those Catholic writers who "ventured to restrict the truth of Sacred Scripture solely to matters of faith and morals, and to regard other matters, whether in the domain of physical science or history, as 'obiter dicta' and—as they contended—in no wise connected with faith" (*DAS*, no. 1)

was that biblical interpretation became one of the most energetically policed areas of Catholic theology down to eve of the Second Vatican Council.

Though the Catholic Church undoubtedly relaxed its discipline after the Second Vatican Council, the extent to which it relaxed the doctrine itself remains moot. *Dei Verbum* suggests that Vatican II did not so much repudiate the antimodernist tradition on inerrancy as bring it into unresolved tension with a salvation-historical perspective.[6] Its central statement on the truth of Scripture reads:

> Therefore, since everything asserted by the inspired authors or sacred writers must be held to be asserted by the Holy Spirit, it follows that the books of Scripture must be acknowledged as teaching solidly, faithfully and without error that truth which God wanted put into sacred writings for the sake of salvation.
>
> (*Cum ergo omne id, quod auctores inspirati seu hagiographi asserunt, retineri debeat assertum a Spiritu Sancto, inde Scripturae libri veritatem, quam Deus nostrae salutis causa Litteris Sacris consignari voluit, firmiter, fideliter et sine errore docere profitendi sunt*).[7]

This sentence, the result of complex drafting history, attempts to honor both neo-scholastic and salvation-historical perspectives. With the neo-scholastic approach, it affirms that whatever the inspired authors "assert" stands asserted by the Holy Spirit. It further characterizes these assertions as "without error." Here we see something like Benoit's framework of inspired human instruments, or even the Rahnerian framework of the author infused with the infallible contents of the Church's mind. In keeping with the salvation-historical approach of the *nouvelle théologie*, however, the very same sentence makes the "books of Scripture" the grammatical subject of the verb "teaching," seemingly relativizing the minds of the individual authors. It also adds a purpose. God wanted revealed truth consigned to writing, says the council, "for the sake of our salvation." This text-centered and teleological approach resonates more with Tracy's idea of the "autonomous text" and

---

6 Reimund Bieringer finds several approaches to Scripture juxtaposed in *Dei Verbum*, no. 2 and no. 11, including "la Bible comme collection de propositions doctrinales" and "la Bible comme récit des actions salvatrices de Dieu dans l'histoire." "Annoncer la vie éternelle (1 Jn 1,2): L'interprétation de la Bible dans les textes officiels de l'Église catholique romaine," *RTL* 37 (2006): 493, 497.

7 *DV*, no. 11.

with Ratzinger's historically progressive understanding of revelation. Without restricting inerrancy to faith and morals or altogether renouncing the regulative role of authorial intention, *Dei Verbum* manages to suggest that inerrancy should not be considered apart from the broader salvific finality of Scripture. Because it leaves the two perspectives on inerrancy in obvious tension, however, *Dei Verbum* is widely viewed as a compromise document.

Theologians have drawn different lessons from this compromise. The American theologian Elizabeth Johnson takes the "salvation" of *nostrae salutis causa* to mean liberation from evil social institutions, and thus concludes that paternal imagery for God falls outside the Bible's normative affirmations: "For the sake of our salvation: on the wings of this principle feminist hermeneutics lifts off from imprisoning discourse and flies around Scriptures seeking what has been lost, to practical critical effect."[8] Without prejudging the nature of salvation so much, the American exegete Raymond E. Brown arguably paved the way for more sweeping conclusions. His *The Critical Meaning of the Bible* contended that *Dei Verbum*'s drafting history reveals a clear trajectory away from the inerrancy of what is asserted to the reliability of what pertains to salvation.[9] The retained neo-scholastic formulas should therefore be construed as an exercise in "face-saving" for the ultra-conservative minority and need not be given the same interpretive weight as the salvation-historical formulas.[10]

Brown's critics, however, objected that he failed to account for all the data. Brown makes much of the fact that the council fathers removed the word "inerrancy" from the working text after Cardinal König and others pointed out that the Bible does in fact contain errors.[11] Avery Dulles agrees that by dropping *inerrantia* the Council wished to avoid the impression of claiming inerrancy for Scripture in every respect. But Dulles also points out what Brown omits—namely, that the Council later replaced the intermediate formula of "saving truths" (*veritates salutares*) with "truth ... for the sake of our salvation" (*veritatem ... nostrae causa salutis*) precisely to avoid the impression that they had restricted the scope of inerrancy to matters of faith

8 Elizabeth A. Johnson, *She Who Is: The Mystery of God in Feminist Theological Discourse* (New York: Crossroad, 1992), 79.

9 Raymond E. Brown, *The Critical Meaning of the Bible: How a Modern Reading of the Bible Challenges Christians, the Church, and the Churches* (New York: Paulist, 1981), 19.

10 Brown, *Critical Meaning of the Bible*, 18 (unnumbered note).

11 Brown, *Critical Meaning of the Bible*, 19.

and morals alone. According to the drafting history, therefore, the dynamic between neo-scholastic and salvation-historical perspectives resembled a tug-of-war more than a linear progression.[12] Indeed, if the last redaction favored any theological tendency, it favored the neo-scholastic minority.[13] Even if this were not the case, however, one might still wonder whether Brown, by using the drafting history to dismiss certain formulas as mere consolation prizes for the losers, shirks his responsibility to text in its final canonical shape.[14] Ratzinger will offer a solution more inclusive of the diverse conciliar affirmations.

Besides inclusiveness, however, Ratzinger's solution will add complexity. Hence discussion of his model of inerrancy will have to proceed in several stages. First, it will review how Ratzinger retools the classical notion of authorial intention by identifying the People of God as Scripture's "subject," and thus as the principal bearer of inerrant intentions. Second, it will turn to Ratzinger's "tests" for discerning the extent to which the People of God intends to affirm any given idea found in Scripture. The section will conclude with a case study: Ratzinger's treatment of whether Scripture teaches the existence of the Devil.

---

12 Avery Dulles, "The Authority of Scripture: A Catholic Perspective," in *Scripture in the Jewish and Christian Traditions: Authority, Interpretation, Relevance*, ed. Frederick E. Greenspahn (Nashville: Abingdon, 1982), 26–27 and 36–37.

13 The text attained its final form when Paul VI personally requested a redrafting to "poter tranquillamente procedere, in tema di tanta responsabilità davanti alla Chiesa e alla propria coscienza." Giovanni Caprile, ed., *Il Concilio Vaticano II: Cronache del Concilio Vaticano II edite da "La Civiltà Cattolica,"* 5 vols. (Rome: La Civiltà Cattolica, 1966–69), 4:331. Gérard Philips landed on the winning formula, it seems, by taking a suggestion of the minority— *veritatem quam Deus, nostrae salutis causa, consignari voluit* (AS IV, 5:708)—and changing the case of *causa* from nominative to ablative, yielding *veritatem quam Deus nostrae salutis causā consignari voluit*. The phrase *nostrae salutis causa* thus changed from a nominative apposition to God—"God, the cause of our salvation"—to an adverbial phrase modifying *consignari*—"to be committed to writing for the sake of our salvation." On this complicated history, see Riccardo Burigana, *La Bibbia nel Concilio: La redazione della constituzione «Dei Verbum» del Vaticano II* (Bologna: Il Mulino, 1998), 427; Alois Grillmeier, "The Divine Inspiration and the Interpretation of Sacred Scripture," in *Commentary on the Documents of Vatican II*, ed. Herbert Vorgrimler, trans. William Glen-Doepl, vol. 3 (New York: Herder & Herder, 1967), 212; Gérard Philips, *Carnets conciliaires de Mgr Gérard Philips: Secrétaire adjoint de la Commission Doctrinale*, ed. K. Schelkens, intro. by L. Declerck (Louvain: Peeters, 2006), 153.

14 Without naming Brown, Thomas Söding calls for a "primacy of the synchronic over the diachronic" in interpreting *Dei Verbum*. "Zeit für Gottes Wort: Die Offenbarungskonstitution des Konzils und die Hermeneutik der Reform," *TRev* 108, no. 6 (2012): 448.

The Layered Intentionality of the People of God

The previous chapter showed that Ratzinger's Bonaventurian-ecclesial model of inspiration identified the People of God—inclusive of Israel, the Apostolic Church, and the Post-Apostolic Church—as the perduring and understanding subject of Scripture. Two elements of this "subject-inclusive" approach to Scripture as revelation will allow Ratzinger to reframe the problem of biblical veracity. First, there exists a historical intentionality that transcends the sundry intentions of individual authors, a corporate intentionality undergirding Scripture's unity as a single book. Second, the collective bearer of this intention, despite the continuity of its faith, has undergone epochal changes across the course of its history. Drawing on the Pauline image of the Church as Christ's "body," Ratzinger compares the People of God to a "human being, who, by physiological and psychological norms, is but a succession of states yet who knows, for all that, that he is always himself."[15] Combining these two elements, Ratzinger reasons that one cannot identify what Scripture *intends* to teach, and thus what it teaches without error, without first discerning the intentions of its corporate author. And this discernment requires retracing ever anew the layered history of the People of God.

The first indications of a theory of inerrancy corresponding to the Bonaventurian-ecclesial model of inspiration appear in Ratzinger's essay "Zum Problem der Entmythologisierung des Neuen Testaments" (1960). Published just a year after his *Theology of History in St. Bonaventure*, the essay takes up a position vis-à-vis Rudolf Bultmann's project of biblical "demythologization," then still dominant in the Germany academy. "People cannot use electric lights and radios," Bultmann famously observed, "and at the same time believe in the spirit and wonder world of the New Testament."[16] The only option for the modern exegete, accordingly, was to detach the Gospel message from this mythical worldview—with its presumption of a three-story cosmos, miraculous deeds, angelic and demonic interference—and recast it "existentially."[17] Ratzinger, for his part, agrees that a certain kind of demythologization is necessary: "Catholic theology has always practiced

15 Joseph Ratzinger, *Principles of Catholic Theology: Building Stones for a Fundamental Theology* (San Francisco: Ignatius, 1987), 132.

16 Rudolf Bultmann, "New Testament and Mythology," in *Kerygma and Myth: A Theological Debate,* ed. Hans Werner Bartsch, trans. Reginald H. Fuller (New York: Harper & Row, 1966), 5.

17 Bultmann, "New Testament and Mythology," 10.

the 'demythologization' of Scripture—that is, the spiritual translation of its social imaginary [*Bildwelt*] into the contemporary intellectual world [*Verständniswelt*] of the believer."[18] He disagrees with Bultmann, however, on the proper criteria for discriminating between mythological periphery and revealed Gospel message: "What is revelation and what is husk [*Schale*] can never be ascertained by the individual theologian—from his own perspective—on the basis of scholarly presuppositions; this, in the end, only the living community of faith can decide, which—as the Body of Christ—is the abiding presence of Christ, who does not let his disposal over his work slip from his grasp."[19] In *Called to Communion*, Ratzinger later connects this idea of distinguishing center and periphery to Bonaventure's ablative model of spiritual progress. Just as a sculptor works essentially by removing stone to reveal the figure "hidden" in the block, so also the Christian works by removing the dross of sin so that God's image may shine forth unimpeded. Extending this reasoning, Ratzinger adds that the Church must always be ready to use "human constructions to help her speak and act in the era in which she finds herself," as well as to dismantle them when they obscure what is truly essential.[20] The People of God in the canonical period presumably represents no exception to this rule. Such statements, taken from Ratzinger's early and later writings, thus imply two convictions. First, one can and must distinguish between Scripture's revealed message, which enjoys an unfading validity, and Scripture's accompanying worldview, which may become obsolete. Second, one can distinguish with confidence only by consulting the transhistorical community of faith.

Just a couple of years after publishing "Das Problem der Entmythologisierung," Ratzinger resumes working out the implications of his Bonaventurian-ecclesial model of inspiration for the problem of inerrancy, now in the form of a critique of *De fontibus revelationis*. In his lecture of October 10, 1962, to the German-speaking bishops, already cited several times in the previous chapter, Ratzinger laments that the "schema speaks very sharply . . . as it works out this deduction: God is supreme truth and cannot err; but God dictated Scripture; therefore, Scripture is precisely just as free of error

---

18 Joseph Ratzinger, "Zum Problem der Entmythologisierung des Neuen Testaments," *Religionsunterricht an Höheren Schulen* 3 (1960): 8.

19 Ratzinger, "Zum Problem der Entmythologisierung," 11.

20 Joseph Ratzinger, *Called to Communion*, trans. Adrian Walker (San Francisco: Ignatius, 1996), 142. Ratzinger cites Bonaventure, *Collationes in Hexameron*, II, 33.

as is God himself—'in qualibet re religiosa vel profana.' . . . Here however the dictation theory that is assumed, as just indicated, expresses no single thought that is specifically Christian."[21] Ratzinger goes on to explain that Hinduism, Buddhism, and Islam understand their respective sacred writings to be "timeless divine dictation,"[22] whereas the best of Christian theology has always understood that the "Bible is the result of God's historical dialogue with human beings and only from this history does it have meaning and significance."[23] A "specifically Christian" theory of inerrancy would, consequently, take into account the salvation-historical locus and relevance of the text. The neo-Thomist model of inerrancy, by focusing on the truth of the authors' discrete propositional judgments, tends to neglect the historical and communal embeddedness of this dialogue.

Pressing his case, Ratzinger adds that the Neo-Thomist theory, besides being insufficiently historical, is also empirically implausible. He suggests that undisputed historical findings have long shown the Bible to contain material errors: Mark's confusion of the high priest Abiathar for his father Ahimelech (Mk 2:26),[24] the historical discrepancies between Chronicles and

---

21 Jared Wicks, "Six Texts by Prof. Joseph Ratzinger as *Peritus* before and during Vatican Council II," *Greg* 89, no. 2 (2008): 280. In his running commentary on the Council, Ratzinger would again characterize the Pontifical Biblical Commission's earlier decisions as symptomatic of an "anti-Modernistic neurosis which had again and again crippled the Church since the turn of the century." *Theological Highlights of Vatican II* (New York: Paulist, 2009), 11; cf. 23.

22 The neo-Thomists themselves would have disputed the justice of this characterization. Pierre Benoit, for instance, associates the "hegemony of dictation theory" with the *res-et-sententia* theory of Cardinal Franzelin, from whom he is at pains to distinguish himself. *Prophecy and Inspiration: A Commentary on the Summa Theologica II–II, Questions 171–178*, trans. Avery Dulles and Thomas L. Sheridan (New York: Desclée, 1961), 116. Sebastian Tromp, who sat on the preparatory theological commission that produced *De fontibus revelationis*, argues in his manual that "dictatio mechanica" was heretical: "Si talis dictatio excludit opus personale intellectuale auctoris sacri, est absolute theologice falsa. Homo non tantum non esset auctor, sed ne secretarius quidem; esset scribendi machina." *De Sacrae Scripturae inspiratione*, 6th ed. (Rome: Gregorian University Press, 1962), 94.

23 Wicks, "Six Texts," 278–79. While in Bonn (1959–63), Ratzinger four times offered lecture cycles on "Religionsphilosophie und Religionsgeschichte," drawing heavily on his colleague Paul Hacker's studies of Hinduism. See Manuel Schlögl, "Sein Werk wird noch vieles zu sagen haben: Biografische und theologische Anmerkung zur Freundschaft von Paul Hacker und Joseph Ratzinger," *MIPB* 5 (2012): 57.

24 This error is not actually undisputed. Some exegetes argue that ἐπὶ 'Αβιαθὰρ ἀρχιερέως (Mark 2:26) may convey a sense that would be historically defensible. Some propose that the Greek construction *epi* + anarthrous genitive may refer to a passage within a larger section, meaning in this case "in the part of about Abiathar." Others suggest that it means "in

Kings, and Daniel's mistaken identification of Belshazzar as Nebuchadnez-zar's son.[25] Yet, according to the usual "dictation theory," to admit that the sacred authors expressly (yet incorrectly) affirmed any of these positions is to implicate the Holy Spirit in error, no less than if one were to admit that the evangelists fabricated Christ's resurrection. A subtler idea of biblical inten-tionality and inerrancy is thus called for: "*Scripture* is and remains inerrant and beyond doubt in everything that *it properly intends to affirm*, but this is not necessarily so in that which accompanies the affirmation and is not part of it. As a result, in agreement with what no. 13 says quite well, the inerrancy of Scripture has to be limited to its *vere enuntiata* [what is really affirmed]. Otherwise historical reason will be led into what is really an inescapable conflict."[26] Though Ratzinger might seem to be merely restating Benoit's position on the various qualifications of authorial judgment, he subtly shifts the locus of the intending subject. Scripture itself, not the hagiographers considered severally, now stands as the grammatical subject of the intention to affirm.[27] Those familiar with Ratzinger's *Habilitationschrift* will realize that

---

the presence of Abiathar the high priest," thus anticipating his future office. See Joel Marcus, *Mark: A New Translation with Introduction and Commentary*, 2 vols., AB 27–27A (New York: Doubleday, 2000–2009), 1:241.

25 Wicks, "Six Texts," 280. It is worth noting that Ratzinger's list of errors resembles the list offered by the Austrian Cardinal Franz König, who, with Cardinal Frings, took turns chair-ing the meetings of the German-speaking bishops. Norbert Trippen, "Kardinal Josef Frings auf dem II. Vatikanischen Konzil," in *Das Zweite Vatikanische Konzil (1962–1965): Stand und Perspektiven der kirchenhistorichen Forschung im deutschsprachigen Raum*, ed. Franz Xaver Bischof (Stuttgart: W. Kohlhammer, 2012), 98. König lists, for example, both the false appellation in Mark 2:26 and the unhistorical claims of Daniel—though with respect to the date of Nebuchadnezzar's siege of Jerusalem rather than to his paternity of Belshazzar (*AS* III, 3:275). Grillmeier considered König's the "most important contribution" to the debate on inerrancy at the Council. "Divine Inspiration and Interpretation of Scripture," 205.

26 Wicks, "Six Texts," 280. "No. 13" here refers to the paragraph of *De fontibus* entitled *Quo-modo inerrantia diiudicanda sit*—"How inerrancy is to be discerned." See *AS* I, 3:18–19.

27 Ratzinger makes Scripture the intending subject more than once in his address: "Accord-ing to a practically irrefutable consensus of historians there definitely are mistakes and errors in the Bible in profane matters of no relevance for what Scripture properly intends to affirm." Wicks, "Six Texts," 280. He continues this *façon de parler* in later writings, such as when identifying the central affirmations of the creation account in Genesis 1: "Scrip-ture would not wish to inform us about how the different species of plant life gradually appeared or how the sun and the moon and the stars were established. Its purpose ulti-mately would be to say one thing: *God* created the world." *In the Beginning . . . : A Catholic Understanding of the Story of Creation and the Fall* (Grand Rapids: Eerdmans, 1995), 5.

"Scripture" here means "Holy Scripture," the biblical text as understood and animated by the People of God.

As the previous chapter also makes clear, however, Ratzinger understands the People of God to derive its transhistorical unity from Christ, toward whom it tends and with whom it has enjoyed various kinds of relationships: prophetic anticipation, direct testimony, retrospective interpretation. Ratzinger's own schema *De voluntate Dei erga hominem*, developed as an early alternative to *De fontibus revelationis*, emphasizes both these points. Its fourth paragraph clearly portrays Christ as the omega of revelation: "In this man, Christ Jesus, the end toward which human history tends has already begun, for he is himself the kingdom of God, in whom 'God is all in all' (1Cor 15:28)." Its fifth paragraph goes on both to distinguish and unite revelation's various "layers" by reference to Christ: "The several revealed truths which are found [*leguntur*] in the Old and New Testaments and developed [*explicantur*] in Holy Mother Church's teaching and preaching, all lead back [*reducuntur*] to the one truth that is Jesus Christ."[28] To discern to what extent Scripture properly intends to affirm the contents of any passage, therefore, one must employ Christological criteria. One can ascertain the *vere enuntiata* only by considering both the passage's historical position vis-à-vis Christ and the relevance of its contents for the Christian mystery.

Already at the Council's beginning, then, one perceives Ratzinger's conviction that Scripture *qua* revelation intends Christ as its end, expressing this intention in a historically differentiated way. He identifies the retrieval of this Christological criterion as the best hope for reconciling the doctrine of inerrancy with the demands of reason.[29] Though direct dependence is difficult to prove, it seems likely that Ratzinger's interventions and others like them convinced the council fathers to supplement the traditional treatment of inerrancy with the abovementioned consideration of its purpose—namely, that God has given this truth "for the sake of salvation."

---

28 Jared Wicks, "Another Text by Joseph Ratzinger as *Peritus* at Vatican II," *Greg* 101, no. 2 (2020): 238.

29 Ratzinger commented retrospectively that, if *De fontibus* had simply reiterated the prohibitions of earlier magisterial statements, this would have resulted "not in the rescue of the faith but in dooming it to sterility, by separating theology once and for all from modern science and confining it in an ivory tower where it would have gradually withered away." *Theological Highlights of Vatican II*, 99.

The "Layered" Intentionality of the Word of God

Though at the outset of Vatican II Ratzinger already considers the Bible's Christological finality relevant for distinguishing its revealed core from its potentially timebound periphery, the relevance of the historical "layering" of the People of God remains underdeveloped. As the last chapter showed, Ratzinger's address to the German-speaking bishops recalled the indirect nature of Old Testament inspiration, noting that the Old Testament "has force not from itself but from Christ and in reference to Christ, who is the one who removes the veil that covered the face of Moses (2 Cor 3:12–18)."[30] But Ratzinger would develop this insight in greater depth during and after the Council, differentiating Scripture's various salvation-historical layers and developing corresponding criteria for identifying what Scripture properly intends to affirm. A fair appraisal of Ratzinger's remodeled inerrancy requires a certain familiarity with these developments.

A better elaborated presentation of Scripture as a stratified reality appears in Ratzinger's inaugural lecture at the University of Münster in 1963, later published as "The Question of the Concept of Tradition" (1965).[31] There Ratzinger notes two major inflection points in the history of the People of God. Christ's reinterpretation of Israel in the Spirit represents, of course, one such watershed. But the early Christian community's reinterpretation of Christ's directive to establish the kingdom of God, their shift from converting Israel to founding a Church of gentiles, represents another nearly as momentous. According to the account of the Council of Jerusalem found in Acts 15, the apostles understood this initiative to be a "new decision taken in the Holy Spirit and[,] thereby, opened up that new interpretation of Christ's message on which the Church is essentially founded."[32] This course correction remains only dimly discernible in Christ's own preaching, perhaps as an implicit contingency plan in the case of Israel's post-Resurrection rejection of his message. Especially in the Apostolic period, then, the Church shows an ability to make decisions that "complete" Christ's foundation, further

---

30 Wicks, "Six Texts," 283.

31 For circumstances and significance of this lecture, see Hansjürgen Verweyen, "Joseph Ratzinger und die Exegese: Die Antrittsvorlesung im Münster im Kontext des Gesamtwerkes," *MIPB* 7 (2014): 48–60.

32 Joseph Ratzinger, "The Question of the Concept of Tradition: A Provisional Response," in *God's Word: Scripture, Tradition, Office,* ed. Peter Hünermann and Thomas Söding, trans. Henry Taylor (San Francisco: Ignatius, 2008), 59.

determining what Christ's own words and deeds have left implied or open-ended. This will be an important point as we look at Ratzinger's understanding of Christ's institution of the Eucharist at the Last Supper.

In light of these two major inflection points, Ratzinger differentiates four strands of tradition "interwoven in the *analogia fidei*." Two of these strands made their debut in the previous chapter's treatment of the "analogous" inspiration of the Old Testament: the "Old Testament theology of the Old Testament" and the "New Testament theology of the Old Testament." But they adumbrate an analogous pairing corresponding to the Christian era: a "New Testament theology of the New Testament," which designates the theology that the historian can reconstruct from within the New Testament; and an "ecclesial theology of the New Testament," which extends the historical meaning of the New Testament without contradicting it. What Ratzinger calls "Holy Scripture," then, comprises four diachronic strata: the two biblical theologies of Old and New Testament, and then the ecclesial theologies of Old and New Testament.[33]

To these diachronic strata Ratzinger also adds what might be considered synchronic layers. He notes that what distinguishes the biblical theologies from the ecclesial theologies is nothing other than the "reality called tradition." At the most global level, tradition encompasses nothing less than the "entire mystery of Christ's presence" in history, the surplus of meaning in revelation that can never be exhaustively captured in writing. Though inexhaustible, tradition does manifest itself concretely in certain media. According to Ratzinger, these are: (1) the faith that Christ's indwelling makes possible, (2) the living authority of the Church that serves as tradition's "organ,"[34] and (3) the dogmas and creeds that this organ has already articulated as a

---

33 Ratzinger, "Question of the Concept of Tradition," 60–61.

34 Ratzinger considers magisterium coeval with the written word: "The teaching office of the apostles' successors does not represent a second authority alongside Scripture but is inwardly a part of it. This *viva vox* is not there to restrict the authority of Scripture." "What in Fact Is Theology?," in *Pilgrim Fellowship of Faith: The Church as Communion*, ed. Stephan Otto Horn and Vinzenz Pfnür, trans. Henry Taylor (San Francisco: Ignatius, 2005), 35. He rehearses New Testament evidence for the interdependence of word and office, including evidence for the incipient distinction between local episcopal office and universal primatial office, in "The Ministerial Office and the Unity of the Church," *JES* 1 (1964): 42–57. For the chronological priority of dogma to Scripture, see Rudolf Voderholzer, "'*Schriftauslegung in Widerstreit*:' Joseph Ratzinger und die Exegese," in *Der Glaube ist einfach*, ed. Gerhard Ludwig Müller (Regensburg: Friedrich Pustet, 2007), 63–67.

"rule of faith." Scripture and tradition together form a complex unity of synchronic and diachronic elements.[35]

For Ratzinger, Scripture discloses its meaning much as a symphony does. Essential to the beauty and power of a symphony is the synchronic complementarity of its many voices and instruments. But the symphony also represents a diachronic form extended over time, whose successive movements must be held together in memory if they are to create tension or give the pleasure of resolution. The dependence of musical intelligibility on this diachronic dimension is apparent from the contrast experience of "skipping" music: all recordings sampled in fractions of a second, without temporal extension, sound unpleasantly alike. In a later writing, Ratzinger opines that something analogous holds for understanding Scripture:

> *Symphonia* serves to express the unity of the Old and New Testaments—which is the unity of law and gospel, of prophets and apostles, but also the unity of the diverse writings of the New Testament among themselves. At issue here is the basic form of the expression of truth in the Church, a form which rests upon a structure enriched by manifold tensions. The truth of faith resonates not as a mono-phony but as symphony, as a polyphonic melody unfolding in the contrapuntal interplay of law, prophets, Gospels, and apostles.[36]

In other words, each element of the word of God—Old Testament, New Testament, dogma, *sensus fidelium*—plays Christ in its own distinct mode; but only as an ensemble does it intelligibly express the Christian mystery.[37]

---

35 Ratzinger, "Question of the Concept of Tradition," 63. Referring elsewhere to the People of God, Ratzinger observes, "When this people speaks . . . from the center of its identity, it speaks in the stages of its own history, yet always as one and the same subject." "The Sign of the Woman: An Introductory Essay on the Encyclical *Redemptoris Mater*," in *Mary: The Church at the Source*, ed. Hans Urs von Balthasar, trans. Adrian Walker (San Francisco: Ignatius Press, 2005), 39.

36 Joseph Ratzinger, *The Nature and Mission of Theology: Essays to Orient Theology in Today's Debates* (San Francisco: Ignatius, 1995), 83–84. For Ratzinger's description of the Gospels as a "choir of four," see Joseph Ratzinger, *Eschatology: Death and Eternal Life*, trans. Michael Waldstein and Aidan Nichols (Washington, DC: The Catholic University of America Press, 1988), 41.

37 For a more detailed discussion of Ratzinger's general identification of truth with the whole, see Dorothee Kaes, *Theologie im Anspruch von Geschichte und Wahrheit: Zur Hermeneutik Joseph Ratzingers* (St. Ottilien: EOS Verlag, 1997), 46–49. For the inclusion of "dogma" among the "profusion of the forms of faith," see Ratzinger, *Nature and Mission of Theology*, 96–97.

In advising theologians to consult the synchronic and diachronic breadth of tradition, Ratzinger tacitly redresses the tendency—often ascribed to the Roman theology of the nineteenth century—to reduce tradition to the ecclesial consciousness of the moment, or even to the latest papal mindset.[38] Ratzinger clearly distances himself from Pius IX's perhaps half-serious claim, "La tradizione sono io,"[39] situating himself, whether wittingly or unwittingly, much closer to John Henry Newman, who makes "preservation of type" the chief note of authentic development.[40] Having entered the Catholic Church at the height of its ultramontane enthusiasm, Newman used to console friends with reminders of the long view: "Looking at early history, it would seem as if the Church moved on to the perfect truth by various successive declarations, alternately in contrary directions, and thus perfecting, completing, supplying each other. Let us have a little faith in her, I say. Pius is not the last of the Popes—the fourth Council modified the third, and the fifth the fourth."[41] Ratzinger and Newman seem to agree, in short, that discerning the "perfect truth" requires attention to patterns of tradition extended over time.

These remarks should suffice to suggest how Ratzinger elaborates his neo-Bonaventurian view of salvation history into a Christologically differentiated map of Scripture. Just as the People of God, through union with Christ her head, has retained her identity across all her historical transformations, so will Scripture exhibit a Christological unity, according to which the "individual part derives its meaning from the whole, and the whole derives its meaning from its end—from Christ."[42]

---

38 Hermann Pottmeyer, *Unfehlbarkeit und Souveränität: Die Päpstliche Unfehlbarkeit im System der ultramontanen Ekklesiologie des 19. Jahrhunderts* (Mainz: Matthias-Grünewald, 1975), 275.

39 Few now doubt the historical authenticity of the statement, made in response to Cardinal Guidi's readiness to compromise with the anti-infallibilist minority at Vatican I. See Klaus Schatz, *Vatikanum I (1869–1870)*, 3 vols. (Paderborn: Schöningh, 1992–94), 3:312–22.

40 John Henry Newman, *Essay on the Development of Christian Doctrine* (London: Longmans, Green, 1909), 171–78. Online: https://www.newmanreader.org/works/development/.

41 Newman, *Letters and Diaries*, xxv, 310. Cited in Ian T. Ker, "Newman, the Councils, and Vatican II," *Communio* 28 (2001): 716.

42 Ratzinger, *In the Beginning*, 9. Ratzinger will advocate for a similarly Christotelic view of Scripture on Thomistic grounds in his 1988 "Biblical Interpretation in Conflict," in *God's Word: Scripture—Tradition—Office*, ed. Peter Hünermann and Thomas Söding, trans. Henry Taylor (San Francisco: Ignatius, 2005), 119–20.

Case Study: The Devil and Galileo

Not long after elaborating this Christologically differentiated model of tradition, Ratzinger translates it into serviceable criteria for discerning the genuine intention of Scripture. A fairly complete set of these criteria appears already in his essay "Farewell to the Devil?," first published in *Dogma and Preaching* (1973). The short reflection attempts to address whether the existence of the Devil belongs to Scripture's *vere enuntiata*, or merely to its accompanying and nonbinding worldview. In answering the question and spelling out his logic, Ratzinger applies a set of four interrelated "standards" that reflect the various strata and elements of tradition distinguished in "The Question of the Concept of Tradition."

"Farewell to the Devil?" responds to a book published under the same title by the Tübingen *Alttestamentler* Herbert Haag. Haag's *Abschied vom Teufel* (1969) argued that Scripture's many references to demonic activity are best understood not as evidence for the existence of fallen angels but as a culturally conditioned manner of expressing Scripture's true and abiding theme: structural sin.[43] Christians may therefore discard the idea of fallen incorporeal intelligences as mere mythological packaging, being obliged to retain only the core concept of systemic evil.

Ratzinger objects not to demythologization per se but to Haag's particular version of it. His 1960 essay "Das Problem der Entmythologisierung" admitted the legitimacy of distinguishing between revelation and worldview, while insisting that only the faith of the whole Church can competently do so. In keeping with this earlier position, "Farewell to the Devil?" undertakes to elaborate criteria for gauging just how much the Church's faith is bound up with such ostensibly outdated ideas: "Although there is no standard that automatically indicates in all particular cases where faith ends and world view begins, there is still a series of aids to judgment that show the way as we look for clarifications."[44] He enumerates four such rules of thumb: (1) the "relationship between the two Testaments,"[45] (2) the relationship to the New Testament portrait of Jesus,[46] (3) the degree of acceptance "as part of the

---

43 Joseph Ratzinger, *Dogma and Preaching*, ed. Michael J. Miller, trans. Michael J. Miller and Matthew J. O'Connell (San Francisco: Ignatius, 2011), 197.

44 Ratzinger, *Dogma and Preaching*, 199.

45 Ratzinger, *Dogma and Preaching*, 199.

46 Ratzinger, *Dogma and Preaching*, 201.

Church's faith,"[47] and (4) "compatibility with scientific [*wissenschaftlicher*] knowledge."[48] The careful reader will notice that these "aids to judgment" correlate closely with strata of tradition that Ratzinger distinguishes in "The Question of the Concept of Tradition." The first aid to judgment sums up the "Old Testament and New Testament Theologies of the Old Testament." The second hinges on Christ's New Testament portrait, thus recalling the "New Testament Theology of the New Testament." The third criterion of the "Church's faith" correlates with the "Church's Theology of the New Testament." The whole structure implies the criterion of scholarly knowledge, inasmuch as it presumes the ability to distinguish between ecclesial senses and those ascertainable by historical reason. Ratzinger's appeal to a series of "aids to judgment" suggests that he sees the Church's mind to be ascertainable, even if never exhaustively "objectifiable."[49]

To differentiate proper and improper demythologization, "Farewell to the Devil?" sets out to apply the four "aids to judgment" to two very different candidates for demythologization. It analyzes in parallel the geocentrism once challenged by Galileo and the existence of the Devil now challenged by Haag, arguing that the latter tests consistently positive for abiding normativity, whereas the former tests consistently negative. Turning to the relation between the Old and New Testaments, for example, Ratzinger attends to the developmental arc of each theme. As the New Testament receives the Old Testament imagery of creation, it shows a trajectory of contraction. "John 1:1 is the New Testament assimilation of the Genesis passage and condenses its colorful depictions into one statement: In the beginning was the Word. Everything else is relegated to the world of imagery."[50] Demonology, by contrast, shows a movement of expansion across Testaments. "The notion of demonic powers enters only hesitantly into the Old Testament, whereas in the life of Jesus it acquires unprecedented weight, which is undiminished

---

47 Ratzinger, *Dogma and Preaching*, 202.

48 Ratzinger, *Dogma and Preaching*, 203.

49 This recalls the French philosopher Maurice Blondel's insistence that the Church, a "summary of collective experience," has a certain moral method of coming to judgments akin the ascetic's expertise in discernment of spirits: "Nothing is more reliable than the light shed by the orderly and repeated performance of Christian practices." *The Letter on Apologetics and History and Dogma*, ed. and trans. Alexander Dru and Illtyd Trethowan (Grand Rapids, MI: Eerdmans, 1994), 277.

50 For a similar deployment of the Christological criterion to discern the abiding content of the creation narratives, see Ratzinger, *In the Beginning*, 15–16.

in Paul's letters and continues into the latest New Testament writings." On the first test, then, the Devil tests positive for permanent normativity while geocentrism tests negative.[51]

Ratzinger takes the second test, an idea's relationship to the New Testament figure of Christ, in a surprising direction. He begins by setting up a weighted contrast: "Statements that remain merely theoretical forms of contemplation but do not enter into the authentic living out of the faith cannot normally be reckoned as part of the core of Christianity."[52] He then focuses on the central significance that Jesus himself attributes to his lived battle against the powers of darkness, evident in his temptations, his exorcisms, his sayings about the strong man and the stronger man, his authorization of his disciples to expel demons. All this stands in clear contrast to Jesus' lack of engagement in the astronomical: "The figure of Jesus, his spiritual physiognomy, does not change whether the sun revolves around the earth or the earth around the sun, but it is critically altered if you cut out the experiential struggle with the power of the demonic kingdom."[53] Inasmuch as the demonic seems closer to Jesus' own experience, as ascertainable even by a historical approach to the New Testament, it would seem to lie closer to the heart of biblical faith than geocentrism.

The criterion of reception into the Church—that is, "into the authentic interior act of faith, into the fundamental form of prayer and life, above and beyond the variations of tradition"—yields a similar result. Here Ratzinger observes that the role a given idea plays in the Church's liturgical and creedal forms often proves decisive. St. Basil, for instance, defended the divinity of the Holy Spirit largely on the grounds of the Spirit's parity with the Father and Son in the baptismal formula. To reject the consubstantiality of the Holy Spirit, in Basil's mind, was to cease to "take baptism at its word, especially in its central action." But the tripersonal nature of God is not the only biblical belief received into the baptismal liturgy. From the beginning, both exorcism and the renunciation of Satan have also belonged to the "central act

---

51 Ratzinger, *Dogma and Preaching*, 200. Hans Albert would later criticize *Jesus of Nazareth*'s presentation of the Devil as a distinctively Christian belief, citing ubiquitous exorcism praxis in Jewish and Hellenistic milieus. "Josef [*sic*] Ratzingers Jesusdeutung: Kritische Bemerkungen zu einigen Aspekten seiner Untersuchung," in *Alla ricerca della verità: Discussioni sul Gesù de Nazaret di Joseph Ratzinger—Benedetto XVI*, ed. Giuseppe Franco (Lecce: Lupo, 2009), 141.

52 Ratzinger, *Dogma and Preaching*, 201.

53 Ratzinger, *Dogma and Preaching*, 202.

of baptism." The great saints, moreover, have continued to experience their pursuit of holiness as an agon against a more-than-human cunning. Jettisoning belief in demonic powers would, therefore, change both the meaning of baptism and the basic "conduct of Christian life."[54] Ratzinger takes it for granted that geocentrism has never penetrated the Church's faith to the same extent. Here we find Ratzinger appealing to the synchronic strata of tradition that correspond to ecclesial interpretation: faith, creeds, and living authority.

The last of the tests, the relation to scholarly knowledge, proves the hardest to apply. Ratzinger agrees that Scripture's central affirmations can never contradict "certified scientific knowledge," concluding that Scripture cannot, consequently, intend to teach geocentrism. But he also points out that legitimate scientific knowledge can easily fuse with scientifically indemonstrable values in such a way as to produce "worldview," a collection of unexamined cultural assumptions assuming the mantle of objective science.[55] The so-called *Deutsche Christen* forgot this, Ratzinger reminds his readers, when they excluded from Scripture's proper affirmations everything that conflicted with Nazi-era eugenic theories.[56] And Haag forgets this too. For the existence of personal evil contradicts no concrete piece of "certified scientific knowledge" but only a kind of narrow empiricism that Ratzinger calls the "functionalist perspective." But if one accepts as plausible only what science can measure and manipulate, Ratzinger reminds Haag, one will end up rejecting much more than just the Devil: "There is no room in a functionalistic perspective for God, either, and no room for man as man, but only for man as function."[57] Only a rational standard hospitable to the central elements of biblical worldview can plausibly claim to guide "demythologization."[58]

According to each of the four "aids to judgment," then, belief in the Devil passes the normativity test while geocentrism fails. Ratzinger thus lays a strong claim to showing two things. First, not all biblical ideas are alike in

---

54 Ratzinger, *Dogma and Preaching*, 202–3.

55 Ratzinger gives this fuller definition of worldview in *Daughter Zion: Meditations in the Church's Marian Belief*, trans. John M. McDermott (San Francisco: Ignatius, 1983), 57–58.

56 Ratzinger, *Dogma and Preaching*, 199.

57 Ratzinger, *Dogma and Preaching*, 203.

58 Ironically, the exegete Klaus Berger would later criticize Ratzinger's *Jesus of Nazareth* (JN 1:174–75) for presenting reasonable faith as what drives out the fear of demons, when it in fact inculcates this fear. "Exegese und Dogmatik: Bermerkungen über das Jesusbuch des Papstes," in *Alla ricerca della verità: Discussioni sul Gesù de Nazaret di Joseph Ratzinger—Benedetto XVI*, ed. Giuseppe Franco (Lecce: Lupo, 2009), 41.

their bearing on the intentions of Holy Scripture. Second, the synchronic and diachronic layers of tradition that Ratzinger enumerates in "The Question of the Concept of Tradition" can generate criteria serviceable for distinguishing between Scripture's central and peripheral notions. Because "Farewell to the Devil?" provides the most methodologically transparent and most comprehensive application of Ratzinger's model of tradition to the problem of biblical worldview, these "layers" and "tests" will serve as the organizing structure for the subsequent chapters dedicated to case studies on Ratzinger as normative interpreter.

This should not obscure the fact, however, that the "tests" serve Ratzinger only as approximate standards. Precisely because tradition can never be "objectified" without remainder, he insists, the "faith of the Church is not something that can be delineated with complete clarity."[59] And when Ratzinger lists criteria for normative interpretation elsewhere, he freely varies the theme. One sees this in the four preaching "standards" he recommends in *Dogma and Preaching* for discerning what in Scripture has perennial and, therefore, contemporary relevance: (1) Sacred Scripture in the "interrelated unity of Old and New Testament", (2) "the Creeds," (3) the "living magisterium of the living Church," and (4) "the concrete faith of the Church in her communities."[60] Here one finds a diagnostic battery of similar complexity, simply adjusted for a different task.

At other times Ratzinger reduces the criteria to those most accessible to a given audience or more decisive for a given question. In a popular piece written just a couple of years before the publication of "Farewell to the Devil?," for instance, Ratzinger defends the existence of the Devil using only two criteria: the "relationship between Old and New Testament" and the "criterion of tradition, of the faith of the Church."[61] Here Ratzinger relies mostly on what falls under the first and third of Ratzinger's tests in "Farewell to the Devil?"

Ratzinger gives the tests yet another complexion in *In the Beginning* (1986), a series of homilies on Genesis that treat, *inter alia*, the "boundaries between image and intention" in the creation narrative.[62] There, when

---

59 Ratzinger, *Dogma and Preaching*, 202.

60 Ratzinger, *Dogma and Preaching*, 26–27.

61 Ratzinger, "Wer ist der Teufel?" *MIPB* 5 (2012): 39. Under the second criterion, Ratzinger mentions only the fact that the Church has repeatedly reaffirmed the existence of the Devil and his minions, such as at Lateran IV in 1215.

62 Ratzinger, *In the Beginning*, 7.

explaining why Scripture does not properly intend to teach the various pic-
turesque details of the creation account scientifically, Ratzinger lists explicitly
only the criteria of the "unity of the Bible" and "Christology."[63] As elaborated
by Ratzinger, these correlate more or less with the first and second criteria of
"Farewell to the Devil?," the relation between Old and New Testament and
the relation to the message of Christ in the New Testament. "Farewell to the
Devil?" thus seems to offer the fullest account of a criteriology that Ratzinger
feels free to abbreviate or reorganize elsewhere.

Taking a step back, then, one can say that Ratzinger's thinking on biblical inerrancy attains its maturity sometime in the early 1970s, after almost
twenty years of refinement. By the mid-1950s he had already arrived at the
conviction that the People of God, by virtue of its union with Christ, represented Scripture's primary intending subject. Building upon that foundation, Ratzinger analyzed this corporate intentionality into diachronic and
synchronic strata, converting these strata into "aids to judgment." But the
variable enumeration of these criteria suggests that Ratzinger often formu-
lates them ad hoc and seldom expects them to function with algorithmic
precision. This will be important to recall when, in the next chapter, we later
encounter Ratzinger's own shifting judgment on the normative import of
Jesus' divorce *logia*.

RATZINGER ON THE FOURFOLD SENSE

Ratzinger's conviction that the reception of Scripture in the Church
retrospectively illuminates its *vere enuntiata* has a positive corollary. Just
as ecclesial reception may reveal the limits of inerrancy, it may also expose
depths of meaning exceeding what one might call Scripture's surface sense.
Ratzinger expresses this conviction in his mature writings in the patristic and
medieval language of Scripture's fourfold sense—namely, the literal sense and
the three "spiritual" senses: allegorical, moral, and anagogical. At the same
time, Ratzinger gives this premodern hermeneutic a more contemporary

---

63 Ratzinger, *In the Beginning*, 8, 15. Though Ratzinger lists only two criteria explicitly, it
should be noted that he scatters throughout data relevant to the third and fourth criteria
of "Farewell to the Devil?" With respect to "scholarly knowledge," for instance, he begins
by conceding that "science has long since disposed of" Genesis as an empirical account of
cosmic origins (3). With respect to acceptance into the Church's faith, he remarks that the
ancient and medieval Church resisted "literalmindedness with respect to particulars" (17).

theoretical foundation, justifying the ongoing relevance of the fourfold sense by appealing to *Dei Verbum*, the findings of contemporary exegesis, and the insights of philosophical hermeneutics. In this way he attempts to do justice to biblical inspiration's positive interpretive consequences, adding to the Bible's presumed immunity from error a presumed inexhaustibility of meaning.

Appreciating Ratzinger's contribution to this question requires, of course, a certain amount of initial framing. A discussion of the relation between *Dei Verbum* 12 and the tradition of the four senses will, therefore, precede Ratzinger's own thoughts, and a Marian illustration will follow. The exposition of Ratzinger's understanding of the spiritual senses will fall in between, focusing on Ratzinger's reconceptualization of the "spiritual senses" as the Bible's divinely superintended "effective history."

The Four Senses as a Reception of *Dei Verbum* 12

Without speaking of the fourfold sense *expressis verbis*, *Dei Verbum* 12 distinguishes two interpretive horizons with regard to Scripture, one human and one divine. It falls to the biblical interpreter to cultivate a kind of binocular vision—that is, to investigate both "what meaning the sacred writers really intended, and [what] God wanted to manifest by means of their words."[64] The former entails determining what "meaning the sacred writer intended to express and actually expressed in particular circumstances by using contemporary literary forms in accordance with the situation of his own time and culture."[65] Here the Dogmatic Constitution distinguishes ever so slightly between what authors mean ("intended to express") and what texts mean ("actually expressed"), but affirms the relevance of immediate historical context in either case. Toward this end, it endorses the toolkit of modern biblical criticism: source criticism, genre criticism, the reconstruction of historical *Sitz im Leben*. The exegete's task is relatively clear and cognate with that of other historical disciplines.

But the third paragraph of *Dei Verbum* 12 complicates this relatively straightforward picture by introducing another interpretive horizon. "But, since Holy Scripture must be read and interpreted in the sacred Spirit in which it was written, no less serious attention must be given to the content

---

64 *DV*, no. 12a.

65 *DV*, no. 12b.

and unity of the whole of Scripture." Here the focus shifts not only more decisively from authorial intention to textual meaning (*"Holy Scripture* must be read . . ."), but from immediate historical context to canonical context. Indeed, the next sentence (in English translation) moves beyond the canon itself, recommending as further interpretive horizons both the "living tradition of the whole Church" and the "harmony that exists between the elements of the faith" (*analogia fidei*). Reading the Bible "in the sacred Spirit in which it was written" means reading it from within the historical trajectory of the People of God, which owes its fundamental coherence to the Holy Spirit's animation. *Dei Verbum* identifies two hermeneutical poles, then, each governed by distinct criteria: an immediate historical context methodologically justified by the Bible's human manner of composition, and a wider ecclesial context methodologically justified by the Spirit's ongoing influence.[66]

As to the manner of integrating these two poles, however, *Dei Verbum* offers more exhortation than explanation. "It is the task of exegetes [*exegetarum*] to work according to these rules toward a better understanding and explanation of the meaning of Sacred Scripture," the Dogmatic Constitution continues, "so that through preparatory study [*praeparato studio*] the judgment of the Church may mature." A careful analysis of *Dei Verbum* 12 indicates that "these rules" comprise both the historical and the ecclesial criteria.[67] Both canons therefore oblige even "exegetes." The Council apparently wanted to forestall the kind of strict disciplinary division that would subsequently emerge in academic theology, whereby two nonoverlapping sets of interpreters ("exegetes" and "systematicians") would each work according to separate criteria to determine two mutually exclusive senses ("what the human authors intended" and "what God wanted to manifest through them"). In the mind of the Council, the two poles interpenetrate too much for such a strict division of labor. On the one hand, the author's intention already represents a moment of inspired meaning. On the other hand, the text starts out signifying more than the author knows. In the final analysis, *Dei Verbum* rather breezily enjoins commentators to integrate both her-

---

66 For all citations in this paragraph, see *DV*, no. 12c.

67 In what is perhaps the most thorough synchronic and diachronic analysis of DV, no. 12, Reimund Bieringer observes, "Thus I conclude that 12,7 refers to the task of the exegete as it is expressed in DV 12 as a whole, both the study of the authorial intention (12, 1–5) and of the meaning of the text (12,6)." "Biblical Revelation and Exegetical Interpretation according to Dei Verbum 12," *SNTSU* 27 (2002): 12.

meneutical poles in such a way as to avoid either collapsing or separating them,[68] showing little appreciation of the difficulties entailed in forming such a methodological "alliance."[69] As in many other questions, it leaves to future generations of theologians the task of elaborating a synthesis.[70]

Though Vatican II speaks of attention to the "sacred Spirit" in which the Bible was written rather than the Bible's "spiritual senses," concurrent developments favored a synergy between these modes of expression. In the years before and during Vatican II, Henri de Lubac published several influential works on premodern biblical interpretation. The first such work, *History and Spirit: The Understanding of Scripture According to Origen* (French: 1950), sought to rehabilitate Origen's exegetical method, which de Lubac described as an "effort to grasp the spirit in the history or undertake the passage from history to spirit."[71] In the late fifties and early sixties, the French Jesuit would follow up this initial effort with his monumental *Medieval Exegesis: The Four Senses of Scripture*. The four-volume work compiles evidence for a claim relevant to our argument—namely, that medieval Latin theology, elaborating the insights of influential patristic authors, consistently teaches multivalence as an entailment of biblical inspiration.[72] John Cassian could already say in the

---

68 According to Beda Rigaux, a *peritus* involved in the drafting of *Dei Verbum*, the document expects the theological and historical to comingle in the interpreter because the historical meaning is also an inspired meaning: "La vérité du fait est unie à la vérité de la signification aussi bien au niveau du commentateur qu'a celui de la source." "L'interprétation de l'Écriture selon la Constitution 'Dei Verbum,'" in *Au service de la parole de Dieu. Melanges offerts à Monseigneur Andre-Marie Charue, Eveque de Namur* (Gembloux: Duculot, 1968), 279.

69 Christopher Seitz criticizes *Dei Verbum* on just these grounds: "In just what sense, one could ask, is this alliance to be made intelligible? Indeed, the entire point of 'objective biblical criticism' may well be to call into question something like the necessity of a churchly context." Christopher Seitz, *Convergences: Canon and Canonicity* (Waco, TX: Baylor University Press, 2020), 95.

70 When addressing a proposed amendment to the first sentence of *DV*, no. 12, the official *relatio* for the session of October 29, 1965, gives the following indication of the Council's desire to avoid taking a position on the relation between the literal sense and the so-called *sensus plenior*: "Tredecim Patres petunt ut, loco *et*, scribatur *quidque*, ut appareat quaestionem *de sensu pleniore* non dirimi." The response: "Omnes concordant de non dirimenda hac quaestione [de sensu pleniore]. Si scribitur *quidque*, quaestio in sensum positivum dirimeretur. Expressio *et* est neutralis" (*AS* IV, 5:710).

71 Henri de Lubac, *History and Spirit: The Understanding of Scripture according to Origen*, trans. Anne Englund Nash and Juvenal Merriell (San Francisco: Ignatius, 2007), 317.

72 Henri de Lubac, *Medieval Exegesis: The Four Senses of Scripture*, trans. Mark Sebanc and E. M. Macierowski, 3 vols. (Grand Rapids: Eerdmans, 1998–2009); partial translation of *Éxegèse médiévale: les quatre sens de l'écriture*, 4 vols., Theologie 41 (Paris: Aubier, 1959–64).

fifth century, "One and the same Jerusalem can be understood in a fourfold manner. According to history it is the city of the Jews. According to allegory it is the Church of Christ. According to anagogy it is the heavenly city of God 'which is the mother of us all' (Gal 4:26). According to tropology it is the soul of the human being."[73] Augustine gives a similar analysis.[74] The fourfold sense would become so standardized in the Middle Ages that Augustine of Dacia condensed the idea into a Latin jingle for pedagogical purposes: *Littera gesta docet, quid credas allegoria, / Moralis quid agas, quo tendas anagogia.*[75] The literal sense of Scripture conceals, in other words, a kind of iconic depth, a transparency to realities of faith, Christian conduct, and eternal destiny. Though framed as a historical exposition, De Lubac's study bore a normative message. No biblical sensibility as ancient and as pervasive as the doctrine of the "spiritual senses," it implied, could be jettisoned altogether.

In the course of things, de Lubac's work influenced the reception of *Dei Verbum* 12. Whereas theologians on the council floor still mooted the nature of Scripture's supra-literal meaning in terms of the *sensus plenior*,[76] postconciliar interpreters, such as the Belgian Jesuit Ignace de la Potterie, began to revive the language of "spiritual sense"—a language whose pedigree de Lubac had shown to be far more ancient.[77] This trend gained additional momentum when, in the early 1990s, the *Catechism of the Catholic Church* dedicated several paragraphs to the "senses of Scripture."[78] The *Catechism* not only

---

For a corroborating presentation of multivalence as a hallmark of this era, see David Steinmetz, "The Superiority of Pre-Critical Exegesis," *ThTo* 37, no. 1 (1980): 27–38.

73 John Cassian, *Coll.* XIV, viii, 4, p. 510.

74 "In all the sacred books, we should consider eternal truths that are taught, the facts that are narrated, the future events that are predicted, and the precepts or counsels that are given." Augustine, *Gn. litt.*, I, 1; p. 19.

75 "The letter teaches events; allegory what you should believe; morality teaches what you should do, anagogy what mark you should be aiming for." See de Lubac, *Medieval Exegesis*, 1:271n1.

76 For a good sense of both the ascendancy and ambiguity of the term *sensus plenior* at the time of the Council, see Raymond E. Brown, "The *Sensus Plenior* in the Last Ten Years," *CBQ* 25 (1963): 262–85. According to Rudolf Voderholzer, the Spanish Jesuit A. Fernández seems to have coined the term *sensus plenior*. *Die Einheit der Schrift und ihr geistiger Sinn: Der Beitrag Henri de Lubacs zur Erforschung von Geschichte und Systematik christlicher Bibelhermeneutik*, Sammlung Horizonte Neue Folge 31 (Einsiedeln: Johannes, 1998), 118.

77 Ignace de la Potterie, "La Lettura della Sacra Scrittura 'nello Spirito': Il metodo patristico di leggere la Bibbia è possibile oggi?" *Civiltà Cattolica* 137 (August 1986): 210–15.

78 *CCC* 115–19.

quotes Augustine of Dacia's couplet but connects it to the concluding directive of *Dei Verbum* 12—namely, that exegetes "work according to these rules toward a better understanding and explanation of the meaning of Sacred Scripture."[79] By this arrangement, the *Catechism* presents reading Scripture according to its fourfold sense as the functional equivalent of expounding Scripture according to the full complement of "rules" laid out by *Dei Verbum* 12, both those oriented toward the immediate historical context and those oriented toward the unfolding ecclesial context. Though it appeared too late to affect the language of the Council itself, de Lubac's retrieval of the fourfold sense became the retrospective key to *Dei Verbum's* reception.[80] Conciliar documents, it seems, take on a life of their own as well.[81]

Ratzinger's Updating of the Fourfold Sense

Given Ratzinger's frank admiration for de Lubac,[82] as well as his prominent role in redacting the *Catechism of the Catholic Church*, it will hardly be surprising to learn that his own thought reflects this postconciliar trajectory. Most of Ratzinger's references to the fourfold sense come later in his career, after the publication of the *Catechism*. Seeking to win a favorable hearing for the premodern hermeneutic, however, Ratzinger gives it a new theoretical underpinning, appealing to the principle that the full meaning of texts comes to light only through their *Wirkungsgeschichte*. Hence, though the language of spiritual senses comes late to Ratzinger, the basic intuition dates back to his discovery that Bonaventure understands Scripture as a garden of "seminal reasons" flowering over the course of history. This creative retrieval of the

---

79 *CCC* 118-19.

80 The reception of *Dei Verbum* in terms of the four senses may thus represent a sort of rough analogy to the reception of *Lumen gentium* in terms of *communio*. As Walter Kasper observes, other images predominate in the documents of the Council itself: body, sacrament, people. Only afterwards, at the extraordinary Synod of Bishops of 1985, did *communio*-ecclesiology emerge as the "central and basic idea of the Council documents." *That They May All Be One: The Call to Unity Today* (London: Burns & Oates & Continuum, 2004), 58. See also Benoît-Dominique de la Soujeole, *Introduction to the Mystery of the Church*, trans. Michael J. Miller, Thomistic Ressourcement Series 3 (Washington, DC: The Catholic University of America Press, 2014), 452. Analogously, though the biblical debate during the Council itself was framed as the opposition between literal sense and *sensus plenior*, one might argue that the doctrine of the four senses retrospectively captures its basic idea.

81 Söding, "Zeit für Gottes Wort," 448–49.

82 See Marie-Gabrielle Lemaire, "Joseph Ratzinger et Henri de Lubac," *Association Internationale de Cardinal de Lubac Bulletin* 15 (2013): 45–62.

patristic and medieval tradition arguably allows Ratzinger to construe the relation between literal and spiritual senses as one of homogeneous development rather than of extrinsic juxtaposition. To the extent that he succeeds in bringing literal and spiritual into a living relationship, I would argue that he offers a more relatively adequate account of the truth of Scripture.

Ratzinger's concern to portray the spiritual senses as the supernatural elevation of a natural process appears unmistakably in his address, *"Is the Catechism of the Catholic Church Up-to-Date?"* (2002). There Ratzinger, then prefect of the Congregation for the Doctrine of the Faith, responds to criticisms that the Catechism had marginalized historical-critical criteria and thereby "slept through a whole century of exegetical research."[83] Ratzinger responds by insisting that the idea of irreducible biblical multivalence corresponds to the latest exegetical findings, especially to source criticism. The very fact that biblical authors could freely reshape, reorder, and reread their source materials implies that these materials possessed a kind of semantic pluripotency from the start. Fifty years earlier Ratzinger's Habilitationsschrift had already pointed out that the evangelists sometimes repurposed "free-floating dominical logia," inserting them into new contexts that "caused a new meaning to become visible."[84] Insofar as the doctrine of the fourfold sense fully acknowledges that the relecture of source materials in a new context, whether canonical or historical, releases their potential meaning, it turns out to be not behind but ahead of its time: "The doctrine of the multiple senses of Scripture, which was developed by the Church Fathers and systematized in the Middle Ages, is recognized again today as being scientifically appropriate, given the nature of this unique structure of texts."[85] The four senses thus square with what critical exegesis has revealed about textual formation and what hermeneutical philosophy has revealed about textual signification.

Later statements will relate the four senses even more clearly to the idea of effective history, accentuating the way that texts accrue meaning even after they achieve a stable form. In his methodological introduction to the first volume of *Jesus of Nazareth*, for instance, Ratzinger returns to the

---

83 Joseph Ratzinger, "Is the *Catechism of the Catholic Church* Up-to-Date? Reflections Ten Years after Its Publication," in *On the Way to Jesus Christ*, trans. Michael J. Miller (San Francisco: Ignatius, 2005), 146–47.

84 JRGS 2:67.

85 Ratzinger, "Is the Catechism of the Catholic Church Up-to-Date?," 150.

Bonaventurian image of the biblical text as seed: "There is a process in which the word gradually unfolds its potentialities, already somehow present like seeds, but needing the challenge of new situations, new experiences and sufferings, in order to open up."[86] Here Ratzinger ascribes to later experiences and historical circumstances the manifestation of new dimensions of the germinal word. He then connects this flowering of signification with the doctrine of the four senses: "There are dimensions of the word that the old doctrine of the fourfold sense of Scripture pinpointed with remarkable accuracy. The four senses of Scripture are not individual meanings arrayed side by side, but dimensions of the one word that reaches beyond the moment."[87] In Ratzinger's mind, the literal and spiritual senses thus lie along a sort of continuum of earlier to later, atomistic to holistic, implicit to explicit. Consequently, the spiritual senses constitute more than a fanciful midrash on the "real" meaning of the text.[88] They represent legitimate meanings of the text revealed in the course of its forward movement.[89]

Indeed, the unfolding of the literal sense into spiritual senses through a Spirit-guided effective history implies a kind of organic permeation of literal and spiritual senses, such that each serves as a kind interpretive standard for the other. The presumption that spiritual senses somehow lie germinally in the literal sense prevents the exegete from forgetting that historical reconstructions can claim only a "relatively certainty," and that "any human utterance of a certain weight contains more than the author may have been aware of at the time."[90] In denying the possibility of neatly separating what the text means from what it meant, Ratzinger succinctly applies to the fourfold

---

86 JN 1:xix.

87 JN 1:xx.

88 What Rowan Williams says of the "apophatic practitioner" Ratzinger would say of the biblical author: "And it is as *participating* in the practices of speaking, imaging and material behaving that the apophatic practitioner works, as someone accepting that their perception is to be handed over into the common life of the worshipping Body, serving that life by underlining the grammar of worship itself." *Understanding and Misunderstanding "Negative Theology,"* The Père Marquette Lecture in Theology 2021 (Milwaukee: Marquette University Press, 2021), 40.

89 "The fundamental and all-important hermeneutical insight here is that subsequent history belongs intrinsically to the inner momentum of the text itself. That is, it does not simply provide retrospective commentary on the text. Rather, through the appearing of the reality which was still to come, the full dimensions of the word carried by the text come to light." Ratzinger, *Eschatology*, 42.

90 JN 1:xix.

sense his earlier-formulated "uncertainty principle." If the point of view of the observer affects experimental outcomes even in the physical sciences, as Heisenberg has shown, how much more will a scholar's sympathies and social location condition historical judgment?[91] "Nothing is 'manifest' to anyone save what he lives," observes Ratzinger in the early 1980s. "For that reason, interpretation is always a question of the whole complex of life."[92] And inasmuch as the post-Enlightenment academy too represents a historically circumscribed tradition of inquiry, its sensibility cannot be automatically presumed to enjoy a greater scientific objectivity, even in historical matters.[93] Ratzinger considers it methodologically naive, then, to construe the "spiritual" understanding as a kind of detachable second story, a pious afterthought whose exclusion in no way prejudices the historical work on the ground floor.

The coinherence of spiritual and literal senses also implies that the literal sense serves as a kind of hermeneutical control on the growth of the spiritual senses. The criteria for legitimate growth remain, of course, notoriously hard to fix.[94] But one minimal yardstick for Ratzinger seems to be the principle of noncontradiction between literal and spiritual senses. The right kind of holistic interpretation "does not contradict historical-critical interpretation, but carries it forward in an organic way toward becoming

---

91 For Ratzinger's invocation of the "uncertainty principle," see "Biblical Interpretation in Conflict," 100.

92 Joseph Ratzinger, "Anglican-Catholic Dialogue: Its Problems and Hopes," *Insight* 1, no. 3 (1983): 4. The accompanying footnote invokes Josef Pieper's observation that even philosophical interpretation, as exemplified by Plato's handling of the traditional judgment myths in the *Gorgias, Phaedo, and Republic*, requires "embedding oneself in a community, through which alone that affinity and *connaturalitas* is achieved, in virtue of which one can examine and interpret what the more-than-human author says and means through the humanly composed text." Pieper, *Buchstabier-Übungen: Aufsätze, Reden, Notizen* (Munich, Kösel, 1980), 30.

93 Ratzinger insists that, given the nature of the Bible, it is scientific to "recognize the faith of the Church as the kind of sympathy without which the text remains a closed book." "Biblical Interpretation in Conflict," 126. Scott Hahn and Benjamin Wiker make a similar point negatively by presenting historical criticism not as a view from nowhere but as the exegetical tradition of the liberal nation-state. *Politicizing the Bible: The Roots of Historical Criticism and the Secularization of Scripture, 1300–1700* (New York: Crossroad, 2013).

94 For a subtle argument in favor of the positive and enduring significance of historical moment with the "telic process" of inspiration, see James Prothro, "Theories of Inspiration and Catholic Exegesis: Scripture and Criticism in Dialogue with Denis Farkasfalvy," in *CBQ* 83, no. 2 (2021): 307–14.

theology in the proper sense."[95] In this respect, Ratzinger merely resumes what he conceded in "The Question of the Concept of Tradition"—namely, that the "literal meaning of Scripture as this can be ascertained historically" functions as a "relatively independent criterion in the dual counterpoint of faith and knowledge."[96] Citations could be multiplied.[97]

As retrieved by Ratzinger, the doctrine of the fourfold sense becomes not a rejection of historical-critical methodology so much as a capsule summary for a hermeneutic of reciprocal influence. The meaning indicated by historical-critical investigation would constitute one relatively independent pole, but the meaning disclosed through the Bible's "effective history" in the Church would constitute another. In his rather pugnacious essay "Biblical Interpretation in Conflict" (1988), Ratzinger already presents "'historical' explanation" and "'holistic' understanding" as the "two sides of interpretation" prescribed by *Dei Verbum* 12.[98] Either side practiced in strict isolation leads to "methodological arbitrariness."[99] By his career's end, however, he prefers to present this bipolar hermeneutic in terms of the fourfold sense. One sees this in his way of describing the proper Christian reception of the Old Testament in "Grace and Vocation without Remorse" (2018): "The original historical meaning of the texts is not to be repealed, but it must be exceeded. The first two lines of the famous *Distychon* on the four senses of Scripture characterize this movement. *Littera facta docet. Quid credas allegoria. Moralis quid agas. Quo tendas anagogia.*"[100] The fourfold sense, now reframed in terms of historical "movement," comes to represent for Ratzinger the ideal synthesis of historical and theological interpretation. "Only harmony in the two methods results in understanding the Bible."[101]

---

95 JN 1:xix. Again: "There is a reciprocal relationship: This society is the essential condition for the growth of the biblical Word; and, conversely, this Word gives the society its identity and its continuity." "What in Fact Is Theology?," *Pilgrim Fellowship of Faith*, 33.

96 Ratzinger, "Question of the Concept of Tradition," 66.

97 For further references on this theme, see my "Ricoeur and Ratzinger on Biblical Historicity and Hermeneutics," *Journal of Theological Interpretation* 8, no. 2 (2014): 203–5; Hansjürgen Verweyen, *Ein unbekannter Ratzinger: Die Habilitationschrift von 1955 als Schlüssel zu seiner Theologie* (Regensburg: Friedrich Pustet, 2010), 102–8.

98 Ratzinger, "Biblical Interpretation in Conflict," 96.

99 Ratzinger, "Biblical Interpretation in Conflict," 121–22.

100 Joseph Ratzinger, "Grace and Vocation without Remorse: Comments on the Treatise *De Iudeais*," *Communio* 45, no. 2 (2018): 167.

101 Ratzinger, "Biblical Interpretation in Conflict," 121.

The basic outlines of Ratzinger's refoundation of the spiritual senses are hopefully by now clear. Ratzinger sought an integration of the two criteriological canons prescribed by *Dei Verbum* 12. Though his language for describing the "two sides" of biblical interpretation has varied, it crystallized around the medieval doctrine of the four senses from the publication of the *Catechism* on. With no doubt self-conscious anachronism, Ratzinger gives the fourfold sense a new theoretical foundation, associating the "literal sense" closely with the Bible's historical-critically indicated meaning and the "spiritual sense" with the meaning opened by its ecclesial *Wirkungsgeschichte*. Recast in this way, the doctrine of the fourfold sense attempts to respond to the demands of both reason and doctrine. It takes seriously the plasticity of textual meaning retrieved by contemporary hermeneutics and implied by source criticism. It also answers well to the exegetical task as prescribed by *Dei Verbum* 12. The fourfold sense thus represents nothing other than the Church's perennial hermeneutic reformulated in light of the new exegetical situation.

The Fourfold Sense of Mary

Lest Ratzinger's theoretical refoundation of the fourfold sense remain too abstract, it will perhaps be helpful to illustrate it briefly through a concrete example. Happily, Ratzinger provides such an example in his treatment of the biblical foundation for the Catholic Marian doctrine and piety in *Daughter Zion*, a book originating from a series of lectures given in the mid-1970s. Though the slim volume tends to use the language of "typology" rather than the fourfold sense, it nevertheless explores literal, allegorical, moral, and anagogical dimensions of the biblical figure of Mary. It thus nicely illustrates how Ratzinger understands the coinherence of the four senses.

According to Ratzinger, the precondition for seeing how the Marian dogmas are truly "in" Scripture, despite being formulated much later, is a holistic and teleological method of interpretation.[102] The mystery of Mary does not yield itself to those who examine atomized texts, but becomes visible only "within a perspective which comprehends and makes its own the

---

102 Ratzinger further elaborates the "teleological principle" elsewhere: "When things have reached their goal, then we can discover the true meaning that lay hidden, so to speak, within them. This meaning, which comes to light at the end of the movement, transcends whatever meaning might be revealed in the individual sections of the course followed." "Biblical Interpretation in Conflict," 119.

'typological' interpretation, the corresponding echoes of God's single history in the diversity of various external histories."[103] Nor will the full significance of Mary appear to those who presume only Christianity's oldest forms to be normative: "The faith of the Church sees in these beginnings something living, that conforms to its own constitution only insofar as it *develops*."[104] If one grants these effective-historical points of departure, then Ratzinger thinks he can show how the contemporary Catholic understanding of Mary lies implicit "in" the Bible itself. I myself will restructure Ratzinger's own arguments so as to clarify how ecclesial reception of the literal sense naturally yields the allegorical, moral, and anagogical senses.

Touching on the allegorical sense, which perceives biblical history as a sign of spiritual realities, Ratzinger notes how the biblical portrait of Mary links her typologically to the doctrine of the spotless Church.[105] As Old Testament reflection progresses, he observes, it both increasingly characterizes Israel as the feminine bride-daughter of God, "daughter Zion,"[106] and increasingly associates the true Israel with a "holy remnant."[107] These twin Old Testament trajectories already find a convergent fulfilment in the Pauline ecclesiology of the Church as God's "holy remnant" (Rom 11:16)[108] and Christ's bride "without spot, wrinkle, or the like" (Eph 5:27).[109] There thus exists in the New Testament a relatively clear doctrine of the Church as the new and immaculate Israel. The Fathers of the Church, Ratzinger notes, develop this idea of the Church as *Ecclesia immaculata* with poetic abandon.[110]

---

103 Ratzinger, *Daughter Zion*, 32. For analogous thoughts on Israel's faith as "das semantische Universum" in which the Marian texts become intelligible, see Ratzinger, Geleitwort zu *Maria, die Mutter Jesu im Neuen Testament*, by Franz Mußner (St. Ottilien: EOS Verlag, 1993), 11. See also Ratzinger, "The Sign of the Woman," 38–41.

104 Ratzinger, *Daughter Zion*, 38.

105 For a fuller development of this point, see Frances McKenna, *Innovation within Tradition: Joseph Ratzinger and Reading the Women of Scripture* (Philadelphia: Fortress, 2015), 166–69.

106 Ratzinger, *Daughter Zion*, 21.

107 Ratzinger, *Daughter Zion*, 64.

108 Ratzinger, *Daughter Zion*, 64.

109 Ratzinger, *Daughter Zion*, 67.

110 For the patristic dialectic of the spotless and sinful Church, see Hans Urs von Balthasar's classic essay "Casta Meretrix," in *Spouse of the Word*, vol. 2 of *Explorations in Theology*, trans. John Saward (San Francisco: Ignatius, 1991), 193–288.

But what does the immaculate Church have to do with Mary? Ratzinger observes that Luke presents Mary as the fulfilment of the very same Old Testament tropes that Paul uses to characterize the Church. The annunciation to Mary (Luke 1:28–32), for instance, unmistakably echoes Zephaniah 3:14–17, the prophetic exhortation to Daughter Zion to rejoice in view of her coming Lord.[111] Through prayerful meditation on such portraits of Mary, the conviction grew that the aboriginal sinlessness belonging corporately to the Church also belonged personally to Mary. The dogma of the Immaculate Conception, therefore, "proclaims that this New Israel (which is simultaneously the true old Israel, the holy remnant preserved by the grace of God) is not an idea, but a person. God does not act with abstractions or concepts; the *type*, of which the ecclesiology of the New Testament and Fathers speak, exists as a *person*."[112] The Immaculate Conception thus turns out to be nothing other than an allegorical sense of Scripture. Faith and prayer slowly plumb the depth of the Marian passages, detect their harmonic resonances, and perceive the hidden yet constitutive role that Mary plays in salvation history.

With the allegorical sense admitted, the anagogical and moral senses lie close to hand. In this respect, Ratzinger appeals to yet another typological synergy between the Gospel of Luke and the Letter to the Ephesians. The Gospel of Luke already presupposes that Mary's faith makes her worthy of special veneration. Elizabeth praises her faith expressly, "Blessed are you who have believed" (Luke 1:45). Ephesians, taking up the theme of faith more generally, presents baptismal faith as a participation in Jesus' own ascension. "God . . . raised us up with him, and seated us with him in the heavens in Christ Jesus" (Eph 2:4–6). Contemplating such texts in conjunction, Ratzinger suggests, Christians began to intuit that Mary's faith already shares in some hidden way in Christ's future glory. And if one goes further, granting that Mary possesses not just any baptismal faith but the perfect faith of the *Ecclesia immaculata*, it follows that Mary will share in Christ's victory in a more definitive way. This provides a biblical foundation for the dogma of the Assumption:

> Thus it is said that, in her, . . . everything still resisting Baptism [faith] has been conquered without remainder through the death of the earthly life. On the basis of the New Testament, through the integration of Luke 1:45

111 Ratzinger, *Daughter Zion*, 42.
112 Ratzinger, *Daughter Zion*, 68.

and Ephesians 2:6, this affirmation refers transparently to Mary, and it forms a bond with the typological contexts which we have been investigating: she who is wholly baptized, as the personal reality of the true Church, is at the same time not merely the Church's *promised* certitude of salvation but its *bodily* certitude also. The Church is already saved in her.[113]

Here Ratzinger alludes to both the moral and anagogical senses. Morally, Mary appears as a model of the virtue of faith and fitting object of veneration for all believers: "From this day all generations will call me blessed" (Luke 1:48). Anagogically, Mary appears as the bodily anticipation of the Church's future destiny. Contemplated and preached throughout the patristic period, these Marian texts, so apparently marginal to the concerns of Scripture, slowly yielded their deeper "typological" or spiritual senses. The "literal" Mary of Nazareth personifies the immaculate aspect of the Church (allegorical), exemplifies baptismal faith (moral), and prefigures our future glory (anagogical).

Having schematically reviewed Ratzinger's understanding of the biblical foundation of the Marian doctrines, one can more readily see why he compares the emergence of the spiritual senses to the growth of meaning that any great text undergoes. As the insights of successive generations accumulate, the People of God—conscious of its mysterious reality, distinctive ethos, and eternal destiny—slowly unspools the literal sense into allegorical, moral, and anagogical threads. This unraveling can generate both pious, symbolic readings (e.g., Mary as the icon of the Christian *anima*) and binding, public interpretations (as in the dogmas of the Immaculate Conception or Assumption). One could almost say that for Ratzinger the spiritual senses are nothing other than the meanings that emerge when the pilgrim Church reads Scripture as an organic whole.

Ratzinger's effective-historical reappropriation of the fourfold sense obliges him to take a stance at once appreciative and critical toward Thomas Aquinas, the standard point of reference for the medieval version of this doctrine. On the one hand, Ratzinger praises Aquinas as a master of teleological hermeneutics, who rightly finds in Christ the culmination of salvation history.[114] What is more, by insisting that the deeper meanings cannot contradict the historically indicated meaning, Ratzinger maintains in his

---

113 Ratzinger, *Daughter Zion*, 80–81.
114 See Ratzinger, "Biblical Interpretation in Conflict," 119–20.

own way Aquinas's principle that the literal sense serves as the foundation for the spiritual senses.[115] The *Catechism*, in fact, cites this Thomistic axiom approvingly.[116] But unlike Aquinas, Ratzinger would hesitate to confine the premises of theological argumentation to the literal sense: "With Thomas Aquinas and his new view of theology, allegory is fundamentally devalued (only the literal sense can be used in arguments). . . . Here the danger of the loss of meaning for the whole Old Testament is obvious."[117] Ratzinger's disagreement owes partly to his anachronistic identification of Aquinas's literal sense with the historical-critically indicated sense.[118] Such an identification may—depending on the exegete—exclude not only the Marian but also the Christological dogmas from Scripture's literal domain.[119] But it also has partly to do with Ratzinger's effective-historical model of the fourfold sense, whereby the literal sense and spiritual senses interpenetrate too much to be isolated with clinical precision.

COMPARATIVE ASSESSMENT ON TRUTH

Ratzinger's explanation of how Scripture rates as preeminently "true," in both privative and positive senses, turns out to flow quite organically from his Bonaventurian-ecclesial model of inspiration. If the People of God is in fact a corporate author of the Bible, then its perduring intentions provide the key to identifying Scripture's *vere enuntiata* and, thereby, the domain of genuine inerrancy. This same people's deepening understanding of the Scripture will likewise advance it along a trajectory, releasing its virtualities

---

115 ST I, q. 1, a. 10, ad 1.

116 See *CCC* 116.

117 Ratzinger, "Grace and Vocation without Remorse," 167. For the implicit Thomistic citation, see ST I, q. 1, a. 10, ad 1. Ratzinger's criticisms of Aquinas's devaluation of the spiritual senses go back to at least 1964. See Santiago Sanz Sánchez, "Joseph Ratzinger y la doctrina de la creación: los apuntes de Münster de 1964 (y III). Algunos temas debatídos," *RET* 74 (2014): 458n10.

118 Stephen Fowl notes the multivalence of Aquinas's literal sense: "Importance of a Multivoiced Literal Sense of Scripture," 40–41. Franklin Harkins notes that Aquinas considers Christ to belong to the literal sense even of Old Testament books, such as Job. "Christ and the Eternal Extent of Divine Providence in the *Expositio super Iob ad Litteram* of Thomas Aquinas," *Viator* 47, no. 1 (2015): 128–51.

119 On this point, see Joseph Ratzinger, "Die Christologie im Spannungsfeld von altchristlicher Exegese und moderner Bibelauslegung," in *Urbild und Abglanz: Festgabe für Herbert Doms zum 80. Geburtstag*, ed. Johannes Tenzler (Regensburg: Josef Habbel, 1972), 359–67.

of meaning. In virtue of its communal subject, then, Scripture will sometimes claim less than (as in the case of cosmology) and sometimes more than (as in the case of Mariology) and sometimes as much as (as in the case of demonology) a surface reading would indicate.

Besides attempting to reconcile the data of the Christian tradition with the demands of reason, Ratzinger's Bonaventurian-ecclesial model also attempts to address the unresolved tensions of *Dei Verbum*. On the one hand, *Dei Verbum* 11 affirms that the Holy Spirit asserts all (irrespective of discipline) that the human authors intended. On the other, it insists that the books of the Bible have as their primary goal to convey that "truth which God wanted put into sacred writings for the sake of salvation." *Dei Verbum* 12, for its part, enjoins upon exegetes two canons of interpretive criteria, one for determining meaning in immediate historical context and one for determining meaning in wider ecclesial context. Here again, the Dogmatic Constitution on Divine Revelation appears to entrust the theoretical integration of these hermeneutical poles to future generations of theologians. A brief comparison of Ratzinger's proposed resolution with Benoit's, Rahner's, and Tracy's will, I think, indicate the greater relative adequacy of Ratzinger's attempted integration.

Review of Ratzinger on Biblical Truth

Ratzinger's chief contribution to resolving the internal tensions of *Dei Verbum* 11 lies in his integration of neo-scholastic and salvation-historical models of authorial intention. By presenting the People of God as the constitutive, intending subject of Scripture, Ratzinger can affirm that the Holy Spirit asserts whatever the "inspired authors" assert, provided, of course, these inspired authors are considered under a certain formality. Ratzinger considers these authors not so much as an aggregate of individuals, whose propositional judgments would be independently inerrant, but as organs of a collective personality, which expresses its mind through the whole ensemble of texts. As mentioned in the previous chapter, *Dei Verbum* took pains to avoid excluding such a collective gloss on the "inspired authors." By taking advantage of this opening, Ratzinger can explain how the "books of Scripture" appear in *Dei Verbum* as the grammatical subject of the activity of teaching "without error." If the People of God has a kind of personality, and if this personality elevates the otherwise inert text into "Holy Scripture," then saying that "Scripture" teaches becomes more than a *façon de parler*.

Ratzinger can also do a fair job of synthesizing the ostensibly variant voices of *Dei Verbum* 11 on the scope of inerrancy. His 2003 essay "Exegesis and the Magisterium of the Church" shows that he, like the neo-scholastics, refuses to exclude profane disciplines a priori from the scope of biblical inerrancy. The relationship between scientific reason and Scripture, he observes, "can never be settled once and for all, because the faith attested to by the Bible also involves the material world; the Bible still makes claims about this world—concerning its origin as a whole and man's origin in particular."[120] Echoing the judgment of *Providentissimus Deus*, he adds that "something analogous can be said with respect to history."[121] When adjudicating the normativity of such historical and scientific ideas, however, Ratzinger also considers the extent that they bear upon faith in Christ, the *telos* of salvation history. This *tantum-quantum* approach requires neither that profane matters be automatically excluded nor that ethical and religious matters be automatically included: "Not only are [Scripture's] literary forms those of the world that produced it, but its manner of thought, even in respect to religious topics, has been determined by the world in which it arose."[122] In short, Scripture intends to affirm all its ideas—historical, scientific, religious—to the extent that they illuminate the face of Christ.

Ratzinger's *tantum-quantum* reading of *Dei Verbum* 11 does not place him so far outside the exegetical mainstream. Raymond Brown comes to a similar conclusion: "It is not as if some parts of Scripture teach without error 'truth for the sake of salvation,' and other parts do not. Everything in Scripture is inerrant to the extent to which it conforms to the salvific purpose of God."[123] But Ratzinger goes beyond Brown in a couple of ways. He gives the "salvific purpose" a Christological complexion. And perhaps even more importantly, he takes care to show how his reading squares with the full gamut of affirmations contained in *Dei Verbum* 11. He does not excise the perspectives of the "losers."

---

120 Joseph Ratzinger, "Exegesis and the Magisterium of the Church," in *Opening Up the Scriptures: Joseph Ratzinger and the Foundations of Biblical Interpretation*, ed. J. Granados, C. Granados, and Luis Sánchez Navarro (Grand Rapids, MI: Eerdmans, 2008), 134.

121 Ratzinger, "Exegesis and the Magisterium of the Church," 134. See *PD*, no. 20.

122 Joseph Ratzinger, *Faith and the Future* (Chicago: Franciscan Herald, 1971), 9.

123 Brown, *Critical Meaning of the Bible*, 19.

Due to the extensive discussion *Dei Verbum* 12 in this chapter, it suffices to recall even more briefly that the Dogmatic Constitution prescribes two canons of interpretive criteria, one justified by Scripture's composition "in human fashion," the other by the "sacred Spirit in which it was written." It does not seem to envision, moreover, the application of one pole to the strict exclusion of the other. Ratzinger's retooled fourfold sense, by aligning the literal sense with the historical-critical meaning and the spiritual senses with their effective-historical meaning, sets the two approaches in a mutually conditioning relationship.

Comparison with Benoit

Though Benoit's Thomist-instrumental model has much to commend it, Ratzinger's model of biblical truth enjoys certain advantages in both its negative and positive aspects. As regards negative immunity from error, Benoit, as was shown in the first chapter, would have the exegete consider not whether an idea has saving import but whether the sacred writer affirms it with a solemn act of judgment. On the one hand, because nothing in the adverbial clause "for the sake of salvation" absolutely requires one to take it as a limiting criterion for inerrancy, Benoit cannot be said to contradict *Dei Verbum* 11. Moreover, since no one can know just how far the biblical author's affirmation extends in any given passage, Benoit's model remains empirically unfalsifiable. As regards positive depth of signification, Benoit can argue that God's principal causality authorizes the exegete to look for a "fuller sense" exceeding the literal sense consciously intended by the human instruments. This comports nicely with the way *Dei Verbum* 12 encourages exegetes simultaneously to investigate what the sacred writers really intended and "what God wanted to manifest by means of their words." Unsurprisingly, given the ascendancy of Benoit's Thomist-instrumental inspiration before the Council, *Dei Verbum* in no way excludes this model of biblical truth.

The chief weakness of Benoit's approach lies not in its incompatibility with *Dei Verbum* 11–12 but in its strained authorial psychology. As regards the *sensus plenior*, one should recall that, for Benoit, only one intrahistorical intention regulates the meaning of the text—namely, the mind of individual authors. But Benoit also defines the *sensus plenior* as a divine meaning hidden from these same minds. With the fuller sense hidden from the mind regulating the meaning of the text, it becomes difficult to see how this more-than-literal meaning really inheres "in" the text from the start. By positing the People of God as another "understanding subject," Ratzinger can supply a historical carrier of these divine intentions, more easily explaining thereby how a more-than-literal sense unfolds continuously "out of" the *sensus literalis*.[124]

Psychological implausibility also dogs Benoit's account of inerrancy. Those who work within Benoit's framework, in order to present a Bible "without error," must suppose that the biblical authors go to great lengths to chronicle historical events tangential to their true concerns, or that they confine themselves exclusively to literary genres unconcerned with historical and scientific exactitude.[125] What is more, they must at least sometimes admit that the biblical authors did not really intend to affirm even central religious ideas, such as the obligation to observe Passover and Sabbath into perpetuity. Can one really say that the authors of Exodus, considered from the perspective of their individual psychologies, did not intend for the day of rest to remain Saturday (Exod 20:8–11), or for Israel to observe the original prescriptions of Passover "as a statute forever" (Exod 12:14, 17, 24)? Christians can naturally point to the Sunday Eucharist as their way of meeting the obligations laid perpetually upon Israel, but can they plausibly claim that the authors of Exodus made private allowances for this alternative mode of fulfillment? Even in the New Testament, Ratzinger would point out, one finds solemn prescriptions that the Church's subsequent experience has been revealed to be "purely of human right."[126] But if the provisional nature of such biblical commands often appears only in light of subsequent events, is it not the transhistorical intention of "Holy Scripture" itself, rather than the private mental reservations of its individual literary agents, that qualifies their

---

124 Lewis Ayres, acknowledging the influence of Ratzinger, proposes the Church as the "bridge" between New Testament and Nicene Christology, in virtue of which one can say that the Nicene belief lies implicitly "in" Scripture. Lewis Ayres, "Is Nicene Trinitarianism 'in' the Scriptures?," *Nova et Vetera* 18, no. 4 (Fall 2020): 1293–97.

125 Sebastian Tromp, SJ, for instance, opts for the carte-blanche solution of supposing that the biblical authors typically wrote in the "genus antiquum vulgare"—where sayings are often compressed and combined, chronology is altered for psychological or logical coherence, and "minor est diligentia et cura in accidentalibus." *De Sacrae Scripturae inspiratione*, 136–37.

126 Joseph Ratzinger, *Church, Ecumenism, Politics: New Essays in Ecclesiology*, trans. Robert Nowell (New York: Crossroad, 1988), 97. Ratzinger elsewhere notes that fathers at Trent, when arguing for the interpretive role of unwritten traditions, had listed several such obsolete commands from the New Testament: "the stipulations of James, the veiling of women, marriage legislation of 1 Corinthians 7." "Question of the Concept of Tradition," 78.

force?[127] By tethering neither inerrancy nor the *sensus plenior* completely to authorial psychology, Ratzinger's view achieves a greater relative adequacy.

Comparison with Rahner

Because Rahner's Molinist-predefinitive model of inerrancy envisions a role not only for individual authors but for the faith consciousness of the Apostolic Church, it differs more subtly from Ratzinger's. Ratzinger's Bonaventurian-ecclesial model nevertheless has the relative advantage of giving greater attention to the variable texture of salvation history itself. This allows it to avoid overburdening authorial psychology and to develop a more differentiated set of criteria for determining what Scripture intends.

The explanatory strengths of Rahner's position are not negligible. By construing inspiration as an act of formal predefinition by which God imbues individual authors with the content of the Apostolic Church's faith, Rahner opens the door to ascribing to these individual authors a range of implicit intentions. His theory assumes, in other words, that every author embraces the universal theology of the whole Church, "even where he himself could not have surveyed it explicitly." [128] It thus becomes hermeneutically sound to read Luke's theology of Mary as the new "immaculate" Israel alongside Paul's theology of the Church as the new "immaculate" Israel, since one can assume that each accepted the other's insights, even if only implicitly. Rahner would thus have little difficulty explaining how the "fuller" or spiritual" senses already inhere "in" the literal sense, since the universal theology of the Church implicitly informs the intention of each individual author.[129] Similar considerations could be brought to bear on problems of

---

127 In this spirit, Norbert Lohfink observes that most interpreters acquit the Old Testament from historical error or moral blindness not by disinterested genre analysis but by critically correlating the historical authors' and the Church's intentions. For instance, it is only from the perspective of the New Testament Church (according to which salvation is no longer envisioned as a promised land) that exegetes can consider the faulty geographical details of Josh 6–8 "so marginal that they can be neglected." "The Inerrancy of Scripture," *The Christian Meaning of the Old Testament* (Milwaukee: Bruce, 1968), 46–48.

128 Karl Rahner, *Inspiration in the Bible*, trans. Charles Henkey, QD 1 (New York: Herder & Herder, 1961), 79–80.

129 Indeed, Rahner's writings on development of doctrine elaborate a certain aspect of Scripture's "effective history," such as the development of Marian dogmas, with great care. See, for example, his "*Virginitas in partu*: A Contribution to the Problem of the Development of Dogma and Tradition," in *More Recent Writings*, trans. Kevin Smith, vol. 4 of *Theological Investigations* (London: Darton, Longman & Todd, 1966), 134–62.

inerrancy. Confronted with the problem of the Passover as perpetual institution, for instance, Rahner could say that the authors of Exodus, writing
within the horizon of universal faith consciousness, implicitly intended to
enjoin Passover observance "only until God should reveal something better."
By inscribing a layer of corporate intentionality into individual authorship,
Rahner goes some distance toward explaining why Scripture means sometimes more, sometimes less, than meets the eye.

In its ability to account for the inerrancy of Scripture, Rahner's account
is roughly comparable to Ratzinger's. One's preference will depend on what
one prefers to leave obscure. In explaining the truth of Exodus's command
to rest on Saturday, for instance, Ratzinger would probably lean heavily on
the idea that Scripture, as the literary sedimentation of the People of God's
historical pilgrimage, intends its contents with different qualifications at
different moments. Since Israel—and, indeed, history itself—was still on the
way to Christ, all Old Testament directives remain subject to Christological
transposition. Though this variable and somewhat hypostasized model of
history remains somewhat obscure, it at least keeps Ratzinger from having
to appeal to implicit ideas somehow latent in historical authors of Exodus.
Rahner naturally has the opposite problem. He need not justify how history itself changes complexion, but he must suppose that the Christological
proviso attached to the Sabbath command inheres in the consciousness of
the authors of Exodus themselves, however implicitly. This is bound to come
across as special pleading.

Ratzinger's salvation-historical sensibility perhaps gives him a more
decided advantage when it comes to developing criteria for discerning what
Scripture intends to affirm. Rahner, as we have seen, presents normative
biblical interpretation largely as a matter of synchronic coordination, as a
dialectic between the partial, explicit, and individual on the one hand, and
the universal, implicit, and ecclesial on the other. His theory of inspiration
thus quite sensibly implies that we should appraise a biblical passage's inerrant content only after critically relating it to the whole.[130] But Rahner never
provides a set of aids-to-judgment for performing this critical correlation.
Nor does he explain why an Old Testament part might relate to the whole

---

130 Robert Gnuse, for instance, sees German Jesuit Norbert Lohfink's model of inerrancy as
a "variation of [Rahner's] position." Gnuse, *Authority of the Bible* (New York: Paulist 1985),
56. Lohfink himself considers inerrant only that meaning of Scripture which emerges after
the meaning intended by individual authors has been "critically related to the whole." *Christian Meaning of the Old Testament*, 46.

differently than a New Testament part. Ratzinger, by contrast, does both. He renders the unwieldy task of critical correlation more manageably by developing four "tests" for normativity. And he adds a diachronic dimension by indexing these tests to the diverse relationships that the People of God has enjoyed with Christ at different historical stages. In this way, Ratzinger renders exegetically practicable Rahner's intuition that Scripture canonizes the mind of the Church. He perhaps thereby keeps his own theology from becoming as "independent of exegesis" as he felt Rahner's became.[131]

Comparison to Tracy

Whereas Benoit and Rahner easily fall within the doctrinal parameters set by *Dei Verbum*, struggling instead to give a plausible authorial psychology, the difficulties of Tracy's hermeneutical-disclosive model run in the opposite direction. Tracy fully embraces the idea that the meaning of Bible, by virtue of its ongoing readership, grows beyond the intentions of its authors: "the Scriptures themselves are the church's book."[132] In treating the Bible as a "Christian classic," however, he marginalizes certain interpretive controls stipulated by *Dei Verbum* 11–12 and retained more robustly by Ratzinger.

As was already noted in the first chapter, Tracy's effective-historical approach to biblical meaning legitimates the positive inexhaustibility of truth so celebrated by premodern exegesis. But it also raises the question of whether any controls exist on arbitrary readings. Tracy himself offers a few: the internal corrective of historical-critical and literary study; the external corrective of ideology critique; the reciprocal corrective of the many voices in canon itself. But it is doubtful that Tracy, by means of these criteria, can uphold the Bible's preeminent veracity in the way that *Dei Verbum* requires. Mostly obviously, *Dei Verbum* 11 teaches that the Holy Spirit vouches for whatever the sacred writers, whether considered severally or corporately, genuinely "assert." The Dogmatic Constitution thus implies that Scripture sometimes makes propositional affirmations. Tracy, by contrast, relocates biblical truth to an existential plane beyond the realm of verification of

---

131 Ratzinger, "Biblical Interpretation in Conflict," 93n2. This characterization of Rahner's theology has been challenged recently in Albert Raffelt, "Karl Rahner und die Bibel," in *Anstöße der Theologie Karl Rahners für gegenwärtige Theologie und Kirche*, ed. Karsten Kreutzer and Albert Raffelt (Freiburg: Katholische Akademie der Erzdiözese, 2019), 187–98.

132 David Tracy, *The Analogical Imagination: Christian Theology in a Culture of Pluralism* (New York: Crossroad, 1981), 249.

falsification. He thus redefines biblical inerrancy as an enduring poetic power, a kind of "indefectibility . . . in spite of errors."[133] By maintaining that Scripture teaches at least some propositions as true "without error," Ratzinger better honors the givens of *Dei Verbum* 11.

Tracy's wholesale abandonment of propositional truth renders his other correctives on arbitrary growth of biblical meaning a bit toothless. If Scripture is "true" primarily because it discloses the primordial dimension of existence, then it matters little whether readers appropriate the text as historically indicated. On this theory, interpretation qualifies as authentic to the extent that it enlarges the reader's existential horizon. Hence, despite tipping his hat to the historical-critical correctives, Tracy cannot really accord normative weight to the canon of historical criteria stipulated by *Dei Verbum* 12 and incorporated into Ratzinger's reprised version of the fourfold sense. Ratzinger would no doubt find in Tracy's hermeneutics the same independence from history he found in medieval allegory, along with the same dangers of "arbitrariness." When one adds Tracy's loose definition of church and his silence on magisterial authority, it becomes clear that Ratzinger offers more resources for clarifying both how Scripture teaches truth "without error" and how its meaning evolves in continuity with its original sense.

In the final analysis, then, Ratzinger's Bonaventurian-ecclesial model of biblical truth lays a strong claim to greater relative adequacy. This should not be taken to mean, of course, that there is no room left for improvement. In the same way that Ratzinger appeals to the People of God as understanding subject without ever carefully delineating the nature of the Church's personality, he also appeals constantly to the growth of Scripture's meaning without himself carefully distinguishing between organic and inorganic developments. To my knowledge, Ratzinger does not really take up the problem of doctrinal development in its own right after 1966.[134] And even there, his description of what it means for a teaching to be virtually precontained in the revealed deposit nowhere reaches the level of sophistication achieved

---

133 Hans Küng, *Infallible? An Inquiry* [I, no. 96], 81–124. Cited approvingly in Tracy, *Analogical Imagination*, 236n15.

134 Joseph Ratzinger, *Das Problem der Dogmengeschichte in der Sicht der katholischen Theologie*, Arbeitsgemeinschaft für Forschung des Landes Nordrhein–Westfalen 139 (Köln: Westdeutscher Verlag, 1966). For references to this theme in Ratzinger's subsequent writings, see my "*Christi Opera Proficiunt*: Ratzinger's Neo-Bonaventurian Model of Social Inspiration," *Nova et Vetera* 13, no. 3 (2015): 703–5.

by either the Thomist school[135] or by Rahner.[136] Ratzinger's thought would especially benefit here from scholastic supplements.

That being said, Ratzinger's thought structure, despite being deeply stamped by the salvation-historical point of departure in theology, remains uniquely open to scholastic annexes. This doubtlessly has much to do with Ratzinger's Bonaventurian point of departure. Whereas other critics of neo-scholastic biblical hermeneutics typically opposed them to a golden age of patristic exegesis, Ratzinger opted instead for an "internal" critique, pitting Bonaventure the scholastic against later neo-scholastic developments.[137] It is arguably for this reason that Ratzinger found himself better able to integrate the neo-Thomist analysis of intentionality and inerrancy with the salvation-historical sensibility emerging in the preconciliar era.

The picture of Ratzinger that emerges from a study of his Bonaventurian-ecclesial model of biblical truth may surprise some. Catholic theology has typically regarded with suspicion Bultmann's project of "demythologization," as well as the postmodern conceit of the autonomous text. But Ratzinger integrates substantial insights from both. The People of God lives by "demythologizing" Scripture—that is, by transposing one set of images and categories into another, by separating essential and inessential elements. This same People of God also lives by appropriating the Bible in altered circumstances, thereby advancing the Word of God along a trajectory of meaning until Christ becomes all in all.

135 In this respect, one does well to consult the still unsurpassed meditations of F. Marín Sola, OP, on "lo virtual revelado." He holds that same deposit of faith can be expressed in new words and even new concepts, but not in such a way as to refer to new realities. *La evolución homogénea del dogma católico*, intro. Emilio Sauras, 2nd ed. (Madrid: Bibliotéca de Autores Cristianos, 1963), 161–66.

136 See especially Karl Rahner, "The Development of Dogma," in *God, Christ, Mary, Grace*, vol. 1 of *Theological Investigations*, trans. Cornelius Ernst (Baltimore: Helicon, 1961), 39–77. The Dominican theologian Aidan Nichols once identified this essay as the high point of Catholic thinking on doctrinal development. See *From Newman to Congar: The Idea of Doctrinal Development from the Victorians to the Second Vatican Council* (Edinburgh: T&T Clark, 1990), 234.

137 See the remarks under "'Der Scholastiker Bonaventure' als Überwinder 'der Scholastik'" in Verweyen, *Ein Unbekannter Ratzinger*, 24–25.

CHAPTER FOUR

The Ethically Normative Interpretation of Scripture: Jesus' Teaching on Divorce

The preceding three chapters surveyed the landscape of Catholic understandings of biblical inspiration and veracity, profiling Ratzinger against that backdrop. They concluded that Ratzinger holds a Bonaventurian-ecclesial model of biblical inspiration that identifies the People of God as the principal (but not exclusive) subject of the charism of inspiration, and thus as the principal (but not exclusive) bearer of Scripture's revelatory intentions. As the People of God, one with itself despite all its historical transformations, reshapes, rereads, and receives the sacred texts, it discloses what "Holy Scripture" intended to affirm all along. So understood, Scripture may mean less than meets the eye, as when it assumes rather than proposes geocentrism. But Scripture may also mean more than meets the eye, as when it presents, through a polyphony of Old and New Testament voices, Mary as the personal face of the *Ecclesia immaculata*.

The previous chapter highlighted Ratzinger's construction of a flexible series of "tests," designed to help the reader discern the intentions of Holy Scripture. These tests boil down to a series of relationships: between the Old and New Testaments, between Scripture and tradition, between Scripture and reason. Applying these yardsticks to the biblical theme of the demonic, Ratzinger rather easily shows that the Devil serves as a load-bearing pillar in the architecture of Scripture whereas geocentrism represents a mere spandrel. But one might still wonder how consistently Ratzinger follows his own method, as well as how serviceable it proves when applied to subtler problems than geocentrism or hexameral creationism. Can it also serve to determine the contemporary relevance of biblical commands? Or the historical value of the Gospels? It is one thing, in short, to sharpen the methodological "knives," but another thing to carve the roast.

Deferring the question of historicity to the fifth and final chapter, this fourth chapter will address Ratzinger's concrete practice of discerning Scripture's normative ethical teaching. Even more specifically, it will focus on Ratzinger's evolving position on the so-called Matthean exception clause— that is, the passages where Jesus seemingly forbids husbands to divorce their wives "except for πορνεία" (Matt 5:32; 19:9).[1] Studying how Ratzinger handles Jesus' divorce *logia* repays the investment for several reasons. For here Ratzinger descends from his habitual concern with the "meta-questions" of moral theology—relativism, conscience and its rights, the distinctive nature of Christian ethics—to determining the normative content of a concrete biblical passage. Here we also find Ratzinger reaching different conclusions in response to the developing ecclesial situation, modeling his conviction that questions of worldview are decided by faith of the whole Church. Finally, the passage's complexity and ambiguity require Ratzinger to reach deep into his criteriological bag of tricks to arrive at his summary judgment. For several reasons, then, the Matthean "exception clause" proves a good testing ground for Ratzinger as a holistic interpreter.

Given the nature of the question and the shifts in Ratzinger's interpretive judgment, it seems best to organize the argument along the following lines. The chapter will begin by rehearsing the difficulties the exception clauses raise for the interpreter applying the narrower canon of historical criteria. The fact that Ratzinger does not deeply engage the exegetical literature makes this preamble necessary. It will then consider how Ratzinger attempts to resolve these difficulties by applying the considerably broader canon of criteria enumerated in "Farewell to the Devil?" Having retraced Ratzinger's thought process, it will go on to consider Ratzinger's evolving conclusions, attempting to reconstruct the development of his thought on the significance of the Matthean exception clause for the question of marital indissolubility.

BIBLICAL BASIS FOR THE INDISSOLUBILITY
OF CHRISTIAN MARRIAGE

Jesus' sayings on divorce have naturally attracted an immense number of learned studies. Because a chapter-length study of Ratzinger's approach

---

1 I leave πορνεία untranslated because to translate it—whether by "fornication," "unchastity," "incest," or "adultery"—is already to take a position on the import of the exception clause.

cannot hope to survey even a fraction of the relevant literature, it will aim instead to lay the necessary foundation for appreciating the distinctiveness of Ratzinger's approach to biblical ethics.[2] This entails identifying the key passages, introducing the interpretive questions raised, as well as taking stock of the intractability of these disputes. The discussion will introduce Synoptic and Pauline parallels, but mostly as a backdrop to the Matthean exception clauses. For it is there in particular that the difference between a narrower and broader historical criteriology makes itself felt.

The Markan, Lukan, and Pauline divorce *logia* differ from their Matthean counterpart in that none includes a disclaimer softening Jesus' well-known prohibition of divorce and remarriage. Asked by the Pharisees what grounds justify divorce, Jesus responds by equating any remarriage after divorce to adultery: "Whoever divorces his wife and marries another commits adultery against her; and if she divorces her husband and marries another, she commits adultery" (Mark 10:12). The parallel passage in Luke bears the same message: "Everyone who divorces his wife and marries another commits adultery, and the one who marries a woman divorced from her husband commits adultery" (Luke 16:18). Paul reinforces the categorical nature of Jesus' prohibition of remarriage after divorce when he relays a dominical word to the church in Corinth: "To the married, however, I give this instruction (not I, but the Lord): A wife should not separate from her husband—and if she does separate, she must either remain single or become reconciled to her husband—and a husband should not divorce his wife" (1 Cor 7:10–11). The narrow field of maneuver that Paul envisions for a separated wife in Christian marriage[3]—remaining single or reconciling—again suggests that he took Jesus to be teaching the indissolubility of the marriage bond.

It is only against this background of unqualified prohibition that the interest in the Matthean exception makes sense. The clause actually appears in two slightly differing wordings in Matthew. First, in the antitheses of the Sermon on the Mount, Jesus declares, "It was also said, 'Whoever divorces his wife must give her a bill of divorce.' But I say to you, whoever divorces

---

2 For a relatively recent survey of this literature, see John Meier, *Law and Love*, vol. 4 of *A Marginal Jew: Rethinking the Historical Jesus* (New Haven: Yale University Press, 2009), 136–38.

3 In 1 Cor 7:15 Paul allows separation, presumably with right to remarriage, for a Christian abandoned by a non-Christian spouse. But it is worth noting that the so-called Pauline privilege does not claim Christ's authority, nor does it apply outside the case of interreligious marriages.

his wife (unless the marriage is unlawful) [παρεκτὸς λόγου πορνείας] causes her to commit adultery, and whoever marries a divorced woman commits adultery" (Matt 5:31–32).[4] A subsequent attempt by the Pharisees to draw Jesus into an intramural debate on the lawfulness of divorce gives Jesus an occasion to expand on this theme:

> Some Pharisees approached him, and tested him, saying, "Is it lawful for a man to divorce his wife for any cause whatever?" He said in reply, "Have you not read that from the beginning the Creator 'made them male and female' and said, 'For this reason a man shall leave his father and mother and be joined to his wife, and the two shall become one flesh'? So they are no longer two, but one flesh. Therefore, what God has joined together, no human being must separate." They said to him, "Then why did Moses command that the man give the woman a bill of divorce and dismiss [her]?" He said to them, "Because of the hardness of your hearts Moses allowed you to divorce your wives, but from the beginning it was not so. I say to you, whoever divorces his wife (unless the marriage is unlawful) [μὴ ἐπὶ πορνείᾳ] and marries another commits adultery." [His] disciples said to him, "If that is the case of a man with his wife, it is better not to marry." He answered, "Not all can accept [this] word, but only those to whom that is granted." (Matt 19:3–11)

Matthew, unlike the other strands of New Testament tradition, seems to present πορνεία as a case apart.

But aside from this rather meager point of consensus, as Ben Witherington has observed, nearly every other aspect of Matthew 5:32 and 19:9 remains disputed.[5] This includes even the characterization of the πορνεία clauses as true "exceptions," since some have proposed translating the prepositional phrases governing πορνεία as something like "irrespective of" rather than "except for." The resulting translation would thus run, "Whoever divorces his wife—the Mosaic permission for cases of πορνεία notwithstanding—causes her to commit adultery."[6] And even among the vast majority who identify the

---

4 The NAB opts to translate πορνεία as "unlawful marriage" rather than "unchastity" or "sexual immorality," thereby indicating that they take Matthew to be affirming the solubility of incestuous marriages—a position to be explored below.

5 Benjamin Witherington, "Matthew 5.32 and 19.9—Exception or Exceptional Situation?," *NTS* 31 (1985): 571.

6 W. D. Davies and Dale C. Allison, *A Critical and Exegetical Commentary on the Gospel according to Saint Matthew*, 3 vols., ICC (Edinburgh: T&T Clark, 1988–97), 1:531.

distinctively Matthean phrases as true exceptions, no clear consensus exists as to the meaning of πορνεία. Some take it to designate an act of "adultery" within marriage, whereas others take it to mean a kind of "incest" rendering the marriage unlawful from the start. Each line of interpretation obviously leads to rather different visions of the indissolubility of Christian marriage.

As a rather representative example of both the possibilities and limitations of sober, historical-critical analysis, one can take the monumental commentary on the Gospel of Matthew by the Protestant scholars W. D. Davies and Dale Allison. Davies and Allison find it "nearly impossible" to choose between incest and adultery. The "incest" interpretation has several considerations in its favor. It is clearly attested in 1 Corinthians 5:1. Matthew consistently designates "adultery" by μοιχεύω and μοιχάομαι elsewhere, including in the very same passages (Matt 5:32; 19:9), suggesting that πορνεία represents a different sin. In Acts 15:20, 15:29, and 21:25, moreover, the Council of Jerusalem requires gentiles to shun blood, what has been sacrificed to idols, and πορνεία. This constellation of stipulations recalls Leviticus 17–18, the part of the Holiness code governing the conduct of both Israelites and those "strangers that sojourn among them." The sexual regulation of the Holiness code that would have most likely conflicted with Gentile customs was the prohibition of intercourse with near kin (Lev 18:6–18). On this reading, the Matthean exception clause finds a plausible *Sitz im Leben*. The Matthean community probably included gentiles who converted to Christianity having already contracted unions contrary to Levitical incest laws. The exception clause would thus clarify that gentiles must still dissolve any bonds declared null by the Council of Jerusalem, Jesus' prohibition of divorce notwithstanding.[7]

Despite the weight of these arguments, Davies and Allison list grounds for favoring the translation of "adultery" that they reckon weightier still. "Adultery," for example, is a well-attested meaning of πορνεία. No patristic sources attest the equation of πορνεία with incest. The decree of the Council of Jerusalem may not be evoking the Levitical Holiness code but instead Deuteronomy 24:1. There Moses permits a husband to divorce his wife when he finds in her "something indecent"—a phrase to which the παρεκτὸς λόγου πορνείας of Matthew 5:32 bears some resemblance. In the first century, Jewish followers of Rabbi Shammai took this "something indecent" to mean her unchastity within marriage. One can also find an alternative communal setting for the exception clause: since Matthew's Gospel alone

---

7 Davies and Allison, *Matthew*, 1:529–30.

relates Joseph's plan to divorce Mary quietly, the exception clause may serve to explain why the righteous Joseph does not violate his foster son's teaching, even proleptically. Finally, two options remain open for squaring an exception for "adultery" with the absolute prohibitions on divorce and marriages found in Mark, Luke, and Paul. One can assume that the other sources took the Matthean exception for granted. Or one can assume that the exception clause qualifies only the prohibition on separation, but not the prohibition on remarriage. The latter would comport well with the policy stated in 1 Corinthians 7:10–11—that is, to stay single or reconcile with one's spouse.[8]

The historian's toolkit alone seems inadequate to resolve the normative questions raised by these passages for the indissolubility of marriage. One can translate πορνεία as "incest" or "adultery" with nearly equal justification. Even when granting the equivalence of πορνεία and adultery, one cannot be certain that adultery justifies more than physical separation. In the judgment of Davies and Allison, "The issue cannot, unfortunately, be resolved on exegetical grounds: Matthew's words are simply too cryptic to admit of definitive interpretation. The question of freedom after lawful divorce is just not addressed, and we cannot wring from the text what it will not give."[9]

The insolubility of such questions by historical methods finds confirmation in the fact of a divided exegetical guild. Among Catholic exegetes, for instance, consensus on the Matthean divorce *logia* has shifted considerably. Proposals already circulated in the nineteenth century to interpret πορνεία as premarital cohabitation, and the exception clause, correspondingly, as permission externally to dissolve a union already intrinsically unlawful.[10] The French Jesuit Joseph Bonsirven breathed new life into the "unlawfulness" solution when in 1948 he proposed that πορνεία referred not to premarital cohabitation but to a union contracted within Levitically prohibited degrees

---

8 Davies and Allison, *Matthew*, 1:530–31.

9 Davies and Allison, *Matthew*, 1:529. When Matt 19:9 gives Allison and Davies occasion to revisit their position eight years later, they construe πορνεία more confidently as adultery, but remain agnostic regarding the entitlements of the wronged party: "The problem of whether 19.9 allows remarriage for the innocent party ... cannot, as Augustine conceded, finally be answered" (Davies and Allison, *Matthew*, 3:17).

10 For the history of this position, beginning with the Italian Jesuit F. S. Patrizi in 1844, see Anton Ott, *Die Auslegung der Neutestamentlichen Texte über die Ehescheidung*, NTAbh III, 1–3 (Münster: Aschendorff, 1911), 261–66.

of sanguinity.[11] Normatively speaking, such solutions have in common the fact that they read πορνεία as grounds not for dividing what God has "joined" but for identifying what God never really "joined" in the first place.

More recent studies among Catholics, however, have tended to interpret the exception clause as something closer to grounds for divorce. One can track this shift in the career of Rudolf Schnackenburg, who served with Ratzinger during the early years of the International Theological Commission.[12] Still sympathetic to Bonsirven's position as late as 1969,[13] Schnackenburg would later declare the πορνεία clause a "real exception in the cause of adultery on the woman's side."[14] The early Jewish-Christian saw no contradiction between this exception and Jesus' prohibition of divorce, he explains, because they understood the latter "not as juridical ruling but as ethical appeal [*sittlicher Anruf*]."[15] The German exegete Heinz Schürmann, when invited to address the Plenary Session of the International Theological Commission (including Ratzinger) in 1977, charts a middle course between the new and the old Schnackenburg. There would have been no need for "casuistic amplifications," such as the Matthean exception clauses or the Pauline instructions on mixed marriages, he argues, had Jesus' words been understood as mere "ethical appeal" (*ethischer Appell*). To the contrary, "All four versions of our dominical saying have the *form of a legal pronouncement* [*Gesetzwortes*], which means to guarantee a binding order within the congregation."[16] At the same time, Schürmann counts Bonsirven's reading of πορνεία among those proposals too exegetically uncertain to serve by themselves as a basis for a

---

11 Joseph Bonsirven, *Le divorce dans le Nouveau Testament* (Paris: Desclée de Brouwer, 1948). For an English-language case for this view, advanced by a well-respected exegete, see Joseph Fitzmyer, "The Matthean Divorce Texts and Some New Palestinian Evidence," *TS* 37, no. 2 (1976): 197–226.

12 See Benedict XVI, "Indirizzo di saluto del Papa Emerito Benedetto XVI in occasione del 50o anniversario di istituzione della Commissione Teologica Internazionale," n.p., cited October 22, 2019, https://www.vatican.va/roman_curia/congregations/cfaith/cti_documents/rc_cti_20191022_saluto-bxvi-50ann-cti_it.html. Ratzinger mentions that the sessions dedicated to the questions of fundamental moral theology (1974) and matrimony (1977), led largely by exegetes and experts in dogmatics, provoked lively debate.

13 Rudolf Schnackenburg, *Schriften zum Neuen Testament* (Munich: Kösel, 1971), 419–20, 433–34.

14 Rudolf Schnackenburg, *Von Jesus zur Urkirche*, vol. 1 of *Die Sittliche Botschaft des Neuen Testaments*, HTKNT Supplementband 1 (Freiburg: Herder, 1986), 152.

15 Schnackenburg, *Von Jesus zur Urkirche*, 151.

16 Schürmann, *Von Jesus zur Urkirche*, 129.

"dependable canonical or pastoral praxis."[17] Catholic exegesis thus remains divided.

Protestant exegesis appears no closer to achieving consensus. It typically resists equating πορνεία narrowly with incest, but continues to disagree as to the normative implications of the Matthean exception clause for the indissolubility of marriage. Even if one grants that πορνεία recalls the sexual regulations of the Levitical Holiness code, observes the American Methodist exegete Richard Hays, the exception would then have to envision not only incest (vv. 6–18) but also adultery, homosexual acts, bestiality, and intercourse during menstruation (vv. 19–23). "The Matthean exception clause," he concludes, "leaves the door open for divorce on the grounds of a variety of offenses related to sexual immorality. No matter what interpretation is put upon the clause, it is undeniable that we see here a process of adaptation, in which Jesus' unconditional prohibition of divorce is applied and qualified in the interest of practicability."[18] The Swiss Protestant exegete Ulrich Luz finds in the exception clause no demonstrable reference to the Holiness code at all, and thus no basis for construing πορνεία as sexual relations within the prohibited degrees of consanguinity. Despite dismissing the arguments of Bonsirven's school as "apologetically motivated 'echappatoires,'" Luz concedes that Matthew's actual meaning may nevertheless find its closest parallel in the Catholic canonical tradition. For in forbidding *both* men and women to marry divorced partners, the Matthean Jesus allows separation for infidelity while foreclosing the possibility of a second marriage. The exclusion of remarriage, which goes beyond the strictness of even the Shammaite school, would account both for the shock of the disciples, a feature of the narrative otherwise difficult to explain, and for the disapproval of second marriages evident in the *Wirkungsgeschichte*. Luz observes frankly, "This corresponds objectively, not terminologically, to the separation of bed, table and board" in the context of a perduring marriage bond—a status long recognized by

17 Heinz Schürmann, *Studien zur neutestamentlichen Ethik*, ed. Thomas Söding, SBAB 7 (Stuttgart: Verlag Katholisches Bibelwerk, 1990) 130n25, 141.

18 Richard Hays, *The Moral Vision of the New Testament: Community, Cross, New Creation, A Contemporary Introduction to New Testament Ethics* (San Francisco: HarperCollins, 1996), 355.

Catholic pastoral practice and canon law.[19] Though opinions could be multiplied, these suffice to show that Protestant exegetes also disagree.

The exegetical survey thus permits a few general observations. The biblical guild has not reached the kind of consensus on Jesus' divorce *logia*, especially the Matthean exception clauses, that could support normative conclusions. Even those who suppose Leviticus 17–18 a relevant background to the exception clauses construe the moral of the story differently. Bonsirven's school construes πορνεία narrowly as an impediment to marriage, whereas Hays construes it broadly as grounds for divorce. Likewise those who reject the relevance of the Levitical Holiness code, preferring to interpret πορνεία as plain sexual infidelity, show little more prospect of reaching consensus. The later Schnackenburg identifies the Matthean exception clause as grounds for dissolving what would have been considered a valid marital bond. Schürmann is not sure what kind of pastoral provisions it envisioned. For Luz the passage probably permits physical separation in the case of sexual infidelity but no right for the wronged party to remarry. The conflict of hypotheses leads Ratzinger, as we will see, to look beyond the historian's standard toolkit for the means to draw normative conclusions.

RATZINGER'S TESTS APPLIED TO THE DIVORCE *LOGIA*

The toolkit for which Ratzinger reaches in the case of the divorce *logia* closely resembles that displayed in "Farewell to the Devil?" This is hardly surprising since Ratzinger's most in-depth studies of the biblical teaching on marriage and divorce, "Zur Theologie der Ehe" (1969)[20] and "Zur Frage nach der Unauflöslichkeit der Ehe" (1972),[21] stem from roughly the same period as his studies on demonology. In these and other essays on marriage, however, Ratzinger proceeds somewhat differently than in "Farewell to the Devil?" No longer trying to give a clinic on the hermeneutical method, he

---

19 Ulrich Luz, *Das Evangelium nach Matthäus*, 4 vols., EKKNT (Zürich: Benzinger und Neukirchener, 1985–2002), I, 1:277. See also his remarks on Matthew 19:9 in *Matthäus* I, 3:98–99.

20 Joseph Ratzinger, "Zur Theologie der Ehe," in JRGS 4:565–92.

21 Joseph Ratzinger, "Zur Frage nach der Unauflöslichkeit der Ehe. Bemerkungen zum dogmengeschichtlichen Befund und zu seiner gegenwärtigen Bedeutung," in *Ehe und Ehescheidung. Diskussion unter Christen*, ed. Franz Henrich and Volker Eid, Münchener Akademie Schriften 59 (Munich: Kösel, 1972), 35–56. Hereafter "Zur Frage nach der Unauflöslichkeit der Ehel."

does not bother to enumerate his "tests" expressly. And he devotes the lion's share of his attention to the reception of Jesus' teaching on marriage and divorce in the Church, giving little to no separate consideration to Jesus' own experience as these are ascertainable on the basis of the New Testament canon. Only three tests factor appreciably into Ratzinger's deliberations: the relationship between Old and New Testament, the extent of reception into the Church's tradition, and the relationship to reason. The exposition will review Ratzinger's deployment of the tests in this order.

Before applying the "tests," however, we do well to recall a peculiarity in the sources for Ratzinger's thought on the subject. Ratzinger shifts his understanding of the normative scope of the divorce *logia* between 1969 and 1972 and perhaps one more time before the end of the 1970s. When he republishes "Zur Frage nach der Unauflöslichkeit der Ehe" in the fourth volume of his *Gesammelte Schriften* (2014), therefore, he feels obliged to replace its summary judgment.[22] But because Ratzinger attaches his new summary judgment to a basically unaltered study of biblical reception history, one can only speculate as to how he would renarrate the same historical data today. At all events, it is important to remember that the texts pertaining to Ratzinger's deployment of the "tests" (as opposed to his normative conclusions) all stem from the late 1960s and early 1970s.

Relationship between Old and New Testament

Ratzinger considers the first of the interpretive canons outlined in "Farewell to the Devil?"—namely, the relationship between Old and Testament—in his 1969 essay "Zur Theologie der Ehe." The fact that Jesus identifies the Mosaic provision for divorce as a concession to Israel's "hardness of heart," not intended "from the beginning," makes such an intertestamental optic almost inevitable. Reading the Matthean teaching on divorce according to the analogy of the testaments, Ratzinger reaches two chief conclusions: Jesus' words should be interpreted prophetically; nature has a history.

Ratzinger opens his reflections by noting that Jesus handles the question of marriage and divorce much as he handles the rest of Israel's legal patrimony in the Sermon on the Mount. "Jesus sets the unconditional call [*unbedingten Anruf*] of God in its totality over and against the historically

---

22 The revised essay is found in JRGS 4:600–621 and will be cited as "Zur Frage nach der Unauflöslichkeit der Ehe."

canalized, attenuated, but also concretized will of God."[23] Important consequences for identifying the genre of Jesus' divorce *logia* follow:

> Because Jesus reaches back behind the plane of the Law to the Beginning, his saying may not again be seen immediately and without further qualification as law; it is inseparable from the domain of faith and discipleship and can make sense only in the context of the new situation opened through Jesus and accepted in faith. . . . If, for a clarification of marriage, Jesus points to Adam's word in the creation account (Gen 2:24) about the unity of man and woman, this saying is not to be built up into a new casuistic position, but understood as a prophecy and actualized [*vergegenwärtigt*] prophetically in faith.[24]

Ratzinger in effect reclassifies Jesus' teachings on divorce in Matthew 5 and Matthew 19 from legal pronouncement to prophetic call. In contrasting Jesus' prophetic words with legal pronouncements and casuistic positions, Ratzinger opposes the position Schürmann would later take—namely, that the divorce *logia* represent the institution of a community order. Ratzinger anticipates instead the later Schnackenburg, who described Jesus' teaching on divorce as a lofty "call" (*Anruf*) perhaps not fully realizable in law.

Continuing the theme of prophetic utterance, Ratzinger then turns to the Letter to the Ephesians and its Christological reinterpretation of the one-flesh union described in Genesis 2:24. Paul too appeals to God's plan from the beginning: "'For this reason a man shall leave [his] father and [his] mother and be joined to his wife, and the two shall become one flesh.' This is a great mystery, but I speak in reference to Christ and the church. In any case, each one of you should love his wife as himself, and the wife should respect her husband" (Eph 5:31–33). Commenting on this series of verses, Ratzinger observes, "It is important, first of all, that Genesis 2:24 is understood henceforth as *christological* prophecy. But because Christian marriage appears as the enduring actuality [*beständige Gegenwart*] of that prophecy, it is really the μυστήριον of Genesis 2:24."[25] According to Ratzinger, then, Paul, by presenting Christ and the Church as the prophetic fulfilment of Genesis 2:24, implies the analogical unity of the two testaments. Here Ratzinger finds yet another illustration of the *analogia fidei*.

---

23 Ratzinger, "Zur Theologie der Ehe," 567.

24 Ratzinger, "Zur Theologie der Ehe," 567.

25 Ratzinger, "Zur Theologie der Ehe," 569.

Discerning the connection between Ephesians 3 and Genesis 2 permits Ratzinger to demonstrate the biblical basis of another analogical pairing. Since Ephesians describes Christ as the fulfilment of Genesis 2:24, which itself refers to God's original plan for creation, this implies that not only Old and New Testament but creation and covenant form an analogical unity. "Creation and Covenant do not stand beside each other and outside each other like secular and spiritual or simply like natural and supernatural; much rather is Christ 'the first creation' (Col 1:15) and creation therefore the potential material of the covenant. . . . The last (the covenant—Christ, the Last Adam) is the true first, the condition for the possibility of the latter."[26] Because God from the beginning intended creation for fulfilment in Christ, only the New Covenant fully clarifies the meaning of creation. Ratzinger here betrays a measured sympathy with the theological ethics of Karl Barth, who likewise attempts to take the concrete, existential unity of creation and covenant as the point of departure for his theological anthropology.[27] The implications of this point of departure for natural-law reasoning will be revisited in the section on scholarly reason.

What does the criterion of intertestamental trajectory reveal about the perennially normative content of Jesus' teaching on divorce? Ratzinger finds the data inconclusive. For the construal of Jesus' words as a call to covenantal faithfulness rather than a "new casuistic position" could serve as grounds for either absolutizing or relativizing their authority. On the one hand, removing them from the legal sphere might seem to render them only more implacable, securing them against all the quibbling and qualifications that normally attend human legislation. As a concrete illustration of this principle, not introduced by Ratzinger, one can point to Luz, who justifies contemporary Protestantism's tolerance for remarriage after divorce on the

---

26 Ratzinger, "Zur Theologie der Ehe," 569.

27 For Karl Barth, God creates only "after" having elected Christ as his covenant partner. Creation is thus the "external basis and possibility of the covenant," and covenant is the "internal basis and possibility of creation, and therefore of the existence of reality distinct from God." Barth, CD III, 2:204. Ratzinger already cites these lines from Barth approvingly in his 1964 seminar on creation. See Santiago Sanz Sánchez, "Joseph Ratzinger y la doctrina de la creación: los apuntes de Münster de 1964 (II). Algunos temas fundamentales," RET 74 (2014): 201–48, 203n6. For evidence of influence that Barth's doctrine of election exercises over Ratzinger's missiology, see my "The Church of the 'Few' for the 'Many': Ratzinger's Missiology of Representation," in Joseph Ratzinger and the Healing of Reformation-Era Divisions, ed. Emery de Gaál and Matthew Levering (Steubenville: Emmaus Academic, 2019), 302–5.

principle that all laws—including Jesus'—apply differently in changed social circumstances.[28] On the other hand, the very supposition that Jesus' teaching on divorce as a whole, just like his teaching in the rest of the Sermon on the Mount, "represents a valid faith-standard, but not the concrete legal form, for humanity's common life," might allow for discrepancy between ideal, "faith standards" and pragmatic, legal standards. In this respect, Ratzinger finds the canonical provisions for divorce in Eastern Orthodoxy understandable, even if not altogether commendable. In the final analysis, he concludes rather blandly that the Matthean divorce clause calls us to "become more aware of the proprium of faith's law and faith's justification, and find new ways to hold the community of faith open to the one who could not maintain the sign of the covenant in all its demands."[29] This tentative conclusion foreshadows the more innovative pastoral proposal of the 1972 essay.

Reception into the Faith of the Church

Faced with an ambiguous intertestamental witness, Ratzinger proceeds to run the case of Jesus' teaching on divorce through the second "test"—that is, its reception into the faith tradition of the Church. Ratzinger offers a few "dogmatic-historical observations" on this theme in "Zur Theologie der Ehe," recalling how Augustine and Bonaventure develop a salvation-historical view of marital ethics, whose demands—for example, monogamy versus polygamy—vary according to covenantal period, despite the underlying constancy of human nature.[30] But perhaps sensing the inadequacy of this highly selective survey, Ratzinger returns to the theme three years later with "Zur Frage nach der Unauflöslichkeit der Ehe," where he broadens the survey of post-biblical authorities and narrows the focus of his investigation to the question of marital indissolubility. The essay provides an ideal occasion for observing Ratzinger apply his second test for normativity.

Beginning with the patristic witness, Ratzinger notes that no authors in the early Church attempt to base a right to a second marriage on the Matthean unchastity clause. He sums up the recently published literature

---

28 Luz, *Matthäus*, I, 3:101. As changed social circumstances, Luz lists, *inter alia*, the emergence of companionate marriages, nuclear families, longer life expectancy, and suspicion of patriarchy.

29 For all citations in this paragraph, see Ratzinger, "Zur Theologie der Ehe," 589–91.

30 Ratzinger, "Zur Theologie der Ehe," 571–73, 576–78.

on the subject, including the influential work of the Jesuit patrologist Henri Crouzel,[31] as follows: "The most surprising aspect of the patristic witness is the fact that there is no attempt to derive from Mt 5:32 and 19:9 a right to remarriage in the case of marital separation through adultery."[32] Up until the fourth century, in fact, theologians generally take the main point of the passage to be a correction of the sexual double-standard operative in the Old Testament and pagan antiquity, a double standard that excused male infidelity and permitted only men to initiate divorce. According to this reading, the man who repudiates his wife would be committing adultery against her in the sense that he would be driving her to cohabitation with another man to whom she is not married. This description of the man's injustice would apply "except for πορνεία" since, in that case, the woman's adultery would precede rather than follow her divorce. Ratzinger writes too early to profit from Crouzel's text-critical study of the Matthean exception clauses, which argues convincingly that the present form of Matthew 19:9—where mention of remarriage follows the exception clause—was unknown to the ante-Nicene fathers.[33] But Ratzinger nevertheless accepts Crouzel's main and still generally accepted point: the early patristic sources do not see in the Matthean Jesus' words the right to divorce an adulterous wife and then remarry.[34]

Ratzinger goes on to observe, in fact, how Augustine's very influential reflections on marriage move the West decisively in the direction of marital indissolubility. In *De bono coniugali* (AD 400–401) Augustine compares the irrevocability of marriage to the sacramental character of priestly ordination, which the sinful priest does not lose "even when it remains for him a source of judgment."[35] Nearly twenty years later in *De nuptiis et concupiscentia* (419–20), the Doctor of Grace compares the definitiveness of marriage with

---

31 Henri Crouzel, *L'Église primitive face au divorce*, Théologie historique 13 (Paris: Beauchesne, 1971).

32 Ratzinger, "Zur Frage nach der Unauflöslichkeit der Ehe," 600–601.

33 Crouzel, "Le texte patristique de Matthieu V.32 et XIX:9," *NTS* 19 (1972): 117–19.

34 Ratzinger, "Zur Frage nach der Unauflöslichkeit der Ehe," 602. In the accompanying footnote, Ratzinger provides instances of this general approach to the Matthean exceptive clauses from Clement of Alexandria, Jerome, Gregory of Nazianzus, and Hilary (602n3).

35 Augustine, *De bono coniugali*, 24, 32 (CSEL 41, 226). Cited in Ratzinger, "Zur Frage nach der Unauföslichkeit der Ehe," 603.

the indelibility of baptismal character.[36] In such cases, Augustine grounds the irrevocability of marriage in the irrevocability of God's decision for humanity.[37] This accords, of course, with Ratzinger's earlier admission that a marital ethos based on the interrelation of creation and covenant may be more stringent than one based in natural law alone. Only the "new situation" brought about by the example of God's fidelity and the prospect of eternal life can justify an unconditional indissolubility.

Having conceded such indissolubility during the lifetime of the spouses to be the classic patristic position, even in cases of adultery, Ratzinger dedicates much of the rest of the essay to exploring mitigating voices. These provide evidence of a more flexible pastoral practice that "is not seen as entirely conformed to the genuine faith of the Church, but is nevertheless not entirely excluded either."[38] He draws attention to Origen's commentary on Matthew, which already notes that some of the Church's pastors "permitted [the divorced to remarry], in contradiction to what was written and laid out [Gesetzten] from the beginning, for the avoidance of greater evils." Origen considers this accommodation "not altogether unreasonable" despite being manifestly unscriptural.[39] Ratzinger goes on to note how a similar reluctance to condemn pastoral accommodations, despite their recognized incompatibility with biblical commands, shows up elsewhere. Augustine, for all his insistence on the indissoluble character of marriage, appears to allow a cuckolded husband to receive communion after divorce and remarriage.[40] Basil seems to permit Christians in a second marriage to return to the faith community, albeit only after seven years of penance.[41]

Moving into medieval thought, Ratzinger dwells at length on the canonist Gratian's attempt to harmonize discrepant authorities in his Decretals. On the one side of the balance stood Augustine's sacramental understanding of

---

36 Augustine, De nuptiis et concupiscentia, I, 10, 11 (CSEL 42, 222). Cited in Ratzinger, "Zur Frage nach der Unauföslichkeit der Ehe," 603.

37 Ratzinger, "Zur Frage nach der Unauföslichkeit der Ehe," 603–4.

38 Ratzinger, "Zur Frage nach der Unauföslichkeit der Ehe," 605.

39 Origen, In Matt 14, 23. Cited in Ratzinger, "Zur Frage nach der Unauföslichkeit der Ehe," 605n10.

40 Augustine, De fide et operibus, 19, 35. Cited in Ratzinger, "Zur Frage nach der Unauföslichkeit der Ehe," 603n8.

41 Basil, Epistolae 217, 77. Cited in Ratzinger, "Zur Frage nach der Unauföslichkeit der Ehe," 605n11.

marital indissolubility. On the other side stood a variety of permissive rulings. A letter of Pope Gregory II to St. Boniface (726 AD) allows German men to remarry if sickness (not spite) prevents their first wives from rendering the marital debt. Continence would be strictly correct, writes Gregory, but is possible only for "ethical heroes." The Provincial Council of Tribur (895) shows similar flexibility, allowing a husband to remarry whose wife has committed incestuous adultery. Gratian ultimately upholds the Augustinian line, explaining the concessions as "something permitted for a time" (*pro tempore permissum*)—that is, as anomalies conceded only during the bumpy transition from paganism to Christianity. The West thus clearly maintained the Augustinian concept of indissoluble marriage as its fundamental form, while sometimes tolerating certain temporary disjunctions between doctrinal and pastoral planes.[42]

In explaining how this tolerated disjunction gradually vanished in the West while becoming the new normal of the Eastern Church, Ratzinger points by and large to the different church-state relationships in the two halves of the Roman Empire. The East's ambition to form a Christian empire meant making Christianity the law of the land, unifying civil and ecclesiastical law. This inevitably entailed, on the one hand, adjusting civil marriage to meet ecclesial requirements and, on the other, treating ecclesial requirements with the pragmatic flexibility characteristic of civic jurisprudence. Under imperial influence, then, and with a view to expediency, Origen's and Basil's tolerance for disparity between biblical doctrine and pastoral praxis became institutionalized. Because marriage law in the West developed under mostly papal (rather than imperial) auspices, it remained more accountable to internal ecclesial requirements.[43]

Ratzinger points to the Council of Trent as a final example of vigorous adherence to Jesus' words on the indissolubility of marriage combined with a willingness to bend in emergency situations. The vigorous adherence is clear enough in canon 7:

> If anyone says that the Church is in error for having taught and for still teaching that in accordance with evangelical and apostolic doctrine [*cf. Mt 5:32; 19:9; Mk 10:11f.; Lk 16:18; 1 Cor 7:11*], the marriage bond cannot be

---

42 Gratian, *Decreta* P 2, C 32, q. 7, c. 17–23. Cited in Ratzinger, "Zur Frage der Unauföslichkeit der Ehe," 607–8.

43 Ratzinger, "Zur Frage nach der Unauföslichkeit der Ehe," 609–10.

dissolved because of adultery on the part of one of the spouses and that neither of the two, not even the innocent one who has given no cause for infidelity, can contract another marriage during the lifetime of the other; and that the husband who dismisses an adulterous wife and marries again and the wife who dismisses the adulterous husband and marries again are both guilty of adultery, let him be anathema.[44]

Relying heavily on the scholarship of the Jesuit Piet Fransen,[45] however, Ratzinger construes the scope of the condemnation rather narrowly. It meant to condemn anyone *claiming the Church has erred* in its teaching on marriage and divorce, thus taking indirect aim at Martin Luther. But it did not intend to anathematize all practices contrary to the Catholic practice. This is evident from the fact that Trent passed over the customs of Eastern Churches in discreet silence, hoping not to endanger prospects of ecclesial reunion. At least to the Ratzinger of 1972, then, Trent represents yet another case of the Catholic Church's long-standing pattern of holding fast to Christ's teaching while finessing emergency situations.[46]

Throughout his review of the Church's reception of Jesus' teaching on divorce, Ratzinger distinguishes between retaining marital indissolubility as "basic form" (*Grundform*) and retaining it as "ideal form" (*Hochform*). The Eastern Churches retain it as "ideal form" but have lost it as "basic form," letting the exception become the rule. The Catholic Church has managed to retain the "ideal form" as "basic form," despite occasionally and temporarily derogating from the norm. As we will see, the possibility of upholding this basic form amid emergency dispensations—whether granted for evangelizing barbarians or advancing ecclesial unity—will factor into Ratzinger's normative conclusions regarding the Matthean exception clauses.

Scholarly Reason

This rather ambivalent conclusion brings us to the last of Ratzinger's criteria: compatibility with scholarly reason. Ratzinger presumes throughout the relevance of historical reason, of course, but does not linger on exegetical

---

44 DH 1807.

45 See Piet Fransen, "Das Thema 'Ehescheidung nach Ehebruch' auf dem Konzil von Trent (1563)," *Concilium* 6 (1970): 343–48.

46 For Ratzinger's interpretation of Trent, see "Zur Frage nach der Unauflöslichkeit der Ehe," 612.

considerations, perhaps because they prove so inconclusive, or because he writes for collections where that task has already been assigned to others. That being said, he does briefly consider the natural moral law, which the Catholic tradition has long taken not to constitute a supernatural revelation, strictly speaking, but human reason's participation in the eternal law by which God orders the universe. Reflecting on what promotes or hinders the flourishing of human nature, in other words, human reason can discern the good to be done and the evil to be avoided.[47] Ratzinger accepts that this rational standard can help identify the normative content of biblical ethics while also underscoring its historical embeddedness and limited usefulness for settling the question of marital indissolubility.

Ratzinger's weighing of natural-law criteria appears mostly in his earlier essay "Zur Theologie der Ehe," which treats questions of marital ethics as a whole. There Ratzinger takes pains to distance himself from what he considers to be cruder scholastic theories of marital ethics, "whose ahistorical rationality is characterized by a peculiar mixture of abstraction and naturalism."[48] A more adequate theory will see natural law as more than respecting the finality of animal processes or observing a timeless catalogue of self-evident precepts. "It is human nature to be not just mere nature [*bloße Natur*], but to have history and rights—to need to have history and rights in order to be able to be 'natural.'"[49] Here one sees the ethical corollary of Ratzinger's more historically inflected anthropology, explored already in chapter 2. Just as human reason exists only in the medium of concrete linguistic communities, with all their particular achievements and burdens, so also natural law exists only as realized in particular ethical and legal cultures. In this respect, Ratzinger anticipates the position of the philosopher Alasdair MacIntyre, who presents moral reason as potentially universal but actually "inseparable from the particularity of history and tradition."[50] Ratzinger's point is not, of

---

47 For the exposition of natural law theory considered classic in Catholic theology, see Thomas Aquinas, ST I-II, q. 94.

48 Ratzinger, "Zur Theologie der Ehe," 578.

49 Ratzinger, "Zur Theologie der Ehe," 585.

50 Gerald McKenny, "Moral Disagreements and the Limits of Reason: Reflections on MacIntyre and Ratzinger," in *Intractable Disputes about Natural Law: Alasdair MacIntyre and Critics*, ed. Lawrence S. Cunningham (Notre Dame, IN: University of Notre Dame Press, 2009), 220. On the similarity between MacIntyre's and Ratzinger's "traditionary" understanding of natural law, see also Russell Hittinger, "Natural Law and Wisdom Traditions," *The Muslim World* 106 (April 2016): 316n15.

course, to deny that natural law contains universal and rationally discernible precepts. It is rather to remind natural lawyers that every culture easily confuses what is obvious to itself with what human reason as such dictates.[51]

This epistemic humility is especially important, in Ratzinger's eyes, when estimating the degree to which natural law prescribes marital indissolubility. Notwithstanding various scholastic arguments to the contrary, Ratzinger insists "that there is no deducibility of the unity and indissolubility of marriage through pure natural law."[52] Ratzinger does not tarry here to engage scholastic nuances on this point, such as Aquinas's distinction between what belongs to natural law's primary precepts and secondary precepts.[53] He is more concerned to identify the firmer point of departure for such specific conclusions: "As the realization of God's covenant faithfulness in human covenant faithfulness, Christian marriage expresses the definitiveness and irrevocability of God's yes in the definitiveness and irrevocability of a human yes."[54] Christian ethical reflection on marriage proceeds not from considering the exigencies of pure nature, in other words, but from reflecting on the "coinherence [*Ineinander*] of creation and covenant," which Ratzinger finds

51 Without denying the species-wide validity of natural law, the early Ratzinger tends to accentuate how social location influences our perception of its requirements: "The idea of natural law is not only colored by Christian ideas but also by the concrete circumstances of history; it thus conceals a double incognito, that of the Bible and that of the ideas of the intervening centuries.... There is a law encompassing all humanity, yet this exists not nakedly, but only in the concrete realizations of the changing times." Ratzinger, "Naturrecht, Evangelium und Ideologie in der katholischen Soziallehre: Katholische Erwägungen zum Thema," in *Christlicher Glaube und Ideologie,* ed. K. von Bismark und W. Dirks (Stuttgart and Mainz: Kreuz Verlag, 1964), 29. Among the reasons teaching authority must extend to morality, observes Ratzinger, is the difficulty of separating reason and the appearance of reason in every age. Ratzinger, "The Church's Teaching Authority—Faith—Morals," in *Principles of Christian Morality,* ed. Joseph Ratzinger, Heinrich Schürmann, and Hans Urs von Balthasar (San Francisco: Ignatius, 1986), 72. Later, in changed social circumstances, Ratzinger will accentuate the universality of natural law. For a review of this development, see Maria Raphaela Hölscher, *Naturrecht bei Joseph Ratzinger/Benedikt XVI. Die Bedeutung des Naturrechts in Geschichte und Gegenwart* (Heiligenkreuz: Be&Be Verlag, 2014), 23–29, 225–30.

52 Ratzinger, "Zur Theologie der Ehe," 589.

53 Aquinas, *Super Sent.,* lib. 4, d. 33, q. 1, a. 1. Thomas explains that because polygamy does not wholly frustrate the primary end of marriage (procreation in the broad sense), it belongs to the secondary precepts of natural law, which passion and custom might more easily obscure. For further exposition, see Kevin Flannery, "Marriage, Thomas Aquinas, and Jean Porter," *Journal of Catholic Social Thought* 8, no. 2 (2011): 282–89.

54 "Zur Theologie der Ehe," 589.

implied in Jesus' and Paul's intertestamental ethics of marriage (Matt 19:8; Eph 5:31; Gen 2:24).[55]

Natural reason, in short, remains undetermined with respect to the question of marital indissolubility. Because it clearly prescribes neither marital indissolubility nor its opposite, it excludes neither the stricter nor the more permissive interpretations of Jesus' divorce *logia*. Here as elsewhere, applying the criterion of scholarly rationality means for Ratzinger distinguishing what reason as such requires from what worldview renders plausible. In this case, however, it is the Christian tradition that assumes the role of the "prejudicing" worldview, inasmuch as it has often led thinkers to overestimate what is self-evident to universal moral reason.

Whereas the application of the "tests" proved quite decisive when applied to the questions of the demonic and geocentrism, they prove less so when used to discern the contemporary ethical relevance of Jesus' teaching on divorce. Situated within their intertestamental trajectory, Jesus' words assume a prophetic rather than legislative character. But this prophetic character could be taken to favor either broader or narrower constructions of the exception clause. The reception history of the Matthean embolisms shows that no one until the time of the Reformation took them as grounds for remarriage after divorce. But the same tradition also shows that exemplary pastors and theologians did not now always energetically suppress the laxer practices they deemed unbiblical, at least in emergency situations. And the criterion of scholarly reason, here assuming the form of natural-law morality, excludes neither interpretation in Ratzinger's eyes. The extent to which πορνεία constitutes an exception to Jesus' principle of marital indissolubility proves difficult to determine.

RATZINGER'S SHIFTING CONCLUSIONS

Given the tenuousness of these preliminary results, it will hardly be surprising to discover that Ratzinger's normative judgment changes over time. Every time he returns to Jesus' teaching on divorce, and to the Matthean *Unzuchtsklauseln* in particular, he gives them a more continuous sense. This continuity increases between ancient biblical and contemporary ecclesial norms, of course, but also between the various layers of early Christian

---

55 "Zur Theologie der Ehe," 575, 581.

tradition. As we shall see, Ratzinger's position also evolves with the ecclesial "signs of the times." This recalls his early recognition that the normative interpretation of Scripture, even when aided by such heuristics as his "tests," remains more an art than a science, always subject to the Church's common faith.

First Interpretation: Adultery as Grounds for Divorce and Remarriage

Ratzinger's first summary judgment, rendered in his 1969 essay "Zur Theologie der Ehe," finds that the Matthean unchastity clause represents a genuine but not altogether commendable exception to the principle of marital indissolubility. Ratzinger observes, "The attempt to construe juridically this supra-legal and supra-juridical call [*Anruf*] leads, in the sector of the Church represented by Matthew, to reintroducing human 'hardheartedness' into the law and to proceeding accordingly." In a footnote attached to the foregoing sentence Ratzinger elaborates: "This presupposes that the so-called 'Matthean clauses' (19:9) are meant in the sense that the Eastern churches understand them: as a possibility of divorce for the innocent party, when a culpable destruction of marriage occurs through adultery on the side of the other partner." Ratzinger dutifully notes Schnackenburg's recent support for Bonsirven's position, according to which πορνεία refers to an incestuous marriage invalid from the start. Intriguingly, Ratzinger does not directly engage Schnackenburg's early position. He merely observes that, if Schnackenburg is right about πορνεία, "the oriental Christian interpretation would then not reach so far back, but would nevertheless have to have arisen very early, after the Jewish marital law was forgotten, along with the peculiar meaning that it assigned to the word πορνεία." Ratzinger clearly finds any narrative predicated on the immediate forgetfulness of the Christian community suspect.[56]

A couple of points are worth noting about Ratzinger's position in 1969. First, he still presumes that the interpretation of the exception clauses embodied in Eastern canon law goes back to the beginning, or nearly so. His subsequent investigation into the reception history would correct this unfounded assumption. Second, Ratzinger, despite assuming that the

---

56 All citations in this paragraph come from Ratzinger, "Zur Theologie der Ehe," 590, 590n13.

Matthean exception clause adumbrates the Eastern policy of concessive remarriage, assigns it little contemporary ethical relevance within the Catholic sphere. "One should not infer from this that the Western Church, in connection with the divorce clauses of Matthew's Gospel, should also make divorce a possibility of her canon law, just like the Orthodox churches of the East."[57] Ratzinger's position will soon become both more historically informed and more pastorally venturesome.

Second Interpretation: Communion for Divorced and Remarried in Hardship

Ratzinger reassesses the abiding normative force of Jesus' teaching on divorce in 1972, in the first version of his essay, "Zur Frage nach der Unauflöslichkeit der Ehe." There Ratzinger stops presenting the Matthean embolism as an attempt to restrict the field of application for Jesus' prohibition on divorce. He nevertheless proposes opening up pastoral exceptions for the divorced and remarried, justifying such accommodations on extrabiblical grounds.

Ratzinger's greater familiarity with the patristic reception of Jesus' teaching on divorce and remarriage leads him to revise his early position on the significance of the Matthean *Unzuchtsklauseln*. Drawing on the work of French patrologists Henri Crouzel and Olivier Rousseau,[58] he makes the following observation:

> Olivier Rousseau's thesis that the laxer praxis later established in the Eastern Church develops neither from a corresponding interpretation of the unchastity clauses nor, therefore, from an interpretation of the New Testament is ... completely supported by the texts, and is further corroborated by Crouzel. After a review of the materials, I must thus correct my supposition ... that there was a praxis of divorce and remarriage in the church community represented by Matthew 5 and 19. This is scarcely probable in light of the complete unanimity of the tradition of the first four centuries in the opposite sense.[59]

---

57 Ratzinger, "Zur Theologie der Ehe," 590–91.

58 Olivier Rousseau, "Scheidung und Wiederheirat im Osten und Westen," *Concilium* 3 (1967): 322–34; Henri Crouzel, *L'Église primitive face au divorce*, Théologie historique 13 (Paris: Beauchesne, 1971).

59 Ratzinger, "Zur Frage nach der Unauflöslichkeit der Ehe," 601n3.

Ratzinger's hermeneutical method remains consistent, then, even if his interpretation of the Matthean exception clauses does not. Ratzinger reads the texts in a new light because his knowledge of their concrete *Wirkungsgeschichte* changes, which he takes to cast a backward light on the Bible's original sense.

Perhaps somewhat counterintuitively, Ratzinger, after concluding that no New Testament precedent exists for allowing remarriage after divorce, moves to relax the Church's sacramental discipline vis-à-vis the divorced and remarried. In this respect, he appeals not so much to the force of the biblical command itself as to the historical record, which shows that the Church sometimes relaxed the norm in the name of pastoral expediency.

> [The Church] cannot cease proclaiming the faith of the new covenant, but she must often enough begin her concrete life a bit beneath the threshold of the biblical word. She can thus permit limited exceptions in clear emergency situations for the prevention of greater evils. The criteria for such an act would have to be: any conduct "standing against what is written" finds its limit in that it may not call into question the very basic form [*Grundform*] from which the Church lives. It is also tied to the character of derogation and of help in urgent need—as the transitional missionary situation was, but also, to some extent, the emergency of Church union.[60]

The "transitional missionary situation" and "emergency of Church union" refer, of course, to cases already mentioned: the Church's gradual introduction of a consistent biblical teaching on marital indissolubility into the German Church as well as Trent's discreet silence on the Orthodox practice of penitential second and third marriages. Ratzinger takes it for granted that these derogations did not call into question the "basic form" of Christian marriage in the West.

Ratzinger goes on to ask whether such emergency situations exist for the divorced and remarried today. He answers affirmatively. The limits and inequities of the annulment process speak against its use as an absolute condition for readmission to communion in the Church. In certain situations, continence remains a practical impossibility—what Gregory II calls the stuff of "ethical heroes"—while access to the sacraments proves needful. He sums up, "Marriage *is* sacramentum, standing in the indissoluble basic form of the definitive decision [*entschiedenen Entscheidung*]. But this does not exclude

60 Ratzinger, "Zur Frage nach der Unauflöslichkeit der Ehel," 53–54.

the possibility that the ecclesial communion embrace those people as well who acknowledge this teaching and principle of life but stand in an emergency situation of a special kind, in which they especially need full communion with the Body of the Lord."[61] According to Ratzinger's summary judgment in 1972, then, the Church may sometimes allow at the pastoral level what Scripture forbids. Ratzinger in 1972 thus more or less anticipates the proposal of Cardinal Walter Kasper to the 2014 extraordinary consistory of cardinals, and, arguably, the provision incorporated into Pope Francis's Apostolic Exhortation *Amoris laetitia*.[62]

It is worth noting that Ratzinger has fully relocated his argumentative basis for more lenient sacramental discipline from the biblical to the pastoral domain. The question for him turns no longer on what the Bible intends to affirm about the indissolubility of marriage, but on whether the Church, for the sake of pastoral expediency, can derogate from what the Bible intends to affirm. He initially concludes that the Church may so do, provided the derogation does not obscure Christian marriage's "basic form."

Mature Interpretation: Matthean Exception Clause as Case-Type

Judging by the subsequent development of his position, Ratzinger soon lost confidence that such concessions could leave the "basic form" intact.[63] The seventies witnessed seismic shifts in marital culture, with most Western societies adopting no-fault divorce policies and with Catholics increasingly taking advantage of them.[64] This new cultural environment seems to have led him to reconsider his position on "emergency" communion for the

---

61 Ratzinger, "Zur Frage nach der Unauflöslichkeit der Ehe," 56.

62 Kasper in fact cites Ratzinger's "Zur Frage nach der Unauflöslichkeit der Ehe" in support of his proposal to admit certain divorced and remarried couples to sacramental communion. See Walter Kasper, *The Gospel of the Family*, trans. William Madges (New York: Paulist, 2014), 40n18. See also *AL*, 300n336.

63 For Ratzinger's many reappraisals of his position between 1980 and 2014, see Gabriel Weiten, "Zur Seelsorge wiederverheirateter Geschiedener 1972–2014," *MIPB* 7 (2014): 109–11.

64 In the German *Sprachraum*, the Schweizer '72 Synode (1972–75) and the Würzburger Synode (1972–75) both moved to admit the divorced and remarried to communion; West Germany likewise undertook a reform of marriage law between 1973 and 1976, allowing for divorce even where no fault could be proven. See Weiten, "Zur Seelsorge wiederheirateter Geschiedener 1972–2014," 105–7.

remarried. In a series of pastoral letters to the Church of Munich-Freising,[65] Ratzinger makes his own the judgment of the Ordinary Synod of Bishops of 1980, which restricted readmission to communion to those remarried Catholics for whom the nullity of the first marriage was morally certain but forensically indemonstrable.[66] In his introduction to the volume by the Congregation for the Doctrine of the Faith on *Pastoral Care for the Divorced and Remarried* (1998), he would later suggest that the new evidentiary standards introduced into the 1983 *Code of Canon Law* rendered even this exception obsolescent.[67] But since this chapter is concerned with Ratzinger the exegete rather than Ratzinger the canonist, it will focus on the evolved exegesis of the Matthean exception clause undergirding these pastoral conclusions. As we shall see, the mature Ratzinger comes to regard the Matthean exception clauses as a sort of "schema" filled in over the course of history.

The first evidence of Ratzinger's shifting exegetical position emerges in the wake of the 1977 plenary session of the International Theological Commission. The International Theological Commission had chosen to study the doctrinal problems of marriage and had invited Heinz Schürmann to serve as expert adviser on matters exegetical. Ratzinger, tasked with writing the preface to the resulting study volume, reveals uneasiness with the accelerating acceptance of divorce among Catholics.

> Certain biblical texts insufficiently elucidated, certain facts, or certain pronouncements from the history of dogma lifted from their context or

---

65 Originally published in several German ecclesial media outlets under the title "Brief an die Priester und Diakone und an alle im pastoralen Dienst Stehenden," the reflection will be cited according to the version republished in JRGS 4:622–49.

66 "[The Synod] names as a separate category those who have arrived at a founded conviction of conscience regarding the nullity of their marriage, even when juridical verification is not possible: In such a case—provided scandal be avoided—admission to communion can be granted in accordance with the founded judgment of conscience" (JRGS 4:633). Having reported the Synod's mind, Ratzinger then expresses his own: "I believe that the Synod has honestly striven to do justice both to the tremendous seriousness of the Lord's words and the biblical tradition, and to the seriousness of the human fortunes [*Schicksale*]" (4:634). For the corroborating opinion of Ratzinger's personal secretary during the 1980 Synod that the report represented Ratzinger's own mind at the time, see Bruno Fink, *Zwischen Schreibmaschine und Pileolus: Erinnerungen an meine Zeit als Sekretär des Hochwürdigsten Herrn Joseph Kardinal Ratzinger in München und Rom September 1978–Dezember 1983*, MMIPB 3 (Regensburg: Schnell und Steiner, 2016), 51.

67 Joseph Ratzinger, introduction to *On the Pastoral Care of Divorced and Remarried Persons*, by the Congregation for the Doctrine of the Faith, Documents and Commentaries (Washington, DC: Libreria Editrice Vaticana, 2012), 10–11.

bearing an obscure meaning, contribute to the disturbance of spirits. . . . Some invoke mercy here as a fundamental Christian attitude. They appeal to it to recommend a certain mitigation of the norms. In this way, they say, Christians will be able to validate [feraient droit à] the liberty of individuals and give full meaning [un sens complet] to certain "foundational" words of the Bible.[68]

How much Ratzinger intends these words—especially the reference to "certain pronouncements from the history of dogma lifted from their context or bearing an obscure meaning"—as a disavowal of his 1972 essay must remain a matter of conjecture. In any event, neither he nor the International Theological Commission shows much sympathy for the position that only a "purely disciplinary law," or even a "certain legalism," stands between the divorced-and-remarried and sacramental communion.[69]

On an analogous occasion nearly twenty years later, Ratzinger speaks a bit more directly to the exegetical situation. In a letter of September 14, 1994, the Congregation for the Doctrine of the Faith, headed by Ratzinger, had reaffirmed that those in irregular second marriages may not approach the eucharistic table. Introducing the accompanying study volume, On the Pastoral Care of Divorced and Remarried Persons (Italian: 1998), Ratzinger returns to the Matthean exception clauses in a rather agnostic mode. "Extensive literature exists regarding the correct understanding of the porneia clauses, with many differing and even conflicting hypotheses. There is no unanimity among exegetes on this point. Many maintain that it refers to invalid marital unions, not to an exception to the indissolubility of marriage. In any case, the Church cannot construct her doctrine and praxis on uncertain exegetical hypotheses."[70] Without citing Bonsirven by name, Ratzinger indirectly appeals to the position that πορνεία designates an impediment of incest. He also tacitly approves a key premise on which Bonsirven's school builds its case—namely, that the Matthean exception clauses reflect the decrees of the so-called Council of Jerusalem: "With reference to the porneia clauses in

---

68 Joseph Ratzinger, preface to Problèmes doctrinaux du mariage chrétien, by the Congregation for the Doctrine of the Faith, ed. P. Delhaye, Lex Spiritus Vitae 4 (Louvain: Centre Cerfaux, 1979), 11.

69 Congregation for the Doctrine of the Faith, Problèmes doctrinaux du mariage chrétien, 121.

70 Ratzinger, "Introduction to Pastoral Care of Divorced and Remarried Persons," 13.

Matthew and in Acts 15:20, the impediments to marriage were established."[71] Though clearly linking Matthew to the Council of Jerusalem, he connects Matthew to the Church's marriage canons much more tentatively, affirming only that the latter were established "with reference to" to the former.

This cautious openness to Bonsirven's position also characterizes Ratzinger's final word on the subject. When the time came to republish "Zur Frage nach der Unauflöslichkeit der Ehe" in the fourth volume of his *Gesammelte Schriften* (2014), Ratzinger opted to add a new summative conclusion to an unaltered historical survey.[72] The new ending accentuates the Church's responsibility to strengthen the faith of believers to the point where they can live the "basic form" of marriage prescribed by Christ, but adds that this does not absolve the Church of an ongoing interpretive task:

> At the same time the Church must try ever anew to sound out the limits and the range of Jesus' word. She must remain true to the Lord's mandate [*Auftrag*], but may not overextend it. It seems to me that the so-called unchastity clauses, which Matthew appended to the dominical word handed down by Mark, already reflect such an effort. There a case-type [*Falltypus*] is named that is not affected by Jesus' saying. The Western Church, under the leadership of Peter's successors, could not follow the path of the Byzantine imperial Church, which accommodated itself ever more to secular law and thereby weakened the distinctive element of living in faith. But she has in her own way highlighted [*herausgestellt*] the limits of the applicability of the Lord's saying and concretely defined its scope withal.[73]

Ratzinger goes on to mention two different ways in which the Western Church has more precisely defined the normative scope of Jesus' command. First, it has clarified that only the marriage of two baptized parties qualifies as a sacramental—and thus indissoluble—marriage. When a marriage between a Christian and non-Christian hinders the faith of the Christian,

---

71 Ratzinger, "Introduction to *Pastoral Care of Divorced and Remarried Persons*," 16.

72 In an interview of April 14, 2015, with Peter Seewald, Ratzinger explains his motivation: "Ich habe gesagt, so wie es da stand, kann man es auch falsch auslegen. Ich kann nicht mit einem zweideutigen Text aufwarten. Es handelt sich dabei nicht um eine neue Position, sondern um eine Klärung; das, was ich im Familienrat gesagt habe—das war nach der Familiensynode 1980, bei der mich Johannes Paulus II. als *Relator* eingesetzt hatte—, habe ich noch mal kurz zusammenzufassen versucht." Peter Seewald, *Benedikt XVI. Ein Leben* (Munich: Droemer, 2020), 562.

73 Ratzinger, "Zur Frage nach der Unauflöslichkeit der Ehe," 617.

the Church considers itself authorized to dissolve it, following the precedent of St. Paul (1 Cor 7:12–16).[74] Second, the Church has gradually identified sacramental marriage's many personal and legal preconditions, the absence of any of which renders a marriage invalid or "null."[75] It is not necessary to enter into the details of these grounds for "annulment" to infer that Ratzinger still considers them distant descendants of the Matthean *Unzuchtsklauseln*.

The precise manner of descendance bears closer examination. His mature position identifies the unchastity clause as a "case-type" to which Jesus' words do not apply. Seeking to build on a point of exegetical consensus, he focuses not on the exact historical case envisioned by the πορνεία clauses but on their status as redactional additions to Jesus' *ipsissima verba*. The fact that those responsible for the Gospel of Matthew felt authorized to gloss a dominical word in this way attests to the early Church's awareness of its competence and responsibility *to* sound out the "limits of the applicability of the Lord's saying." Ratzinger thus attempts to establish the πορνεία clause as a precedent not for any particular marital impediment, but for the whole centuries-long process of defining such impediments and establishing their existence in concrete cases.

Ratzinger's final position on the unchastity clause thus turns out to be, in one respect, a middle way between his earlier positions. He begins in 1969 with an ill-founded confidence that Matthew meant the exception clause as a casuistic softening of Jesus' command, authorizing even remarriage in the case of adultery. When better acquainted with the reception history in 1972, he abandons this position. He declines to replace it, however, with any positive speculation on the meaning on πορνεία. In 1998 and 2014 he again attempts to give some positive content to the *Unzuchtsklauseln*, but only a rather schematic one. The exception clause, accordingly, now represents a "case-type" unaffected by Jesus' words, whose exact parameters the Church knew itself competent to delimit. This is not so much a reversal of Jesus' words as a clarification of their scope. Ratzinger thus interprets the exception clause as something like a "schema" waiting to be fleshed out by the "reality of

---

74 Ratzinger, "Zur Frage nach der Unauflöslichkeit der Ehe," 617–18. The Catholic canonical tradition calls this authority the "Pauline Privilege" (see CIC 1143–50).

75 Ratzinger, "Zur Frage nach der Unauflöslichkeit der Ehe," 618–20. For the various impediments and requirements for marriage according to canonical form, see CIC 1073–133.

subsequent history,"[76] or a seed "needing the challenge of new situations, new experiences and new sufferings in order to open up."[77] It foreshadows all the clarifying questions that would be posed to the divorce *logia* in the course of history, as well as the delimiting answers that would be given. In this respect, Ratzinger's final position hearkens back to the effective-historical model of Scripture that he proposed as early as his Bonaventure Habilitation.

EVALUATING RATZINGER'S MATURE INTERPRETATION

Ratzinger's attempts to determine the contemporary ethical relevance of the Matthean unchastity clauses represent in many respects an unusual case. Ratzinger revisits the question several times between 1969 and 2014, even republishing his 1972 essay with an altered conclusion. The case is also unusual in that Ratzinger attends little to the criterion of Christ's own mentality as historically indicated, an interpretive background that this chapter supplied by way of its initial exegetical survey. And yet, for all these idiosyncrasies, Ratzinger's typical hermeneutical method shines through enough to permit something like an evaluation against two standards: historical reason and internal coherence. Ratzinger's mature position, I would argue, receives the highest marks on both counts.

Ratzinger's final position can hardly be said to ignore the requirements of historical reason. One might even go so far as to say that it finds good historical support. For Ratzinger reads the unchastity clauses not as true exceptions to the principle of marital indissolubility, but as an attempt by the Matthean redactor to define marriage and divorce more precisely. The magisterial Protestant commentaries of Davies and Allison on the one hand and Luz on the other do not contradict this. They concur with Ratzinger in ascribing "except for πορνεία" to the Matthean redactor.[78] Moreover, they both favor—Luz much more strongly than Davies and Allison—the idea that the Matthean redaction means to identify adultery as a case justifying something like a "separation of table, bed, and board." This would be a way of further defining what counts as "divorce" and "marriage," insofar as it would

---

76 Joseph Ratzinger, *Eschatology: Death and Eternal Life*, trans. Michael Waldstein and Aidan Nichols (Washington, DC: The Catholic University of America Press, 1988), 43.

77 JN 1:xix.

78 Luz, *Matthäus*, I, 1:269; Davies and Allison, *Matthew*, 3:16.

clarify that social separation does not necessarily imply a will to separate "what God has united." Ratzinger's rather capacious frame can thus accommodate the favored solution of leading Protestant exegetes.

The more interesting question, however, is whether Ratzinger's frame proves too capacious. Ratzinger construes the unchastity clause as a formal "case-type," it seems, to avoid excluding Bonsirven's identification of πορνεία as a union within the Levitically prohibited degrees of consanguinity. On this construal, of course, Matthew would be addressing not the requirements of the "divorce" but the requirements of "marriage." The strongest argument against this position—which Luz values more than Allison and Davies—is the absence of patristic attestation. Just as no ante-Nicene fathers attempt to derive from Matthew's exceptive clauses a right to remarriage in the case of marital infidelity, so none attempts to construe them as grounds for "annulment" *avant la lettre*. Does Ratzinger, in excluding the former but not the latter, allow his historical judgment to be drawn into what Luz calls "apologetically motivated 'echappatoires'"? Perhaps. But Ratzinger might have good reasons, not expressly mentioned in his new conclusion, for weighing the two effective-historical lacunae differently. Because the desire to divorce and remarry after betrayal presumably recurs in every time and location, the early Church's consistent refusal to gratify this desire has a certain interpretive force. The need to dissolve unions prohibited by the Levitical Holiness code may, by contrast, reflect a highly transient historical situation, a time when the Twelve had already authorized the mission to the gentiles but had not yet given up conceiving of them as "strangers among the Jews." If this transitional "solution along Jewish lines"[79] commenced with the so-called Council of Jerusalem and lost steam after the destruction of Jerusalem, it might explain why the Levitical interpretation finds no echo in extracanonical literature—even if it came closest to the intentions of the Matthean redactor. Ratzinger is well aware of these intracanonical inflection points, as

---

79 I owe the phrase to Robert Louis Wilkens, *The First Thousand Years: A Global History of Christianity* (New Haven: Yale University Press, 2012), 21. Old Testament Scholar Christopher Seitz likewise reads the situation this way: "Christians in time, after the parting of the ways with Israel, ceased living in strict conformity to the ruling of Acts 15, for example, which was derived from Leviticus." "The Ten Commandments: Positive and Natural Law and the Covenants Old and New—Christian Use of the Decalogue and Moral Law," in *I Am the Lord Your God: Christian Reflections on the Ten Commandments*, ed. Carl E. Braaten and Christopher R. Seitz (Grand Rapids, MI: Eerdmans, 2005), 34.

well as of the Church's tendency—even in the premodern period—to regard the "stipulations of James" as culture-specific legislation.[80]

There still remain many commentators, including the younger Ratzinger himself, who take the Matthean clausules as straightforward permission to remarry in case of spousal adultery, and who make their case on historical grounds. They would no doubt want to dispute the mature Ratzinger's commitment to tough-minded historical reason. It is worth noting, however, that proponents of this reading often betray the antinomian prejudices regnant among exegetes of the 1960s and 1970s. Though Ratzinger typically insists on the analogous unity of Old and New Testament, his first judgment frames the controversy between Jesus and the Pharisees according to a thinly veiled dialectic of Law and Gospel. Jesus "shreds casuistry" (*die Kasuistik zerreißt*), he observes in 1969, with a "supralegal and superjuridical call."[81] The later Schnackenburg would follow the early Ratzinger's lead, sharply opposing the domain of community order and that of Jesus' exalted "ethical calling." Protestant exegetes tend to agree that Jesus' prohibition of divorce has love as its "last instance," and cannot thus serve a "casuistic legal or ecclesial order."[82] Taking up the question of Jesus' teaching on divorce more recently, however, the German Catholic exegete Thomas Söding notes that readings of this ilk savor of both liberal Protestant confessional commitments and the *Zeitgeist* of the 1960s and 1970s. Most nowadays agree that the portrayal of the primitive Church as an "unregulated space" (*rechtsfreier Raum*) is no more than a "projection."[83] Such judgments, in other words, reflect what Ratzinger calls "worldview," a fusion of knowledge and value. As such, they cannot be presumed to occupy the high ground of historical objectivity.

80 See Joseph Ratzinger, "The Question of the Concept of Tradition: A Provisional Response," in *God's Word: Scripture, Tradition, Office*, ed. Peter Hünermann and Thomas Söding, trans. Henry Taylor (San Francisco: Ignatius, 2008), 59, 78. For Ratzinger's awareness that Christian leaders fled Jerusalem before its destruction, see JN 2:28–41.

81 Ratzinger, "Zur Theologie der Ehe," 590.

82 Wolfgang Schrage, *Ethik des Neuen Testaments*, 4th ed., GNT 4 (Göttingen: Vandenhoeck & Ruprecht, 1982), 98. For Eduard Lohse the Matthean "adultery clauses" serve to indicate that one acquires Jesus' new vision of marriage "not through legal prescriptions but from the liberating power of the new creation." *Theologische Ethik des Neuen Testaments*, Theologische Wissenschaft 5, no. 2 (Stuttgart: Kohlhammer, 1988), 68.

83 Thomas Söding, "In favorem fidei: Die Ehe und das Verbot der Scheidung in der Verkündigung Jesu," in *Zwischen Jesu Wort und Norm: Kirchliches Handeln angesichts von Scheidung und Wiederheirat*, ed. Markus Graulich und Martin Seidnader, QD 264 (Freiburg: Herder, 2014), 74.

Even the historical survey on which Ratzinger based his later case for "emergency" communion has not always stood the test of time. The Jesuit patrologist Gilles Pelland would later show how strongly Origen disapproves the divorce practices he describes.[84] Henri Crouzel would later argue that the second marriages Basil permitted after lengthy penance were in fact those of widows.[85] Piet Fransen's interpretation of Trent, which Ratzinger effectively made his own, has likewise come under heavily scrutiny. E. Christian Brugger challenges its two key interpretive positions on the abovementioned canon 7: that it meant to defend papal prerogative rather than define the nature of marriage,[86] and that it meant to avoid dogmatizing anything contrary to Greek divorce praxis.[87] That being said, Brugger does concede that Trent intended to avoid excommunicating the Greeks, despite having defined marital indissolubility in terms incompatible with the Eastern marriage canons. Hence, such emendations to the historical record may not invalidate Ratzinger's general conclusion—namely, that the Church has sometimes been reluctant to condemn marital arrangements found to lie beneath the "threshold of the biblical word."[88] But such discreet silence obviously differs from a positive declaration of emergency dispensations.

Evaluated according to the exigencies of historical reason, Ratzinger's mature teaching fares best. Nothing in the historical record unambiguously contradicts the idea that the Matthean community inserted the unchastity clauses to "sound out the limits and the range of Jesus' word" rather than to overrule it on their own authority. Ratzinger's openness to Bonsirven's position might attract criticism on grounds of historical discontinuity, but even these objections are not insuperable. The mature position tends to be less

---

84 Gilles Pelland, "Le pratique de l'église ancienne concernant les divorcés remarries," in *La pastorale des divorcés remarries*, ed. Congregation for the Doctrine of the Faith (Paris: Bayard, Centurion, Cerf, 1999), 109.

85 Henri Crouzel, "Encore sur divorce et remariage selon Épiphane," VC 38 (1984): 273.

86 Here Brugger points to the canon's emphasis on the truth of what the Church teaches (*docere, docuit*), not just the validity of the authority by which it teaches. E. Christian Brugger, *The Indissolubility of Marriage and the Council of Trent* (Washington, DC: The Catholic University of America Press, 2017), 134–39.

87 Brugger suggests that the complex phrasing of canon 7 is meant to avoid excommunicating the Greeks, not to avoid doctrinally defining positions contrary to their practice. *Indissolubility of Marriage and the Council of Trent*, 139–41.

88 For Brugger's criticism of Ratzinger, see *Indissolubility of Marriage and the Council of Trent*, 142n40.

burdened, moreover, by antinomian "worldview" and tendentious constructions of the historical record.

The second standard of evaluation is that of internal consistency. How faithful is Ratzinger in practice to his hermeneutical theory, especially to the principle that biblical meaning grows "in continuity with its original sense"? I would argue that Ratzinger, measured against this internal standard, becomes increasingly self-consistent. His 1969 essay tolerates the most "discontinuous" reading of various layers of tradition, but appears to be motivated, ironically, by a desire to maintain continuity between the earliest and latest layers, between the "real" Jesus and contemporary Catholic practice. While still under the impression that the Matthean exception clauses directly anticipate the penitential remarriages allowed by the Eastern Churches, Ratzinger moves to relativize their normative value. He portrays them as a kind of regressive tendency in the Matthean community, a ploy to restore Old Testament concessions to "hardness of heart" and thus weaken the "earnestness of the beginning."[89] Though Ratzinger typically insists that the Jesus of the Gospels is none other than the "real" Jesus, here he comes close to accusing the Gospel of Matthew of misrepresenting its protagonist. Ratzinger seems to feel obliged to open distance between the Matthean Jesus and the "real" Jesus in order to close distance between the "real" Jesus and the Catholic Church.

When he examines the patristic record more closely in preparation for his 1972 essay, however, Ratzinger realizes that the Western Church before the Renaissance had not construed the *Unzuchtsklauseln* in a sense opposed to Catholic teaching on marital indissolubility. Having rediscovered the continuity between Matthew's teaching and Catholic teaching, he allows the distance between the Matthean Jesus and the "real" Jesus to close. He instead proposes opening a different kind of distance. The question he considers is whether the Church may readmit to eucharistic communion certain remarried people, doubtlessly exceptional, who find themselves "a bit beneath the threshold of the biblical word"?[90] The issue of communion for the remarried thus turns no longer on the normative content of any particular dominical word—Ratzinger no longer suspects that the πορνεία clause affects the indissolubility of valid marriages—but on the disjunction tolerable between any

---

89 Ratzinger, "Zur Theologie der Ehe," 590.

90 Ratzinger, "Zur Frage nach der Unauflöslichkeit der Ehe!," 53.

biblical norm and pastoral praxis. Since the adjudication of this problem pertains more to moral and sacramental theology, this study will leave it to others. It is worth noting, however, that Ratzinger's 1972 essay implies that not all norms laid down by Jesus are directly "pastoral." A vestigial gap still remains between Gospel norm and community ordinance.

The 2014 version of "Zur Frage nach der Unauflöslichkeit der Ehe" will close even this gap. Without attempting to determine the exact historical exigency to which the unchastity clause responds, the mature Ratzinger characterizes it both as a Matthean addition to Jesus' original words and as a reference to a "case-type" falling outside Jesus' normative intention. As in his 1972 essay, Ratzinger allows no discontinuity between Jesus and Matthew at the level of intended meaning. But he also implies that a certain "preservation of type"—to borrow a phrase of Newman—must govern the Church's way of delimiting the marital bond. A contemporary extension of the Matthean pattern, he suggests, might probe the assumption, still operative in the background of the Church's annulment procedures, that couples understand marital permanence "by nature."[91] With this assumption removed, of course, far fewer unions would be reckoned sacramental marriages. Evidently, the mature Ratzinger, like the Ratzinger of 1969, holds that those formed in a Christian "worldview" may easily overestimate the self-evident contents of natural law. But unlike in 1969, Ratzinger here shows far less antinomian sentiment. He presents the unchastity clause as a "case-type"—that is, a *casus* inviting casuistic analysis—immediately applicable even to pastoral praxis.

In characterizing the πορνεία clause as a "case-type" (*Falltypus*), of course, Ratzinger does more than moderate his youthful antinomianism. He also evokes the whole "typological" approach to Scripture to which he appealed when demonstrating the biblical basis for the Marian dogmas. The Church arrived at this meaning only after meditating for centuries on the Marian passages in canonical context, gradually perceiving that both Mary and the Church were successor types to Israel's immaculate "remnant." It was likewise by reading the Matthean "case-type" in both canonical and changing historical contexts, Ratzinger implies, that the Church developed its theology of sacramental marriage and its corresponding canon law. This does not commit Ratzinger to holding that these concepts lie on the surface of Scripture, accessible to any disinterested historian. It commits him only to holding that the proposed interpretation does not demonstrably contradict

91 Ratzinger, "Zur Frage nach der Unauflöslichkeit der Ehe," 618–19.

historical evidence, and that it stands in some typological continuity with the historical precedent to which it appeals.

But does the Matthean exception clause show this kind of continuous development into canonical legislation? If one takes it as an early warrant for "separation of bed, table, and board," then the historical record abounds with attestations. Paul's directive to wives either to separate or be reconciled to their husbands (1 Cor 7:10–11) comes even earlier. But if one takes the *porneia* clause to refer to a kind of proto-annulment on grounds of incest, then one can agree in only a highly qualified way. Though there is much evidence to suggest that the Levitical Holiness code influenced the canonical definition of incest,[92] there is little to indicate that canonists linked the Holiness code specifically to Matthew 5:32 and 19:9. One might counter that the Western Church did not begin to systematize its marital impediments until after the collapse of the Roman legal order, long after the original concern of the unchastity clauses had faded from memory.[93] This would explain why the πορνεία clauses did not generate a canonical *Wirkungsgeschichte*, even if Matthew originally inserted them with the intention that Bonsirven proposes. Still, one could not say that reception history positively supports Bonsirven's view. Maybe for this reason Ratzinger affirms only a loose historical connection in 1998, affirming only that the impediments to marriage were established "with reference to the *porneia* clauses in Matthew and in Acts 15:20."

Despite such liabilities, Ratzinger's mature interpretation of the *Unzuchtsklauseln* still proves most consistent with his interpretive principles. For interpreting the unchastity clauses as license for remarriage after adultery, as Ratzinger does in 1969, is neither historically continuous with their reception history nor conceptually continuous with the Church's current theology of marriage. Ratzinger's mature position avoids this double continuity. For it takes the normative content of the unchastity clause as a way of proceeding by which the Church discerns the limits of Jesus' command without presuming the authority to separate what God has united.

---

92 For the general indebtedness of Augustine and others to the Jewish definition of a ratified marriage, see Joseph Freisen, *Geschichte des canonischen Eherechts: Bis zum Verfall der Glossenlitteratur* (Paderborn: Ferdinand Schöningh, 1893), 154. For the application of the Levitical Holiness code to questions of permissible consanguinity in the German missions, see Freisen, *Geschichte des canonischen Eherechts*, 157.

93 Hans-Wolfgang Strätz, "Ehe VIII: Rechtshistorisch," *LThK3* 3:476–77.

This procedural "case-type" can naturally accommodate both Bonsirven's position (πορνεία as incest impeding marriage) and Luz's interpretation (πορνεία as adultery justifying physical separation), inasmuch as both circumscribe Jesus' intentions without implying the dissolubility of the marital bond. Bonsirven's position exhibits at least conceptual continuity with later Catholic theology. Luz's position exhibits this as well as a continuous attestation among the fathers—and should probably for this reason be preferred.

Summing up, one can say that Ratzinger, even if he reaches varying assessments, deploys consistent criteria for determining the normative scope of Jesus' words. These are more or less the "tests" that he used to discriminate between revelation and worldview in "Farewell to the Devil?" In the case of the Matthean exception clause, the lack of exegetical consensus seems to deter Ratzinger from dwelling on the second "test"—that is, Jesus' own mentality as the historian can ascertain it. But the other tests do factor in: relationship between testaments, relationship to the faith of the Church, relationship to rational inquiry. Ratzinger also seems to imply that the Church's sacramental theology and marital canons evolved from the exception clauses in much the same way that the Marian doctrines evolved from the Marian pericopes in Luke—namely, by meditative *relecture* in a canonical context. In the end, Ratzinger concludes that the Matthean unchastity clauses do not intend to affirm a real exception to the principle of marital indissolubility. But they do typify an effort to clarify what the Lord means by marriage and divorce, a task that the Church must face anew in every age.

Though this chapter has traced only one question of biblical ethics over the course of Ratzinger's career, it is nevertheless instructive for the "historiography" of Ratzinger. According to a tenacious narrative, the student uprisings of 1968 mark the moment when Ratzinger started his "defection from the progressive camp"[94] of the Catholic Church and entered into personal possession of "an entire and unchanging truth."[95] His shifting summary judgments on the question of communion for the divorce and remarried suggest that the narrative has its explanatory limits. Undeniably, Ratzinger becomes gradually more opposed to the disjunction of biblical teaching and pastoral practice, and thus to changing the Church's sacramental discipline

94 John Allen, *Joseph Ratzinger: The Vatican's Enforcer of Faith* (New York: Continuum, 2000), I was once invited to speak on Ratzinger at a multidisciplinary conference on the year 1968, which was assumed to be the year of his "turn."
95 Gary Wills, "A Tale of Two Cardinals," *New York Review of Books* 48, no. 7 (2001): 26.

for the divorced and remarried. Still, 1968 marks no noticeable watershed for him on this question. In some respects his position grows more "permissive" between 1969 and 1972, moving from a defense of the Church's marriage canons despite the presumed lack of biblical warrant to a plea for pastoral flexibility despite the clarity of the biblical witness. The 2014 conclusion to "Zum Problem der Unauflöslichkeit der Ehe" does not so much end the historically conscious search for greater pastoral flexibility as refocus it. Ratzinger stops pondering whether the Church finds itself in a state of permanent marital emergency and begins interrogating the canonical presumption that spouses in every time and place can be said to know the permanence of marriage "by nature." There are different pastoral conclusions, in short, but not different Ratzingers.

CHAPTER FIVE

The Historicity of the Gospels through the Lens of the Last Supper

Building on the first three chapters, which laid out Ratzinger's theory of Scripture against the background of other influential Catholic approaches, the final two chapters have been attempting to capture Ratzinger in the act of interpreting. How does he identify what Scripture intends to affirm, especially in disputed questions? The previous chapter took up an ethical question—namely, How does Ratzinger determine the perennial normative content of Jesus' teaching on divorce, especially in light of the so-called "unchastity clauses"? The present chapter will address the historical truth of the Gospels, exploring how Ratzinger forms his judgment concerning the historicity of one particular narrative: the Last Supper.

Among the many Gospel narratives whose historicity could be studied, the Last Supper offers several advantages. First, Ratzinger has offered historically informed interpretations of the Last Supper at several points along his lengthy career.[1] The exposition found in the second volume of his *Jesus of Nazareth* trilogy represents, therefore, the fruit of years of meditation. Second, the question of the historicity of the Last Supper intersects with the larger questions of Jesus of Nazareth's prophetic knowledge, messianic consciousness, claims to authority, intention to found a community, and so on.[2] Finally, the Last Supper offers a strenuous proving ground for Ratzinger's

---

1 Besides *Jesus of Nazareth*, see especially "Form and Content in the Eucharistic Celebration," in *Feast of Faith: Approaches to a Theology of the Liturgy*, trans. Graham Harrison (San Francisco: Ignatius, 1986), 33–66; *Many Religions—One Covenant: Israel, the Church, and the World* (San Francisco: Ignatius, 1999), 57–66.

2 Brant Pitre offers a helpful overview in *Jesus and the Last Supper* (Grand Rapids, MI: Eerdmans, 105), 1–28. Joachim Gnilka observes, "One will admittedly only ascribe to Jesus

hermeneutic of faith and reason. Calendrical and verbal discrepancies pose serious challenges to Ratzinger's attempt to "portray the Jesus of the Gospels as the real, 'historical' Jesus in the strict sense of the word,"[3] and thus offer an occasion for clarifying just what Ratzinger means by "real" and "historical."

Since the aim of this chapter is, once again, not only to exposit Ratzinger's thought but to evaluate it against the twofold criterion of doctrinal tradition and historical reason, the following order of argumentation recommends itself. I will begin by providing additional doctrinal and rational criteria relevant to the specific question of Gospel historicity. This means a brief study of the development of *Dei Verbum* 19, as well as a review of Ratzinger's philosophical analysis of historical criticism in "Biblical Interpretation in Conflict." Adding these additional criteria to the four tests, I will then show how Ratzinger uses the whole criteriological ensemble to form his judgment concerning the historicity of the Last Supper. Two aspects of this historical question will receive closer scrutiny: whether the so-called institution narrative goes back to Jesus himself and whether it took place on Passover. Finally, I will stage a brief conversation between Ratzinger and the many critics of his *Jesus of Nazareth* trilogy. Ratzinger remains methodologically consistent, I argue, even though his method is not strictly historical-critical.

ADDITIONAL CRITERIA
RELEVANT TO GOSPEL HISTORICITY

The reason for introducing new criteria in this final chapter is rather simple. Both the magisterial tradition and Ratzinger treat the historicity of the four canonical Gospels as a case apart. This greater circumspection vis-à-vis questions of historicity is already evident in the antimodernist period.

---

the facilitation of a renewed covenant ratification with Israel, which is given through his surrender unto death, if one grants him knowledge of death and a messianic mission-consciousness." *Das Evangelium nach Markus*, 2 vols., EKKNT (Zürich: Benziger und Neukirchener, 1979), II, 2:248. Hansjürgen Verweyen notes the plausibility of Jesus' intention to "found" a cultic meal depends greatly on whether one ascribes to him an "imminent expectation" of a glorious parousia. "Vom Abschiedsmahl Jesu zur Feier der Eucharistie," in *Passion aus Liebe: Das Jesus-Buch des Papstes in der Diskussion*, ed. Jan-Heiner Tück (Ostfildern: Matthias Grünewald, 2011), 168. Peter Fiedler lists the incompatibility of Jesus' imminent expectation with his institution of a perpetual rite as one of the arguments against the historicity of the Last Supper narratives. "Sünde und Vergebung im Christentum," *Internationale Zeitschrift für Theologie Concilium* 10 (1974): 569.

3 JN 1:xxii.

Whereas Leo XIII's *Providentissimus Deus* (1893) seems quite content to admit that Scripture describes the physical world according to "what sensibly appeared,"[4] the Pontifical Biblical Commission a dozen years later warns exegetes against conceding too readily that "those books of Sacred Scripture regarded as historical . . . only have the appearance of history." This may be admitted "only if it is not opposed to the mind and decision of the Church—when it can be proved with solid arguments."[5] Tellingly, the Biblical Commission, even at this early stage of magisterial reflection, identifies its principal criteria for discerning historicity as the "mind of the Church" (*sensus ecclesiae*) and the "solid arguments" of historical reason.

The greater circmspection counseled in historical matters applies a fortiori to the Gospels. For stories about Jesus engage the *sensus ecclesiae* in a particularly direct way. Massgoers celebrate Christ's Transfiguration as if an event; retreatants contemplate the Sermon on the Mount as if Christ's own voice. Celebrating and inwardly reverencing mysteries that one believes unhistorical arguably leads to what Brian McNeil calls "religious schizophrenia."[6] The Gospels thus pose a special challenge for the integration of faith and historical reason. A closer look at *Dei Verbum*'s treatment of the New Testament and at Ratzinger's understanding of what counts as "solid arguments" will bear this out.

Gospel Historicity in *Dei Verbum* 19

The circumstance prompting the fathers of the Second Vatican Council to give special attention to the historical truth of the Gospels, supplementing the sort of general treatment of inerrancy and interpretation offered by *Dei Verbum* 11–12, was the growing influence of Rudolf Bultmann on exegesis. There arose a fear that Catholic exegetes, combining Bultmann's program of "demythologization" with the genre criticism already endorsed by *Divino afflante Spiritu*, would simply reclassify the Gospels as a "myth" on par with the prehistory of Genesis 1–11.[7] The Council thus sought to forestall

---

4 *PD*, no. 18.

5 Response of the Biblical Commission "Concerning Historical Narratives" (June 23, 1905). Dean P. Béchard, ed. *The Scripture Documents: An Anthology of Official Catholic Teachings*, trans. Dean P. Béchard (Collegeville, MN: Liturgical, 2002), 188. For the Latin, see DH 3373.

6 Brian McNeil, CRV, "Meditating on the Jesus of History," *Angelicum* 62, no. 3 (1985), 416.

7 For the long shadow that Bultmann cast over the Council, see Helmut Hoping, "Theologischer Kommentar zur Dogmatischen Konstitution über die göttliche Offenbarung,"

any wholesale dehistoricization of the Gospels by explicitly affirming their historical truth. The struggle for a formulation that would achieve near unanimity among council fathers spanned the length of the Council, eventually issuing in *Dei Verbum* 19. Despite its complex and pendular prehistory, this final statement affirms a degree of historicity for the Gospels greater than is commonly acknowledged among historical critics.[8]

The Council's first attempt to address the historical value of the Gospels, found in *De fontibus revelationis* 20–22, adopts a sharply antimodernist tonality. Paragraph 20 teaches, "The same Holy Mother Church with firm and most constant faith has believed and believes [*credidit et credit*] that the four received Gospels sincerely hand down what Jesus the Son of God, for the eternal salvation of men, really [*reapse*] did and taught while sojourning among men (cf. Act. 1:1)." This positive statement, the only one to survive substantially intact in the final version, then gives way to the condemnation of opposing errors. Paragraph 21 admonishes those who weaken the "genuine, historical, and objective truth [*germana veritas historica et obiectiva*] of the deeds of the life of our Lord Jesus Christ, as these are narrated in the Holy Gospels," especially those who call into doubt the "facts of the infancy of Christ, the signs and miracles of the Redeemer, and his miraculous resurrection from the dead and glorious ascension to the Father, which affect the faith itself." Paragraph 22 goes on to put those on notice who would ascribe Jesus' words not to Jesus himself but to the evangelists or to the primitive Christian community, "at least as regards the very reality signified by the words" (*saltem quoad ipsam rem verbis significatam*). When the Council sent the whole of this draft schema back for reworking, those responsible for revision naturally looked for ways to find a formulation satisfactory to theologians of varying theological orientations. This proved to be a protracted undertaking.[9]

---

in *HThKZVK*, vol. 3 of 5, ed. Peter Hünermann and Bernd Jochen Hilberath (Freiburg: Herder, 2005), 786–787; Juan Luis Caballero and Pablo Edo, "La redacción del capítulo V de *Dei Verbum*," *ScTh* 47 (2015): 187.

8 For this drafting history I am especially indebted to Caballero and Edo, "La redacción del capítulo V de *Dei Verbum*," esp. 186–93; Hoping, "Theologischer Kommentar zur Dogmatischen Konstitution über die göttliche Offenbarung," esp. 720–35, 782–90; Anthony Giambrone, "The Quest for the *Vera et Sincera de Jesu: Dei Verbum* §19 and the Historicity of the Gospels," *Nova et Vetera* 13, no. 1 (2015): 87–123, and conversation with John Finnis.

9 *AS* I, 3:22–23. Hoping notes that rifts over Gospel historicity, inerrancy, and the nature of tradition divided the Preparatory Theological Commission from the start. "Theologischer Kommentar zur Dogmatischen Konstitution über die göttliche Offenbarung," 717.

The publication of *Sancta mater ecclesia: De historica evangeliorum veritate* (April 21, 1964), the fruit of a study of Gospel historicity commissioned by John XXIII and entrusted to the Pontifical Biblical Commission, inaugurated the final phase of this debate. Appearing between the second and third conciliar sessions, the statement both distinguished three stages in the formation of the Gospels—Jesus' words and deeds themselves, their apostolic preaching, and their written expression[10]—and acknowledged that Jesus' words and deeds underwent a strategic reshaping at each successive stage. The Instruction concluded that the evangelists, despite adapting their material with an eye to literary coherence, the situations in the churches, and personal inspirations, in no way compromised the veracity of the Gospels: "For the truth of the story is not at all affected by the fact that the evangelists related the words and deeds of the Lord in a different order, and express his sayings not literally but differently, while preserving (their) sense."[11] In his influential commentary on *Sancta mater ecclesia*, the American Jesuit exegete Joseph Fitzmyer presented the document as a clear rejection of the "fundamentalistic view" embodied in the first draft of *De fontibus revelationis*. Observing that the document appeals to the "truth of the story" (*veritati narrationis*), Fitzmyer ventures the opinion that it may be a category error to speak of the "historical truth" of the Gospels at all: "If one were to ask, 'Well, then, if it is not a question of historical truth, of what kind is it?' the answer would have to be, 'of the Gospel truth.'" Because Fitzmyer never defines "Gospel truth," however, the attempted explanation verges on tautology.[12]

The scholastically inclined minority worried increasingly that the draft schemas mooted in the conciliar aula would only reproduce the ambiguities of *Sancta mater ecclesia*, thus leaving the "truth of the story" open to a Bultmannian gloss. They appealed to Pope Paul VI, who, on October 18, 1965, sent a letter encouraging the Theological Commission to underscore the historical nature of the claims being made on behalf of the Gospels. The Theological Commission eventually agreed to add the clause: "whose

---

10 *SME*, no. 2.

11 *SME*, no. 2.

12 *SME*, no. 2. Joseph A. Fitzmyer, "The Biblical Commission's Instruction on the Historical Truth of the Gospels," *TS* 25 (1964): 395. At this stage in his career, Fitzmyer systematically avoided the word "historicity." For instance, when overseeing the translation of Augustin Bea's *La storicità dei Vangeli*, a commentary on *Sancta Mater Ecclesia*, he retitled it. See Augustin Bea, *The Study of the Synoptic Gospels*, ed. Joseph Fitzmyer (New York: Harper & Row, 1965). I owe this observation to a conference presentation by John Finnis.

historical character [*historicitatem*] the Church unhesitatingly affirms." In
his official *relatio* Joannes van Dodewaard explains that *historicitas*, unlike
the word *historia*, which some theologians use to designate "supramundane
realities apprehended by faith," "is not exposed to ambiguity."[13] They agreed
to close a loophole.

In light of this contrapuntal drafting history, the nature of the claims
made by *Dei Verbum* 19 come into sharper focus. The carefully balanced
paragraph merits citation *in extenso*:

> Holy Mother Church has firmly and with absolute constancy held, and
> continues to hold [*tenuit ac tenet*], that the four Gospels just named, whose
> historical character [*historicitatem*] the Church unhesitatingly asserts,
> faithfully hand on what Jesus Christ, while living among men, really did
> and taught for their eternal salvation until the day He was taken up into
> heaven (see Acts 1:1). Indeed, after the Ascension of the Lord the Apostles
> handed on to their hearers what He had said and done. This they did with
> that clearer understanding [*pleniore intelligentia*] which they enjoyed after
> they had been instructed by the glorious events of Christ's life and taught
> by the light of the Spirit of truth. The sacred authors wrote the four Gospels,
> selecting some things from the many which had been handed on by word
> of mouth or in writing, reducing some of them to a synthesis, explaining
> some things in view of the situation of their churches and preserving the
> form of proclamation but always in such fashion that they told us the
> honest truth about Jesus [*vera et sincera de Iesu*]. For their intention in writ-
> ing was that either from their own memory and recollections, or from the
> witness of those who "themselves from the beginning were eyewitnesses
> and ministers of the Word" we might know "the truth" concerning those
> matters about which we have been instructed (see Luke 1:2–4).[14]

When *Dei Verbum* is viewed against the backdrop of its predecessor documents, the nature of the balance it aims to strike becomes clearer.

On the one hand, it affirms more clearly than *De fontibus revelationis*
the evangelists' freedom to reshape memories and eyewitness testimonies
for kerygmatic ends. Notably, it drops the catalogue of authentic historical
events, such as the much-debated infancy narratives. It further admits that
the evangelists write from a post-Resurrection perspective, having received
through Christ's resurrection and the Spirit's unction a certain *intelligentia*

---

13 *AS* IV, 5:723.
14 *DV*, no. 19.

plenior. It goes on to list several redactional activities compatible with the genuine historicity of the Gospels: at the oral phase, adopting the form of preaching; and at the written phase, selecting, synthesizing, and explaining with an eye to the situation in the churches. Historicity need not mean photorealism.

On the other hand, *Dei Verbum* insists in certain respects even more unmistakably than its forerunners on the historical character of the Gospel portrait of Jesus. It adds the word *historicitas*, whose absence from *Sancta mater ecclesia* Fitzmyer considered so portentous. It also replaces the verbs *credidit et credit* found in *De fontibus revelationis* with the verbs *tenuit ac tenet*. The commission preferred the language of "holding" over the language of "believing," the *relator* Dodewaard informs us, "because in this way it is better expressed that this historicity is held by faith *and reason*, and not faith alone."[15] According to the mind of the Council, then, the historical basis for the Gospel narratives lies patent even to unbiased historical judgment.[16] However much the evangelists may have stylized Jesus' words and deeds, it insists, they did not distort the truth of his historical person.

Ratzinger's Philosophical Challenge to Historical Criticism

Though Ratzinger does not cite *Dei Verbum* 19,[17] he knows its teaching well. Beginning with the third session of Vatican II (mid-1964), he sat on

---

15 *AS* IV, 5:723.

16 Indeed, as a wave of recent research has confirmed, ancient biographers felt that good history required a creative fidelity to their sources not unlike that described by *Dei Verbum*. For the pioneering work in this field, see Richard A. Burridge, *What Are the Gospels?: A Comparison with Greco-Roman Biography*, 2nd ed. (Grand Rapids, MI: Eerdmans, 2004). According to Craig Keener, Burridge's book "swiftly and successfully shifted the consensus of scholarship about the Gospels." Keener, *Christobiography: Memory, History, and the Reliability of the Gospels* (Grand Rapids, MI: Eerdmans, 2019), 13. Richard Bauckham holds that eyewitnesses and evangelists exercised the freedom "to tell a good story effectively and to vary the details around a stable core." *Jesus and the Eyewitnesses: The Gospels as Eyewitness Testimony*, 2nd ed. (Grand Rapids, MI: Eerdmans, 2017), 595. Closely related are approaches such as Helen K. Bond's, which stress the inevitably approximate and constructive nature of human memory: "Deterioration and change in memory begins within hours, as we relive experiences and struggle to make sense of them. Over time, we may retain the gist of what happened, but not the specific details." "Dating the Death of Jesus: Memory and the Religious Imagination," *NTS* 59 (2013): 472.

17 Interestingly, though Ratzinger seems to assume *Dei Verbum*, no. 19, he prefers to reference no. 12. See JN 1:xv, xviii; JN 2:xv. Even Church documents cite it seldom, one recent exception being the Pontifical Biblical Commission's *Inspiration and Truth of Sacred*

the Theological Commission responsible for revising the whole Dogmatic Constitution on Divine Revelation.[18] Moreover, as we shall see, he uses the language and redactional concepts of *Dei Verbum* 19 when interpreting the Last Supper. Indeed, among the major concerns of his treatment of the Last Supper narratives is to show that one can responsibly "hold" to their historicity by both faith and reason.

But the criterion of reason, as we have already seen in chapter 3, proves slippery in application. As Ratzinger meant to show through his analysis of both the Galileo affair and Haag's demythologizing exegesis, scholarly knowledge easily fuses with extradisciplinary value judgments to form a kind of "worldview," which then masquerades as reason pure and simple. In his prefatory remarks to the second volume of *Jesus of Nazareth*, Ratzinger suggests that exegetes, by and large, still have not sufficiently disambiguated historical reason as such from scientistic assumptions:

> One thing is clear to me: in two hundred years of exegetical work, historical-critical exegesis has already yielded its essential fruit. If scholarly exegesis is not to exhaust itself in constantly new hypotheses, becoming theologically irrelevant, it must take a methodological step forward and see itself once again as a theological discipline, without abandoning its historical character. It must learn that the positivistic hermeneutic on which it has been based does not constitute the only valid and definitively evolved rational approach; rather, it constitutes a specific and historically conditioned form of rationality that is both open to correction and completion and in need of it.[19]

Before historical-critical methodology can serve as a solid counterpoint to faith, in other words, its practitioners must bracket the "positivistic" or "functionalist" worldview into which they have been socialized.

Such observations are hardly new. Already at the close of the nineteenth century Ernst Troeltsch, one of the fathers of German sociology, would admit that his version of critical historiography "involves a definite approach to the whole sphere of culture, constitutes a method of representing the past and

---

Scripture (2014), which nevertheless gives much more attention to *Dei Verbum*, no. 11. See *IVSS*, nos. 63–64, 84.

18 Hoping, "Theologische Kommentar zu *Dei Verbum*," 731.

19 JN 2:xiv–xv.

the present, and therefore implies some extraordinary consequences."[20] At the turn of the twentieth century the French Catholic philosopher Maurice Blondel would make analogous observations: "To claim to constitute the science of history without any speculative preoccupation ... is to be influenced by prejudices on the pretext of attaining to an impossible neutrality. . . . In default of an explicit philosophy, a man ordinarily has an unconscious one. And what one takes for simple observations of fact are often simply constructions."[21] Ratzinger, for his part, insists that the contemporary field of university-based historical criticism has largely forgotten what Troeltsch and Blondel knew—namely, that the historical method cannot independently establish but must import its "approach to the whole sphere of culture," its "explicit philosophy," or its "worldview."

But what exactly are the elements of this uncritically assumed hermeneutic? In his essay from the late 1980s, "Biblical Interpretation in Conflict," Ratzinger offers a kind of catalogue of the philosophical axioms that guided mid-twentieth-century exegetes such as Bultmann and Dibelius and, as a result, preoccupied the drafters of Vatican II. Attempting to grasp the tree by the root, Ratzinger observes that what unites this exegetical school is the attempt "to apply the methods of models of natural science in the realm of history."[22] This also seems be what Ratzinger, in the lengthy passage cited above, means by a "positivistic hermeneutic."

Two principal interpretive prejudices follow from unreflective positivism. The first is an aspiration toward univocal results—that is, toward assigning a single scientifically determined meaning to each text: "The historical-critical method is in fact based on the attempt to reach a similar degree of accuracy, and thereby of certainty, in its results as is exhibited in natural science."[23] The second is what Ratzinger calls the "simple transfer of the

20 Ernst Troeltsch, "Historical and Dogmatic Method in Theology," in *Religion in History*, trans. James Luther Adams and Walter F. Bense, Fortress Texts in Modern Theology (Philadelphia: Fortress, 2007), 23.

21 Maurice Blondel, *The Letter on Apologetics and History and Dogma*, ed. and trans. Alexander Dru and Illtyd Trethowan, (Grand Rapids, MI: Eerdmans, 1994), 237.

22 Joseph Ratzinger, "Biblical Interpretation in Conflict," in *God's Word: Scripture—Tradition—Office*, ed. Peter Hünermann and Thomas Söding, trans. Henry Taylor (San Francisco: Ignatius, 2005), 111. For more references to historical-critical exegesis' "orientation toward natural-scientific models," see Ratzinger's introduction to the German edition of *Biblical Interpretation in Conflict* (*JRGS* 9, 2:787).

23 Ratzinger, "Biblical Interpretation in Conflict," 100.

evolutionary model from natural science to the history of the mind."[24] This allows exegetes to classify theological ideas along a spectrum ranging from primitive to sophisticated and to date their emergence accordingly.

Though Ratzinger also accepts that the Christian idea developed, as we have seen, he works from a different developmental paradigm. His germinal model imagines the growth of biblical meaning like the continuous maturation of a single organism, a kind of self-maintenance across change. But the evolutionary model imagines this development more like Darwinian speciation, a process of mutation yielding new forms of life ever more remote from their common ancestor. This same evolutionary paradigm, moreover, supposes a notion of theological "complexity" impatient of historical verification. Exegetes influenced by Bultmann often suppose that Jesus' eschatological pronouncements represent the primitive core, to which the early community first added narrative settings, and then cultic elements, legal concerns, and Hellenistic metaphysics.[25] Consequently, exegetes inevitably find what their evolutionary a priori prepares them to see—namely, a "discontinuity that holds good in all phases of the tradition."[26]

Though Ratzinger is well aware that Bultmann and Dibelius no longer exercise their former influence among exegetes, he nevertheless holds that aspects of their "worldview" have long outlived their particular exegetical positions. There is no doubt some justice in this position. More recent exegetes agree that evolutionary assumptions still tacitly inform the standard dating of New Testament writings and the reconstruction of hypothetical sources such as the Q tradition.[27] John Meier's *A Marginal Jew*, a magisterial

---

24 Ratzinger, "Biblical Interpretation in Conflict," 106.

25 For Ratzinger's fuller exposition of this ramifying dialectic between the simple and complex, see Ratzinger, "Biblical Interpretation in Conflict," 102–11.

26 Ratzinger, "Biblical Interpretation in Conflict," 104.

27 In the mid-1970s John A. T. Robinson was already complaining, "Unexamined assumptions have tended to lead to the unwarranted conclusions that the more the documents tell us about the early church (a) the less they tell us about Jesus and (b) the longer they took to develop." *Redating the New Testament* (London: SCM, 1976), 354. Taking aim at the tendency of scholars to date "higher" Christologies later, Martin Hengel observes, "Fundamentally, more happened christologically in these few years [after the Resurrection] than in the following 700 years of Church history." *Son of God: The Origin of Christology and the History of Jewish–Hellenistic Religion*, trans. John Bowden (Philadelphia: Fortress, 1976), 2. In a paper intended to inform Ratzinger on the current state of Gospel exegesis, Hengel also expressed skepticism regarding the Q hypothesis, which, to his mind, too quickly assumes that Luke developed his material from other texts rather than from eyewitness accounts.

synthesis of historical Jesus research, still lists "embarrassment" and "discontinuity" among the principal criteria for identifying Jesus' historically unassailable words and deeds.[28] These tip the scales of authenticity in favor of those episodes that would have run against the grain either of ancient Jewish or early Christian thinking. Peter Stuhlmacher notes how contemporary exegetes' own sense of what is embarrassing often subtly guides the application of such criteria.[29] One must keep these disciplinary biases in mind, Ratzinger would argue, when exegetes declare the early Church responsible for whatever in Jesus' words and deeds recalls Old Testament traditions, anticipates early Christian life, or departs from the values of the modern academy. It should be obvious that such an oppositional construction of the layers of tradition runs counter to Ratzinger's *analogia fidei*.

When Ratzinger describes his quest, therefore, as "guided by the hermeneutic of faith, but at the same time adopting a responsible attitude toward historical reason,"[30] he signals a complex undertaking. It involves more than simply splitting the difference between the teachings of *Dei Verbum* 19 and the positions of the exegetical guild. It means applying a hermeneutic of mutual refinement, using solid historical arguments to concretize *Dei Verbum*'s notion of "historicity," while allowing the perspective of faith to chasten the pseudo-scientific pretensions of historical criticism. And this faith perspective, he recalls once again, becomes accessible primarily through a transhistorical community: "I have attempted to develop a way of observing and listening to the Jesus of the Gospels that can indeed lead to personal encounter and that, through collective listening with Jesus' disciples' across the ages, can indeed attain sure knowledge of the real historical figure of Jesus."[31] Ratzinger's "collective listening" to the Gospels will thus involve the

---

Gespräch über Jesus: Papst Benedikt XVI. im Dialog mit Martin Hengel, Peter Stuhlmacher und seinen Schülern in Castelgandolfo 2008 (Tübingen: Mohr Siebeck, 2010), 13, 33.

28 John Meier, *The Roots of the Problem and the Person*, vol. 1 of *A Marginal Jew: Rethinking the Historical Jesus* (New York: Doubleday, 1991), 168–74.

29 In a 2008 paper meant to update Ratzinger on the current state of exegesis, Peter Stuhlmacher, after defending the substantial historicity of the Jewish trial scenes, suggested that the countervailing consensus stemmed largely from prevailing ideology: ignorance of the Old Testament among Gospel scholars, discomfort with the image of God as judge, uncritical adoption of the Kantian ideals of moral autonomy, fear of charges of anti-Judaism. *Gespräch über Jesus*, 89–93, 106–8.

30 JN 2:xvii.

31 JN 2:xvii.

"tests" corresponding to the different ages of the People of God. It is to the application of all these criteria to the case of the Last Supper that we now turn.

RATZINGER'S TESTS APPLIED TO THE LAST SUPPER

In "Farewell to the Devil?," it will be remembered, Ratzinger held that the careful discrimination between revealed core and peripheral worldview could take place only on a case-by-case basis. The tests were only "aids to judgment," not algorithmic inputs generating unambiguous results. Something analogous obtains for the discrimination between the historical "ground" of the Gospels and the redactional elements introduced by faith-filled evangelists. Ratzinger uses this language, at any rate, when noting an unresolved ambiguity in the final portrait of Jesus sketched by the formerly leading Catholic exegete Rudolf Schnackenburg. "Schnackenburg shows us the Gospel's image of Christ," observes Ratzinger, "but he considers it to be the product of manifold layers of tradition, through which the 'real' Jesus can only be glimpsed from afar. He writes: 'The historical ground is presupposed but is superseded in the faith-view of the evangelists.' Now, no one doubts that; what remains unclear is how far the 'historical ground' actually extends." [32] In saying that "no one doubts" that the evangelists' faith perspectives rests on a "historical ground," Ratzinger joins those who understand the Gospel stories to be a mixture of historical fact and theological elaboration. At the same time, he hints that he reckons the proportion of historical fact much higher than Schnackenburg.

However high Ratzinger may reckon this proportion of ground to faith-view, he does not thereby commit to a uniform ratio. When responding to criticisms of his treatment (later modified) of the Virgin Birth in *Introduction to Christianity*, Ratzinger notes that "those events that lie after death as the end of 'historical existence' stand in a different relationship to history [*Historie*] than those events through which historical existence is founded [*begründet*]: conception and birth."[33] A higher symbol-to-ground ratio is presumably needed to narrate eschatological events.

---

32 JN I:xiii.

33 Joseph Ratzinger, "Glaube, Geschichte, und Philosophie," *Hochland* 61 (1969): 539.

The *Jesus of Nazareth* trilogy offers a similar take on this variable proportion. On the one hand, it treats the post-Resurrection meal fellowship of
Jesus and his disciples as if significant distance intervened between empirical reality and narrative representation: "What this table fellowship with the
disciples actually looked like is beyond the powers of our imagination."[34]
On the other hand, Ratzinger vigorously defends the substantial historicity
of the infancy narratives, locating their probable origin in "family traditions" preserved by Mary and others.[35] At all events, it is worth noting that
Ratzinger attempts to hold propositions in tension: some Gospel narratives
draw heavily on what Richard H. Bell calls "theological symbol"; and yet the
"Jesus of the Gospels . . . is a historically plausible and convincing figure."[36]
Following his treatment of the Last Supper, we will also see how Ratzinger
thinks he escapes self-contradiction.

But if Ratzinger admits that the evangelists "package" their history with
varying degrees of theological elaboration, how does he decide in practice
where historical core ends and theological wrapping begins? Here, I would
argue, Ratzinger makes an analogous application of the tests featured in the
previous two chapters,[37] combining them with the Gospel-specific criteria
of *Dei Verbum* 19 and a chastened version of historical criticism. To show
how this is so, I will reorganize two threads of Ratzinger's argument for the
substantial historicity of the Last Supper—namely, chronology and narrative
content—according to the four tests. Along the way, we will have occasion

---

34 JN 2:272.

35 JN 3:16.

36 JN 2:xxii. Richard H. Bell, "The Transfiguration: A Case Study in the Relationship
between 'History' and 'Theological Symbol' in the Light of Pope Benedict's Book," in *The
Pope and Jesus of Nazareth: Christ, Scripture, and the Church*, ed. Adrian Pabst and Angus
Paddison (London, SCM, 2009), 160.

37 Tellingly, Franz Mußner characterizes the first volume of *Jesus of Nazareth* as a "book
of relations," embracing not only the relationship between Son and Father, but also the
relationship between selected Gospel themes and the whole New Testament, the Old Testament, and the Fathers of the Church. Franz Mußner, "Ein Buch der Beziehungen," in *Das
Jesus-Buch des Papstes. Die Antwort der Neutestamentler*, ed. Thomas Söding (Freiburg:
Herder, 2007), 87–98. The Protestant exegete Jörg Frey likewise characterizes Ratzinger's
method as historical, canonical, and ecclesial. "Historisch-kanonisch-kirchlich: Zum Jesusbild Joseph Ratzingers," in *Das Jesus-Buch des Papstes: Die Antwort der Neutestamentler*, ed.
Thomas Söding (Freiburg: Herder, 2007), 43–53. Both of these methodological lists closely
map Ratzinger's four "tests."

to note where Ratzinger both echoes *Dei Verbum* and corrects for the bias
of what he calls "positivistic hermeneutics."

Tests Applied to Last Supper Chronology

Among the many impediments to taking the Last Supper narratives as
unvarnished historical transcripts stands an apparent calendrical discrepancy. Put simply, the Synoptics and the Gospel of John seem to place different events on 15 Nisan, the Jewish Passover. The Synoptic Gospels follow
Mark's rather precise dating: "On the first day of Unleavened Bread, when
they sacrificed the Passover lamb, his disciples said to him, 'Where will you
have us go and prepare for you to eat the Passover?'" (Mark 14:12). Since
the Jews typically reckoned days from evening to evening, the first day of
Unleavened Bread (14 Nisan) and the Passover (15 Nisan) occupied the daytime and evening portions of the same Thursday, reckoned from midnight
to midnight.[38] The Synoptic chronology thus has Jesus celebrating his Passover meal Thursday evening, suffering death on the Passover itself (Friday),
resting in the tomb on the Sabbath (Saturday), and rising on the "first day
of the week" (Sunday).

John's Gospel, however, implies a different chronology. It reports that
the Jewish authorities, after hauling Jesus before Pilate, avoided entering the
Praetorium "so that they might not be defiled, but might eat the Passover"
(John 18:28). This motivation seems to indicate that Jesus was crucified not
on Passover but *before* it, presumably at the time the Passover lambs were
being sacrificed that would be eaten that night.[39] On this supposition, Passover (Nisan 15) would have run that year from Friday evening to Saturday
evening, largely coinciding with the Sabbath. If Jesus died on the "Day of
Preparation" (Friday daytime and Nisan 14), as John 19:14 suggests, then
he celebrated his Last Supper the day before Passover (Thursday evening
and Nisan 14), rested in the tomb on Saturday (Passover and Sabbath), and

---

38 Joel Marcus, *Mark: A New Translation with Introduction and Commentary*, 2 vols., AB
27–27A (New York: Doubleday, 2000–2009), 2:944.

39 Raymond E. Brown notes that Jesus was condemned at noon, "the very hour at which
the priests began to slaughter the paschal lambs in the temple area." *The Gospel according to
John*, 2 vols., AB 29–29A (New York: Doubleday, 1966–70), 2:556. Brant Pitre counters, however, that both Second Temple and rabbinic sources place the sacrifice of the lambs later in
the day, between 3 pm and 5 pm. *Jesus and the Last Supper*, 327.

rose on Sunday morning.[40] For present purposes, the most significant difference in the Johannine chronology is its placement of the Last Supper on
the evening before the Jewish Passover Feast. Bound up with the question of
Synoptic and Johannine chronologies, therefore, is the question of whether
Jesus chose the calendrically indicated Passover (Nisan 15) as the setting for
his symbolically charged meal.

In deciding which way of relating Jewish Passover and Last Supper
enjoys greater historical probability, exegetes have until recently felt obliged
to choose among three options: Synoptics, John, or both. The German Protestant exegete Joachim Jeremias made an influential case for the Synoptic
calendar, pointing to references to the Jewish Passover ritual in the Synoptic
accounts of the Last Supper.[41] The American Catholic exegete John Meier
favors the Johannine chronology, according to which Jesus' meal anticipated
the calendrical Passover: "Both the pre-Synoptic and Johannine traditions
are much better explained by a special farewell meal, planned and executed
by Jesus according to his own desires and peculiar circumstances."[42] The
French Catholic exegete Annie Jaubert, for her part, argued that John and
the Synoptics can both be right, since they place the Last Supper on different Passovers. She noted that some Jews, especially those associated with
Qumran, calculated Passover according to the solar calendar, with the result
that the Passover Feast fell on a Tuesday evening. Jesus could thus have celebrated the Passover of the Qumran calendar Tuesday and died Friday, on the
Passover of the lunar Temple calendar.[43] Most recent interpreters, including
Ratzinger himself, have felt compelled to choose among these three options.

Still, it is worth noting that a fourth proposal, worthy of serious consideration, has entered the field since the publication of the second volume of
Ratzinger's *Jesus of Nazareth*. Brant Pitre's *Jesus and the Last Supper* (2015)
argues that John's Gospel, rightly interpreted, also places the Last Supper

---

40 JN 2:108–9.

41 Joachim Jeremias, *Die Abendmahlsworte Jesu*, 4th ed. (Göttingen: Vandenhoeck &
Ruprecht, 1967).

42 Meier, *Marginal Jew*, 1:399.

43 Annie Jaubert, "La Date de la dernière Cène," *RHR* 146 (1954): 140–73. There exist
numerous variations on this argument. Colin J. Humphreys proposes that the Synoptics
make use of Israel's pre-exilic way of reckoning the Passover, surviving only in pockets,
according to which Passover would fall on Wednesday. *The Mystery of the Last Supper:
Reconstructing the Final Days of Jesus* (Cambridge: Cambridge University Press, 2011),
193–94.

on the Jewish Passover.[44] According to Pitre, exegetes have largely failed to notice that the word Passover (πάσχα) has four biblically attested meanings: (1) the Passover lamb, sacrificed on 14 Nisan in the afternoon; (2) the Passover meal, eaten on 15 Nisan in the evening; (3) the Passover Peace Offering, offered and eaten daily during 15–21 Nisan; and (4) Passover week, spanning 15–21 Nisan.[45] With the full semantic range of πάσχα taken into account, Pitre claims, nothing in John's narrative proves incompatible with placing both the Last Supper and Passion on 15 Nisan, the same Passover Feast identified in the Synoptics. For example, when Jewish leaders refuse to enter the Praetorium so that, by avoiding defilement, they "might eat the Passover" (φάγωσιν τὸ πάσχα) (John 18:28), "Passover" may here bear the third meaning, the Passover Peace Offering performed daily during 16–21 Nisan.[46] Again, when John depicts Pilate condemning Jesus on the "Preparation of the Passover" (παρασκευὴ τοῦ πάσχα) (John 19:14), "Passover" may here bear the fourth meaning, such that the whole phrase means simply "Friday of Passover week."[47] On this hypothesis, the calendrical discrepancy would turn out to be only apparent.

Because this chapter aims to study Ratzinger's way of estimating the historical value of the Gospels, it will consider Pitre's arguments only tangentially, focusing instead on how Ratzinger evaluates the Synoptic, Johannine, and two-calendar solutions. In the end, Ratzinger accepts that the Gospel chronologies are irreconcilable and deems John's timeline more historically plausible, explaining the Synoptic chronology as a theological symbol. The four "tests," along with a certain tendency to optimize for symbolic realism, guide him to this conclusion. By reorganizing the historical reasoning of *Jesus of Nazareth* according to the four tests, I hope to make these points clear.

The first test, the relationship between Old and New Testament, proves largely inconclusive with regard to the Synoptic, Johannine, and

---

44 Pitre, *Jesus and the Last Supper*, 251–373.

45 Pitre, *Jesus and the Last Supper*, 333.

46 Pitre, *Jesus and the Last Supper*, 352–56.

47 Pitre, *Jesus and the Last Supper*, 357–60. Pitre notes that because Friday was the weekly day of preparation for the Sabbath, παρασκευὴ had come to mean simply "Friday" by the first century AD. Though Pitre furnishes many examples of παρασκευὴ in isolation meaning just "Friday," he provides no ancient parallels for the whole phrase παρασκευὴ τοῦ πάσχα meaning "Friday of Passover Week."

two-calendar solutions. As we saw in previous chapters, this criterion pre-disposes Ratzinger toward solutions that exhibit an analogical pattern across Testaments, especially one of surprising intensification. The waxing profile of the demonic and the increasing strictness regarding divorce in the New Testament both indicated that Scripture properly intends to affirm these ideas. When presuming the Johannine chronology to be historical, Ratzinger finds a similar pattern of continuity-across-discontinuity.[48] For then Jesus would have celebrated something like a Passover meal "off-calendar," depart-ing from legal prescriptions. Here lies discontinuity.[49] At the same time, Jesus would have organized his meal in the atmosphere of the Passover festival, died as the Passover lambs were being slaughtered, and experienced divine rescue afterward. Here lies a typological continuity. The whole conjunction of events suggests that Jesus intended to celebrate a "new" and definitive Passover: "Even though the meal that Jesus shared with the Twelve was not a Passover meal according to the ritual prescriptions of Judaism, neverthe-less, in retrospect, the inner connection of the whole event with Jesus' death and Resurrection stood out clearly. It was Jesus' Passover . . . . The old was not abolished; it was simply brought to its full meaning."[50] A similar pat-tern of continuity-in-discontinuity would also, of course, characterize Jesus' actions on the supposition of the Synoptic chronology or Jaubert's recon-struction. For if Jesus celebrated his Last Supper on any ritually prescribed Passover, according to either solar or lunar calendar, he would still have added elements of his own to the Passover script.[51] At best, one can say that the criterion of the *analogia fidei* does not weigh against the historicity of the Johannine narrative more than that of any other.

48 For Ratzinger's debt to Meier, see JN 2:113–14; Meier, *Marginal Jew*, 1:429–30.

49 Rabbi Walter Homolka argues that Jesus behaves at the Last Supper just like a pious Jew celebrating a Seder. "Jesu Letztes Abendmahl," in *Der Jesus Buch des Papstes: Passion, Tod, und Auferstehung im Disput*, ed. Herman Häring (Berlin: LIT, 2011), 199. As Josef Wohlmuth notes, however, the Seder as we know it today may postdate the Last Supper, making its celebration an unlikely intention for Jesus. "Die Sicht auf Judentum in Zweiten Band des Jesusbuches," in *Der Jesus des Papstes: Passion, Tod, Auferstehung im Disput*, ed. Herman Häring (Berlin: LIT, 2011), 187.

50 JN 2:113–14.

51 Even when he supposed a closer relation between Last Supper and Jewish Passover, Ratz-inger observed, "There is nothing fortuitous in this interplay of old and new. It is the exact and necessary expression of the new existing situation in salvation history. Jesus prays his new prayer within the Jewish liturgy." "Form and Content in the Eucharistic Celebration," 41.

The second test, that of compatibility with the broader New Testament image of Christ, proves a bit more discriminating. For it weighs against Jaubert's solution and begins to suggest a theological motive for the Synoptic dating. Jaubert's hypothesis, as we have seen, supposes that Jesus followed a calendar linked principally to the Qumran and Essene communities, who shunned the calendar of the Temple aristocracy out of contempt for the Herodian Temple.[52] Yet elsewhere in the Gospels, Ratzinger notes, Jesus "still followed the Jewish festal calendar, as is evident from John's Gospel in particular."[53] Ratzinger finds it unlikely, in short, that Jesus, in departing from the lunar Temple calendar, would have acted so unlike himself, or at least so unlike his broader New Testament portrait.

Applying this same test to John and the Synoptics does not so much positively favor the historicity of the Johannine account as redress the long-standing prejudice against it. Ratzinger notes that the exegetes have typically presumed John's presentation to be a "theological chronology."[54] John, they reason, artfully develops a paschal-lamb Christology throughout the whole course of his Gospel, introducing Christ from the outset as the "Lamb of God" (John 1:29, 36) and comparing the unbroken bones of his corpse to a paschal lamb properly slaughtered (John 19:36; cf. Ex 12:46). It would be entirely in keeping with John's favored typologies, therefore, to redate Jesus' Passion to the Day of Preparation, to the hour of the slaughter of the lambs.

As Ratzinger sees things, however, theological motivations could just as easily explain why Mark sets the Last Supper on the "first day of the Feast of Unleavened Bread, when they sacrificed the Passover lamb" (Mark 14:12a; cf. Mark 14:1). The Christological interpretation of this succession of feasts begins quite early in the New Testament tradition. Paul can, without any further explanation, exhort the Corinthian community in the following terms: "Cleanse out the old leaven that you may be new dough, as you really are unleavened. For Christ, our Paschal Lamb, has been sacrificed" (1 Cor 5:7). Building on the commentary of John Meier,[55] Ratzinger explains its

---

52 JN 2:33.

53 JN 2:111.

54 JN 2:108.

55 Referring to 1 Corinthians 5:7, Meier remarks, "[Paul] apparently can presuppose that his Gentile converts understand the metaphor without any explanation. This implies that as early as the mid-fifties of the 1st century the idea of Christ's death as a Passover sacrifice was common Christian tradition." *Marginal Jew*, 1:429n108.

significance, "The first day of Unleavened Bread and the Passover follow in rapid succession, but the older ritual understanding is transformed into a Christological and existential interpretation. Unleavened bread must now refer to Christians themselves, who are freed from sin by the addition of yeast. But the sacrificial lamb is Christ."[56] In other words, one could easily construe the Synoptics' careful setting of the Last Supper at the transition from Unleavened Bread to Passover as an attempt to bring out the paschal significance of the Eucharist. This would be no more fanciful than construing the Johannine dating as an attempt to bring out the paschal significance of the Passion. Indeed, the fact that paschal-lamb Christology enjoys such universal diffusion throughout the New Testament (see also 1 Pet 1:19; Rev 5:6) suggests that there may be a striking historical basis for it, such as the coincidence of Jesus' Passion with the slaughter of the lambs. The second test, then, weighs against Jaubert's two-calendar solution, inasmuch as it supposes that Jesus and his disciples, when planning the Last Supper, adhered to a calendar they otherwise ignored in the New Testament. It still does not put much distance between Johannine and Synoptic historicity.

The third "test," that of reception into the faith of the Church, yields more robust results, tending to exclude Jaubert's thesis and indirectly supporting Johannine historicity. Jaubert's thesis, it will be remembered, places the Last Supper on a Tuesday evening. Knowing that this represents something of a novelty, she attempts to show that the third-century *Didascalia Apostolorum* preserves an authentic memory of this chronology.[57] Ratzinger counters, however, that a less ambiguous and more enduring tradition, evident already in the second century, places the Last Supper on Thursday.[58] Though Ratzinger does not himself provide references, he doubtlessly has in mind the same passages that Jaubert herself cites in the course of anticipating objections. According to a fragment of Clement of Alexandria known as Περὶ τοῦ πάσχα, to name just one such example, Jesus washed his disciples' feet on

---

56 JN 2:114–15.

57 Jaubert provides a translation of the relevant excerpts of *Didascalia Apostolorum* (cap. 21, x–xx) in "Date de la Dernière Cène," 142–44. Joachim Jeremias argues that Jaubert's citations placing the Last Supper earlier in the week derive from the weekly Wednesday and Friday fast, which Christians began to associate retrospectively with Jesus' arrest and execution. Jeremias, *Abendmahlsworte Jesu*, 19.

58 JN 2:111. Ratzinger mentions sources starting in the second century but does not provide references. Jaubert, however, provides a list of such references in the course of denying their probative force. "Date de la Dernière Cène," 149–58.

the day of "the consecration of the unleavened bread and the preparation of the feast" (ὁ ἁγιασμὸς τῶν ἀζύμων καὶ ἡ προετοιμασία τῆς ἑορτῆς) and suffered "the next day" (τῇ ἐπιούσῃ).[59] Here Clement allows but a single day's time between meal and death. Other late second-century sources, such as Irenaeus' *Against Heresies*, corroborate the same one-day interval.[60] Since the early Church universally reckoned Friday the day of Christ's death, one could say that the Western Christian liturgy implicitly "received" this one-day interval when, in the fourth century, it began celebrating the annual commemoration of the Lord's Supper on a Thursday.[61] In the final analysis, Ratzinger finds it unlikely that so much of the Church misremembered these events from the beginning.

In appealing to the Church's corporate memory against Jaubert's hypothesis, Ratzinger arrives at the same conclusion as Meier. But he does so by a somewhat different path. Meier finds Jaubert's hypothesis implausible largely by the criterion of multiple attestation. Jaubert disregards the one calendrical fact about which Mark and John agree: "the Last Supper was on Thursday evening and Jesus died on the next day, Friday."[62] Meier's historical reasoning no doubt made an impression on Ratzinger, who as recently as 2007 had shown much more sympathy for Jaubert's hypothesis.[63] But *Jesus of Nazareth* places the accent elsewhere. It faults Jaubert's proposal not so much for

59 Clement of Alexandria, *Stromata Buch VII und VIII, Excerpta ex Theodoto, Eclogae Propheticae, Quis Dives Salvetur, Fragmente*, ed. Otto Stählin and Ludwig Früchtel, 2nd ed., GCS 17 (Berlin: Akademie, 1970), 216–17.

60 In *Against Heresies* II, 22, 3, Irenaeus of Lyons reports that Jesus went up from Bethany to Jerusalem, "eating the Pasch and suffering the following day" (*manducans pascha et sequenti die passus*). *Contra les hérésies: Livre II*, 2 vols., SC 293–94 (Paris: Cerf, 1982), 2:218.

61 The Third Council of Carthage (397 AD) witnesses indirectly to the practice of celebrating the annual *coena domini* on Thursday when it dispenses participating priests from fasting that day, presumably in view of the fasting required on Good Friday and Holy Saturday. See *Mansi* 3:885.

62 Meier, *Marginal Jew*, 1:429n109. In the same footnote, Meier also draws a "rough analogy from textual criticism": just as textual criticism sees accepting a "hypothetical reconstruction that is witnessed in none of the manuscripts or versions" as a last resort, so also to create "a scenario for the date of Jesus' death that is supported by none of the Gospel traditions and to prefer it over Gospel traditions that are by no means impossible brings us close once again to writing a novel."

63 In at least one Holy Thursday homily, Ratzinger presented Jesus' celebration of the Passover according to the Qumran calendar as a "plausible hypothesis." "Homily at the Mass of the Lord's Supper," n.p., cited April 5, 2007, http://www.vatican.va/content/benedict-xvi/en/homilies/2007/documents/hf_ben-xvi_hom_20070405_coena-domini.html.

failing to retain what is multiply attested as for failing to explain the Last Supper's patristic and liturgical trajectory. Ratzinger's tendency to reason from the "world in front of the text" back to proportionate historical cause arguably represents one of the distinctives of his exegetical style.

Besides casting doubt upon Jaubert's solution, considerations related to the Last Supper's ecclesial reception history also appear indirectly to dispose Ratzinger toward Johannine historicity. I say "indirectly" because the strength of the historical case for either Synoptic or Johannine chronology depends in part on how plausibly it explains the origin of the alternative: the more compelling the theological rationale for Mark's chronology, the easier the historical case for John's chronology, and vice versa. Since both Johannine and Markan sequences can claim a plausible theological symbolism—Jesus as the paschal lamb for John, Jesus as the true Passover for Mark—the criterion ostensibly decides little.[64] But Ratzinger's conviction that Scripture's ecclesial *Wirkungsgeschichte* illuminates rather than occludes the "real" Jesus leads him to discern in Mark an additional rationale seldom considered by historical critics. After observing that all the Gospels present Jesus' dying and rising as the "Passover that endures," Ratzinger suggests that Mark's chronology supposes a kind of sacramental transference between Paschal Mystery and Last Supper: "On this basis, one can understand how it was that very early on, Jesus' Last Supper—which includes not only a prophecy, but *a real anticipation of the Cross and Resurrection in the eucharistic gifts*— was regarded as a Passover: as *his* Passover."[65] The key phrase here is "real anticipation." In a passage cited earlier, Ratzinger also speaks of an "inner connection" between the events of Thursday evening and those of Friday through Sunday. In both cases Ratzinger implies that Mark already realized inchoately what the Council of Trent would teach explicitly fifteen hundred years later: namely, that the Mass "represents"—or makes really present, whether prospectively or retrospectively—Christ's sacrificial death-unto-resurrection.[66] Mark may have felt authorized to treat the received histori-

---

64 Xavier Léon-Dufour, for instance, understands the Passover setting of the Last Supper to be an artful theological construction, whose point is the "transposition from rites to person." *Sharing the Eucharistic Bread: The Witness of the New Testament*, trans. Matthew J. O'Connell (New York: Paulist, 1987), 193.

65 JN 2:115. Italics mine.

66 Trent teaches that Jesus offered his body and blood under the species of bread and wine at the Last Supper "in order to leave to his beloved Spouse the Church a visible sacrifice . . .

cal chronology flexibly because from "very early on" he knew that the Last Supper, like the Mass in Tridentine teaching, transcends its spatio-temporal location, coinciding mysteriously with Jesus' death-unto-resurrection.[67]

By allowing later eucharistic teaching to guide his thinking on the theology of Mark's chronology, Ratzinger finds indirect grounds for favoring Johannine historicity. He can more easily understand, it seems, why Mark would feel compelled to tamper with the time signatures than why John would. For if Mark believed that the Last Supper somehow formed a single event with what followed later in time—that is, with the death-unto-Resurrection bracketing Passover—he could hardly convey such a mysterious unity by a strictly historical narration. Only by symbolically restructuring historical source material could Mark effectively express certain *vera et sincera de Jesu*. On the supposition that Markan chronology is symbolically structured, moreover, the calendrical symbol would enjoy a greater share of metaphysical realism. On the hypothesis that John shifts dates to portray Jesus as sacrificed paschal lamb, the Jesus-lamb connection would lie principally in the mind of the evangelist. It is John who connects the typological dots. On the hypothesis that Mark shifts dates to show the Last Supper as part of a single Paschal Mystery, the connection between Last Supper and death-unto-resurrection would have a deeper *fundamentum in re*, or basis in reality. The evangelist would simply be highlighting dots that God himself connected, as it were, in establishing the Mass as a real *repraesentatio* of Jesus' Cross and Resurrection. By attending to the test of ecclesial reception, Ratzinger begins to find reasons to favor Markan symbolism and, by implication, Johannine historicity.

---

by which the bloody <sacrifice> that he was once for all to accomplish on the Cross would be re-presented [*repraesentaretur*]." DH 1740.

67 Ratzinger's appeal to this "inner connection" or "real anticipation" perhaps reveals the influence of the "commemorative representation" theory shared broadly by figures such as Maurice de la Taille, Odo Casel, and Charles Journet, all of whom present the Eucharist as a "sacramental sacrifice in which the cross of Christ is 'represented.'" Frederick Bauerschmidt, "The Eucharist," in *The Oxford Handbook of Catholic Theology*, ed. Lewis Ayres and Medi Ann Volpe (Oxford: Oxford University Press, 2019), 286–87. Ratzinger's mentor Gottlieb Söhngen also promoted such a view. Colman E . O'Neill, "The Mysteries of Christ and the Sacraments," *The Thomist* 25, no. 1 (January 1962): 1–2. Accoring to O'Neill, Thomists sometimes distinguish between applying the effects of the cross and representing the cross *qua* historical event (41–42), but this would seem to affect Ratzinger's point little. In either case the reality of the Paschal Mystery "touches" other moments to which it is not connected by strictly historical lines of influence.

The fourth of the tests, that of scholarly knowledge, only further inclines Ratzinger toward the historicity of Johannine chronology. Here we do well to recall that, for Ratzinger, applying this test always requires discerning between solid findings and extradisciplinary "worldview." In the case of history, this means distinguishing especially between historical reason as such and the evolutionary schemata that often invisibly guide historical criticism. Applying this principle of discrimination to Meier's arguments, Ratzinger again finds himself persuaded that the balance of probability favors the Johannine argument. The argument adduced by Meier that Ratzinger seems to find particularly impressive is the unlikelihood that the Temple authorities could have chosen the Passover itself as the day for undertaking the whole series of actions culminating in Jesus' execution.[68] Far from marginalizing the cultic, this argument seems to take the liturgical reverence of Jesus' Jewish contemporaries very seriously.[69] Indeed, some critics have chided Ratzinger for following Meier in "making too much of *a priori* reasoning in the study of history."[70] But this argument appears to have merit in Ratzinger's eyes precisely because it owes so little to evolutionary presuppositions.

Still, it is worth noting that Ratzinger does not find all Meier's arguments for Johannine historicity so unencumbered. For example, when Meier moves to classify Mark's Passover references (14:1a, 12–16) as later redactional additions, Ratzinger discounts this effort as "artificial."[71] Though Ratzinger does not explain his reasons for this negative judgment, broader context gives us some basis for responsible conjecture. One possible reason has already

68 JN 2:106–8.

69 For the importance of liturgy to Ratzinger's anthropology, see Christopher Ruddy, "*Deus adorans, Homo adorans*: Joseph Ratzinger's Liturgical Christology and Anthropology," in *The Center Is Jesus Christ Himself: Essays on Revelation, Salvation & Evangelization in Honor of Robert P. Imbelli*, ed. Andrew Meszaros (Washington, DC: The Catholic University of American Press, 2021), 173–88.

70 John P. Joy, "Ratzinger and Aquinas on the Dating of the Last Supper: In Defense of the Synoptic Chronology," *NBf* (2012): 330. On the same page, Joy points to the fact, recounted by Ratzinger himself, that Jewish Zealots slaughtered pilgrims on the Temple on 14 Nisan 70 AD. The fact that Jews were willing to defile the Temple for political reasons suggests that they may have been willing to disregard some of the finer points of Passover observance. To this point, however, it might be objected that Zealots are more plausible candidates for sacrilege against the Temple than the Temple authorities themselves. Pitre argues that none of the happenings mentioned in the Synoptics is strictly prohibited on Passover, adding that later rabbinic sources even required certain criminals to be held for punishment until major feast days. *Jesus and the Last Supper*, 295–304.

71 JN 2:112–13.

been explored during the discussion of the third test. Ratzinger may think Meier's proposal "artificial" because it attributes too much "artifice" to Mark, portraying the redactional process as an imposition of theological meaning on events rather than an explication of meaning from events. Another possibility is that Ratzinger detects in Meier's reasoning the kind of evolutionary *parti pris* criticized in "Biblical Interpretation in Conflict." Meier is arguably giving the sort of explanation that, according to Ratzinger, guild exegetes have been conditioned to find satisfying: he carves the text into developmental layers, postdating those elements that he had previously traced back to a cultic theologoumenon—the Pauline trope of Christ as paschal lamb. Now Ratzinger, as we saw in chapter 4's treatment of the Matthean exception clause, has no principled objection to classifying certain passages as "redactional." But he does seem to resist the assumption that a genetic account "explains" the text, or that a later date can be presumed for cultic theologoumena.

Despite the need to fill Ratzinger's occasionally elliptical logic, a few results emerge clearly from the foregoing investigation. Ratzinger continues to employ all four tests, even when he does not expressly enumerate them. But when treating Gospel historicity, he applies the tests analogously, adding his own philosophical criticism of critical historiography and the precisions of *Dei Verbum* 19. The Dogmatic Constitution's insistence that evangelists always redacted their material "in such fashion that they told us the honest truth about Jesus" becomes a kind of optimizing criterion. If historical evidence obliges him to treat one or another chronology as a theological symbol, Ratzinger opts for the more "realistic" symbolic chronology, the one having the greater *fundamentum in re*. This gives us grounds for speculating that Ratzinger would have favored Pitre's "Passover solution" had he been aware of it. For if Pitre is right, then the Last Supper not only coincided metaphysically with Passover-spanning events (Cross and Resurrection), but coincided calendrically with the Jewish Passover itself. The alignment of metaphysical and historical perspectives gives maximal realism. Whatever the case may be, it is worth noting that Ratzinger does not feel obliged to reconcile every detail on the historical plane. Nor does he think that conceding the theological nature of Synoptic Passion chronology undermines his position that the Gospels give us "the real, 'historical' Jesus in the strict sense of the word."[72]

---

72 JN 1:xxii.

Institution Narrative

Analogous to the critical issues raised by the chronology of the Last Supper are the questions raised by its narrative content. Just as a comparison of John and the Synoptics revealed calendrical disagreement, so a comparison of the various accounts of the Lord's Supper reveals verbal disagreement. Because the Pauline (1 Cor 11:23–25) and Lukan (Luke 22:15–20) versions of the institution narrative track each other closely, whereas Matthew (Matt 26:26–29) tends to follow Mark's phrasing (Mark 14:22–25), one can get a good sense of the critical problems confronting the exegete simply by comparing the Pauline and Markan accounts.

In what is generally agreed to be the earliest complete document containing a Last Supper narrative, 1 Corinthians (ca. AD 55) informs the Corinthian community about the origins of their common worship:

> For I received from the Lord what I also handed on to you, that the Lord Jesus, on the night he was handed over, took bread, and, after he had given thanks, broke it and said, "This is my body that is for you. Do this in remembrance of me." In the same way also the cup, after supper, saying, "This cup is the new covenant in my blood. Do this, as often as you drink it, in remembrance of me" (1 Cor 11:23–25).

Mark's version, by contrast, unfolds in a continuous narrative, reading as follows:

> While they were eating, he took bread, said the blessing, broke it, and gave it to them, and said, "Take it; this is my body." Then he took a cup, gave thanks, and gave it to them, and they all drank from it. He said to them, "This is my blood of the covenant, which will be shed for many. Amen, I say to you, I shall not drink again the fruit of the vine until the day when I drink it new in the kingdom of God" (Mark 14:22–25).

The two accounts agree that Jesus spoke solemn words over bread and a cup, identifying them with his body and blood.

But the two accounts also disagree in several respects. In Paul's letter Jesus speaks of his body as given "for you" (ὑπὲρ ὑμῶν), whereas in Mark's gospel he speaks of his blood being shed "for many" (ὑπὲρ πολλῶν). Again, the Pauline Jesus speaks of the "new covenant in my blood" (ἡ καινὴ διαθήκη ... ἐν τῷ ἐμῷ αἵματι), whereas the Markan Jesus speaks of "my blood of the covenant" (τὸ αἷμα μου τῆς διαθήκης). Perhaps most significantly, Mark does not contain the Pauline injunction to repeat, "Do this, as often as you drink it, in remembrance of me" (1 Cor 11:25; cf. v. 24).[73] The Gospels disagree to some extent over the words that most clearly express expiatory self-understanding and founding intention.

These discrepancies have led scholars to question just how much any of the narratives matches the actual words and deeds of Jesus of Nazareth the night before he suffered.[74] Some consider the whole episode an invention of the early Christian community, who attributed it to Jesus as a way of justifying a form of worship they initially adopted for other reasons,[75] perhaps in imitation of Jesus' table fellowship with sinners.[76] Others doubt not that Jesus ate with his disciples shortly before his death, but that he himself used the opportunity to express the expiatory finality of his execution or to institute a new form of worship.[77] Ratzinger himself concludes that the meal, the expiatory theology, and the founding intent all go back to Jesus himself. At the same time, he allows that the evangelists lightly redacted Jesus' words to bring out their full theological significance. Ratzinger arrives at these results, once again, by an analogous application of the tests.

---

73 Verweyen points to the absence of Jesus' instituting command in Matthew and Mark as the "hardest problem for a rapprochement between ecclesial and historical-critical exegesis." "Vom Abschiedsmahl Jesu zur Feier der Eucharistie," 172.

74 For a recent and thorough overview of scholarly opinion against the historicity of the Last Supper, see Pitre, *Jesus and the Last Supper*, 5–27.

75 See Rudolf Bultmann, *Theologie des Neuen Testaments*, 9th ed. (Tübingen: J.C.B. Mohr 1984), 150; Paul Bradshaw, *Reconstructing Early Christian Worship* (London: SPCK, 2009), 18; David N. Power, "Sacraments in General," in *Systematic Theology: Roman Catholic Perspectives*, 2nd ed., ed. Francis Schüssler Fiorenza and John P. Galvin (Minneapolis: Fortress, 2011), 464; Jens Schröter, *Das Abendmahl: Frühchristliche Deutungen und Impulse für die Gegenwart* (SBS 210; Stuttgart: Katholisches Bibelwerk, 2006), 132–33.

76 Ansgar Wucherpfennig, "Wie hat Jesus Eucharistie gewollt? Neutestamentlichen Gedanken zur eucharistischen Gastfreundschaft," *StZ* 143 (2018): 856–57.

77 Fiedler, "Sünde und Vergebung," 568–71. Anton Vögtle thinks Jesus foresaw his death and attributed salvific significance to it, but leaves open "whether the whole result [*Gesamtbefund*], above all the salvific interpretation of death found in the Last Supper tradition, is more convincingly explained as originating from Jesus or after Easter." "Todesankündigungen und Todesverständnis Jesu," in *Der Tod Jesu: Deutungen im Neuen Testament*, ed. Karl Kertelge, QD 74 (Freiburg: Herder, 1976), 113. Heinz Schürmann grounds the Last Supper narrative not in Christ's *ipsissima verba* but in his *ipsissima facta*, his symbolic action at the Last Supper and elsewhere. *Jesu ureigener Tod: Exegetische Besinnungen und Ausblick* (Freiburg: Herder, 1975), 16–65. David Power deems the expiatory interpretation of the Eucharist a corruption that began to take hold in the fourth century. *The Eucharistic Mystery: Revitalizing the Tradition* (New York: Crossroad, 1992), 321–22.

With respect to the historicity of the Last Supper narratives, the criterion of relationship between Old and New Testaments plays a significant role in Ratzinger's deliberations. Here again it leaves him unsympathetic to any interpretation that, following the ancient pattern of Marcion, starkly opposes Jesus' image of God to that of the Old Testament. Ratzinger shows little sympathy, for instance, with Peter Fiedler's attempt to chalk the Last Supper narrative up to the re-judaizing tendencies of the early Christian community.[78] Fiedler reasons in the following way. The Gospel accounts of Jesus' preaching, their most reliable historical material, announce a God of unconditional forgiveness. But the Last Supper narratives point instead to a God who requires bloody expiation. The latter must therefore represent a theological regression on the part of the early Church.[79]

Ratzinger finds that Fiedler's construction of Jesus' authentic mission overlooks Old Testament continuities of both content and form. For the content of Jesus' preaching reveals not only promises of forgiveness but self-comparison to Isaiah. He too preaches in order that people "'may look and see but not perceive, and hear and listen but not understand, in order that they may not be converted and be forgiven'" (Mark 4:12; Isa 6:9). Consequently, even those historical strata supposedly closest in origin to Jesus liken him to the Old Testament's most developed type of expiatory suffering.[80] Formally, Fiedler's conclusion fails to consider Jesus' ministry from the "perspective of the whole structure of the biblical image of God and salvation history," thus overlooking the possibility of development in Jesus' attitude. Just as God treats humanity's hardness of heart in the Old Testament with fresh initiatives—responding to Babel with Abraham, and to Israel's rebellious desire for a king with the Davidic monarchy—so also a similar change of strategy on Jesus' part is, for Ratzinger, "entirely plausible."[81] Even so, the evidence does not support a sharp break. Where Fiedler finds stark opposition between Jesus' image of God on the one hand, and the Old Testament and Last Supper images on the other, Ratzinger sees only differences of accent.

---

78 JN 2:119–20.

79 Fiedler, "Sünde und Vergebung," 569.

80 JN 2:123.

81 JN 2:120–21. Ratzinger here adapts Erik Peterson's argument that God's "Plan A" was to renew Israel by placing it at the head of the nations. See Erik Peterson, "Die Kirche," in *Ausgewählte Schriften*, ed. Barbara Nichtweiß, vol. 1 of *Theologische Traktate* (Würzburg: Echter, 1994), 245–57.

The criterion of intertestamental analogy also factors subtly into Ratzinger's arguments in favor of the substantial historicity of what Germans call the *Deuteworte*, or the "interpretive words" spoken by Jesus over the bread and cup. Aware that many exegetes appeal to the effervescent creativity of the early community to explain discrepancies in the *Deuteworte*, Ratzinger offers an alternative explanation rooted in the *analogia fidei*: "We take it as a given that the tradition of Jesus' words would not exist without reception by the early Church, which was conscious of a strict obligation to faithfulness in essentials, but also recognized that the enormous resonance of these words, with their subtle references to Scripture, permitted a degree of nuanced redaction."[82] The "subtle references to Scripture" mean Old Testament allusions. If Jesus managed to convey at the Last Supper that he was giving the Old Testament's multilayered covenantal history a new "depth and density,"[83] striking a chord rather than a single string, then this too would explain how variants emerged. Words such as "blood" and "covenant," for example, common to all the accounts of Jesus' words over the chalice, could plausibly evoke either the "blood of the covenant" sprinkled on Sinai (Exod 24:8), or Jeremiah's promise of a "new covenant" (Jer 31:31).[84] Each evangelist, remembering these words in light of the Resurrection, might "choose to place the accent more on one or on the other, without thereby being unfaithful to the Lord's words."[85] Because discrepancies in Jesus' *Deuteworte* can be explained by differing sensitivities to their subtle Old Testament harmonics, this need not weigh against their substantial historicity.

The second test, that of relation to the broader New Testament image of Christ, functions less as an authenticating pattern than as a recurring question: Would excising the Last Supper from Jesus' "critical biography" change the basic image of Christ proposed for belief by the New Testament?

---

82 JN 2:127.

83 Ratzinger, *Many Religions—One Covenant*, 63.

84 With reference to Ratzinger's arguments, Ermenegildo Manicardi suggests "covenant" (διαθήκη) as an *ipsissimum verbum Jesu* from which various redactional elaborations stem. "The Last Supper: The Meaning Given by Jesus to His Death," in *The Gospels: History and Christology: The Search of Joseph Ratzinger-Benedict XVI / I Vangeli: Storia e Cristologia: La ricerca di Joseph Ratzinger-Benedetto XVI*, vol. 1, ed. Bernardo Estrada, Ermenegildo Manicardi, and Armand Puig i Tàrrech (Rome: Libreria Editrice Vaticana, 2013), 632–33.

85 JN 2:127. Ratzinger elsewhere observes that the Markan and Pauline accounts hearken back to Old Testament covenant traditions, "but each strand selects a different reference point." *Many Religions—One Covenant*, 59.

Ratzinger ultimately concludes that the historicity of the Last Supper is even more central than the reality of the Devil to the New Testament portrait of Jesus. For the words and deeds ascribed to Jesus the night before he suffered imply without exception a figure of unprecedented authority and originality.[86] After reflecting on the theological audacity of the Last Supper narratives, Ratzinger comments: "Only from the mind of Jesus himself could such an idea have emerged. Only he could so authoritatively weave together the strands of the Law and the Prophets—remaining entirely faithful to Scripture while expressing the radically new quality of his sonship."[87] In transferring creative responsibility for such an original religious vision to an anonymous community, Ratzinger argues, exegetes inevitably diminish Jesus' spiritual stature, reducing him to a "friendly rabbi," "political revolutionary," or some other such stock character drawn from the sociology of religion. Far from representing a minor tweak, then, such a reattribution "concerns the very heart of Christianity and the essence of the figure of Jesus."[88]

It is worth noting that, in rejecting the portrait of Jesus as "friendly rabbi," Ratzinger recalls arguments from the first volume of *Jesus of Nazareth* regarding Jesus' implicit authority. There he considers at length the episode where Jesus, reprimanded for allowing his disciples to pick grain on the Sabbath, refuses to stop them, saying, "The Son of Man is Lord of the Sabbath" (Mark 2:28; Matt 12:8; Luke 6:5). Aware that contemporary Western Christians instinctively give this passage an antinomian gloss, taking it as a charter for a less demanding and legalistic religion, Ratzinger draws attention to Rabbi Jacob Neusner's impression of what Jesus' comportment would have meant for his Jewish contemporaries, who understood the Sabbath to be of divine institution. According to Neusner, "Jesus was not just another reforming rabbi, out to make life 'easier' for people.... Jesus' claim to authority is at issue."[89] Were he at the scene, Neusner continues, he would feel obliged to put pointed questions to Jesus' disciples: "Is it really so that your master, the

---

86 John Meier, for instance, observes: "If we should allow the basic historicity of the eucharistic narrative (Mark 14:22–25 parr.), we would have to admit that Jesus did and said some astounding and unprecedented things at the Last Supper, things that cannot be explained simply by positing the context of some Jewish ritual meal, Passover or otherwise." *Marginal Jew*, 1:399.

87 JN 2:125.

88 JN 2:117–18.

89 Jacob Neusner, *A Rabbi Talks with Jesus* (Montreal: McGill-Queen's University Press, 2000). Cited in JN 1:110.

son of man, is lord of the Sabbath? . . . I ask again—is your master God?"[90]
The first volume of *Jesus of Nazareth* thus focuses on an implicit claim to
divine authority found in the Synoptic preaching material, the very stratum
of tradition where Fiedler claimed to find a Jesus so different from that of
the Last Supper.

This sets the stage for the second volume of *Jesus of Nazareth* to find in
the Jesus of the Last Supper more than a "friendly rabbi." It is entirely consistent with the character of one who claimed to be Lord of the Sabbath, in other
words, that he should also act as Lord of the Passover, reconfiguring the feast
and recentering it on his own person.[91] In appealing to Jesus' authority over
ritual prescription, Ratzinger subtly employs the criterion of compatibility
with the broader New Testament portrait of Jesus.

Considerations relevant to the third test—namely, reception into the
Church's faith and life—only strengthen the case for historicity in Ratzinger's
mind. Here as elsewhere,[92] he focuses on a special form of "effective history":
the eucharistic praxis of the early Church. He engages especially the findings
of Rudolf Pesch, who, on historical and philological grounds, traces both
the Pauline and the Markan versions of the institution narrative back to
the Jerusalem community, assigning them a date no later than the 30s AD.[93]
Evidence for the Eucharist thus goes back as far as evidence for Christianity
itself. Given its aboriginal status, Ratzinger finds it highly implausible that
the idea for the Eucharist came from anyone other than Christ: "The idea
that the Eucharist originated within the 'community' is quite absurd, even

---

90 Neusner, *Rabbi Talks with Jesus*, 88. Cited in JN 1:110.

91 Here Ratzinger perhaps betrays the influence of Romano Guardini's *The Lord*, which
he calls a "masterpiece" (JN 2:xv) and a successful portrayal of Jesus as "God . . . made visible" (JN 1:xi): "The last time [Jesus celebrated the Passover] he did not strictly adhere to
the ritual. The very day was changed from Friday to Thursday, for was not he who called
himself Lord of the Sabbath also Lord of the Passover? During the meal there were other,
incomparably weightier, innovations." Guardini, *The Lord*, trans. Elinor Castendyk Briefs,
8th printing (Chicago: Henry Regnery, 1954), 369.

92 Speaking of the sacrificial nature of the Mass, Ratzinger observes, "The Church's liturgy
being the original interpretation of the biblical heritage has no need to justify itself before
historical reconstructions: it is rather itself the standard, sprung from what is living, which
directs research back to its initial stages. . . . To live by faith and die for faith is possible, only
because the power of the living community, which it created and still creates, opens up the
significance of history and renders it unequivocal, in a way that no amount of mere reasoning could do." Joseph Ratzinger, "Anglican-Catholic Dialogue: Its Problems and Hopes,"
Insight 1, no. 3 (1983): 8.

93 JN 2:116.

from a historical point of view. Who could possibly have dreamed up such an idea, such a reality? How could the first generation of Christians—as early as the 30s—have accepted such an invention without anyone calling it into question?"[94] Here Ratzinger echoes the criticism that Vincent Taylor long ago made of German form-criticism and its faith in uninhibited collective creativity: "If the Form-Critics are right, the disciples must have been translated to heaven immediately after the Resurrection."[95] Not a few exegetes find themselves in sympathy with such objections.[96]

But if Jesus founded the Eucharist at the Last Supper, and the Church began celebrating it so soon afterward, why the variations in Jesus' *Deuteworte*? Here Ratzinger suggests that much can be explained by their diverse reception into the eucharistic liturgy. Ratzinger grants that Jesus established only the "essentials of the new 'worship,'" leaving it to the post-Resurrection community to elaborate its "definitive liturgical form."[97] As the early Christians began using Christ's words liturgically, they naturally adapted them slightly to this new context, accentuating diverse aspects of what Jesus said, did, or implied. And this diverse ritual reception may have in turn affected how the biblical authors remembered or narrated the original events. Referring to Paul's version of the institution narrative, for instance, Ratzinger concludes, "There is no contradiction between holding that the text is intended for liturgy, having been crafted earlier with the liturgy in mind, and holding that it represents a strict tradition of the Lord's own words and intentions."[98] Differences in the *Deuteworte* thus reflect not only the various Old Testament harmonics of Jesus' discourse, but also their liturgical resonances.

94 JN 2:125. Again, on the same page: "Only because he himself spoke and acted thus could the Church in her various manifestations 'break bread' from the very beginning, as Jesus did on the night he was betrayed."

95 Vincent Taylor, *The Formation of the Gospel Tradition*, 2nd ed. (London: MacMillan, 1935), 41.

96 Rudolf Pesch, *Das Abendmahl und Jesu Todesverständnis* (QD 80; Freiburg: Herder, 1978), 21; Jeremias, *Abendmahlsworte Jesu*, 118; Craig Evans, "The Last Days of Jesus' Life: Did Jesus Anticipate the Cross?," in Estrata et al., *Gospels: History and Christology*, 527; Manicardi, "Last Supper," 632.

97 JN 2:139. This involved, inter alia, separating the Eucharist from the agape meal, adding prayers and biblical readings after estrangement from the synagogue, and fixing Sunday for weekly eucharistic celebrations. JN 2:138–40.

98 JN 2:117.

In its eucharistic practice, in short, the early Church acted not as if they were inventing something but as if they were receiving the same event within different horizons of experience. The unity and diversity of the Last Supper narratives suggests to Ratzinger that exegesis has often presented a false dichotomy: either Jesus or the Christian community. He finds the facts much better explained by a synergy of both Jesus (in institution) and the early Church (in diversely accentuated reception).[99]

The fourth "test," compatibility with scholarly knowledge, once again takes the form of a complex negotiation with historical criticism, an attempt to extract sound historical reasoning from the "worldview" that university-based exegesis often uncritically assumes. One can see this complex negotiation at work especially in Ratzinger's engagement with Fiedler and Pesch. Reading between the lines, one sees that Ratzinger has little use for Fiedler's arguments because they so clearly exhibit the tendency to strap historical evidence to the procrustean bed of an a priori evolutionary schema. On the surface of things, it is theological tensions internal to the Gospel tradition itself that lead Fiedler to conclude that the early Church retrojected the Last Supper narratives onto Jesus: Jesus presents God as unconditionally forgiving in his preaching but as score-settling in the Last Supper discourses. Yet Ratzinger suspects that the real incompatibility lies elsewhere, in the way the very "idea of expiation is incomprehensible to the modern mind." If we want to form a picture of the real Jesus of Nazareth, it is necessary not to "dismantle the texts according to our preconceived ideas, but to let our own ideas be purified and deepened by his word."[100] Shorn of their evolutionary suppositions about whether expiation is advanced or primitive, Fiedler's arguments demonstrate at best a differing emphasis in Jesus' Last Supper discourse, and one easily accounted for by changing context.[101]

Ratzinger engages Pesch much more appreciatively than Fiedler, but even there feels obliged to contest Pesch's claim to univocal conclusions. The occasion for Ratzinger's critique is the sharp generic contrast that Pesch finds

---

99 Ratzinger would thus seem to agree with something like Pitre's conclusion that the words of Jesus are historical in their "*substantia.*" Pitre, *Jesus and the Last Supper*, 46–50.

100 JN 2:119–20.

101 For an *Altestamentler*'s concurring opinion that an unexamined *Kultkritik* conditions New Testament scholarship, see Ludger Schwienhorst-Schönberger, "Der verleugnete Tempel: Warum Benedict XVI. mit seinem Zölibats-Artikel Recht hat," *Herder Korrespondenz* 74, no. 3 (March 2020): 46–49.

between the Markan and Pauline accounts, whereby Mark constitutes the primary "historical narrative" (*berichtende Erzählung*) and Paul the secondary "etiology of worship" (*Kultätiologie*).[102] The difference is evident, inter alia, from the fact that Mark lacks Paul's emphasis on the ritual "repeatability" of Jesus' action: "Do this, as often as you drink it, in remembrance of me" (1 Cor 11:25).[103] Pesch infers, therefore, that Mark's account originated from Jesus himself rather than the Church's eucharistic praxis. Pesch's terminology at least still suggests that he envisions an evolutionary process—however compressed—that yields discontinuous theological "species:" a mutation from the exclusively narrative to the exclusively cultic. All this leaves open the possibility that the *Deuteworte*, as Jesus spoke them, were not true words of institution, but merely words of prophecy interpreting his imminent death. The Church would thus have invented at least the idea of making them the center of its new worship.

Though Ratzinger agrees that the Markan account goes back to Jesus, he refuses to accept Pesch's strict genre binary. In place of Pesch's eliminative either-or, Ratzinger suggests an analogical difference of relative emphasis. Though Paul's version has clearer liturgical markers, it still "represents a strict tradition of the Lord's own words *and intentions*."[104] And though Mark's version retains a more "narrative" character, it too results from the "selection and shaping of material for liturgical purposes."[105] By such "selection and shaping" Ratzinger seems to mean what Thomas Söding calls "targeted reduction" (*gezielte Reduktion*), a tendency to crop out all elements of the meal except "what in retrospect seemed essential—two gestures and two statements, bearing upon bread and wine."[106] Nor does Ratzinger's analogical reading lack the support of eminent exegetes. French exegete Xavier Léon-Dufour, for instance, groups the Synoptic and Pauline accounts together,

102 Rudolf Pesch, "Das Abendmahl und Jesu Todesverständnis," in *Der Tod Jesu: Deutungen im Neuen Testament*. ed. Karl Kartelge, QD 74 (Freiburg: Herder, 1976), 155; cf. Pesch, *Das Markusevangelium*, 2 vols., HTKNT (Freiburg: Herder, 1977), II, 1:369.

103 Pesch, *Markus*, II, 1:354–55; Pesch, *Abendmahl und Jesu Todesverständnis*, 53–59.

104 JN 2:117. Italics mine.

105 JN 2:117.

106 Thomas Söding, "Brot und Wein: Die Gaben beim Letzen Abendmahl," *Internationale Katholische Zeitschrift Communio* 42 (2013): 239.

in contrast to the "testamentary" tradition of John 13–17, as a single "cultic" tradition admitting diverse theological accents.[107]

The way Ratzinger defends the unity of intention underlying these diverse theological accents recalls *Dei Verbum*. Both the Pauline and Markan accounts, he argues, reveal "selection and shaping of material for liturgical purposes." The language recalls the redactional processes expressly acknowledged by *Dei Verbum* 19: "The sacred authors wrote the four Gospels, *selecting* some things from the many which had been handed on by word of mouth or in writing . . . *explaining* some things in view of the situation of their churches . . . but always in such fashion that they told us the honest truth about Jesus." Ratzinger finds, in short, nothing in the deliverances of sober historical reason incompatible with the picture of New Testament composition painted by the Dogmatic Constitution on Divine Revelation.

Unsurprisingly, it turns out that Ratzinger handles the historicity of the institution narrative much as he handled the chronology of the Last Supper. He discreetly applies the same fourfold hermeneutic of faith and reason, adding to the three faith-based criteria the extra precisions of *Dei Verbum* 19. At the same time, when applying the criterion of historical reason, he corrects for what he sees as an unreflective misappropriation of scientific models by the exegetical guild. Against Fiedler he insists that theology does not follow the laws of animal genealogy, making it possible to locate expiatory models along a developmental spectrum. In dialogue with Pesch, he insists that genre analysis does not return unambiguous results, such that one could tidily compartmentalize historically and ritually oriented texts, assigning the former to Christ and the latter to the Church. At the same time, Ratzinger draws important insights from each of these authors about the "world behind the text": the possibility that Jesus corrected course in the face of rejection by Israel's leaders, as well as the fact that eucharistic praxis goes back to the 30s AD. In his treatment of the Last Supper, in short, Ratzinger illustrates very concretely what he means when he claims that a "properly developed faith-hermeneutic is appropriate to the [biblical] text and can be combined with a historical hermeneutic, aware of its limits, so as to form a methodological whole."[108]

---

107 Léon-Dufour, *Sharing the Eucharistic Bread*, 82–101.
108 JN 2:xiv–xv.

The application of this methodological whole to the Last Supper narratives leads Ratzinger to an important conclusion. Despite minor discrepancies in both chronology and *Deuteworte*, the historical ground turns out to be nearly coterminous with the narrative. Yes, the Synoptic authors redacted the dating and tenor of Jesus' words and gestures to sharpen their reference to either the Old Testament types or to the community's eucharistic praxis. But Jesus of Nazareth himself forged the basic synthesis narrated in the Gospels, combining paschal atmosphere, bread, wine, expiatory interpretation, and founding intention. It is worth recalling that Ratzinger does not always insist on so much historicity. Already in his 1955 Bonaventure *Habilitation* he acknowledges that the evangelists sometimes inserted Jesus' "free-floating sayings" (*freischwebende Logien*) into new narrative contexts, thereby developing their meaning.[109] Given the particular nature and effective history of the Last Supper narratives, however, Ratzinger doubts they arose from a pastiche of recollections of inclusive commensality. In estimating how far the historical ground subtends the Gospel narrative, Ratzinger proceeds on a case-by-case basis.

OBJECTIONS AND EVALUATION

Just how successfully has Ratzinger made his case for the viability of his "methodological whole"? The answer depends greatly, of course, on whom one asks and which evaluative standards one chooses. But since Ratzinger has consistently structured his thought around faith and historical reason, an evaluation according to these standards seems appropriate. We will let *Dei Verbum* represent the demands of faith and the criticism of the exegetical guild represent the exigencies of reason. Since representatives of historical reason have registered far more objections, their criticisms will receive greater attention.

Standard of Faith

The strongest faith-based objection to Ratzinger's approach to the historicity of the Gospels would almost certainly concern his implicit relegation of Synoptic chronology to the realm of theological symbol. According to Ratzinger, it will be remembered, Mark places the Last Supper on the

109 JRGS 2:67.

Jewish Passover because he perceived retrospectively the "inner connection" between it and the Passion itself, which, if John is more historically accurate, took place as the ritually prescribed Passover was about to commence. Ratzinger treats other passages analogously, identifying the Matthean and Lucan genealogies of Christ, for instance, as a "symbolic structuring of historical time."[110] But by construing even the Synoptic Passover as such a symbolic structuring, does Ratzinger weaken the credibility of the Gospels, "whose historical character," according to Dei Verbum 19, "the Church unhesitatingly asserts"?

I think it fairly clear that Ratzinger is not answerable to this charge. As was shown above, Ratzinger, when admitting differences between the empirical and narrated Jesus, takes care to explain the difference through the redactional techniques expressly recognized in Dei Verbum 19. When Ratzinger suggests that the evangelists realized the "inner connection" between the Last Supper and the Cross, redating the Last Supper accordingly, he implies that they were "reducing some of [the things handed down about Jesus] to a synthesis" and "explaining some things in view of the situation of their churches." Mark synthetically "reduces" the historical timeline, in other words, with a view to "explaining" to the churches how Jesus refounds the Jewish Passover in the Eucharist. Ratzinger certainly allows a higher ratio of theological symbol to historical fact here than many exegetes of the premodern era,[111] and possibly more than even certain redactors of Dei Verbum.[112] But we should not forget that Ratzinger himself was a redactor

---

110 JN 3:9.

111 When Thomas Aquinas learns that certain Greek theologians considered the Passion chronology of the Synoptic Gospels simply mistaken, he responds with the following hermeneutical principle: "But it is heresy to say that there is anything false not only in the Gospels but anywhere in the canonical scriptures. Consequently, we have to say that all the evangelists state the same thing and do not disagree." Super Ioannem, cap. 13, lec. 1. I owe the English translation to Joy, "Ratzinger and Aquinas on the Dating of the Last Supper," 332.

112 For example, Augustin Bea, SJ, whom Paul VI sent to the Theological Commission to advocate for a more robust affirmation of Gospel historicity, appears to reject anything like Ratzinger's distinction between center and periphery when he insists on the accuracy of even the historical "background" to salvation history: "Our question, therefore, about the possible existence of a limit set to inerrancy refers, not to the events in which God truly reveals himself, but to those events which form their historical setting, and which Scripture frequently describes in great detail.... In other words, is the historical background also described without error?... For my own part I think that this question must be answered affirmatively, that is, that these 'background' events also are described without error." The Word of God and Mankind (London: Geoffrey Chapman, 1967), 190.

of *Dei Verbum*. Because different council fathers understood *Dei Verbum* 19 differently, the Council's teaching on *historicitas* must ultimately be decided by the "way the words run."[113] Ratzinger makes a good case that he meets these requirements.

But Ratzinger does more than simply color inside the doctrinal lines. After conceding the irreconcilability of the Johannine and Synoptic chronologies at the historical level, he turns this discrepancy from a problem for Gospel historicity into a witness for the eucharistic faith of the early Church. Here Ratzinger allows his speculation to be guided by the Last Supper's ecclesial *Wirkungsgeschichte*, which in some respects culminates in the Council of Trent's teaching that the Mass "represents"—or participates on the reality of—Christ's sacrificial death-unto-resurrection.[114] If it is Mark who has construed the chronology theologically, then this very flexibility may give evidence of an inchoate form of this Tridentine doctrine. Mark may well have felt authorized to adjust the festal dating of the Last Supper, in other words, because he intuited that the Last Supper and Paschal Mystery somehow form a single event, even if separated from a historical point of view. He thus arguably illustrates concretely how communicating the *vera et sincera de Iesu* not only proves compatible with a degree of chronological restructuring but actually requires it, since certain events have effects transcending their historical location. Ratzinger's approach to the symbolic—or, better yet, sacramental—nature of the Markan chronology thus recalls his approach to the redactional nature of the Matthean exception clause. Just as he turned the latter into evidence that the Church had realized very early its competence to develop a casuistry of marriage, he turns the former into evidence of the Church's primordial belief in eucharistic representation. Here as elsewhere,

---

113 Council fathers had divergent understandings of the degree of Gospel historicity. On September 25, 1965, the conciliar *peritus* Albert Prignon records in his journal the very mixed reception Jean Daniélou received when campaigning to reintroduce into *Dei Verbum* "un texte affirmant de façon exagérée, l'historicité des évangiles de l'enfance, sans tenir compte du difficile problème qui se pose à ce sujet." *Journal conciliaire de la 4e Session*, ed. Declerck and A. Haquin (Louvain: Peeters, 2003), 73. Apropos the priority of the canonical text, Thomas Guarino notes that Trent's removal of *partim-partim* language to describe the relationship between Scripture and tradition was probably merely stylistic. Since the words now run this way, however, one is not obliged to hold that revelation is contained "partly" in Scripture and "partly" in tradition. Guarino, "Catholic Reflections on Discerning the Truth of Sacred Scripture," in *Your Word Is Truth: A Project of Evangelicals and Catholics Together*, ed. Charles Colson and Richard John Neuhaus (Grand Rapids, MI: Eerdmans, 2002), 83–84.

114 DH 1740.

Ratzinger more readily concedes redactional discontinuities that betoken deeper continuities in the faith tradition.

Standard of Historical Reason

As might be expected, Ratzinger's *Jesus of Nazareth* received much more criticism for failing to meet the standards of historical reason than for failing to meet the standards of faith. These include many errors of fact, which need not detain us.[115] But they also include charges of systemic inconsistency or opacity. These criticisms come from many different angles, but they cluster around two centers of gravity: overhasty harmonization of diverse canonical voices, and uneven use of historical-critical methodology. It is hoped that Ratzinger's treatment of the historicity of the Last Supper, profiled against the backdrop of *Dei Verbum* and restructured according to the tests, will offer a basis for evaluating the justice of these criticisms.

Not a few exegetes complain that Ratzinger reduces the internal pluralism of Scripture to a kind of monolithic Johannine perspective. The American exegete Richard Hays spoke for many when he observed of the first volume of *Jesus of Nazareth*, "Because of Ratzinger's pervasive tendency to treat the texts as transparent to historical facts about Jesus, he also fails to be sufficiently attentive to the individual narrative shape and content of the four distinct witnesses of the canonical evangelists."[116] Catholic *Neutestamentler* Michael Theobald finds that the second volume of *Jesus of Nazareth*

---

115 Richard Hays mentions, for instance, Ratzinger's claim that Galatians was written to Jewish Christians. "Ratzinger's Johannine Jesus: A Challenge to Enlightenment Historiography," in *The Pope and Jesus of Nazareth: Christ, Scripture, and the Church*, ed. Adrian Pabst and Angus Paddison (London: SCM Press, 2009), 117.

116 Hays, "Ratzinger's Johannine Jesus," 115. Referring to Ratzinger's tendency to privilege John, Lothar Wehr protests, "One cannot simply force [the Gospels] by making one of the New Testament theologies into a yardstick for the whole." "Theologien als Bereicherung der Theologie—Eine Verteidigung der Redaktionskritik," in *Alla ricerca della Verità: Discussioni sul* Gesù di Nazaret *di Joseph Ratzinger—Benedetto XVI*," ed. Guiseppe Franco (Lecce: Lupo, 2009), 56. Again, E. Jüngel, reviewing the first volume, insists that the "inner unity of Scripture" is "more complex, richer in tensions and more fraught with problems than Ratzinger's book leads us to suspect." "Der Hypothetische Jesus: Anmerkungen zum Jesus-Buch des Papstes," in *Annäherungen an "Jesus von Nazareth*," ed. J.-H. Tück (Ostfildern: Grünewald, 2007), 101. Rosino Gibellini notes that Ratzinger departs from the "historical method" by making "extended use of the Gospel of John, which he attributes, despite knowing well the Johannine question, to an eyewitness testimony." "Il libro del papa su Gesù nel conflitto delle interpretazioni," in *Alla ricerca della verità: Discussioni sul Gesù de Nazaret di Joseph Ratzinger—Benedetto XVI*, ed. Giuseppe Franco (Lecce: Lupo, 2009), 105.

makes John the "key signature for the Gospel score or harmony in the whole book."[117] In characterizing Ratzinger's exegetical style as insufficiently attentive to intracanonical diversity, exegetes imply a fixed standard of judgment. To evaluate the justice of their claims, however, one would need to know what this standard of judgment is and how they themselves determine it.

Ratzinger's critics might respond in a couple of ways. They might show that Ratzinger forces the evangelists to agree where they demonstrably disagree, thus offering a fairly objective standard for declaring him insufficiently attentive to intracanonical differences. Lothar Wehr claims, for instance, that Ratzinger ignores "contradictions" within the Gospel tradition.[118] To my knowledge, however, neither Wehr nor anyone else makes Ratzinger's treatment of the Last Supper the basis for such an argument. There, as we have seen, he confronts chronological, theological, and linguistic discrepancies rather candidly. Exegetical critics seem to have in mind something more like the harmonizing tendency evident in Ratzinger's treatment of Rudolf Pesch. Pesch, as we saw, underscores the difference between the Markan and Pauline perspectives on the institution narrative by placing them in hermetically sealed genres: Mark has left us an original historical narrative (without reference to worship) and Paul a derivative cultic etiology (without reference to history). Ratzinger does not deny the force of the literary evidence that Pesch adduces, especially the absence of elements of "repeatability" in the Markan account. But he considers both accounts to straddle the narrative-etiological divide, differing in relative emphasis rather than in generic species. Ratzinger perhaps harmonizes more than Pesch does, but he hardly violates the principle of noncontradiction.

The fact that exegetes seldom present evidence of Ratzinger papering over downright contradictions suggests that they fault him for something subtler. They fault him for deviating from a kind of golden mean between excessive and insufficient attention to difference, whose position "virtuous" interpreters are in the best position to estimate. I agree that in many domains the judgment of the virtuous remains the last court of appeal. I also agree that exegesis more attentive to difference turns up insights about the biblical text

---

117 Michael Theobald, "Um der Begegnung mit Jesus willen: Der zweite Teil des Jesus-Buches von Joseph Ratzinger/Benedikt XVI," *BK* 66 (2011), 174.

118 According to Wehr, the Gospels preserve their inherited traditions "even at the price of certain tensions or even contradictions [*Widersprüche*]." "Theologien als Bereicherung der Theologie," 56.

that Ratzinger's writings do not. One need only think of Richard Hays' profound comparative analysis of Jesus' parable discourses, which, by noticing a revelatory strategy unique to Mark—"Nothing is hidden except *in order to* (ἵνα) be revealed" (Mark 4:22a)—does much to explain why Mark's coyness about Jesus' identity need not imply a "diminished Christology."[119] There is little literary analysis so fine-grained in Ratzinger. Nevertheless, to speak of "Christology" is already to direct one's gaze beyond the kaleidoscopic plane of diverse textual worlds toward their one referent. As long as there are four Gospels and one Christ, Gospel studies cannot avoid aiming for a balanced attention to unity and difference. Determining the just mean in this regard, like finding the right position from which to take in a work of art, falls inevitably to the virtuous interpreter.

But contemporary virtue ethics, besides recalling our inevitable recourse virtuous judgment, has also emphasized how virtue and its appraisal depend at least in part on context.[120] Virtues regulate communal pursuits. Hence, the temperance of sumo wrestlers may look rather different from the temperance of marathoners. And even among communities that profess to pursue the same goal (e.g., justice), different sensibilities about how to achieve this goal inevitably emerge. One's estimate of hermeneutical virtuosity may, therefore, depend on the interpretive community into which one has been socialized.

Ratzinger long ago anticipated this contextual turn. Early on he develops Bonaventure's "rationally corrective" account of faith into a historically inflected account of human reason. Reason inherits from its surrounding linguistic community not only isolated facts but, for better or for worse, a value-laden "worldview." Ratzinger returns repeatedly to the point that university-based research into the historical Jesus can claim no immunity from these general epistemological limitations. Housed in interdisciplinary institutions dominated by the physical sciences, academic exegesis developed its sense of readerly virtuosity under a constant pressure to produce unambiguous, "scientific" results. It too, therefore, represents "a specific and historically conditioned form of rationality that is both open to correction

---

119 Richard Hays, *Reading Backwards: Figural Christology and the Fourfold Gospel Witness* (Waco, TX: Baylor University Press, 2014), 28–29.

120 See Alasdair MacIntyre, *After Virtue: A Study in Moral Virtue*, 3rd ed. (Notre Dame, IN: University of Notre Dame Press, 2007); Stanley Hauerwas, *A Community of Character: Toward a Constructive Christian Social Ethic* (Notre Dame, IN: University of Notre Dame Press, 1991).

and completion and in need of it." Because the exegetical guild inculcates its own evolutionary metaphysics of history and its own sense of "plausible" explanation, neither of which can be justified on purely historical grounds, it cannot rightly claim, as Joseph Fitzmyer does, that its method is "per se neutral."[121]

Ratzinger's position on the non-neutrality of university-based exegesis has arguably begun to find broader support. Protestant exegetes have also suggested, for instance, that the tendency to privilege univocal and discontinuous readings of Scripture has its roots not only in university culture but in their own confessional histories. A. K. M. Adam suggests that the inter-confessional strife arising in the wake of the Reformation pressured toward univocity as a regulative ideal: "As factional polemicists draft the (silent) Bible as witness for partisan pleading, those who volunteer to tell us what the Bible really means show an increasing tendency toward minimizing the ambiguity of their evidence."[122] The Lutheran theologian David Yeago makes an analogous observation, taking as his point of departure not inter- but intra-confessional discord: "Criticism that privileges difference and diversity *protects* denominational institutions from disruptive normative claims that might upset their fragile containment of highly centrifugal factions. If no coherent appeal can be made to a shared norm of scriptural faithfulness, we are all allowed to continue on our parallel tracks, doing and saying the different and incompatible things ... with which we feel comfortable."[123] Various exegetes may unwittingly find univocal and contrastive reading styles more satisfying, not because they offer a more satisfying explanation in historical terms but because they reflect their own experience of church.[124]

For other thinkers, historical criticism and its version of readerly virtuosity represent the confessional exegesis not of divided Christendom but of

---

121 Joseph Fitzmyer, *The Inspiration of Scripture: In Defense of the Historical-Critical Method* (New York: Paulist, 2008), 69.

122 A. K. M. Adam, "Poaching on Zion: Biblical Theology as Signifying Practice," in *Reading Scripture with the Church: Toward a Hermeneutic for Theological Interpretation* (Grand Rapids, MI: Baker Academic, 2006), 20.

123 David S. Yeago, "The Spirit, the Church and the Scriptures: Biblical Inspiration and Interpretation Revisited," in *Knowing the Triune God: The Work of the Spirit in the Practices of the Church*, ed. David S. Yeago and James J. Buckley (Grand Rapids, MI: Eerdmans, 2001), 78.

124 Jon D. Levenson, *The Hebrew Bible, the Old Testament, and Historical Criticism* (Louisville: Westminster/John Knox, 1993), 1–32.

the modern liberal state. According to this line of thinking, it is no accident that historical criticism emerges alongside the postconfessional state and the privatization of religion. Historical criticism, they argue, has always embodied a statist agenda: to detach theologians from their confessional traditions of interpretation and render them more docile citizens of the secular political order. This it does by "privatizing" such confessionally divisive criteria as canonical coherence, dogmatic interpretation, and liturgical reception. This statist genealogy does not necessarily contradict the Protestant-confessional genealogy since, as Jon Levenson suggests, the "privatization" of exegesis is more congenial to Protestant *sola scriptura* than to Jewish or Catholic styles of interpretation.[125] In any event, one can naturally consider such privatization more "objective" only if one presumes at the outset that all confessional traditions are prejudicial.[126]

The effort to describe historical criticism as a value-laden, cultural-political project usually reflects a desire to contest its hegemony. But some of its most ardent defenders actually champion it on the same grounds. For John Collins, for instance, "[Historical criticism] has created an arena where people with different faith commitments can work together and have meaningful conversations. The historical focus has been a way of getting distance from a text, of respecting its otherness. The neutrality and objectivity at which the discipline has aimed has allowed Jews and Christians to work together and has allowed feminists to make their case in ways that initially unsympathetic scholars have found compelling."[127] Notably, Collins does not praise historical criticism for having actually produced more objective history. He instead praises it because it has, by *aiming at* historical objectivity,

---

125 Levenson, *Hebrew Bible*, 23–24.

126 For convincing genealogies of this sort, see Jeffrey Morrow, "Spinoza and the Theo-Political Implications of his Freedom to Philosophize," *NBf* 99 (2018): 374–87; Morrow, "Secularization, Objectivity, and Enlightenment Scholarship: The Theological and Political Origins of Modern Biblical Studies." *Logos* 18, no. 1 (2015): 14–32; Scott Hahn and Benjamin Wiker, *Politicizing the Bible: The Roots of Historical Criticism and the Secularization of Scripture, 1300–1700* (New York: Crossroad, 2013), passim. Michael Legaspi calls the disciplines of modern criticism a "cultural-political project shaped by the realities of the university." *The Death of Scripture and the Rise of Biblical Studies* (Oxford: Oxford University Press, 2010), 7. Angus Paddison also argues against reading Scripture according to the modern university's definition of neutrality: *Scripture: A Very Theological Proposal* (Edinburgh: T&T Clark, 2009), 122–24.

127 John Collins, *The Bible after Babel: Historical Criticism in a Postmodern Age* (Grand Rapids, MI: Eerdmans, 2005), 10.

fostered the intellectual habits of mind conducive to frictionless citizenship in the postconfessional political order.[128]

John Meier offers a similar rationale for questing after the historical Jesus. He admits that objectivity in this discipline is an "asymptotic goal," an ideal that scholars can never fully realize but that they must nevertheless resolutely pursue.[129] He also acknowledges frankly, as was noted in the introduction, that the application of historical-critical methods does not yield even a relatively complete historical portrait of Jesus, let alone the Christ of faith. What would be gained, then, by using such methods to produce minimal consensus statements about Jesus? "We would have a rough draft of what that will-o'-the-wisp, 'all reasonable people,' could say about the historical Jesus. The document could serve as a common ground, a starting point for dialogue between Christians and Jews, between various Christian confessions, and between believers and nonbelievers, as well as an invitation to further research by both historians and theologians."[130] What recommends the method is, once again, not so much the richness or impartiality of its results as the kind of civil and inclusive conversations it makes possible.

To the extent that the interpretive sensibilities of university-based exegesis reflect the exigencies of the liberal political order and its educational organs, its criticisms of Ratzinger's readerly habits remain subject to criticism. For to demonstrate convincingly that Ratzinger's comparatively more "harmonizing" reading style is less "virtuous," or less adequate to the reality under investigation, exegetes will need to establish that their more "differentiating" sensibility reflects a less historically conditioned form of rational inquiry. In light of recent reflections by both friends and foes of historical criticism, this will prove no easy task.

The second criticism often leveled against Ratzinger's Jesus book is inconsistent application of the historical-critical method. Reviewing the first volume of *Jesus of Nazareth*, for instance, Richard Hays speaks of Ratzinger's "grudging and very uneven acknowledgment of any historical distance between Jesus of Nazareth and the narrative representations of him in our canonical Gospels."[131] Peter Stuhlmacher, an exegete from whom

---

128 On this point, see Michael Legaspi, "What Ever Happened to Historical Criticism?" *Journal of Religion & Society* 9 (2007): 1–11.

129 Meier, *Marginal Jew*, 1:4.

130 Meier, *Marginal Jew*, 1:2.

131 Hays, "Ratzinger's Johannine Jesus," 115.

Ratzinger solicited critical feedback, finds this defect unremedied in the second volume: "He still avoids as far as possible the differentiation between historical facticity and the faith perspective opened only from Easter."[132] Nor is Ratzinger's treatment of the Last Supper narratives excepted from this vein of criticism. Michael Theobald warns his readers, for instance, that Ratzinger "clandestinely inscribes a later eucharistic understanding onto the texts."[133] Here again, examples could be multiplied,[134] even from scholars sympathetic to Ratzinger's overall project.[135]

---

132 Peter Stuhlmacher, "Joseph Ratzingers Jesus-Buch (Teil II): Eine Kritische Würdigung," in *Passion aus Liebe: Das Jesus-Buch des Papstes in der Diskussion*, ed. Jan-Heiner Tück (Ostfildern: Matthias Grünewald, 2011), 76.

133 Theobald, "Um der Begegnung mit Jesus willen," 174.

134 Marcus Bockmuehl considers the failure to make transparent the negotiation between historical and theological considerations one of the "more validly recurring criticisms of the Pope's book." "Saints' Lives as Exegesis," in *The Pope and Jesus of Nazareth: Christ, Scripture and the Church*, ed. Adrian Pabst and Angus Paddison (London: SCM Press, 2009), 132. Rudolf Hoppe finds incomprehensible Ratzinger's "verdict against a consistently [*konsequent*] historical-critical approach—even if he nevertheless considers it 'indispensable.'" "Historische Rückfrage und deutende Erinnerung an Jesus: Zum Jesusbuch von Joseph Ratzinger/Benedikt XVI," in *Das Jesus-Buch des Papstes: Die Antwort der Neutestamentler*, ed. Thomas Söding (Freiburg: Herder, 2007), 62. Martin Ebner criticizes Ratzinger for insisting that the Gospels present the "real Jesus" while admitting that the disciples' post-Easter preaching had a different center of gravity from Jesus' kingdom-centered preaching. "Jede Ausleger hat seine blinden Flecken," in *Das Jesus-Buch des Papstes: Die Antwort der Neutestamentler*, ed. Thomas Söding (Freiburg: Herder, 2007), 34–36. Luke Timothy Johnson criticizes Ratzinger for presuming excessive continuity between pre- and post-Resurrection—that is, for insisting that "Jesus was just as the Gospels (read, it is true from the perspective of their 'deep harmony') say he was." Review of Joseph Ratzinger, *Jesus of Nazareth: From the Baptism in the Jordan to the Transfiguration*, *Modern Theology* 24, no. 2 (2008): 319. For roundups of the major European-language reviews of the first volume of *Jesus of Nazareth*, see Joseph O'Leary's blog entries: Joseph O'Leary, "German Reception of the Pope's Jesus-Book," n.p., cited August 9, 2008, https://josephsoleary.typepad. com/my_weblog/2008/08/german-receptio.html; "Non-German Reviews of the Pope's Jesus-Book (Updated)," n.p., cited March 12, 2009, https://josephsoleary.typepad.com/ my_weblog/2009/03/nongerman-reviews-of-popes-jesusbook-updated.html; and the bibliography provided in G. Anger and J.-H. Tück, "Vorstudien und Echo: Ein erster bibliographischer Überblick zu Joseph Ratzingers *Jesus von Nazareth*," in *Annäherungen an "Jesus von Nazareth,"* ed. J.-H. Tück (Ostfildern: Grünewald, 2007), 182–99.

135 The American Old Testament scholar Gary Anderson concedes, for instance, that Ratzinger may sometimes exaggerate the explicitness of Jesus' foreknowledge of his expiatory destiny. "The Baptism of Jesus: On Jesus' Solidarity with Israel and Foreknowledge of the Passion," in *Explorations in the Theology of Benedict XVI*, ed. John C. Cavadini (Notre Dame: University of Notre Dame Press, 2012), 249–51.

There is one sense in which I consider such critiques justified. *Jesus of Nazareth* is not altogether methodologically transparent in its historical judgments. The introduction to the first volume contains perhaps the best capsule summary of Ratzinger's hermeneutic of faith and reason, but it enumerates neither the relevant strata of tradition nor their corresponding hermeneutical tests. Moreover, *Jesus of Nazareth* does not, like the earlier "Farewell to the Devil?," structure its exposition along methodological lines. And even when Ratzinger appeals to the Catholic doctrinal tradition, he can be somewhat selective. He cites *Dei Verbum* 12 as a methodological template, for instance, but not *Dei Verbum* 19, which seems to guide his judgment no less palpably. He uses phrases like "words of transformation" or "words of institution" to describe the *Deuteworte*, but does not name the conciliar decisions they anticipate, such as those of Lateran IV and Trent. For all these reasons, then, Ratzinger's admission of distance between Jesus of Nazareth and the Jesus of the Gospels, or even between the Jesus of the Gospels and Catholic doctrine, is bound to look uneven and sometimes capricious.

This chapter's methodologically reorganized survey of *Jesus of Nazareth* on the Last Supper, however, suggests that Ratzinger is anything but arbitrary in assessing historicity. It is true that he does not maintain a fixed ratio of historical ground and faith-based redaction. And from a historical-critical perspective, this suggests a certain unevenness. But behind this variable ratio stands a stable set of criteria: the four tests, the redactional processes of *Dei Verbum*, and the critique of university-based exegetical "worldview." Different events enjoy different relationships to history, with some more squarely unfolding within its continuous fabric (e.g., the Last Supper) and others straddling the boundary between time and eternity (e.g., Resurrection). *The sensus ecclesiae* is also differently invested in the historicity of various episodes, as the Pontifical Biblical Commission recognized already in 1905. Inasmuch as the Catholic Church has received the Eucharist as a divine rather than a human institution—Paul himself says he receives it "from the Lord" (ἀπὸ τοῦ κυρίου) (1 Cor 11:23)—faith arguably requires that a more substantial historical ground subtend this narrative. It is true, in the end, that Ratzinger does not measure a uniform distance between Jesus of Nazareth and the narrated Jesus. But it is untrue that he lacks a consistent method for estimating this distance, however it may vary.

A related line of criticism observes that Ratzinger, by offering such a high estimate of Gospel historicity, must inevitably trace the evangelists' imbalances back to Jesus himself. Richard Hays raises this objection not against Ratzinger's treatment of the Last Supper, but against his tendency to ascribe a high historical value to John's Gospel—a tendency also evident in his study of the Last Supper. When reviewing Ratzinger's first volume of *Jesus of Nazareth*, for instance, Hays observes that the author defends the historicity of John to such an extent that he ends up with a "Jesus who tells 'the Jews' that their father is the devil (8:44)."[136] In order to save Jesus of Nazareth from complicity in John's antisemitism, Hays implies, one has to admit that the evangelist puts his own (very different) views in Jesus' mouth. From what we have learned so far, however, it is obvious that Ratzinger would not be satisfied with any solution that exonerates Jesus by indicting John. To do so would ultimately make faith's true norm not the Jesus of the Gospels but a historical reconstruction, built on the shifting sand of academic consensus. Though Hays could not have known it when he gave the example, Ratzinger would address this problem in the second volume of *Jesus of Nazareth*. There he points out that John uses "the Jews" as a cipher for the Temple aristocracy, not for the Jewish people as a whole.[137] Ratzinger thus admits that the evangelist may have expressed Jesus' judgment against the Jewish authorities in anachronistic terms. But he never suggests that John fails to tell us the "honest truth about Jesus" by imputing to Jesus a bigotry that Jesus himself would have rejected.

Ratzinger thus insists on the historical character of all the Gospel portraits of Jesus without imagining this historicity as a kind of photorealism. Christopher Seitz has helpfully remarked that Ratzinger's *Jesus of Nazareth* trilogy combines concerns seldom joined: canonical criticism's attention to the Bible's final literary form and historical criticism's attention to "ostensive reference"—that is, to the "real" Jesus.[138] In keeping with the former, he concedes both a symbolic chronology for Mark and a degree of theologically motivated redaction in the institution narratives. In keeping with the latter, however, he tends to make historicity a defeasible presumption. And in the case of Last Supper, he prefers to identify as symbolic that chronology which, so read, enjoys the deepest *fundamentum in re*. In this sense, one might justifiably, like Hays, call his admission of distance between Jesus of Nazareth and the Jesus of the Gospels "grudging." But one could just as easily describe

---

136 Hays, "Ratzinger's Johannine Jesus," 116.

137 JN 2:185.

138 Christopher Seitz, *Convergences: Canon and Canonicity* (Waco, TX: Baylor University Press, 2020), 159.

this inclination as "optimizing," showing a tendency to adjust for the best "fit" between the twin criteria of faith and reason. If the attitude of faith sees the New Testament, at least in its substance, as a "history that unfolded upon this earth" rather than mere "symbols of meta-historical truths,"[139] one might say that it belongs to a faith-and-reason hermeneutic to presume historicity until proven otherwise, or to favor symbolic narratives with the most realistic foundation.

Much of the criticism directed at Ratzinger's handling of the Gospels, in short, imagines that he is precritical, naively unaware of both the tensions within the biblical canon and the distance between historical reality and narrative representation. Old Testament scholar Pauline Viviano, for instance, claims that the "faith-hermeneutics that [Ratzinger] applies to the New Testament . . . is a return to the spiritual interpretation of the early church fathers which renders the contributions of historical critical-scholarship null and void."[140] Ratzinger's faith-hermeneutic, however, is not so much precritical as postcritical. Ratzinger is acutely sensitive to the situatedness of reason. He knows that he arrives at different conclusions concerning Gospel historicity precisely because he has apprenticed himself to a different tradition of inquiry: not primarily to the university-centered tradition of the last two centuries, but to the ecclesial tradition of the last two millennia—within which the historical-critical tradition represents but a segment. Each inculcates a different set of readerly virtues. The university tradition esteems critical autonomy and differentiating analysis, while the ecclesial tradition esteems receptive trust and analogical synthesis. At the heart of the dispute is not whether Ratzinger reads "virtuously," but whether his tradition of readerly "virtuosity" is less adequate to biblical realities than that of the post-Enlightenment research university. The concluding reflection will take up this question, among others.

---

139 JN 2:104.

140 Pauline Viviano, "Fighting Biblical Fundamentalism," in *Vatican II: 50 Personal Stories*, ed. William Madges and Michael J. Daley (Maryknoll, NY: Orbis, 2012), 143.

Three Achievements

Having examined in some depth Ratzinger's theology of Scripture, placing it in dialogue with both dogmatic and exegetical voices, we are in a better place to evaluate its achievement. Where has Ratzinger's career-long engagement with Scripture and its interpretation left us? In passing, I have already had a chance to note *lacunae* in Ratzinger's theology of revelation, where he presupposes rather than elaborates key premises of his Bonaventurian-ecclesial hermeneutical, such as the personality of the Church or the nature of "organic" doctrinal development. But here in conclusion I would like to suggest three positive achievements. He has left us, first, a more convincing balance between a priori and a posteriori moments in biblical interpretation; second, a strong case for the superiority of a historical-ecclesial hermeneutic properly aware of its epistemological limits; finally, a new paradigm for understanding biblical inspiration and truth "without error," creatively faithful to the doctrinal tradition. The first point will lead us to place Ratzinger in conversation with Raymond E. Brown and Romano Guardini; the second will turn to the philosopher Alasdair MacIntyre; and the third will bring us back to John H. Newman.

When I say that Ratzinger helpfully recalibrates the balance between a priori and a posteriori moments of biblical interpretation, I borrow a conceptual pairing from Raymond E. Brown. In his influential treatment of inerrancy found in *The Critical Meaning of the Bible*, Brown notes, "Many of us think that at Vatican II the Catholic Church 'turned the corner' in the inerrancy question by moving from the *a priori* toward the *a posteriori* in the statement of *Dei verbum* 11: 'The Books of Scripture must be acknowledged as teaching firmly, faithfully and without error that truth which God wanted put into the sacred writings for the sake of our salvation."[1] Ratzinger called for the Council to turn this same corner when he criticized *De fontibus revelationis* for its aprioristic treatment of inerrancy: "Here the schema speaks very sharply, as it works out this deduction: God is supreme truth and cannot err; but God dictated the Scripture; therefore, the Scripture is precisely just as free of error as is God himself."[2] Both Brown and Ratzinger felt that that preconciliar biblical theology employed an excessively deductive approach to determining what inspired Scripture will tolerate in terms of error, suppressing any inductive consideration of the kinds of errors that Scripture does in fact contain. As the schoolmen used to say, "The inference from actuality to possibility is valid"—*ab esse ad posse valet illatio.*

Though both Brown and Ratzinger agreed on the need to revalorize the a posteriori moment, their final recommendations differ. Brown presents his synthesis this way: "In the inerrancy question Vatican II assumes as *a priori* that God wants the salvation of his people. The extent to which truth in Scripture conforms to that purpose is an *a posteriori* issue."[3] With the a priori and a posteriori moments so reconfigured, Brown concludes, one no longer needs to consider Scripture inerrant in its historically indicated literal sense. Ratzinger might agree with this modest conclusion, but not with the more sweeping premise from which Brown derives it—namely, that the extent to which this saving purpose requires true ideas is an "*a posteriori* issue." For this seems to suggest that determining how much truth is necessary for salvation is a matter of reading the Bible as one would read any other historical document, and then keeping track of how much it happens to get right. Ratzinger, being more sensitive to the elusive nature of objectivity, cannot follow Brown so far down the a posteriori path.

To understand Ratzinger's desire to retain a more robust a priori of faith, even in determining how far biblical inerrancy extends, one does well to note his debt to Romano Guardini, another great twentieth-century student of Bonaventure. In the methodological remarks prefacing *Das Christusbild der paulinischen und johanneischen Schriften* (1962), which Ratzinger considers "among the most important yet expressed on the problem of method in the

---

1 Raymond E. Brown, *The Critical Meaning of the Bible: How a Modern Reading of the Bible Challenges Christians, the Church, and the Churches* (New York: Paulist, 1981), 18.

2 Jared Wicks, "Six Texts by Prof. Joseph Ratzinger as *Peritus* before and during Vatican Council II," *Greg* 89, no. 2 (2008): 280.

3 Brown, *Critical Meaning of the Bible*, 19.

interpretation of Scripture,"[4] Guardini points to the inescapability of the "hermeneutical circle" (*Denkzirkel*).[5] Successful human knowing, he argues, does not entail approaching all phenomena—mineral, vegetable, animal, rational—with the same "cognitive posture" (*Erkenntnishaltung*).[6] It would be the very opposite of "scientific," for instance, to study anthropology exclusively through the mineralogist's *instrumentarium*, sorting and classifying the human species according to density, hardness, and index of refraction. Critical thinking means much rather expanding one's cognitive posture with each qualitatively higher phenomenon until it reaches a certain equilibrium with the phenomenon, an adequacy to all its dimensions. Here lies the problem of the circle: finding the right cognitive posture requires getting a "grip" on the new object; but recognizing the object as new presupposes that one has already found the right grip.[7]

Guardini here points to an insight dear to the Romantics and rediscovered by modern cognitive psychology. Goethe, who fancied himself more a scientist than a poet, was convinced that the kind of world we meet depends greatly on the kind of attention we bring to bear on it. "Every new object clearly seen opens up a new organ of perception in us."[8] Cognitive scientists, for their part, have confirmed this intuition by drawing attention to the phenomenon of "perseveration." Afflicting especially those with right-brain deficit, the side specialized in holistic attention, perseveration refers to the incapacity to shift mental frames according to changing situations. "For example," says Iain McGilchrist, "having found an approach that works for one problem, subjects seem to get stuck, and will inappropriately apply it to a second problem that requires a different approach."[9] Here again, one needs

---

4 Joseph Ratzinger, "Biblical Interpretation in Conflict," in *God's Word: Scripture—Tradition—Office*, ed. Peter Hünermann and Thomas Söding, trans. Henry Taylor (San Francisco: Ignatius, 2005), 116n29.

5 Romano Guardini, *Das Christusbild der paulinischen und johanneischen Schriften* (Würzburg: Werkbund Verlag, 1961), 10.

6 Guardini, *Christusbild*, 10.

7 "Wherever a genuine *novum* occurs . . . its intelligibility (*Sinnverhalt*) can only be thought in the form of a circle." Guardini, *Christusbild*, 11.

8 Johann Wolfgang von Goethe, *Goethe: Scientific Studies*, ed. and trans. D. Miller (New York: Suhrkamp, 1988), 39.

9 Iain McGilchrist, *The Master and His Emissary: The Divided Brain and the Making of the Western World*, exp. ed. (New Haven: Yale University Press, 2019), 40.

somehow to recognize in advance what kind of problem one has in order to know what approach to take.

The problem of the circle is only exacerbated in the case of faith and revelation. For there one deals not just with the relative beginning of a higher link in the chain of created being but with the absolute beginning of God's new initiative. One can therefore judge revelation adequately only from the cognitive posture of faith:

> Faith is obedience to the "phenomenon," namely the "epiphany of God." . . . Not the abandonment of reason but the final consequence of the demands of genuine reason. Faith means the beginning of a conversion not only of the will and moral behavior but of thought as well; the decision taken in all seriousness to accept as true what is true from revelation's point of view; as possible what is possible from revelation's point of view—and thereby even the acceptance of the risk of appearing foolish to a reason closed up in the world.[10]

Because revelation demands to be evaluated by the rational standards that it itself awakens, the question of how far revelation extends cannot be settled simply by a posteriori considerations. The more error one anticipates, the more one will in fact find.[11]

Indeed, it is not hard to imagine interpretive scenarios in which the result depends almost entirely on cognitive posture adopted. Take, for instance, the question of whether Jesus' participation in John's baptism of repentance indicates that he considered himself a sinner. Critical interpreters will doubt-lessly be aware that the Letter to the Hebrews describes Jesus as "without sin" (Heb 4:15). But absent any a priori assumptions about the theological coher-ence of the canon, there will be no reason to "bend" the interpretation of the baptism in the Jordan in the direction of Hebrews. A strictly a posteriori approach to biblical error would lead us to conclude that the Synoptics and Hebrews have contradictory Christologies, one admitting Jesus' sinfulness,

---

10 Guardini, *Christusbild*, 12.

11 An indication of the kinship between Ratzinger's and Guardini's positions is the fact that Michael Theobald, who appeared in the previous chapter, criticizes both on similar grounds. "Die Autonomie der historischen Kritik—Ausdruck des Unglaubens oder the-ologische Notwendigkeit? Zur Schriftauslegung Romano Guardinis," in *Auslegung des Glaubens: Zur Hermeneutik christlicher Existenz*, ed. L. Honnenfelder and M. Lutz-Bach-mann (Berlin: Hildesheim, 1987), 30–31.

one denying it.[12] If one starts with the *parti pris* of a coherent canon, by contrast, then one might find it more natural to interpret Jesus' baptism as a gesture of solidarity with *others'* sins. In view of the many prayers of collective repentance offered by representative individuals in the Old Testament, this interpretation too could claim plausibility even in historical terms.[13] But only a prior expectation of Christ's sinlessness would likely induce the interpreter to prefer the impeccable reading to the peccable. Because many biblical passages, like the baptism of the Jordan, remain multivalent even from a historical point of view, the amount of internal contradiction one finds a posteriori will often reflect how much one expected to find a priori.

More sensitive to the problem of the "circle," Ratzinger arrives at a model of inerrancy by working both deductively and inductively. As early as his dissertation on Augustine, Ratzinger was already citing approvingly his mentor Gottlieb Söhngen's characterization of Christianity as "Truth in the double counterpoint" (*Wahrheit im doppelten Kontrapunkt*).[14] In the case of biblical interpretation, this means proceeding from twin givens: that Scripture both participates in God's changeless truth and that it shows signs of the cultural and scientific limitations of its human authors. Ratzinger finesses both ends until reaching what he considers an optimal fit. This involves tweaking limited theological formulations in light of the "facts"—for example, relocating the inerrant intention of Scripture from the level of the individual author to the level of the People of God. But this also involves tweaking the supposed "facts" in light of the dogmatic tradition, puncturing pretensions to pseudo-scientific certainty prevalent in critical exegesis. Adjusting both ends, Ratzinger finds that his Bonaventurian-ecclesial model accommodates both the more enduring doctrinal affirmations and the deliverances of more sober historical research.

In moving rhythmically between two poles, one could say that Ratzinger has groped his way toward a theology of biblical inspiration in much the same way that James Watson and Francis Crick discovered the structure

---

12 For an argument along these lines, see Paul Hollenbach, "The Conversion of Jesus: From Jesus the Baptizer to Jesus the Healer," *ANRW* II, 25.1 (1982): 201–2.

13 For such an interpretation, appealing to Ezra 9 and Tobit, see Gary Anderson, "The Baptism of Jesus: On Jesus' Solidarity with Israel and Foreknowledge of the Passion," in *Explorations in the Theology of Benedict XVI*, ed. John C. Cavadini (Notre Dame, IN: University of Notre Dame Press, 2012), 239–43.

14 JRGS 1:64–65, n14.

of DNA. The two scientists had learned from the X-ray diffraction experiments of other researchers two important features of the molecule. It was shaped somewhat like a corkscrew and exhibited a repeating nucleotide sequence. Watson and Crick began "tinkering" with both these underdetermined givens, trying different combinations of shape and sequence until they came up with something that elegantly harmonized the data—namely, a *double*-helix shape with the famous G-A-C-T nucleotide sequencing.[15] One could say that Ratzinger attempts something analogous, determining the scope of Scripture's revelatory intentions through both deductive and inductive moments.

Ratzinger is not alone, of course, in attempting a new synthesis of a priori and a posteriori perspectives. His uniqueness lies rather in his more even attention to both. Brown, for instance, left behind a vast body of biblical commentary guided by the ordinary evidentiary standards accepted by critical scholars. But he devoted comparatively little attention to what distinguishes Scripture as God's Word or to the complexities of *Dei Verbum*. At the outset of his treatment of inspiration in *The Critical Meaning of the Bible*, Brown informs us,

> My contribution will be entirely from the vantage point of biblical criticism. I do not plan to consider the word of God philosophically (e.g., what human activities are possible to the Supreme Being) or in the context of historical (e.g., what various past church writers have through about the word of God) or of systematic theology (e.g., whether there is a magisterial position or a unanimous theological position on what "the word of God" means).[16]

As Gregory Vall has noted, this horizonal restriction to the competencies of the biblical critic is itself a kind of "*a priori* orientation."[17] Kevin Duffy, though more appreciative of Brown's contributions, nevertheless concedes, "As regards hermeneutical theory, Brown travels light."[18]

---

15 Brenda Maddox, "The Double Helix and the 'Wronged Heroine,'" *Nature* 421 (2003): 407–8. Cited January 23, 2003, https://www.nature.com/articles/nature01399.

16 Brown, *Critical Meaning of the Bible*, 5.

17 Gregory Vall, "Ratzinger, Brown, and the Reception of *Dei Verbum*," *JJT* 23, 1–2 (2016): 215.

18 Kevin Duffy, "The Ecclesial Hermeneutic of Raymond E. Brown," *HeyJ* 39 (1998): 52.

Those theologians who travel "heavier" hermeneutically, however, tend not to engage in workaday exegesis. Among the Catholic theologians surveyed in the first chapter, only Benoit can claim to have been a practicing exegete. Ironically, Benoit's Thomist-instrumental attracts more charges of excessive apriorism than Rahner's Molinist-predefinitive or Tracy's hermeneutic-disclosive models. Among Catholic theologians active since the Second Vatican Council, at least, Ratzinger remains one of the few to travel "heavy" in both doctrinally based hermeneutical theory and historical-critical fluency.

But even among this elite company of theologian-exegetes, which would surely include figures such as Edward Schillebeeckx and Walter Kasper, Ratzinger still stands out for his willingness to let the vector of critique run with equal vigor in both directions. Though Schillebeeckx and Kasper allow exegetical consensus to temper biblical Christologies that they deem excessively high or naïve, they venture less by way of criticism of exegetical consensus. Schillebeeckx, for instance, allows as historical only the two miracles attested in the Q tradition.[19] He likewise classifies the narrative about the women finding the empty tomb as an "etiological cult legend" legitimating the tomb as an annual pilgrimage site.[20] Though generally more moderate, Kasper, at least in the original version of *Jesus the Christ*, grants that a broad swath of miracle stories—the calming of the storm, the Transfiguration, the feeding of the multitudes, the miraculous catch of fish, the raising of Jairus's daughter and Lazarus—constitute "projections of the experiences of Easter back into the earthly life of Jesus, or anticipatory representations of the exalted Christ."[21] The slope of criticism runs largely in one direction.

With Ratzinger, as we have seen, things are rather different. Not only does he not limit the authentic miracles to those found in the Q source; he expresses "fundamental doubts" about whether such a collection of sayings

---

19 Edward Schillebeeckx, *Jesus: An Experiment in Christology*, 3rd ed., trans. Hubert Hoskins (New York: Seabury, 1979), 185–88.

20 Schillebeeckx, *Jesus*, 333–34. Schillebeeckx accepts that the Resurrection was an event of sorts, a conversion-inducing appearance of Jesus, but not the kind incompatible with a remaining corpse (704n45).

21 Walter Kasper, *Jesus the Christ*, rev. ed. (New York: Continuum, 2011), 78. In the new foreword written in 2011, Kasper notes that he would now give a "more positive judgment" regarding the historicity of such events (xixn10).

ever existed.[22] In this he anticipates today's waxing Q skepticism.[23] He also shows, generally speaking, a greater readiness to use faith as a critical standard by which to puncture what he sees as the inflationary tendencies of historical reason. Over the course of his career, of course, Ratzinger's campaign against excessive apriorism has to some extent shifted fronts, from neo-scholastic deductions to the evolutionary schemata structuring critical biographies of Jesus. This second front has led some exegetes to characterize his method as so dogmatic as to be "immune to historical criticism."[24] Ratzinger's changing attitude toward both the Matthean exception clause and Jaubert's harmonizing hypothesis, however, suggests that he can be persuaded by arguments from historical plausibility. He simply does not find all such historical arguments persuasive, even those that momentarily enjoy majority favor. For his attempts to embrace a priori and a posteriori postures as mutually informative moments of a single method, Ratzinger has won the appreciation of even Protestant interpreters.[25]

Given Ratzinger's willingness to admit that reason is something of a wax nose, one might reasonably ask how he can present his own Bonaventurian-ecclesial hermeneutic as anything more than an exercise in self-confirming bias. Here I would like to suggest that the probative force of Ratzinger's case roughly parallels Alasdair MacIntyre's case for the superiority of an Aristotelian-Thomist virtue ethics. Although I have no evidence that Ratzinger read MacIntyre directly, they share a common tendency to emphasize the situatedness of human reason without endorsing wholesale cultural relativism. Both must therefore face the problem of arguing across rival traditions of rational inquiry. The problem can be posed this way: If there is no view from nowhere, and if our social location influences not only the evidence

---

22 Ratzinger, *Gespräch über Jesus*, 33.

23 For a recent challenge to the Q hypothesis and bibliography, see Francis Watson, *Gospel Writing: A Canonical Perspective* (Grand Rapids, MI: Eerdmans, 2013).

24 Hans Albert, "Josef [*sic*] Ratzingers Jesusdeutung: Kritische Bemerkungen zu einigen Aspekten seiner Untersuchung," in *Alla ricerca della verità: Discussioni sul Gesù de Nazaret di Joseph Ratzinger—Benedetto XVI*, ed. Giuseppe Franco (Lecce: Lupo, 2009), 145.

25 Kevin Vanhoozer, "Expounding the Word of the Lord: Joseph Ratzinger on Revelation, Tradition, and Biblical Interpretation," in *The Theology of Benedict XVI: A Protestant Appreciation*, ed. Tim Perry (Bellingham: Lexham, 2019), 85. For the ecumenical importance of Ratzinger's attempts to unite metaphysics and scriptural exegesis, see Katherine Sonderegger, "Writing Theology in a Secular Age: Joseph Ratzinger on Theological Method," in *The Theology of Benedict XVI: A Protestant Appreciation*, ed. Tim Perry (Bellingham: Lexham, 2019), 43.

we notice but the rational standards by which we evaluate that evidence, it seems impossible to argue successfully for the superiority of one tradition of inquiry over another. For even if one admitted that, in theory, one tradition must be best, it still seems impossible, in practice, to determine which is best. For on both Ratzinger's and MacIntyre's premises, there is no nonpartisan rationality available to referee the contest between rival traditions. And if two teams compete, each with a different understanding of how points are scored, both will likely go away declaring themselves winner.

MacIntyre deals with this problem more explicitly than Ratzinger, clarifying in the prologue to the third edition of *After Virtue* just how much he thinks his arguments in the book achieved. He does not claim to have shown that "Aristotelian moral theory is able to exhibit its rational superiority in terms that would be acceptable to the protagonists of the dominant post-Enlightenment moral philosophies."[26] He claims, rather, to have shown only this: "From the standpoint of an ongoing way of life informed by and expressed through Aristotelian concepts it is possible to understand what the predicament of moral modernity is and why the culture of modernity lacks the resources to proceed further with its own moral enquiries, so that sterility and frustration are bound to afflict those unable to extricate themselves from these predicaments."[27] According to MacIntyre, among the factors contributing to the internal contradictions of modern moral discourse is the vestigial presence of very solemn and absolute-sounding moral categories dislocated from the broader metaphysical framework that once rendered them intelligible (e.g., a doctrine of creation, a "metaphysical biology" of human nature). Because MacIntyre admits that different traditions of moral inquiry have different internal standards of justification, he doubts that he can satisfy the objections of Kantians, utilitarians, and contractarians on their own terms. The most he can hope to do is provide an account of moral inquiry both internally coherent and capable of explaining incoherence in rival traditions (even if not in terms that would convince adherents of rival traditions).

Though Ratzinger does not spell out the claim for the rational superiority of his Bonaventurian-ecclesial hermeneutic so explicitly, he offers arguments in each of these categories. In the case of both Jesus' teaching on divorce and the historicity of the Last Supper, Ratzinger takes pains to argue

---

26 Alasdair MacIntyre, *After Virtue: A Study in Moral Virtue*, 3rd ed. (Notre Dame, IN: University of Notre Dame Press, 2007), x.

27 MacIntyre, *After Virtue*, x.

that his conclusions do not contradict the historical record. In this sense they meet the criterion of internal consistency. But his hermeneutic of faith and historical reason also explains historical-critical tradition's lack of discernible progress, its alternation of contradictory hypotheses, the tendency of each new generation of exegetes to dismiss the previous generation's portrait of the historical Jesus as a projection of the Zeitgeist. If Jesus' filial anchoring in God really is the central feature of his personality, and if historical criticism must bracket this feature methodologically, then historical critics will inevitably compile many valuable historical findings but paint no coherent picture of Jesus' person, aims, and historical impact. Ratzinger diagnoses historical-critical "exhaustion" this way when he writes, "In two hundred years of exegetical work, historical-critical exegesis has already yielded its essential fruit. If scholarly exegesis is not to exhaust itself in constantly new hypotheses, becoming theologically irrelevant, it must make a methodological step forward and see itself once again as a theological discipline."[28] Somewhat ironically, exegetes seem to corroborate this picture of their field when they criticize Ratzinger for engaging mostly "dated" exegesis.[29] Now it has to be admitted that major discoveries can revolutionize a field, as when the Dead Sea Scrolls (1947–56), with their wealth of information about Second Temple Judaism, quickly rendered much previous biblical scholarship obsolete. But this sort of information gap does not seem to separate the exegesis of 1970s from that of the new millennium. The irrelevance of one generation's work to the next appears to rest much more on shifting "worldview" than on the advent of new data.

Ratzinger also has the equivalent of MacIntyre's explanation of incoherence from vestigial "survivals." Just as terms such as "moral law" may survive long after the idea of a divine lawgiver has faded, revealing a moral discourse at odds with itself,[30] so concepts like "canon" may survive even in a supposedly nonconfessional discipline, revealing a conflicted relationship between faith and exegesis. On the one hand, mainstream biblical scholarship takes

---

28 JN 2:xiv.

29 Timothy Johnson, Review of Joseph Ratzinger, *Jesus of Nazareth: From the Baptism in the Jordan to the Transfiguration, Modern Theology* 24, no. 2 (2008): 319; Richard Hays, "Ratzinger's Johannine Jesus: A Challenge to Enlightenment Historiography," in *The Pope and Jesus of Nazareth: Christ, Scripture, and the Church*, ed. Adrian Pabst and Angus Paddison (London: SCM Press, 2009), 115.

30 MacIntyre, *After Virtue*, 53.

over the canon *materially* from the churches, accepting the list of books handed on by ecclesial tradition rather than the so-called gnostic gospels. On the other hand, mainstream exegesis disavows the *formal* understanding of the canon as a body of writings unified by a collective "subject that organically traverses the whole of history."[31] As Ratzinger sees things, the death of formal canonicity has led to a way of dealing with the biblical texts focused on genetic analysis: "The tendency to search for the most ancient and most original behind present developments is the logical conclusion of the loss of the binding element which holds history together and unifies it in the midst of contradictions."[32] With the canon's "understanding subject" bracketed, Scripture dissolves into contradictions, drawing the exegetical guild in tow. The interminability of debate reflects the fact that the canon in the academy, like the moral law in modernity, survives as only a ghost of its former self.

One can see Ratzinger's point illustrated indirectly by Raymond E. Brown's response to his Erasmus Lecture of January 1988. In remarks prepared in advance, Brown praised historical criticism as a safeguard against too quickly presuming a unified belief among canonical sources: "Too often very conservative interpreters have appealed to the analogy of other biblical writings to determine what the author must have known, e.g., Paul must have known the virginal conception narrated in Matthew and Luke."[33] Here Brown's idea of biblical meaning seems centered in individual rather than corporate intentionality, resulting in a weaker sense of canonicity than Ratzinger's *analogia fidei*. After hearing Ratzinger's Erasmus lecture, however, Brown took pains to clarify that he too rejects a kind of "radical criticism . . . more concerned with the sources than with the written text, so that what the text should have said becomes the message."[34] In light of Brown's rejection of both conservative canonicity and radical anti-canonicity, however, one might ask what makes for a "moderate" approach? For Brown, it seems, it comes down to admitting a moderate amount of ecclesial preunderstand-

---

31 Joseph Ratzinger, *The Nature and Mission of Theology: Essays to Orient Theology in Today's Debates* (San Francisco: Ignatius, 1995), 95.

32 Ratzinger, *Nature and Mission of Theology*, 95.

33 Raymond E. Brown, "The Contribution of Historical Biblical Criticism to Ecumenical Church Discussion," in *Biblical Interpretation in Crisis. The Ratzinger Conference on Bible and Church*, ed. Richard John Neuhaus, Encounter Series 9 (Grand Rapids, MI: Eerdmans, 1989), 26.

34 Brown, "Contribution of Historical Biblical Criticism," 38.

ing: "The 'lines of development' approach in my paper shows that the so-called moderate positions are accepted because of the thesis that the Bible is the book of the church and that liturgy, church history, and the *sensus fidelium* are major hermeneutical tools."[35] Ecclesial criteria have their place, in other words, so long as one does not anachronistically read them back into the first-century sources. Here one finds Brown candidly spectrifying the exegetical field—conservative, moderate, radical—according to degree of ecclesial precommitment. Judging by his previous remarks, Ratzinger would probably agree that these different appraisals of the churches' role in exegesis are the real factor dividing exegetical camps. But he might add that this is exactly his point. Since historical criticism cannot by its own methods determine whether Jesus is the Son of God or the Bible the Church's book, it lacks a principled means of resolving its persistent disagreements.[36] This issues in what Ratzinger calls the "exhaustion" of critical exegesis, a phenomenon similar to what MacIntyre calls the frustrations of "moral modernity."

Like MacIntyre, then, Ratzinger does not claim to be able to establish the superiority of his interpretive method by arguments acceptable to historical criticism. His project is much rather to model a hermeneutic of faith accountable to historical reason that others can "try on." He is confident that those who do so will find that it fits best: that it both yields a stable and coherent way of interpreting Scripture and explains why the alternative, purely historical "cognitive posture" fails to produce lasting consensus.

Though Ratzinger is perhaps best known for his deconstruction of historical criticism, these efforts serve as a preamble to a more constructive project: proposing a paradigm shift in the Catholic theology of biblical inspiration. One way to think about Ratzinger's paradigm shift is as a contemporary reframing of Bonaventurian insights. Guided by Bonaventure's subject-inclusive notion of *inspiratio*, Ratzinger took preexisting blocks, filed down the protruding edges, and built his own house. He combined elements of Rahner and Benoit by appealing to the intention not of individual authors but of the People of God. He combined elements of Rahner and Tracy by explaining Scripture's growth in meaning as a function of its ongoing reception by the People of God. In synthesizing the elements this way, he arguably

---

35 Brown, "Contribution of Historical Biblical Criticism," 40; cf. 34.

36 Kevin Duffy notes that Raymond E. Brown's self-designation as a "centrist" exegete flows from his twin commitment to both a Catholic (especially Chalcedonian) preunderstanding and objective biblical criticism. Duffy, "Ecclesial Hermeneutic of Raymond E. Brown," 37.

better spanned the doctrinal "pegs" laid down by Trent, Vatican I, and especially Vatican II. Ratzinger's efforts have not eliminated all strains, but they have provided a workable pattern that can be further refined. This has been the main argument so far.

But there is another way of thinking about the paradigm shift. One can also understand Ratzinger to have finally "received" Newman, even if unwittingly. Newman, it will be remembered, wanted above all to still the "questionings and perplexities in the secret heart, which cut at the root of devotion, and dry up the founts of love."[37] He dimly foresaw that a successful strategy would imagine Scripture as if God had "spoken the whole of it over again," introducing an inspired sense that integrated all the regional senses without coinciding entirely with any of them. In 1884 he suggested that the ideas of Scripture enjoy a divine guarantee only insofar as they bear upon faith and morals, which he took to be Scripture's "drift." But the idea lacked both a certain nuance and the metaphysical integration expected by scholastically formed theologians. Its potential thus remained largely unrealized.

Ratzinger seems to arrive at the main lines of Newman's solution independently, but, by building on the theological proposals developed after Newman, provides a kind of metaphysical—and especially Christological—integration. Forgetfulness of the limits of historical methods, he writes in the introduction to his *Jesus of Nazareth* trilogy, has become a kind of scandal to the faith: "Intimate friendship with Jesus, on which everything depends, is in danger of clutching at thin air."[38] For Ratzinger and Newman alike, then, an "optimal" view of inspiration would be flexible enough to dispel constant fear of contradiction yet robust enough to unseal the founts of devotion. It is especially important for Ratzinger that the Scriptures facilitate devotion to Christ.

Turning to the inspired sense of Scripture, Ratzinger again inclines toward a solution along Newman's lines, albeit with a stronger Christological accent. Like Newman, Ratzinger calls for a model of inspiration that would allow God to speak the whole of Scripture "over again," imparting its inspired sense. Unlike Newman, Ratzinger provides the historical organ through which God performs this *relecture*. God speaks of the whole of

---

37 John Henry Newman, "Essay on the Inspiration of Scripture (1861–1863)," in *Newman's Doctrine on Holy Scripture: According to His Published Works and Previously Unpublished Manuscripts*. ed. Jaak Seynaeve (Louvain: Publications Universitaires de Louvain, 1953), 70.

38 JN 1:xii.

Scripture "over again" by guiding the People of God in their continual reread-ing and redaction of the Scriptures. God spoke Scripture over again in the formation of the Old Testament canon. God spoke it yet again in Christ, who reread the Old Testament from God's own perspective, redrawing the "dividing line between center and periphery, between the will of God and the work of man."[39] God continues to speak the whole of Scripture in the Church, the region of Christ's Spirit, whence it follows that "one cannot determine the meaning of its individual texts from what the first author—who in most cases is hypothetically ascertained—intended to say historically."[40] One must look instead to the "living Christ" as the "genuine norm for interpreting the Bible."[41] Transposing Ratzinger's theory into Newman's terms, one could say that God "repeats" the words of individually inspired prophets and apostles by also guiding how Christ and the People of God receive them. It is by attending to this "ecclesial drift" that one discerns what Scripture properly intends to affirm and what it includes merely obiter.

The theological movement from Newman to Ratzinger opens up the possibility of a kind of *relecture* of *Providentissimus Deus* itself. In a passage that was commonly (but mistakenly) taken to condemn Newman, Pope Leo XIII rejected any solution conceding that "divine inspiration regards the things of faith and morals, and nothing beyond." In retrospect it becomes clear that Leo was right to shut this door. For a strict narrowing to faith and morals claimed both too little and too much. It claimed too little for the potential relevance of history and science to matters of faith and morals. Yet it claimed too much for the possibility of translating even certain biblical ideas on religion and morality directly into the present. Even here one must avoid what Ratzinger calls "false directness," sifting carefully what applies to a particular time and place from what remains a matter of perpetual observance.

But *Providentissimus Deus* seems to have been prescient in another way. After denying the possibility that God allowed the biblical authors to fall into error, the encyclical invokes the authority of St. Augustine's *De consensu*

---

39 Joseph Ratzinger, *Principles of Catholic Theology: Building Stones for a Fundamental The-ology* (San Francisco: Ignatius, 1987), 98.

40 Joseph Ratzinger, "Is the *Catechism of the Catholic Church* Up-to-Date? Reflections Ten Years after Its Publication," in *On the Way to Jesus Christ,* trans. Michael J. Miller (San Fran-cisco: Ignatius, 2005), 150.

41 Ratzinger, "Is the Catechism Up-to-Date?," 152.

evangelistarum: "'Therefore,' says St. Augustine, 'since they wrote the things which He showed and uttered to them, it cannot be pretended that He is not the writer; for His members executed what their Head dictated.'"[42] More interesting than Augustine's denial of error on the part of the evangelists is his grounds for doing so: the unity between Christ the Head and his members. Ratzinger likewise appeals to the varied yet constant connection between the People of God and Christ when relativizing the criterion of individual authorial intention. Though Leo generally cited patristic authorities with a view demonstrating a rather strict view of inerrancy, he nevertheless supplied resources for elaborating a more flexible model.

Ratzinger thus arguably completes Newman's seminal insights by extending the reasoning of the encyclical that was thought to have condemned him. He respects the negative boundary established by Leo and maintained in *Dei Verbum* 11—namely, that inspiration and inerrancy cannot be reduced to matters of faith and morals and nothing beyond. He proposes instead a sliding scale, whereby inspiration and inerrancy extend to all Scripture's ideas—whether historical, scientific, ethical, or cultic—to the degree that they bear upon faith in Christ. In this way Ratzinger integrates both *Dei Verbum* 11's affirmation that God consigned truth to Scripture "for the sake of our salvation" and Newman's idea that God gives Scripture a "drift" polarizing the biblical field into central affirmations and *obiter dicta*. At the same time, he makes the faith of the *totus Christus*, highlighted by Leo, the criterion for discerning those central affirmations. This he does with the theoretical grounding of Bonaventure's theology of *inspiratio* and greater familiarity with the results of twentieth-century biblical criticism. By practicing the kind of return to the sources that he preached, Leo XIII laid the foundation for the house that Ratzinger would build.

All this allowed Ratzinger to bring the Catholic quest for an adequate theory of biblical inspiration and inerrancy, palpable already in Newman, to a certain preliminary synthesis. I say *preliminary* synthesis because Ratzinger's theology of Scripture itself remains open to further development and clarification. But I nevertheless say preliminary *synthesis* because Ratzinger has brought the data of faith and reason into a stable configuration. He has rebalanced the a priori and a posteriori moments with a serenity that proved elusive to both pre- and post-conciliar exegetes. He has made a case, analogous to MacIntyre's argument for the superiority of Thomist-Aristotelian ethical

42 *De consensu evang.* 1, I, cap. 35. Cited in *PD* 20.

tradition, that his hermeneutic of faith and reason represents a cognitive posture more adequate to the biblical phenomenon. The fact that Ratzinger engages in contemporary debates while echoing premodern sensibilities, such as Bonaventure's theology of revelation or Newman's patristic reading strategies, suggests that his central insights may survive this generation as well. They stand as both an endpoint and a beginning.

Bibliography

WRITINGS BY JOSEPH RATZINGER

"Anglican-Catholic Dialogue: Its Problems and Hopes." *Insight* 1, no. 3 (1983): 2–11.

"Anmerkungen zur Aktualität von Johann Sebastian Dreys *Kurze Einleitung in das Studium der Theologie*." In *Theologie, Kirche, Katholizismus: Beiträge zur Programmatik der Katholischen Tübinger Schule*, edited by Michael Kessler and Max Seckler, 1–6. Tübingen: Francke, 2003.

Behold the Pierced One: An Approach to a Spiritual Christology. San Francisco: Ignatius, 1986.

"Biblical Interpretation in Conflict." In *God's Word: Scripture—Tradition—Office*, edited by Peter Hünermann and Thomas Söding, translated by Henry Taylor, 91–126. San Francisco: Ignatius, 2005.

"Brief von Joseph Ratzinger an P. Karl Rahner vom 19. Juni 1963." *Mitteilungen. Institut Papst Benedikt XVI.* 5 (2012): 13–16. Manuscript: ADPSJ Abt. 1010 [Karl Rahner Archiv] II, A, Nr. 2418.

"Die Christologie im Spannungsfeld von altchristlicher Exegese und moderner Bibelauslegung." In *Urbild und Abglanz: Festgabe für Herbert Doms zum 80. Geburtstag*, edited by Johannes Tenzler, 359–67. Regensburg: Josef Habbel, 1972.

Called to Communion. Translated by Adrian Walker. San Francisco: Ignatius, 1996.

Church, Ecumenism, Politics: New Essays in Ecclesiology. Translated by Robert Nowell. New York: Crossroad, 1988.

"The Church's Teaching Authority—Faith—Morals." In *Principles of Christian Morality*, edited by Joseph Ratzinger, Heinrich Schürmann, and Hans Urs von Balthasar, 45–73. San Francisco: Ignatius, 1986.

Daughter Zion: Meditations in the Church's Marian Belief. Translated by John M. McDermott, SJ. San Francisco: Ignatius, 1983.

Dogma and Preaching. Edited by Michael J. Miller. Translated by Michael J. Miller and Matthew J. O'Connell. San Francisco: Ignatius, 2011. Translation of *Dogma und Verkündigung*. Munich: Erich Wewel Verlag, 1973.

"Dogmatic Constitution on Divine Revelation." In *Commentary on the Documents of Vatican II*, vol. 3, edited by Herbert Vorgrimler, translated by William Glen-Doepl, 170–98, 260–72. New York: Herder & Herder, 1967.

"Erich Przywaras Alterswerk" (review of *Alter und Neuer Bund* and *Gespräch Zwischen den Kirchen*). *Wort und Wahrheit* 13 (1958): 220–21.

Eschatology: Death and Eternal Life. Translated by Michael Waldstein and Aidan Nichols. Washington, DC: The Catholic University of America Press, 1988.

"Exegesis and the Magisterium of the Church." In *Opening Up the Scriptures: Joseph Ratzinger and the Foundations of Biblical Interpretation*, edited by J. Granados, C. Granados, and Luis Sánchez-Navarro, 126–36. Grand Rapids, MI: Eerdmans, 2008.

Faith and the Future. Chicago: Franciscan Herald, 1971.

"Form and Content in the Eucharistic Celebration." In *Feast of Faith: Approaches to a Theology of the Liturgy*, translated by Graham Harrison, 33–66. San Francisco: Ignatius, 1986. Translation of *Das Fest des Glaubens*. Einsiedlen: Johannes, 1981.

Geleitwort zu *Maria, die Mutter Jesu im Neuen Testament*, by Franz Mußner. St. Ottilien: EOS Verlag, 1993.

Gespräch über Jesus: Papst Benedikt XVI. im Dialog mit Martin Hengel, Peter Stuhlmacher und seinen Schülern in Castelgandolfo 2008. Tübingen: Mohr Siebeck, 2010.

"Glaube, Geschichte, und Philosophie." *Hochland* 61 (1969): 533–43.

"Grace and Vocation without Remorse: Comments on the Treatise *De Iudeais*," *Communio* 45, no. 2 (2018): 163–84. Translation of "Gnade und Berufung ohne Reue: Anmerkung zum Traktat «De Iudaeis»," *Internationale Katholische Zeitschrift—Kommunio* 47 (2018): 387–406.

"Homily at the Mass of the Lord's Supper." No pages. Cited April 5, 2007. Online: http://www.vatican.va/content/benedict-xvi/en/homilies/2007/documents/hf_ben-xvi_hom_20070405_coena-domini.html.

"Indirizzo di saluto del Papa Emerito Benedetto XVI in occasione del 50° anniversario di instituzione della Commissione Teologica Internazionale." No pages. Cited October 22, 2019. Online: http://www.vatican.va/roman_curia/congregations/cfaith/cti_documents/rc_cti_20191022_saluto-bxvi-50ann-cti_it.html.

In the Beginning . . . : A Catholic Understanding of the Story of Creation and the Fall. Grand Rapids, MI: Eerdmans, 1995.

Introduction to Christianity. San Francisco: Ignatius, 1990.

Introduction to *On the Pastoral Care of Divorced and Remarried Persons*. Documents and Commentaries. Washington, DC: Libreria Editrice Vaticana, 2012.

"Is the *Catechism of the Catholic Church* Up-to-Date? Reflections Ten Years after Its Publication." In *On the Way to Jesus Christ*, translated by Michael J. Miller, 142–65. San Francisco: Ignatius, 2005. Translation of "Lehrmässige Aktualität des 'Katechismus der katholischen Kirche' zehn Jahre nach seiner Veröffentlichung." *L'Osservatore Romano Deutsche Ausgabe* 46 (November 15, 2002): 9–11.

Many Religions—One Covenant: Israel, the Church, and the World. San Francisco: Ignatius, 1999.

"Der Mensch und die Zeit im Denken des heiligen Bonaventura." In *L'Homme et son destin d'après les penseurs du moyen âge*, 473–83. Louvain and Paris: Neuwelaerts, 1960.

"Message of His Holiness Benedict XVI to Participants in the Plenary Meeting of the Pontifical Biblical Commission." May 2, 2011. No pages. Online: http://www.vatican. va/content/benedict-xvi/en/messages/pont-messages/2011/documents/hf_ben-xvi_ mes_20110502_plenaria_pcb.html.

Milestones: Memoirs, 1927–1977. San Francisco: Ignatius, 1998.

"The Ministerial Office and the Unity of the Church." *Journal of Ecumenical Studies* 1 (1964): 42–57.

The Nature and Mission of Theology: Essays to Orient Theology in Today's Debates. San Francisco: Ignatius, 1995.

"Naturrecht, Evangelium und Ideologie in der katholischen Soziallehre: Katholische Erwägungen zum Thema." In *Christlicher Glaube und Ideologie*, edited by K. von Bismark und W. Dirks, 24–30. Stuttgart and Mainz: Kreuz Verlag, 1964.

"Offenbarung—Schrift—Überlieferung." *Trierer Theologische Zeitschrift* 67 (1958): 13–27.

Preface to *Problèmes doctrinaux du mariage chrétien*, by the Congregation for the Doctrine of the Faith. Edited by P. Delhaye. Lex Spiritus Vitae 4. Louvain: Centre Cerfaux, 1979.

"Primacy, Episcopacy, and *Successio Apostolica*." In *God's Word: Scripture—Tradition—Office*, edited by Peter Hünermann and Thomas Söding, translated by Henry Taylor, 13–39. San Francisco: Ignatius, 2005.

Principles of Catholic Theology: Building Stones for a Fundamental Theology. San Francisco: Ignatius, 1987.

Das Problem der Dogmengeschichte in der Sicht der katholischen Theologie. Arbeitsgemeinschaft für Forschung des Landes Nordrhein–Westfalen 139. Köln: Westdeutscher Verlag, 1966.

"Das Problem der Mariologie." *Theologische Revue* 61, no. 2 (1965): 73–82.

"The Question of the Concept of Tradition: A Provisional Response." In *God's Word: Scripture, Tradition, Office*, edited by Peter Hünermann and Thomas Söding, translated by Henry Taylor, 41–89. San Francisco: Ignatius, 2008.

Review of Karl Rahner, *Visionen und Prophezeiungen*, 2nd ed. *Theologische Revue* 56, no. 6 (1960): 249–50.

"Sacred Scripture in the Life of the Church." In *Commentary on the Documents of Vatican II*, vol. 3, edited by Herbert Vorgrimler, translated by William Glen-Doepl, 262–72. New York: Herder & Herder, 1967.

Salt of the Earth: The Church at the End of the Millennium—An Interview with Peter Seewald San Francisco: Ignatius, 1997.

"The Sign of the Woman: An Introductory Essay on the Encyclical *Redemptoris Mater.*" In *Mary: The Church at the Source*, edited with foreword by Hans Urs von Balthasar, translated by Adrian Walker, 37–60. San Francisco: Ignatius, 2005. Translation of "Die Zeichen der Frau: Versuch einer Hinführung zur Enzyklika 'Redemptoris Mater' von Papst Johannes Paulus II," in *Maria: Gottes Ja zum Menschen* (Freiburg: Herder, 1987), 105–28.

The Spirit of the Liturgy. Translated by John Saward. San Francisco: Ignatius, 2000.

Theological Highlights of Vatican II. New York, Paulist, 2009.

"Theologie im Präsens." (review of *Über die Schriftinspiration*, by Karl Rahner, *Zur Theologie des Todes*, by Karl Rahner, and *Mächte und Gewalten im Neuen Testament*, by Heinrich Schlier). *Wort und Wahrheit* 13 (1958): 644–46.

The Theology of History in St. Bonaventure. Chicago: Franciscan Herald, 1989.

"The Transmission of Divine Revelation." In *Commentary on the Documents of Vatican II*, vol. 3, edited by Herbert Vorgrimler, translated by William Glen-Doepl, 181–98. New York: Herder & Herder, 1967.

"Wer ist der Teufel?" *Mitteilungen. Institut Papst Benedikt XVI.* 5 (2012): 38–39. Translation of *Famiglia Cristiana* 41, no. 40 (October 10, 1971): 7.

"Wesen und Weisen der auctoritas im Werk des hl. Bonaventura." In JRGS 2:744–66. Repr. in *Die Kirche und ihre Ämter und Stände. Festschrift für Joseph Kardinal Frings zum goldenen Priesterjubiläum*, edited by W Corsten, A. Frotz, und P. Linden, 58–72. Köln: Bachem, 1960.

"What in Fact Is Theology?" In *Pilgrim Fellowship of Faith: The Church as Communion*, edited by Stephan Otto Horn and Vinzenz Pfnür, translated by Henry Taylor, 29–37. San Francisco: Ignatius, 2005.

"Zur Frage nach der Unauflöslichkeit der Ehe." In JRGS 4:600–621.

"Zur Frage nach der Unauflöslichkeit der Ehe¹." In *Ehe und Ehescheidung: Diskussion unter Christen*, edited by Franz Henrich and Volker Eid, 35–56. Münchener Akademie Schriften 59. Munich, Kösel, 1972.

"Zum Problem der Entmythologisierung des Neuen Testaments." *Religionsunterricht an Höheren Schulen* 3 (1960): 2–11.

"Zur Theologie der Ehe." In JRGS 4:565–92. Repr. from *Theologische Quartalschrift* 149 (1969): 53–74.

LITERATURE

Adam, A. K. M. "Poaching on Zion: Biblical Theology as Signifying Practice." In *Reading Scripture with the Church: Toward a Hermeneutic for Theological Interpretation*, 17–34. Grand Rapids, MI: Baker Academic, 2006.

Aguzzi, Steven D. "One Step Forward, Two Steps Back: Supersessionism and Pope Benedict XVI's Eschatological Ecclesiology Concerning Israel and the Jewish People." *Journal of Ecumenical Studies* 49, no. 4 (2014): 601–12.

Albert, Hans. "Josef [*sic*] Ratzingers Jesusdeutung: Kritische Bemerkungen zu einigen Aspekten seiner Untersuchung." In *Alla ricerca della verità: Discussioni sul Gesù de Nazaret di Joseph Ratzinger—Benedetto XVI*, edited by Giuseppe Franco, 131–48. Lecce: Lupo, 2009.

Allen, John. *Joseph Ratzinger: The Vatican's Enforcer of Faith.* New York: Continuum, 2000.

Alonso Schökel, Luis. *The Inspired Word.* Translated by Francis Martin. New York: Herder & Herder, 1969.

Anderson, Gary. "The Baptism of Jesus: On Jesus' Solidarity with Israel and Foreknowledge of the Passion." In *Explorations in the Theology of Benedict XVI*, edited by John C. Cavadini, 236–53. Notre Dame, IN: University of Notre Dame Press, 2012.

Anger, G., and J.-H. Tück. "Vorstudien und Echo: Ein erster bibliographischer Überblick zu Joseph Ratzingers *Jesus von Nazareth*." In *Annäherungen an "Jesus von Nazareth*," edited by J.-H. Tück, 182–99. Ostfildern: Grünewald, 2007.

Ayres, Lewis. "Is Nicene Trinitarianism 'in' the Scriptures?" *Nova et Vetera* 18, no. 4 (Fall 2020): 1285–1300.

Balthasar, Hans Urs von. "Casta Meretrix." In *Spouse of the Word*, vol. 2 of *Explorations in Theology*, translated by John Saward, 193–288. San Francisco: Ignatius, 1991.

Bauckham, Richard. *Jesus and the Eyewitnesses: The Gospels as Eyewitness Testimony.* 2nd ed. Grand Rapids, MI: Eerdmans, 2017.

Bauerschmidt, Frederick Christian. "The Eucharist." In *The Oxford Handbook of Catholic Theology*, edited by Lewis Ayres and Medi Ann Volpe, 277–93. Oxford: Oxford University Press, 2019.

Bea, Augustin, SJ. "Deus auctor Sacrae Scripturae. Herrkunft und Bedeutung der Formel." *Angelicum* 20 (1943): 16–31.

———. *The Study of the Synoptic Gospels.* Edited by Joseph Fitzmyer, SJ. New York: Harper & Row, 1965. Translation of *La storicità dei Vangeli.* Brescia: Morcelliana, 1964.

———. *The Word of God and Mankind.* London: Geoffrey Chapman, 1967.

Béchard, Dean P., ed. *The Scripture Documents: An Anthology of Official Catholic Teachings.* Translated by Dean P. Béchard. Collegeville, MN: Liturgical, 2002.

Bell, Richard H. "The Transfiguration: A Case Study in the Relationship between 'History' and 'Theological Symbol' in the Light of Pope Benedict's Book." In *The Pope and Jesus of Nazareth: Christ, Scripture and the Church*, edited by Adrian Pabst and Angus Paddison, 159–75. London, SCM Press, 2009.

Benoit, Pierre. "Analogies of Inspiration." In *Aspects of Biblical Inspiration*, translated by J. Murphy-O'Connor, OP, and S. K. Ashe, OP, 13–35. Chicago: Priory, 1965. Translation from "Les analogies de l'inspiration," in *Sacra pagina: Miscellanea biblica Congressus Internationalis Catholici de re biblica*, vol. 1, ed. J Coppens, A. Descamps, E. Massaux, 86–99. Gembloux: Duculot, 1959.

———. "Inspiration and Revelation." *Concilium* 10 (1965): 6–24.

———. *Prophecy and Inspiration: A Commentary on the Summa Theologica II–II, Questions 171–178*. Translated by Avery Dulles and Thomas L. Sheridan. New York: Desclée, 1961. Translation from *Traité de la prophétie*. Tournai: Desclée & Cie, 1947.

Berger, Klaus. "Exegese und Dogmatik: Bermerkungen über das Jesusbuch des Papstes." In *Alla ricerca della verità: Discussioni sul Gesù de Nazaret di Joseph Ratzinger—Benedetto XVI*, edited by Giuseppe Franco, 25–43. Lecce: Lupo, 2009.

Bieringer, Reimund. "Annoncer la vie éternelle (1 Jn 1,2): L'interprétation de la Bible dans les textes officiels de l'Église catholique romaine." *RTL* 37 (2006): 498–512.

———. "Biblical Revelation and Exegetical Interpretation according to Dei Verbum 12," *Studien zum Neuen Testament und seiner Umwelt* 27 (2002): 5–40.

Blankenhorn, Brendan, OP. "God Speaks: Divine Authorship of Scripture in Karl Rahner and Pierre Benoit," *Angelicum* 93, no. 3 (2016): 445–61.

Blondel, Maurice. *The Letter on Apologetics and History and Dogma*. Edited and translated by Alexander Dru and Illtyd Trethowan. Grand Rapids, MI: Eerdmans, 1994.

Bockmuehl, Marcus. "Saints' Lives as Exegesis." In *The Pope and Jesus of Nazareth: Christ, Scripture and the Church*, edited by Adrian Pabst and Angus Paddison, 119–33. London: SCM Press, 2009.

Bond, Helen K. "Dating the Death of Jesus: Memory and the Religious Imagination." *New Testament Studies* 59 (2013): 461–75.

Bonsirven, Joseph, SJ. *Le divorce dans le Nouveau Testament*. Paris: Desclée de Brouwer, 1948.

Bradshaw, Paul. *Reconstructing Early Christian Worship*. London: SPCK, 2009.

Brotherton, Joshua. "Revisiting the *Sola Scriptura* Debate: Yves Congar and Joseph Ratzinger on Tradition." *Pro Ecclesia* 24, no. 1 (2015): 85–114.

Brown, Raymond E., SS. "The Contribution of Historical Biblical Criticism to Ecumenical Church Discussion." In *Biblical Interpretation in Crisis. The Ratzinger Conference on Bible and Church*, edited by Richard John Neuhaus, 24–49. Encounter Series 9. Grand Rapids, MI: Eerdmans, 1989.

———. *The Critical Meaning of the Bible: How a Modern Reading of the Bible Challenges Christians, the Church, and the Churches*. New York: Paulist, 1981.

———. "Difficulties in Using the New Testament in American Catholic Discussions," *Louvain Studies* 2 (1976): 144–58.

———. *The Gospel according to John.* 2 vols. Anchor Bible 29–29A. New York: Doubleday, 1966–70.

———. "The *Sensus Plenior* in the Last Ten Years," *Catholic Biblical Quarterly* 25 (1963): 282–85.

Brugger, E. Christian. *The Indissolubility of Marriage and the Council of Trent.* Washington, DC: The Catholic University of America Press, 2017.

Bultmann, Rudolf. "New Testament and Mythology." In *Kerygma and Myth: A Theological Debate,* edited by Hans Werner Bartsch, translated by Reginald H. Fuller, 1–44. New York: Harper & Row, 1966.

———. *Theologie des Neuen Testaments.* 9th ed. Tübingen, J.C.B. Mohr, 1984.

Burigana, Riccardo. *La Bibbia nel Concilio: La redazione della constituzione «Dei Verbum» del Vaticano II.* Bologna: Il Mulino, 1998.

Burridge, Richard A. *What Are the Gospels?: A Comparison with Greco-Roman Biography.* 2nd ed. Grand Rapids, MI: Eerdmans, 2004.

Burtchaell, James Tunstead. *Catholic Theories of Biblical Inspiration since 1810: A Review and Critique.* Cambridge: Cambridge University Press, 1969.

Caballero, Juan Luis, and Pablo Edo. "La redacción del capítulo V de *Dei Verbum.*" *Scripta Theologica* 47 (2015): 177–200.

Canty, Aaron. "Bonaventurian Resonances in Benedict XVI's Theology of Revelation." *Nova et Vetera* 5, no. 2 (2007): 249–66.

Caprile, Giovanni, SJ, ed. *Il Concilio Vaticano II: Cronache del Concilio Vaticano II edite da "La Civiltà Cattolica."* 5 vols. Rome: La Civiltà Cattolica, 1966–69.

Collins, Christopher S., SJ. *Word Made Love: The Dialogical Theology of Joseph Ratzinger/Benedict XVI.* Collegeville, MN: Liturgical, 2013.

Congar, Yves-Marie, OP. "Ecclesia ab Abel." In *Abhandlungen über Theologie und Kirche. Festschrift für Karl Adam,* edited by Marcel Reding, 79–108. Düsseldorf: Patmos, 1952.

———. *I Believe in the Holy Spirit.* 3 Vols. Translated by David Smith. New York: Crossroad Herder, 1997.

———. "Inspiration des écritures canoniques et apostolicité de l'Église." *Revue des sciences philosophiques et théologiques* 45 (1961): 32–42.

———. *The Mystery of the Temple: Or the Manner of God's Presence to His Creatures from Genesis to Apocalypse.* Translated by Reginald Trevett. London: Burns & Oates, 1962. Translation of *Le mystère du temple.* Paris: Cerf, 1958.

———. *Vraie et fausse réforme dans l'Église.* Paris: Cerf, 1950.

Congregation for the Doctrine of the Faith. "Nota Doctrinalis *Professionis Fidei* Formulam Extremam Enucleans," *AAS* 90 (1998): 544–51.

———. *Problèmes doctrinaux du mariage chrétien.* Edited by P. Delhaye. Lex Spiritus Vitae 4. Louvain: Centre Cerfaux, 1979.

Clement of Alexandria. *Stromata Buch VII und VIII, Excerpta ex Theodoto, Eclogae Propheticae, Quis Dives Salvetur, Fragmente.* 2nd ed. Edited by Otto Stählin and Ludwig Früchtel. GCS 17. Berlin. Akademie, 1970.

Collins, James. *The Bible after Babel: Historical Criticism in a Postmodern Age.* Grand Rapids, MI: Eerdmans, 2005.

———. *What Are Biblical Values?* New Haven: Yale University Press, 2019.

Crouzel, Henri, SJ. *L'Église primitive face au divorce.* Théologie historique 13. Paris: Beauchesne, 1971.

———. "Encore sur divorce et remariage selon Épiphane," *Vigiliae Christianae* 38 (1984): 271–80.

———. "Le texte patristique de Matthieu V.32 et XIX:9," *New Testament Studies* 19 (1972): 98–119.

Davies, W. D. and Dale C. Allison. *A Critical and Exegetical Commentary on the Gospel according to Saint Matthew.* 3 vols. International Critical Commentary. Edinburgh: T&T Clark, 1988–97.

De Lubac, Henri, SJ. *History and Spirit: The Understanding of Scripture according to Origen.* Translated by Anne Englund Nash and Juvenal Merriell. San Francisco: Ignatius, 2007.

———. *Medieval Exegesis: The Four Senses of Scripture.* 3 Vols. Translated by Mark Sebanc and E. M. Macierowski. Grand Rapids, MI: Eerdmans, 1998–2009. Partial translation of *Éxegèse médiévale: les quatre sens de l'écriture.* 4 Vols. Theologie 41. Paris: Aubier, 1959–1964.

DiCenso, James J. *Hermeneutics and the Disclosure of Truth: A Study in the Work of Heidegger, Gadamer, and Ricoeur.* Charlottesville: University of Virginia Press, 1990.

Doyle, John P. "Hispanic Scholastic Philosophy." In *The Cambridge Companion to Renaissance Philosophy,* edited by James Hankins, 250–69. Cambridge: Cambridge University Press, 2007.

Duffy, Kevin. "The Ecclesial Hermeneutic of Raymond E. Brown." *Heythrop Journal* 39 (1998): 37–56.

Dulles, Avery, SJ. "The Authority of Scripture: A Catholic Perspective." In *Scripture in the Jewish and Christian Traditions: Authority, Interpretation, Relevance,* edited by Frederick E. Greenspahn, 14–40. Nashville: Abingdon, 1982.

———. *The Craft of Theology: From Symbol to System.* New expanded ed. New York: Crossroad, 1992.

———. "The Interpretation of the Bible in the Church." In *Kirche Sein,* edited by Wilhelm Geerlings and Max Seckler, 29–37. Freiburg: Herder, 1994.

Ebner, Martin. "Jede Ausleger hat seine blinden Flecken." In *Das Jesus-Buch des Papstes: Die Antwort der Neutestamentler,* edited by Thomas Söding, 30–42. Freiburg: Herder, 2007.

Evans, Craig. "The Last Days of Jesus' Life: Did Jesus Anticipate the Cross?" In *The Gospels: History and Christology: The Search of Joseph Ratzinger-Benedict XVI / I Vangeli: Storia e Cristologia: La ricerca di Joseph Ratzinger-Benedetto XVI*, vol. 1 of 2, edited by Bernardo Estrada, Ermenegildo Manicardi, and Armand Puig i Tàrrech, 511–27. Rome: Libreria Editrice Vaticana, 2013.

Farkasfalvy, Denis M., OCist. *Inspiration and Interpretation: A Theological Introduction to Sacred Scripture.* Washington, DC: The Catholic University of America Press, 2010.

———. "Inspiration and Interpretation." In *Vatican II: Renewal within Tradition*, edited by Matthew Levering and Matthew L. Lamb, 77–100. Oxford: Oxford University Press, 2008.

———. *A Theology of the Christian Bible: Revelation, Inspiration, Canon.* Washington, DC: The Catholic University of America Press, 2018.

Fastiggi, Robert L. "Communal or Social Inspiration: A Catholic Critique." *Letter and Spirit* 6 (2010): 247–63.

Fiedler, Peter. "Sünde und Vergebung im Christentum." *Internationale Zeitschrift für Theologie Concilium* 10 (1974): 568–71.

Fink, Bruno. *Zwischen Schreibmaschine und Pileolus: Errinerungen an meine Zeit als Sekretär des Hochwürdigsten Herrn Joseph Kardinal Ratzinger in München und Rom September 1978–Dezember 1983.* Monographische Beiträge zu den Mitteilungen. Institut Papst Benedikt XVI. 3. Regensburg: Schnell und Steiner, 2016.

Finnis, John. "Apostolicity and Historicity: Scripture, Development, and a Truly Critical History." Paper presented at a private, virtual conference, December 17–18, 2021.

Fitzmyer, Joseph A., SJ. "The Biblical Commission's Instruction on the Historical Truth of the Gospels." *Theological Studies* 25 (1964): 386–408.

———. *The Inspiration of Scripture: In Defense of the Historical-Critical Method.* New York: Paulist, 2008.

———. "The Matthean Divorce Texts and Some New Palestinian Evidence." *Theological Studies* 37, no. 2 (1976): 197–226.

Flannery, Kevin, SJ. "Marriage, Thomas Aquinas, and Jean Porter." *Journal of Catholic Social Thought* 8, no. 2 (2011): 277–89.

Forestell, J. T., CSB. "The Limitation of Inerrancy." *Catholic Biblical Quarterly* 20, no. 1 (1958): 9–18.

Fowl, Stephen E. "The Importance of a Multivoiced Literal Sense of Scripture: The Example of Thomas Aquinas." In *Reading Scripture with the Church: Toward a Hermeneutic for Theological Interpretation*, 35–30. Grand Rapids, MI: Baker Academic, 2006.

Fransen, Piet, SJ. "Das Thema 'Ehescheidung nach Ehebruch' auf dem Konzil von Trent (1563)." *Concilium* 6 (1970): 343–48.

Franzelin, Johann-Baptist, SJ. *De Divina Traditione et Scriptura.* Rome: S. C. Propagandae Fidei, 1896.

Frei, Hans. *The Eclipse of Biblical Narrative*. New Haven: Yale University Press, 1974.

Freisen, Joseph. *Geschichte des canonischen Eherechts: Bis zum Verfall der Glossenlitteratur*. Paderborn: Ferdinand Schöningh, 1893.

Frey, Jörg. "Historisch-kanonisch-kirchlich: Zum Jesusbild Joseph Ratzingers." In *Das Jesus-Buch des Papstes: Die Antwort der Neutestamentler*, edited by Thomas Söding, 43–53. Freiburg: Herder, 2007.

Gabel, Helmut. *Inspirationsverständnis im Wandel: Theologische Neuorientierung im Umfeld des Zweiten Vatikanischen Konzils*. Mainz: Matthias Grünewald, 1991.

———. "Inspiration und Wahrheit der Schrift (DV 11): Neue Ansätze und Probleme in Kontext der gegenwärtigen wissenschaftlichen Diskussion." *Theologie der Gegenwart* 45 (2002): 121–36.

Gadamer, Hans-Georg. *Truth and Method*. 2nd rev. ed. Translation revised by Joel Weinsheimer and Donald G. Marshall. New York: Crossroad, 1989.

Gadenz, Pablo T. "Magisterial Teaching on the Inspiration and Truth of Scripture: Precedents and Prospects." *Letter & Spirit* 6 (2010): 67–91.

Gertz, Bernhard. "Was ist Analogia Fidei: Klarstellungen zu einem Kontrovers-Thema." *Catholica* 26 (1972): 309–24.

Giambrone, Anthony, OP. "The Quest for the *Vera et Sincera de Jesu*: Dei Verbum §19 and the Historicity of the Gospels." *Nova et Vetera* 13, no. 1 (2015): 87–123.

Gibellini, Rosino. "Il libro del papa su Gesù nel conflitto delle interpretazioni." In *Alla ricerca della verità: Discussioni sul Gesù de Nazaret di Joseph Ratzinger—Benedetto XVI*, edited by Giuseppe Franco, 101–9. Lecce: Lupo, 2009.

Gnilka, Joachim. *Das Evangelium nach Markus*. 2 vols. Evangelisch-Katholischer Kommentar zum Neuen Testament. Zürich: Benziger und Neukirchener, 1979.

Gnuse, Robert. *The Authority of the Bible*. New York: Paulist, 1985.

Goethe, Johann Wolfgang von. *Goethe: Scientific Studies*. Edited and translated by D. Miller. New York: Suhrkamp, 1988.

Gordon, Joseph K. *Divine Scripture in Human Understanding: A Systematic Theology of the Bible*. Notre Dame, IN: University of Notre Dame Press, 2019.

Gosse, Philip H. *Omphalos: An Attempt to Untie the Geological Knot*. London, John Van Voorst, 1857.

Gregory the Great. *Homiliae in Hiezechielem prophetam*. Edited by Marcus Adriaen. CCSL 142. Turnhout: Brepols, 1971.

Grillmeier, Alois, SJ. "The Divine Inspiration and the Interpretation of Sacred Scripture." In *Commentary on the Documents of Vatican II*, vol. 3, edited by Herbert Vorgrimler, translated by William Glen-Doepl, 199–246. New York: Herder & Herder, 1967.

Guardini, Romano. *Das Christusbild der paulinischen und johanneischen Schriften*. Würzburg: Werkbund Verlag, 1961.

———. *The Lord.* Translated by Elinor Castendyk Briefs. Eighth printing. Chicago: Henry Regnery, 1954.

Guarino, Thomas. "Catholic Reflections on Discerning the Truth of Sacred Scripture." In *Your Word Is Truth: A Project of Evangelicals and Catholics Together,* ed. Charles Colson and Richard John Neuhaus, 79–101. Grand Rapids, MI: Eerdmans, 2002.

Hahn, Scott. *Covenant and Communion: The Biblical Theology of Pope Benedict XVI.* Grand Rapids, MI: Brazos, 2009.

Hahn, Scott, and Benjamin Wiker. *Politicizing the Bible: The Roots of Historical Criticism and the Secularization of Scripture, 1300–1700.* New York: Crossroad, 2013.

Harkins, Franklin T. "Christ and the Eternal Extent of Divine Providence in the *Expositio super Iob ad Litteram* of Thomas Aquinas." *Viator* 47, no. 1 (2015): 123–52.

Harrison, Brian W. "Restricted Inerrancy and the 'Hermeneutic of Discontinuity.'" *Letter and Spirit* 6 (2010): 225–46.

Hauerwas, Stanley. *A Community of Character: Toward a Constructive Christian Social Ethic.* Notre Dame, IN: University of Notre Dame Press, 1991.

Hays, Richard. *The Moral Vision of the New Testament: Community, Cross, New Creation, A Contemporary Introduction to New Testament Ethics.* San Francisco: HarperCollins, 1996.

———. "Ratzinger's Johannine Jesus: A Challenge to Enlightenment Historiography." In *The Pope and Jesus of Nazareth: Christ, Scripture, and the Church,* ed. Adrian Pabst and Angus Paddison, 109–18. London: SCM Press, 2009. Repr. "The Catholic Quest for the Historical Jesus." In *Reading with the Grain of Scripture,* 123–31. Grand Rapids, MI: Eerdmans, 2020.

———. *Reading Backwards: Figural Christology and the Fourfold Gospel Witness.* Waco, TX: Baylor University Press, 2014.

Heidegger, Martin. *Basic Writings.* Edited by David Farrell Krell. Revised and expanded ed. San Francisco: HarperCollins, 1993.

———. *Poetry, Language, Thought.* Translated by Albert Hofstadter. New York: Harper & Row, 1971.

Helm, Paul. "B. B. Warfield's Path to Inerrancy: An Attempt to Correct Some Serious Misunderstandings," *Westminster Theological Journal* 72 (2010): 23–42.

Hengel, Martin. *Son of God: The Origin of Christology and the History of Jewish–Hellenistic Religion.* Translated by John Bowden. Philadelphia: Fortress, 1976.

Hittinger, Russell. "Natural Law and Wisdom Traditions." *The Muslim World* 106 (April 2016): 313–36.

Hodge, A. A., and B. B. Warfield. "Inspiration," *Presbyterian Review* (1881): 225–60.

Hollenbach, Paul. "The Conversion of Jesus: From Jesus the Baptizer to Jesus the Healer." *Aufstieg und Niedergang der römischen Welt* II, 25.1 (1982): 196–219.

Holmes, Derek, and Robert Murray, SJ, introduction to *On the Inspiration of Scripture: John Henry Newman*, edited by Derek Holmes and Robert Murray, 3–96. Washington, DC: Corpus Books, 1967.

Hölscher, Maria Raphaela. *Naturrecht bei Joseph Ratzinger/Benedikt XVI. Die Bedeutung des Naturrechts in Geschichte und Gegenwart*. Heiligenkreuz: Be&Be Verlag, 2014.

Homolka, Walter. "Jesu Letztes Abendmahl." In *Der Jesus Buch des Papstes: Passion, Tod, und Auferstehung im Disput*, edited by Herman Häring, 195–99. Berlin: LIT, 2011.

Hoping, Helmut. "Theologischer Kommentar zur Dogmatischen Konstitution über die göttliche Offenbarung." In *Herders Theologischer Kommentar zum Zweiten Vatikanischen Konzil*, vol. 3 of 5, edited by Peter Hünermann and Bernd Jochen Hilberath, 695–831. Freiburg: Herder, 2005.

Hoppe, Rudolf. "Historische Rückfrage und deutende Erinnerung an Jesus: Zum Jesusbuch von Joseph Ratzinger/Benedikt XVI." In *Das Jesus-Buch des Papstes: Die Antwort der Neutestamentler*, edited by Thomas Söding, 45–65. Freiburg: Herder, 2007.

Humphreys, Colin J. *The Mystery of the Last Supper: Reconstructing the Final Days of Jesus*. Cambridge: Cambridge University Press, 2011.

Irenaeus of Lyons. *Contra les hérésies: Livre II*. 2 vols. SC 293–94. Paris: Cerf, 1982.

Jaubert, Annie. "La Date de la dernière Cène." *Revue de l'histoire des religions* 146 (1954): 140–73.

Jeremias, Joachim. *Die Abendmahlsworte Jesu*. 4th ed. Göttingen: Vandenhoeck & Ruprecht, 1967.

Johnson, Elizabeth A. *She Who Is: The Mystery of God in Feminist Theological Discourse*. New York: Crossroad, 1992.

Johnson, H. J. T. "Leo XIII, Cardinal Newman and the Inerrancy of Scripture." *Downside Review* 69 (1951): 411–27.

Johnson, Luke Timothy. Review of *Jesus of Nazareth: From the Baptism in the Jordan to the Transfiguration* by Joseph Ratzinger. *Modern Theology* 24, no. 2 (2008): 318–20.

Journet, Charles. *L'Église du Verbe incarnée*. 2 vols. Paris. Desclée de Brouwer, 1951–55.

———. *La volonté divine salvifique sur les petits enfants*. Paris. Desclée de Brouwer, 1958.

Joy, John P. "Ratzinger and Aquinas on the Dating of the Last Supper: In Defense of the Synoptic Chronology." *New Blackfriars* (2012): 224–339.

Jüngel, E. "Der Hypothetische Jesus: Anmerkungen zum Jesus-Buch des Papstes." In *Annäherungen an "Jesus von Nazareth*," edited by J.-H. Tück, 94–103. Ostfildern: Grünewald, 2007.

Kaes, Dorothee. *Theologie im Anspruch von Geschichte und Wahrheit: Zur Hermeneutik Joseph Ratzingers*. St. Ottilien: EOS Verlag, 1997.

Kasper, Walter. *The Gospel of the Family*. Translated by William Madges. New York: Paulist, 2014.

———. *Jesus the Christ*. Rev. ed. New York: Continuum, 2011.

———. *That They May All Be One: The Call to Unity Today*. London and New York: Burns & Oates & Continuum, 2004.

Keener, Craig. *Christobiography: Memory, History, and the Reliability of the Gospels*. Grand Rapids, MI: Eerdmans, 2019.

Ker, Ian. T. "Newman, the Councils, and Vatican II." *Communio* 28 (2001): 708–28.

Koch, Kurt. "Benedict XVI. und Bonaventura." In *Das Geheimnis des Senfkorns: Grundzüge des theologischen Denkens von Papst Benedikt XVI*, 45–68. Regensburg: Friedrich Pustet, 2010.

La Potterie, Ignace de, SJ. "La Lettura della Sacra Scrittura 'nello Spirito': Il metodo patristico di leggere la Bibbia è possibile oggi?" *Civiltà Cattolica* 137 (August 1986): 209–23.

La Soujeole, Benoît-Dominique de, OP. *Introduction to the Mystery of the Church*. Translated by Michael J. Miller. Thomistic Ressourcement Series 3. Washington, DC: The Catholic University of America Press, 2014.

Legaspi, Michael. *The Death of Scripture and the Rise of Biblical Studies*. Oxford: Oxford University Press, 2010.

———. "What Ever Happened to Historical Criticism?" *Journal of Religion & Society* 9 (2007): 1–11.

Lemaire, Marie-Gabrielle. "Joseph Ratzinger et Henri de Lubac." *Association Internationale de Cardinal de Lubac Bulletin* 15 (2013): 45–62.

Léon-Dufour, Xavier, SJ. *Sharing the Eucharistic Bread: The Witness of the New Testament*. Translated by Matthew J. O'Connell. New York: Paulist, 1987.

Levenson, Jon D. *The Hebrew Bible, the Old Testament, and Historical Criticism*. Louisville: Westminster/John Knox, 1993.

Levering, Matthew. *Participatory Biblical Exegesis: A Theology of Biblical Interpretation*. Notre Dame, IN: University of Notre Dame Press, 2008.

Lindbeck, George A. *The Nature of Doctrine: Religion and Theology in a Postliberal Age*. Philadelphia: Westminster, 1984.

Lohfink, Norbert, SJ. "The Inerrancy of Scripture." In *The Christian Meaning of the Old Testament*, 24–51. Milwaukee: Bruce, 1968.

Lohse, Eduard. *Theologische Ethik des Neuen Testaments*. Theologische Wissenschaft 5/2. Stuttgart: Kohlhammer, 1988.

Luz, Ulrich. *Das Evangelium nach Matthäus*. 4 vols. Evangelisch-Katholischer Kommentar zum Neuen Testament. Zürich: Benzinger und Neukirchener, 1985–2002.

———. *Theologische Hermeneutik des Neuen Testaments*. Neukirchen-Vluyn: Neukirchener Verlag, 2014.

MacIntyre, Alasdair. *After Virtue: A Study in Moral Virtue*. 3rd ed. Notre Dame, IN: University of Notre Dame Press, 2007.

MacKenzie, Roderick A. F. "Some Problems in the Field of Inspiration." *CBQ* 20, no. 1 (1958): 1–8.

Maddox, Brenda. "The Double Helix and the 'Wronged Heroine.'" *Nature* 421 (2003): 407–8. Cited January 23, 2003. Online: https://www.nature.com/articles/nature01399.

Manicardi, Ermenegildo. "The Last Supper: The Meaning Given by Jesus to His Death." In *The Gospels: History and Christology: The Search of Joseph Ratzinger-Benedict XVI / I Vangeli: Storia e Cristologia: La ricerca di Joseph Ratzinger-Benedetto XVI*, vol. 1 of 2, edited by Bernardo Estrada, Ermenegildo Manicardi, and Armand Puig i Tàrrech, 605–33. Rome: Libreria Editrice Vaticana, 2013.

Marcus, Joel. *Mark: A New Translation with Introduction and Commentary.* 2 vols. Anchor Bible 27–27A. New York: Doubleday, 2000–2009.

Marín-Sola, Francisco, OP. *La evolución homogénea del dogma católico.* Introduction by Emilio Sauras, OP. 2nd ed. Madrid: Bibliotéca de Autores Cristianos, 1963.

Marschler, Thomas. "Analogia Fidei: Anmerkungen zu einem Grundprinzip theologischer Schrifthermeneutik," *Theologie und Philosophie* 87 (2012): 208–36.

McCarthy, Dennis J. "Personality, Society, and Inspiration." *Theological Studies* 24, no. 4 (1963): 553–76.

McGilchrist, Iain. *The Master and His Emissary: The Divided Brain and the Making of the Western World.* Expanded ed. New Haven: Yale University Press, 2019.

McKenna, Frances. *Innovation within Tradition: Joseph Ratzinger and Reading the Women of Scripture.* Philadelphia: Fortress, 2015.

McKenny, Gerald. "Moral Disagreements and the Limits of Reason: Reflections on MacIntyre and Ratzinger." In *Intractable Disputes about Natural Law: Alasdair MacIntyre and Critics*, edited by Lawrence S. Cunningham, 195–226. Notre Dame, IN: University of Notre Dame Press, 2009.

McKenzie, John L., SJ. "The Social Character of Inspiration." *Catholic Biblical Quarterly* 24, no. 2 (1962): 115–24.

McNeil, Brian, CRV. "Meditating on the Jesus of History." *Angelicum* 62, no. 3 (1985): 403–418.

Meier, John. *The Roots of the Problem and the Person.* Vol. 1 of *A Marginal Jew: Rethinking the Historical Jesus.* New York: Doubleday, 1991.

———. *Law and Love.* Vol. 4 of *A Marginal Jew: Rethinking the Historical Jesus.* New Haven: Yale University Press, 2009.

Möhler, Johann Adam. *Unity in the Church or The Principle of Catholicism: Presented in the Spirit of the Church Fathers of the First Three Centuries.* Edited and translated by Peter C. Erb. Washington, DC: The Catholic University of America Press, 1996. Translation of *Die Einheit in der Kirche Oder das Prinzip des Katholizismus dargestellt im Geiste der Kirchenväter der ersten drei Jahrhunderte.* Tübingen: Heinrich Laupp, 1825.

Moller, Phillip, SJ. "What Should They Be Saying about Biblical Inspiration? A Note on the State of the Question." *Theological Studies* 74 (2013): 605–31.

Morrow, Jeffrey. "Secularization, Objectivity, and Enlightenment Scholarship: The Theological and Political Origins of Modern Biblical Studies." *Logos* 18, no. 1 (2015): 14–32.

———. "Spinoza and the Theo-Political Implications of his Freedom to Philosophize." *New Blackfriars* 99 (2018): 374–87.

Mußner, Franz. "Ein Buch der Beziehungen." In *Das Jesus-Buch des Papstes. Die Antwort der Neutestamentler*, edited by Thomas Söding, 87–98. Freiburg, Herder, 2007.

Neusner, Jacob. *A Rabbi Talks with Jesus*. Montreal: McGill-Queen's University Press, 2000.

Newman, John Henry. *Essay on the Development of Christian Doctrine*. London: Longmans, Green, 1909. Online: https://www.newmanreader.org/works/development/.

———. "Essay on the Inspiration of Scripture (1861–1863)." In *Newman's Doctrine on Holy Scripture: According to His Published Works and Previously Unpublished Manuscripts*, edited by Jaak Seynaeve, WF, 60–144. Louvain: Publications Universitaires de Louvain, 1953.

———. "Further Illustrations." In *On the Inspiration of Scripture: John Henry Newman*, edited by Derek Holmes and Robert Murray, 131–53. Washington, DC: Corpus Books, 1967.

———. "Inspiration in Its Relation to Revelation." In *On the Inspiration of Scripture: John Henry Newman*, edited by Derek Holmes and Robert Murray, 101–31. Washington, DC: Corpus Books, 1967.

Nichols, Aidan, OP. *From Newman to Congar: The Idea of Doctrinal Development from the Victorians to the Second Vatican Council*. Edinburgh: T&T Clark, 1990.

———. *The Shape of Catholic Theology: An Introduction to its Sources, Principles, and History* Edinburgh: T&T Clark, 1991.

Niebuhr, H. Richard. *The Meaning of Revelation*. 2nd ed. Library of Theological Ethics. Louisville, KY: Westminster John Knox, 2006.

O'Leary, Joseph. "German Reception of the Pope's Jesus-Book." Personal blog. No pages. Cited August 9, 2008. Online: https://josephsoleary.typepad.com/my_weblog/2008/08/german-receptio.html.

———. "Non-German Reviews of the Pope's Jesus-Book (Updated)." Personal blog. No pages. Cited March 12, 2009. Online: https://josephsoleary.typepad.com/my_weblog/2009/03/nongerman-reviews-of-popes-jesusbook-updated.html.

O'Malley, John, SJ. *What Ever Happened at Vatican II?* Cambridge, MA: Belknap, 2008.

O'Neill, Colman E., OP, "The Mysteries of Christ and the Sacraments." *The Thomist* 25, no. 1 (January 1962): 1–53.

Ott, Anton. *Die Auslegung der Neutestamentlichen Texte über die Ehescheidung*. Neutestamentliche Abhandlungen III, no. 1–3. Münster: Aschendorff, 1911.

Otto, Rudolf. *The Idea of the Holy: An Inquiry into the Non-rational Factor in the Idea of the Divine and Its Relation to the Rational*. 2nd ed. Translated by John W. Harvey. London: Oxford University Press, 1958.

Paddison, Angus. *Scripture: A Very Theological Proposal*. Edinburgh: T&T Clark, 2009.

Pech, Justinus C., OCist. *Paradox und Wahrheit: Henri de Lubac und Joseph Ratzinger im gnadentheologischen Gespräch.* Frankfurter Theologische Studien 77. Münster, Aschendorff, 2020.

Pelland, Gilles, SJ. "Le pratique de l'église ancienne concernant les divorcés remarries." In *La pastorale des divorcés remariés,* edited by the Congregation for the Doctrine of the Faith, 101–33. Paris: Bayard, Centurion, Cerf, 1999.

Perrone, Giovanni. *Continens tractatus de locis teologicis partes secundam et tertiam.* Vol. II, no. 2, of *Praelectiones theologicae.* Rome: Typis Collegii Urbani, 1842.

Pesch, Rudolf. "Das Abendmahl und Jesu Todesverständnis." In *Der Tod Jesu: Deutungen im Neuen Testament,* edited by Karl Kartelge, 137–87. Gaben beim Letzen Abendmahl. QD 74. Freiburg: Herder, 1976.

——. *Das Abendmahl und Jesu Todesverständnis.* QD 80. Freiburg: Herder, 1978.

——. *Das Markusevangelium.* 2 vols. Herders Theologischer Kommentar zum Neuen Testament. Freiburg: Herder, 1977.

Peterson, Erik. "Die Kirche." In *Ausgewählte Schriften,* edited by Barbara Nichtweiß, 245–57. Vol. 1 of *Theologische Traktate.* Würzburg: Echter, 1994.

Philips. Gérard. *Carnets conciliaires de Mgr Gérard Philips: Secrétaire adjoint de la Commission Doctrinale.* Edited by K. Schelkens. Introduced by L. Declerck. Louvain: Peeters, 2006.

Pidel, Aaron. "*Christi Opera Proficiunt:* Ratzinger's Neo-Bonaventurian Model of Social Inspiration." *Nova et Vetera* 13, no. 3 (2015): 693–711.

——. "The Church of the 'Few' for the 'Many': Ratzinger's Missiology of Representation." In *Joseph Ratzinger and the Healing of Reformation-Era Divisions,* edited by Emery de Gaál and Matthew Levering, 295–316. Steubenville, OH: Emmaus Academic, 2019.

——. "Joseph Ratzinger on Biblical Inerrancy." *Nova et Vetera* 12, no. 1 (2014): 307–30.

——. "Ricoeur and Ratzinger on Biblical History and Hermeneutics." *Journal of Theological Interpretation* 8, no. 2 (2014): 37–56.

Pieper, Josef. *Buchstabier-Übungen: Aufsätze, Reden, Notizen.* Munich: Kösel, 1980.

Pitre, Brant. *Jesus and the Last Supper.* Grand Rapids, MI: Eerdmans, 2015.

Plantinga, Alvin. *The Nature of Necessity.* Oxford: Clarendon, 1974.

Pottmeyer, Hermann Josef. *Unfehlbarkeit und Souveränität: Die Päpstliche Unfehlbarkeit im System der ultramontanen Ekklesiologie des 19. Jahrhunderts.* Mainz: Matthias-Grünewald, 1975.

Power, David N., OMI. *The Eucharistic Mystery: Revitalizing the Tradition.* New York: Crossroad, 1992.

——. "Sacraments in General." In *Systematic Theology: Roman Catholic Perspectives,* 2nd ed., edited by Francis Schüssler Fiorenza and John P. Galvin, 461–96. Minneapolis: Fortress, 2011.

Prignon, Albert. *Journal conciliaire de la 4ᵉ Session*. Edited by L. Declerck and A. Haquin. Louvain: Peeters, 2003.

Prothro, James. "Theories of Inspiration and Catholic Exegesis: Scripture and Criticism in Dialogue with Denis Farkasfalvy." *Catholic Biblical Quarterly* 83, no. 2 (2021): 294–314.

Przywara, Erich, SJ. *Alter und Neuer Bund: Theologie der Stunde*. Wien: Herold Verlag, 1956.

Raffelt, Albert . "Karl Rahner und die Bibel." In *Anstöße der Theologie Karl Rahners für gegenwärtige Theologie und Kirche*, edited by Karsten Kreutzer and Albert Raffelt, 187–98. Freiburg: Katholische Akademie der Erzdiözese, 2019.

Rahner, Karl, SJ. "The Development of Dogma." In *God, Christ, Mary, Grace*, vol. 1 of *Theological Investigations*, translated by Cornelius Ernst, OP, 39–77. Baltimore: Helicon, 1961.

———. "Exegesis and Dogmatic Theology." In *Theological Investigations*, vol. 5, 67–93. London: Darton, Longman & Todd, 1966.

———. *Inspiration in the Bible*. Translated by Charles Henkey. QD 1. New York: Herder and Herder, 1961.

———. "Reflection on the Concept of '*Ius Divinum*' in Catholic Thought." In *Theological Investigations*, vol. 5, 219–243. London: Darton, Longman & Todd, 1966.

———. "Theology in the New Testament." In *Theological Investigations*, vol. 5, 23–41. London: Darton, Longman & Todd, 1966.

———. "*Virginitas in partu*: A Contribution to the Problem of the Development of Dogma and Tradition." In *More Recent Writings*, vol. 4 of *Theological Investigations*, translated by Kevin Smith, 134-62. London: Darton, Longman & Todd, 1966.

Ramage, Matthew. *Dark Passages of the Bible: Engaging Scripture with Benedict XVI and Thomas Aquinas*. Washington, DC: The Catholic University of America Press, 2013.

———. *Jesus, Interpreted: Benedict XVI, Bart Ehrman, and the Historical Truth of the Gospels*. Washington, DC: The Catholic University of America Press, 2017.

Rausch, Thomas, SJ. *Pope Benedict XVI: An Introduction to His Theological Vision*. New York: Paulist, 2009.

Ricoeur, Paul. *Essays on Biblical Interpretation*. Edited by Lewis Mudge. Philadelphia: Fortress, 1980.

———. *Hermeneutics and the Human* Sciences. Edited and translated by John B. Thompson. Cambridge: Cambridge University Press, 1981.

Ricoeur, Paul, and André LaCocque. *Thinking Biblically: Exegetical and Hermeneutical Studies*. Translated by David Pellauer. Chicago: University of Chicago Press, 1998.

Rigaux, B. "L'interprétation de l'Écriture selon la Constitution 'Dei Verbum.'" In *Au service de la parole de Dieu. Melanges offerts à Monseigneur Andre-Marie Charue, Eveque de Namur*, 263–84. Gembloux: Duculot, 1968.

Robinson, John A. T. *Redating the New Testament*. London: SCM, 1976.

Rogers, Paul. "Pierre Benoit's 'Ecclesial Inspiration': A Thomistic Notion at the Heart of Twentieth-Century Debates on Biblical Inspiration." *Thomist* 80, no. 4 (2016): 521–62.

Rousseau, Olivier. "Scheidung und Wiederheirat im Osten und Westen," *Concilium* 3 (1967): 322–34.

Ruddy, Christopher. "*Deus adorans, Homo adorans*: Joseph Ratzinger's Liturgical Christology and Anthropology." In *The Center Is Jesus Christ Himself: Essays on Revelation, Salvation & Evangelization in Honor of Robert P. Imbelli*, edited by Andrew Meszaros, 173–88. Washington, DC: The Catholic University of American Press, 2021.

Sanz Sánchez, Santiago. "Joseph Ratzinger y la doctrina de la creación: los apuntes de Münster de 1964." *Revista española de teología* 74 (2014): 31–70.

———. "Joseph Ratzinger y la doctrina de la creación: los apuntes de Münster de 1964 (II). Algunos temas fundamentales." *Revista española de teología* 74 (2014): 201–48.

———. "Joseph Ratzinger y la doctrina de la creación: los apuntes de Münster de 1964 (y III). Algunos temas debatídos." *Revista española de teología* 74 (2014): 453–96.

Schatz, Klaus, SJ. *Vatikanum I (1869– 1870)*. 3 vols. Paderborn: Schöningh, 1992–94.

Schenk, Richard, OP. "Bonaventura als Klassiker der analogia fidei: Zur Rezeption der theologischen Programmatik Gottlieb Söhngens im Frühwerk Joseph Ratzingers." In *Gegenwart der Offenbarung: Zu den Bonaventura-Forschungen Joseph Ratzingers*, edited by Marianne Schlosser and Franz-Xaver Heibl, 18–49. Ratzinger-Studien 2. Regensburg: Friedrich Pustet, 2010.

Schillebeeckx, Edward. *Jesus: An Experiment in Christology*. 3rd ed. Translated by Hubert Hoskins. New York: Seabury, 1979. Translation of *Jesus: Die Geschichte von einem Lebenden*. 3rd ed. Freiburg: Herder, 1975.

Schleiermacher, Friederich. *The Christian Faith*. Edited by H. R. Mackintosh and J. S. Stewart. Philadelphia: Fortress, 1976.

Schlögl, Manuel. *Am Anfang eines großen Weges: Joseph Ratzinger in Bonn und Köln*. MMIPB 1. Regensburg: Schnell & Steiner, 2014.

———. "Sein Werk wird noch vieles zu sagen haben: Biografische und theologische Anmerkung zur Freundschaft von Paul Hacker und Joseph Ratzinger." *Mitteilungen. Institut Papst Benedikt XVI.* 5 (2012): 49–61.

Schlosser, Marianne. "Zu den Bonaventura-Studien Joseph Ratzingers." JRGS 2:29–37.

Schmidt, Eckart D. "*. . . das Wort Gottes immer mehr zu lieben:" Joseph Ratzingers Bibelhermeneutik im Kontext der Exegesegeschichte der römischkatholischen Kirche*. Stuttgarter Bibelstudien 233. Stuttgart: Katholisches Bibelwerk, 2015.

Schmucki, Oktavian, OFMCap. "Joseph Ratzingers 'Die Geschichtstheologie des hl. Bonaventura: Nachwirken in der Forschung und der Folgezeit." In *Gegenwart der Offenbarung: Zu den Bonaventura Forschungen Joseph Ratzingers*, edited by Marianne Schlosser and Franz-Xaver Heibl, 344–59. Ratzinger-Studien 2. Regensburg: Friedrich Pustet, 2010.

Schnackenburg, Rudolf. *Schriften zum Neuen Testament*. München. Kösel Verlag, 1971.

———. *Von Jesus zur Urkirche*. Vol. 1 of *Die Sittliche Botschaft des Neuen Testaments*. Herders Theologischer Kommentar zum Neuen Testament Supplementband 1. Freiburg: Herder, 1986.

Schrage, Wolfgang. *Ethik des Neuen Testaments*. 4th ed. Grundrisse zum Neuen Testament 4. Göttingen: Vandenhoeck & Ruprecht, 1982.

Schröter, Jens. *Das Abendmahl: Frühchristliche Deutungen und Impulse für die Gegenwart*. Stuttgarter Bibelstudien 210. Stuttgart: Katholisches Bibelwerk, 2006.

Schürmann, Heinz. *Jesu ureigener Tod: Exegetische Besinnungen und Ausblick*. Freiburg: Herder, 1975.

———. *Studien zur neutestamentlichen Ethik*. Edited by Thomas Söding. Stuttgarter Biblische Aufsatzbände 7. Stuttgart: Verlag Katholisches Bibelwerk, 1990.

Schwienhorst-Schönberger, Ludger. "Der verleugnete Tempel: Warum Benedict XVI. mit seinem Zölibats-Artikel Recht hat." *Herder Korrespondenz* 74, no. 3 (March 2020): 46–49.

Seewald, Peter. *Benedikt XVI. Ein Leben*. München: Droemer Verlag, 2020.

Seitz, Christopher R. *Convergences: Canon and Canonicity*. Waco, TX: Baylor University Press, 2020.

———. "The Ten Commandments: Positive and Natural Law and the Covenants Old and New—Christian Use of the Decalogue and Moral Law." In *I Am the Lord Your God: Christian Reflections on the Ten Commandments*, edited by Carl E. Braaten and Christopher R. Seitz, 18–40. Grand Rapids, MI: Eerdmans, 2005.

Senior, Donald, CP. *Raymond E. Brown and the Catholic Biblical Renewal*. New York: Paulist, 2018.

Söding, Thomas. "Bekennen und Bezeugen: Perspektiven personalisierter Christologie im Neuen Testament." *Zeitschrift für Theologie und Kirche* 116, no. 2 (June 2019): 133–52.

———. "Brot und Wein: Die Gaben beim Letzen Abendmahl." *Internationale Katholische Zeitschrift Communio* 42 (2013): 237–48.

———. "In favorem fidei: Die Ehe und das Verbot der Scheidung in der Verkündigung Jesu." In *Zwischen Jesu Wort und Norm: Kirchliches Handeln angesichts von Scheidung und Wiederheirat*, edited by Markus Graulich und Martin Seidnader, 48–81. QD 264. Freiburg: Herder, 2014.

———. "Zeit für Gottes Wort: Die Offenbarungskonstitution des Konzils und die Hermeneutik der Reform." *Theologische Revue* 108, no. 6 (2012):443–58.

Söhngen, Gottlieb. "Bonaventura als Klassiker der analogia fidei." *Wissenschaft und Weisheit* 2, no. 2 (1935): 97–111.

Sonderegger, Katherine. "Writing Theology in a Secular Age: Joseph Ratzinger on Theological Method." In *The Theology of Benedict XVI: A Protestant Appreciation*, edited by Tim Perry, 28–45. Bellingham: Lexham, 2019.

Stallsworth, Paul T. "The Story of an Encounter." In *Biblical Interpretation in Crisis. The Ratzinger Conference on Bible and Church*, edited by Richard John Neuhaus, 102–90. Encounter Series 9. Grand Rapids, MI: Eerdmans, 1989.

Steinmetz, David, "The Superiority of Pre-Critical Exegesis." *Theology Today* 37, no. 1 (1980): 27–38.

Strätz, Hans-Wolfgang. "Ehe VIII: Rechtshistorisch." In *LThK*³ 3:476–77.

Stuhlmacher, Peter. *Biblische Theologie des Neuen Testaments*. 2 vols. Göttingen: Vandenhoeck & Ruprecht, 1992–99.

———. "Joseph Ratzingers Jesus-Buch (Teil II): Eine Kritische Würdigung." In *Passion aus Liebe: Das Jesus-Buch des Papstes in der Diskussion*, edited by Jan-Heiner Tück, 62–76. Ostfildern: Matthias Grünewald, 2011.

Taylor, Vincent. *The Formation of the Gospel Tradition*. 2nd ed. London: MacMillan, 1935.

Theobald, Michael. "Die Autonomie der historischen Kritik—Ausdruck des Unglaubens oder theologische Notwendigkeit? Zur Schriftauslegung Romano Guardinis." In *Auslegung des Glaubens: Zur Hermeneutik christlicher Existenz*, edited by L. Honnenfelder and M. Lutz-Bachmann, 21–45. Berlin: Hildesheim, 1987.

———. "Um der Begegnung mit Jesus willen: Der zweite Teil des Jesus-Buches von Joseph Ratzinger/Benedikt XVI." *Bibel und Kirche* 66 (2011): 173–78.

Thomas, Stephen. *Newman and Heresy: The Anglican Years*. Cambridge: Cambridge University Press, 1991.

Tracy, David. *The Analogical Imagination: Christian Theology in a Culture of Pluralism*. New York: Crossroad, 1981.

———. *Blessed Rage for Order: The New Pluralism in Theology*. New York: Seabury, 1975.

———. "Hans Küng: Loving Critic of His Church." *The Christian Century* 88, no. 20 (May 19, 1971): 631–33.

Trippen, Norbert. "Kardinal Josef Frings auf dem II. Vatikanischen Konzil." In *Das Zweite Vatikanische Konzil (1962–1965): Stand und Perspektiven der kirchenhistorichen Forschung im deutschsprachigen Raum*, edited by Franz Xaver Bischof, 93–103. Stuttgart: W. Kohlhammer, 2012.

Troeltsch, Ernst. "Historical and Dogmatic Method in Theology." In *Religion in History*, translated by James Luther Adams and Walter F. Bense, 20–43. Fortress Texts in Modern Theology. Philadelphia: Fortress, 2007. Translation of "Über die historische und dogmatische methode in der Theologie." In vol. 2 of *Gesammelte Schriften*, 728–53. Aalen: Scientia Verlag, 1962.

Tromp, Sebastian, SJ. *De Sacrae Scripturae inspiratione*. 6th ed. Rome: Gregorian University Press, 1962.

Vall, Gregory. "Ratzinger, Brown, and the Reception of *Dei Verbum*." *Josephinum Journal of Theology* 23, no. 1–2 (2016): 204–26.

Vanhoozer, Kevin J. "Expounding the Word of the Lord: Joseph Ratzinger on Revelation, Tradition, and Biblical Interpretation." In *The Theology of Benedict XVI: A Protestant Appreciation*, edited by Tim Perry, 66–86. Bellingham: Lexham, 2019.

Vanhoozer, Kevin J., and Daniel J. Treier. *Theology and the Mirror of Scripture: A Mere Evangelical Account*. Downers Grove, IL: IVP Academic, 2015.

Vanhoye, Albert. "The Reception in the Church of the Dogmatic Constitution '*Dei Verbum*.'" In *Opening Up the Scriptures: Joseph Ratzinger and the Foundations of Biblical Interpretation*, edited by J. Granados, C. Granados, and Luis Sánchez-Navarro, 104–25. Grand Rapids, MI: Eerdmans, 2008.

Vawter, Bruce. *Biblical Inspiration*. Philadelphia: Westminster, 1972.

Verweyen, Hansjürgen. *Ein unbekannter Ratzinger: Die Habilitationschrift von 1955 als Schlüssel zu seiner Theologie*. Regensburg: Friedrich Pustet, 2010.

———. "Joseph Ratzinger und die Exegese: Die Antrittsvorlesung im Münster im Kontext des Gesamtwerkes." *Mitteilungen. Insitut Papst Benedikt XVI*. 7 (2014): 48–60.

———. "Vom Abschiedsmahl Jesu zur Feier der Eucharistie." In *Passion aus Liebe: Das Jesus-Buch des Papstes in der Diskussion*, edited by Jan-Heiner Tück, 163–92. Ostfildern: Matthias Grünewald, 2011.

Viviano, Pauline A. "Fighting Biblical Fundamentalism." In *Vatican II: 50 Personal Stories*, edited by William Madges and Michael J. Daley, 140–43. Maryknoll, NY: Orbis, 2012.

Voderholzer, Rudolf. *Die Einheit der Schrift und ihr geistiger Sinn: Der Beitrag Henri de Lubacs zur Erforschung von Geschichte und Systematik christlicher Bibelhermeneutik*. Sammlung Horizonte Neue Folge 31. Einsiedeln: Johannes Verlag, 1998.

———. "Joseph Ratzinger und das Zweite Vatikanische Konzil." In *Erneuerung in Christus. Das Zweite Vatikanische Konzil (1962–1965) im Spiegel Münchener Kirchenarchiv*, edited by Peter Pfister, 91–108. Schriften des Archivs des Erzbistums München und Freising 16. Regensburg: Schnell & Stein, 2012.

———. "'Schriftauslegung in Widerstreit:' Joseph Ratzinger und die Exegese." In *Der Glaube ist einfach*, edited by Gerhard Ludwig Müller, 54–84. Regensburg: Friedrich Pustet, 2007.

Vögtle, Anton. "Todesankündigungen und Todesverständnis Jesu." In *Der Tod Jesu: Deutungen im Neuen Testament*, edited by Karl Kertelge, 51–113. QD 74. Freiburg: Herder, 1976.

Watson, Francis. *Gospel Writing: A Canonical Perspective*. Grand Rapids, MI: Eerdmans, 2013.

———. "Literal Sense, Authorial Intention, and Objective Truth: In Defense of Some Unfashionable Concepts." In *Text and Truth: Redefining Biblical Theology*, 95–124. Grand Rapids, MI: Eerdmans, 1997.

Wehr, Lothar. "Theologien als Bereicherung der Theologie—Eine Verteidigung der Redaktionskritik." In *Alla ricerca della Verità: Discussioni sul Gesù di Nazaret di Joseph Ratzinger—Benedetto XVI*," edited by Guiseppe Franco, 45–62. Lecce: Lupo, 2009.

Weiten, Gabriel. "Zur Seelsorge wiederverheirateter Geschiedener 1972–2014." *MIPB* 7 (2014): 103–16.

Wicks, Jared, SJ. "Another Text by Joseph Ratzinger as *Peritus* at Vatican II," *Gregorianum* 101, no. 2 (2020): 233–49.

———. "Biblical Criticism Criticized." *Gregorianum* 72, no. 1 (1991): 117–28.

———. "Joseph Ratzinger Warming the Christic Imagination, October 1962." In *The Center Is JESUS CHRIST Himself: Essays on Revelation, Salvation, and Evangelization in Honor of Robert P. Imbelli,* edited by Andrew Meszaros, 29–51. Washington, DC: The Catholic University of America Press, 2021.

———. *La Divina Rivelazione e la sua trasmissione.* 3rd ed. Rome: Editrice Pontificia Università Gregoriana, 2008.

———. "Six Texts by Prof. Joseph Ratzinger as *Peritus* before and during Vatican Council II," *Gregorianum* 89, no. 2 (2008): 233–311.

Wilkens, Robert Louis. *The First Thousand Years: A Global History of Christianity.* New Haven: Yale University Press, 2012.

Williams, Rowan. *Understanding and Misunderstanding "Negative Theology."* The Père Marquette Lecture in Theology 2021. Milwaukee: Marquette University Press, 2021.

Wills, Gary. "A Tale of Two Cardinals." *New York Review of Books* 48, no. 7 (2001): 24–26.

Witherington, Benjamin. "Matthew 5.32 and 19.9—Exception or Exceptional Situation?" *New Testament Studies* 31 (1985): 571–76.

Wittgenstein, Ludwig. *Philosophical Investigations.* Oxford: Blackwell, 1997.

Wohlmuth, Josef. "Die Sicht auf Judentum in Zweiten Band des Jesusbuches." In *Der Jesus des Papstes: Passion, Tod, Auferstehung im Disput,* edited by Herman Häring, 179–93. Berlin: LIT, 2011.

Wucherpfennig, Ansgar, SJ. "Wie hat Jesus Eucharistie gewollt? Neutestamentlichen Gedanken zur eucharistischen Gastfreundschaft." *Stimmen der Zeit* 143 (2018): 855–60.

Yeago, David S. "The Spirit, the Church and the Scriptures: Biblical Inspiration and Interpretation Revisited." In *Knowing the Triune God: The Work of the Spirit in the Practices of the Church,* edited by David S. Yeago and James J. Buckley, 49–93. Grand Rapids, MI: Eerdmans, 2001.</bibtext>

Index

A

Abraham, 58–59, 209

Adam, A. K. M., 223

Ad tuendam fidem. See John Paul II

Aeterni Patris. See Leo XIII

Aguzzi, Steven, 96n150

Albert, Hans, 118n51, 238n24

Allen, John, 180n94

Allison, Dale C., 148n6, 149–51, 173–74

Alonso Schökel, Luis, 34n66

Amoris laetitia. See Francis

analogia fidei, 88–92, 113, 123, 155, 193, 199, 210, 241

Anderson, Gary, 226n135, 235n13

Anger, G., 226n134

Anthony of the Desert, 43

Augustine of Dacia, 125–26, 130

Assumption, Doctrine of the, 62n33, 133–34

Augustine of Hippo, 43, 54, 65, 66n44, 78, 125, 150n9, 157–59, 179n92, 235, 244–45

authorial intention, 9, 20n19, 32, 43, 45, 51, 99, 123, 138, 140, 188, 245; collective or ecclesial, 11, 32–33, 47, 64, 103–6, 116, 120, 139, 235, 242, and thus layered, 107–15; divine, 3, 21; implied by world of text, 38, 40–41; limiting the scope of inerrancy, 22–25, 104–6, 136, 235

Ayres, Lewis, 139n124

B

baptism, 118–19, 133–34; in Jordan, 234–35

Balthasar, Hans Urs von, 132n110

Bañez, Domingo, 26

Barth, Karl, 61–62, 89n122, 156

Basil of Caeserea, 118, 159–60, 176

Bauckham, Richard, 189n16

Bea, Augustin, 27n42, 187n12, 218n112

Bell, Richard H., 195

Benedict XV, 103n5

Benedict XVI. *See* Ratzinger, Joseph

Benoit, Pierre, 9, 11, 15, 31, 36, 42, 45, 48–50, 52, 53–54, 56, 74, 103, 104, 109n22, 142, 237; compared with Ratzinger, 76–77, 81, 86–87, 94, 97–98, 109, 138–40, 242; on ecclesial inspiration, 33, 64, 69; evaluation of, 23–25; proponent of Thomist-Instrumental Model of Inspiration, 16–20, 28n43, 46, 60; on the truth of scripture, 20–23

Berger, Klaus, 119n58

Bible. *See* Scripture

Bieringer, Reimund, 104n6, 123n67

Blankenhorn, Brendan, 34n66, 35n69

Blondel, Maurice, 117n49, 191

Bockmuehl, Marcus, 226n134

Bonaventure, 232; on the apostles, 85; influence on Ratzinger, 8, 11, 53–63,

65–71, 73, 88–89, 93, 97, 144, 172–73, 222, 242, 245–46; on marriage, 157; on seminal reasons, 126–27; on spiritual progress, 108; on *theologia*, 81

Bond, Helen K., 189n16

Boniface, Saint, 160

Bonsirven, Joseph, 150–53, 165, 170–71, 174, 176, 179–80

Bradshaw, Paul, 208n75

Brotherton, Joshua, 68n57

Brown, Raymond E., 5–6, 10, 11n32, 18, 105–6, 125n76, 137, 196n39, 231–32, 236, 241–42

Brugger, E. Christian, 176

Bultmann, Rudolf, 107–108, 144, 185, 187, 191–92, 208n75. *See also* demythologization

Burigana, Riccardo, 106n13

Burridge, Richard A., 189n16

Burtchaell, James Tunstead, 16, 19n16, 27n39, 31n53, 77n86, 85n113

C

Caballero, Luis, 185n7, 186n8

canon. *See* Scripture

Canty, Aaron, 54n1

Carthage, Third Council of, 202n61

Cassian, John, 124–25

casuistry, 151, 155–56, 172, 175, 178, 219

Catechism of the Catholic Church, 125–27, 131, 135

Church, 45, 47, 51, 53, 64, 67, 69, 74, 76, 82n99, 83–84, 87–88, 92, 101–2, 114, 123, 125, 130, 139n124, 143, 161, 168, 170–72, 175–78, 181, 188, 202, 213, 218, 242; from Abel, 93–94, 99; apostolic or early, 29–35, 49, 84, 68, 81, 84–86, 94, 97, 107, 112–13, 140, 193, 209–10, 212, 214–16, 219; according to Augustine, 54; bride of Christ, 155; corporate personality, 77–78, 79–80, 98–99, 107, 231; Eastern or Orthodox, 65, 102, 157, 160–61, 165–66,

171, 176–77; the mind/faith/subjectivity of, 11, 43, 59–62, 65, 77, 79–80, 89, 93, 96–99, 116, 117n49, 118, 120–21, 129, 140, 142, 146, 157–61, 180, 185–86, 201, 227; Protestant, 223; site of inspiration, 63, 66n47, 91, 93, 95, 244; spotless counterpart to Mary, 132–35, 140; *See also* People of God; Mary, the Virgin

classic, Bible as. *See* Tracy, David

Clement of Alexandria, 158n34, 201–2

Collins, Christopher, 68n57

Collins, John, 224

Congar, Yves, 13, 33–35, 88–89, 93n143.

Congregation for the Doctrine of the Faith, 1n3, 5, 7, 127, 169–70

covenant, 14, 157, 163, 167; and creation, 156, 159, 163; and Last Supper or eucharist, 183n2, 207, 210; old and new, 89–91, 93, 96n150. *See also* Last Supper

Crick, Francis, 235–36

Crouzel, Henri, 158, 166, 176

Cullman, Oscar, 54

D

Daniélou, Jean, 219n113

Darwin, Charles, 3, 192

Davies, W. D., 148n6, 149–51, 173–74

Dead Sea Scrolls, 240

Dei filius. See Vatican I

Dei verbum, 39, 82, 84, 87, 227; on biblical interpretation, 122–26, 130–31, 136; on collective authorship, 74; on the historicity of Scripture, 12–13, and the Gospels, 51, 184–90, 193, 195, 206, 216–20; on the Old Testament, 52, 87–88; on the literal sense, 20nn19–20, 22n27, 23n29; on the role of individual biblical authors, 49–50, 74–75; on Scripture and tradition, 19n14, 48–49, 81; a standard for evaluating theology, 8–9, 52, 67, 73–74, 81–82, 103, 136–38, 142–43; on the truth of Scripture, 50–51, 103–6, 231, 245; *See also* Vatican II

De fontibus revelationis, 111; on Gospel historicity 186, 188–89; Ratzinger's criticisms of, 57–58, 61–63, 67, 73, 80, 90–91, 108–10, 232

de la Potterie, Ignace, 125

de la Soujeole, Benoît-Dominique, 99, 126n80

de Lubac, Henri, 10, 90n126, 124–26

demythologization, 107–8, 116–19, 144, 185, 190

Deuteworte, 210, 213, 215, 217, 227. *See also* Institution Narrative

Devil, 12; as properly affirmed by Scripture, 116–21

d'Hulst, Maurice, 5n14

Dibelius, Martin, 191–92

DiCenso, James J., 37n71

Dionysius the Areopagite, 81n97

discernment (normative) of Scripture, 12, 14, 20n19, 46–47, 50, 103, 106–8, 110n26, 111–12, 115–21, 141, 145–46, 164, 179, 185, 244–45

Divino afflante Spiritu, 5, 16, 18n12, 20nn19–20, 21n24, 22n26, 23n29, 88n119, 103, 185

divorce *logia*: and admission to communion, 169–70, 177–78; the exegesis of, 146–81; the normative ethical interpretation of, 12, 46, 121, 183, 199, 239

DNA, its discovery as analogy for faith-reason hermeneutic, 235–36

Dodewaard, Joannes van, 188–89

dogma. *See* doctrine

doctrine: development of, 143–44, 231; interpreting Scripture, 32–33, 44–47, 82–83; and the articulation of tradition, 113–14; subordinate to Scripture, 19, 81, 85

Doyle, John P., 26nn35–36

Drey, Johann Sebastian von, 85n113, 90n126

Duffy, Kevin, 236, 242

Dulles, Avery, 78, 105

E

Ebner, Martin, 226n134

Edo, Pablo, 185n7, 186n8

effective history, 37–39, 43, 52, 76n84, 97, 122, 126–28, 130–32, 134, 135, 138, 140n129, 142, 152, 167, 173–74, 179, 203, 211–12, 217, 219

ethics, *See* morals

Eucharist, 6, 95, 98, 113, 139, 170, 177, 201, 203–4, 208n77, 211n86, 212–19, 226–27. *See also* Last Supper

Evans, Craig, 213n96

exegesis: individual-ecclesial dialectic, 32–33, 61, 77, 214, 240, 242; premodern 102, 124–25, 142, 144; and virtue ethics, 221–22. *See also* demythologization, historical criticism, spiritual senses.

F

faith: consciousness or "soul" of Church, 30–33, 48, 64–65, 71, 79, 98–99, 116–20, 129n93, 140–41, 245; criterion for demythologization, 116; and mysticism, 61; and the meaning of tradition, 113; principle of continuity across testaments, 92–96, 98, 107; and reason, 3, 9, 12, 14n40, 70, 130, 137, 184–85, 189–90, 193, 216–17, 222, 227, 229, 238, 240, 242, 246; standard of biblical interpretation, 57, 61, 97, 108, 114, 132n103, 146, 157–161, 180, 193, 201, 212, 227, 232, 234, 243; standard of evaluation for theology, 8, 183, 186, 217–20. *See also analogia fidei*, morals, Church

Fastiggi, Robert L., 86n115

Farkasfalvy, Denis, 7n22, 8n23, 11n33, 27n42, 49n112, 50n114, 51n115

Fiedler, Peter, 184n2, 208n77, 209, 212, 214, 216

Finnis, John, 186n8, 187n12

Fitzmyer, Joseph, 10, 151n11, 187, 189, 223

Florence, Council of, 47n103

Flannery, Kevin, 163n53

Forestell, J. T., 21n22

Fowl, Stephen E., 24n31, 135n118

Francis of Assisi, 43

Francis, Pope, 168

Fransen, Piet, 161, 176

Franzelin, Johann Baptist, 2, 77n86, 109n22

Frei, Hans, 46

Freisen, Joseph, 179n92

Frey, Jörg, 195n37

Frings, Josef, 57–58, 71, 110n25

G

Gabel, Helmut, 33n62, 75n80

Gadenz, Pablo T., 7n20

Gadamer, H.-G., 36–38

Galilei, Galileo, 116–17, 190

geocentrism, 12, 117–19, 145, 164. *See also* Galilei, Galileo

Gertz, Bernhard, 89n122

Giambrone, Anthony, 186n8

Gibellini, Rosino, 220n116

Gnilka, Joachim, 183n2

Gnuse, Robert, 32n56, 141n130

Goethe, Johan Wolfgang von, 233

Gordon, Joseph, 11n33

Gosse, Philip, 1

Gratian, 160

Gregory the Great, 38

Gregory II, 160, 167

Grillmeier, Alois, 49n112, 50n114, 51n115, 75, 106n13, 110n25

Guardini, Romano, 212n91, 231–34

Guarino, Thomas, 219n113

Guidi, Filippo Maria, 115n39

H

Haag, Herbert, 116–17, 119, 190

Hahn, Scott, 14n37, 129n93, 224n126

Harrison, Brian W., 51n115

Harkins, Franklin, 135n118

Hauerwas, Stanley, 222n120

Hays, Richard, 152–53, 220, 222, 225, 225, 227–28, 240n29

Heidegger, Martin, 36–39, 42, 73, 80. *See also* Tracy, David.

Heilsgeschichte. See salvation history

Hengel, Martin, 192n27

historical-critical method, 6, 14, 82n102, 127, 149, 208n73, 220, 237, 240, 242; bearer of worldview, 12, 129n93, 184, 189–95, 205, 214, 223–27, 229; endorsed cautiously by magisterium, 5; external corrective to ideology, 44, 142–43, 238, 241; and the literal sense, 135, 138; standard of theological evaluation, 8, 129–31

historicity, 146; compared with "history-like" narrative, 46; constitutive of humanity, 72; in *Dei Verbum*, 50, 184; and doctrine, 82n100; of the Gospels, 183–229; and normative biblical interpretation, 12–13, 16. *See also* Last Supper

Hittinger, Russell, 162n50

Hodge, A. A., 9

Holiness Code (Levitical), 149, 152–53, 174, 179

Hollenbach, Paul, 235n12

Holmes, Derek, 5n14, 77n86

Hölscher, Maria Raphaela, 163n51

Holy Spirit: divinity of, 118; guiding apostles, 85n110, 85n13; guiding magisterium, 81, 96; inspiring Scripture, 17n7, 18n12, 20, 21n25, 50, 84, 87, 89, 102, 104, 110, 112, 136, 142; superintending Bible's effective history, 123, 128. *See also* inspiration

Homolka, Walter, 199n49

Hoping, Helmut, 185n7, 186nn8–9, 190n18

Hopko, Thomas, 82

Hoppe, Rudolf, 226n134

Humphreys, Colin J., 197n43

I

Immaculate Conception, Doctrine of the, 133–34, 178; *see also* Mary, the Virgin

inerrancy. *See* truth.

inspiration, 124; an analogical concept, 24–25, 60, 65, 74; 87–96, 98, 113; equivalent to *revelatio* in Bonaventure, 56–58, 62, 73, 89, 93, 97; and the Old Testament, 34–35, 87–96, 113, 136; the *res-et-sententiae* theory of, 19n16, 26–27, 29, 31, 77–78, 109n22; the search for a new paradigm of, 3–8, 15–53, 231, 241–43; a social or collective charism, 11, 24–25, 33n61, 34–35, 64, 74–75, 79, 86, 95n146, 97, 99, 107, 136, 213; teleological, 3–4, 65–73, 95–96, 104, 111, 131–32, 134–35, 137. *See also analogia fidei*; Benoit, Pierre; Rahner, Karl; Ratzinger, Joseph; Tracy, David.

Inspiration and Truth of Scripture, The. See Pontifical Biblical Commission

International Theological Commission, 151, 169–70

Irenaeus of Lyons, 202

J

Jaubert, Annie, 197, 199–203, 238

Jeremias, Joachim, 197, 201n57, 213n96

Jerusalem, City of, 110n25, 125, 202n60, 212

Jerusalem, Council of, 112, 149, 170–71, 174

Jerusalem, destruction of, 174, 175n80

Jesus Christ: Ascension of, 133; devotion to, 243; and divorce, 12, 146–53, 171; end of salvation history and Scripture, 30, 66–69, 73, 93, 95–96, 111–112, 114–15, 118, 134, 137, 141–42, 144, 156, 245; inspirer of Scripture, 40, 58–59, 85n113, 92–93, 98, 244; and Institution Narrative,

207–17; peccability of, 234–35; real v. historical, 6, 13, 177, 184, 186, 188, 194, 206, 225, 227; revelatory preeminence and reason for Scripture's authority, 81, 83–87; united with the Church, 63, 65n40, 91, 99n152, 108, 111, 121, 155, 244–45; Transfiguration of, 185. *See also* divorce *logia*, Last Supper

Jewish-Christian dialogue, 35, 95–96, 225; and Johannine antisemitism, 228

John Paul II, 7

Johnson, Elizabeth, 105

Johnson, H. J. T., 5n14

Johnson, Luke Timothy, 226n134, 240n29

John XXIII, 187

Journet, Charles, 98n151, 99, 204n67

Joy, John P., 205n70, 218n111

Jüngel, E., 220n116

K

Kaes, Dorothee, 13n36, 114n37

Kasper, Walter, 126n80, 168, 237

Keener, Craig, 189n16

Ker, Ian T., 115n41

Koch, Kurt, 55n9

König, Franz, 105, 110n25

Küng, Hans, 47, 143n133

L

LaCocque, André, 38n76

Last Supper: historicity of, 12–13, 113, 183–221, 226–29

Lateran IV, 120n61, 227

Legaspi, Michael, 124n126, 225n128

Lemaire, Marie–Gabrielle, 126n82

Lenormant, François, 5n14

Léon-Dufour, Xavier, 203n64, 215

Leo XIII, 4, 15–16, 21n25, 22nn26–27, 103, 185, 244–45

Levering, Matthew, 11n33

Levenson, Jon D., 223n124, 224

Lindbeck, George A., 78

literal sense: counterpart to spiritual senses or *sensus plenior*, 19–21, 128, 139; Thomas Aquinas on, 24n31, 135–136; dimension of fourfold sense, 121–32, 135, 140; identified with historically indicated meaning, 131, 136, 138, 232; of Mary, 134. *See also* authorial intention, spiritual senses.

Lohfink, Nobert, 32n56, 140n127, 141n130

Lohse, Eduard, 175n82

Luz, Ulrich, 76n84, 152–53, 156, 157n28, 173–74, 180

M

magisterium: attitude toward exegesis, 5, 16, 20nn19–20, 21n25; on the historicity of the Gospels, 184–89; organ of tradition, 49, 63, 113, 81n96, 120; relation to Scripture, 83, 86, 113n34, 143, 236; standard for theologians, 8, 23, 33. *See also* doctrine.

MacIntyre, Alasdair, 162, 222n120, 231, 238–42, 245

MacKenzie, Roderick A. F., 24n31

Maddox, Brenda, 236n15

Manicardi, Ermenegildo, 210n84, 213n96

Marcus, Joel, 109n24, 196n38

Marín Sola, F., 144n135

Marschler, Thomas, 92n136

Mary, the Virgin: faith of, 111; fourfold sense of, 131–35, 140, 145, 178, 180; impending divorce from Joseph, 150; virginal birth, 194–95. *See also* Church

Mass. *See* Eucharist

Matthean exception clause. *See* divorce *logia*

McCarthy, Dennis J., 34n65

McGilchrist, Iain, 233

McKenna, Frances, 14n38, 132n105

McKenny, Gerald, 162n50

McKenzie, John L., 95n146

McNeil, Brian, 185

Meier, John P., 6, 10, 147n2, 192, 193n28, 197, 199n48, 200, 202, 205–6, 211n86, 225

Möhler, J. A., 2, 85n113

Molina, Luis de, 25–26, 28, 31

Moller, Philip, 11n33

morals: application of biblical teaching to, 12, 46–47, 37, 145–81, 183; and authenticity, 36–37; faith and, 4, 15, 22, 51, 103, 105–6, 243–45. *See also* divorce *logia*, virtue ethics

Morrow, Jeffrey, 224n126

Moses, 16, 112, 148–49, 154

Murray, Robert, 5n14, 77n86

Mußner, Franz, 195n37

N

National Socialism, 119.

natural law, 156, 159, 162–64, 178–79, 181

neo-scholasticism, 8, 11, 22, 54, 62, 70, 80, 81n96, 104–6, 109, 136–37, 144, 238.

neo-Thomism. *See* neo-scholasticism

Neusner, Jacob, 211, 212n90.

Newman, John Henry, 2–5, 8, 15, 102, 115, 178, 231; compared with Ratzinger, 243–46

Nichols, Aidan, 18, 144n136

Niebuhr, H. R., 9

O

O'Leary, Joseph, 226n134

Ott, Anton, 150n10

Otto, Rudolf, 41

Origen of Alexandria, 101–2, 124, 159–60, 176.

Orthodoxy. *See* Church

P

Paddison, Angus, 224n126

Pascendi Dominici gregis, 22n26, 23n28, 103n5

paschal lamb, 196n39, 200–201, 203–4, 206. *See also* Jesus Christ, Last Supper.

Passover: and the dating of the Last Supper, 184, 196–206, 211–12, 218; perpetual observance, 139–41; refounded by Jesus, 218. *See also* Eucharist.

Patrizi, F. S., 150n10

Paul VI, 5, 50n114, 106n13, 187, 218n112

Pech, Justinus, 13n36, 71n65

Pelland, Gilles, 176

People of God, 12; author/subject of Scripture, 64–66, 74–77, 89, 91, 94, 97, 103, 106–7, 121, 123, 134–36, 139, 141, 143–45, 194, 235, 240, 242, 244; body of Christ, 91, 99, 107–8, 111, 115; faith of, 61; in Latin American theology, 93n143; spanning Israel and Church, 34, 89, 92, 98, 112, 114–15, 141–42, 145. *See also* authorial intention, Church

Perrone, Giovanni, 2, 26–27, 29, 31

perseveration, problem of, 233

Pesch, Rudolf, 212, 213n96, 214–16, 221

Peterson, Erik, 209n81

Philips, Gérard, 106n13

Pieper, Josef, 129n92

Pitre, Brant, 183n2, 196n39, 197–98, 205n70, 206, 208n74, 214n99

Pius IX, 115

Pius X, 103n5

Pius XII, 5, 20n19, 103

Plantinga, Alvin, 10n31

Pontifical Biblical Commission, 1n1, 5, 7–8, 16, 21n25, 23n28, 51n115, 103, 109n21, 185, 187, 189n17, 227

porneia. See divorce *logia*

Pottmeyer, Hermann, 115n38

Power, David N., 208n75, 208n77

Prignon, Albert, 219n113

prophecy, 17–18, 21, 24–25, 28, 65, 79–80, 84, 87, 111, 114, 133, 154–55, 164, 18, 203, 211, 215. *See also* Benoit, Pierre; Thomas Aquinas

Prothro, James, 129n94

Providentissimus Deus, 4, 5n14, 9, 15, 16, 18n12, 21n25, 22nn26–27, 88n119, 103, 137, 185, 244–45

Przywara, Erich, 89–92

Pusey, Edward, 3

Q

Q hypothesis, 192, 237–38

R

Raffelt, Albert, 142n131

Ramage, Matthew, 14nn39–40

Rahner, Karl, 9–11, 15, 19n16, 25, 36, 42–43, 53, 54, 56, 60, 64, 69, 74, 103–4, 136, 237; collaborator with Ratzinger, 67, 83; compared with Ratzinger, 77–80, 85–86, 94–98, 140–44, 242; exegetical principles, 31–33, 45; evaluation of, 33–35; in light of *Dei Verbum*, 48–52; Molinist-predefinitive model of inspiration, 25–31

Ratzinger, Joseph: on the analogous inspiration of testaments, 87–94; applying normativity to Devil and geocentrism, 12, 116–21; author of *Jesus of Nazareth*, 183–84, 198, 227, 228; on the Bible's unique authority, 14, 80–87; Bonaventurian-ecclesial model of inspiration, 11, 15, 54–73; as mystical, 56; subject-inclusive, 63–65, 107; historically progressive, 65–69; and rationally corrective, 69–73; on the divorce *logia*, 12, 146, 153–81; on the historicity of the Last Supper, 12–13, 196–206, and the Institution Narrative, 207–17, as evaluated by the standards of faith, 217–19, and of historical reason, 220–29, 239; more adequate model of inspiration, 74–94, 127; on the organic unity of Scripture and Church, 74–80; philosophical criticism of historical criticism, 189–94; rebalancing a priori and a posteriori approaches to exegesis, 231–38; retriever of doctrine of inspiration, 1–2, 7–9; on Scripture's layered intentionality, 107–15; similarity to Alasdair MacIntyre, 238–42; on tradition, 51n117, 91–92, 113–14; on the truth of Scripture, 103–7, 136–44; updating the fourfold sense, 126–31. *See also* historical-critical method, inspiration, tradition, truth

Rausch, Thomas 14n40

reason: and inspiration, 17, 28, 56, 69–73; standard of theological evaluation, 8–9, 13, 110–11, 117, 119, 131, 137, 145, 154, 161–64, 173, 175–76, 184–85, 189–90, 193, 205, 214, 216–17, 220–29. *See also* faith.

Reformation, Protestant, 2, 9–10, 164, 175, 223–24

Renan, Ernest, 3

Ricoeur, Paul, 10, 36, 38–39, 43, 45

Rigaux, Beda, 124n68

Robinson, John A. T., 192n27

Rogers, Paul, 33n61

Rousseau, Olivier, 166

Ruddy, Christopher, 205n69

S

salvation history, 29–30, 56, 93, 115, 134, 141, 209, 218n112; contrasted with neo–scholasticism, 50–51, 54, 70, 71n65, 88–89, 104–6, 109, 111–12, 136–37, 140, 144, 157; Mary's role in, 133. *See also* Bonaventure, Jesus Christ

Sancta mater ecclesia, 187–89

Sanz Sánchez, Santiago, 135n117, 156n27

Schatz, Klaus, 115n39

Schenk, Richard, 89n122

Schleiermacher, Friedrich, 10

Schlögel, Manuel, 57nn15–16, 109n23

Schlosser, Marianne, 55n9

Schmaus, Michael, 55n5

Schmidt, Eckart D., 10n30, 82n102

Schmucki, Oktavian, 55n6, 66n44

Schnackenburg, Rudolf, 151, 153, 155, 165, 175, 194

Schoiswohl, Joseph, 49n108

Schrage, Wolfgang, 175n82

Schwienhorst-Schönberger, Ludger, 214n101

Sedula cura. See Paul VI

Schillebeeckx, Edward, 237

Schröter, Jens, 208n75

Schürmann, Heinz, 151–53, 155, 169, 208n77

Scripture: canon of, 8, 35, 41, 43–45, 56, 69, 97, 101–3, 123, 127, 142, 154, 178, 180, 220–25, 228–29, 234, 241–42; authority of, 3, 18, 34, 36, 45–46, 53, 74, 76, 78, 80–87, 97–98, 101, 113n34. *See also* inspiration, truth, exegesis, *sola scriptura*

Seewald, Peter, 171n72

Seitz, Christopher, 95, 124n69, 174n79, 228

Senior, Donald, 11n32

Sensus plenior. See spiritual senses

Sermon on the Mount, 147, 154, 157, 185

sola scriptura, 2, 63, 74, 224

Sonderegger, Katherine, 238n25

Söding, Thomas, 106n14, 126n81, 175, 204n67, 215

Söhngen, Gottlieb, 54, 78, 88, 89n122, 235

spiritual senses: components of fourfold sense, 121–31; of Mary, 131–35, 178, 180; and the *sensus plenior*, 21, 28n43, 45–46, 50, 51, 124n70, 125, 126n80, 138–40. *See also Dei Verbum.*

Spiritus Paraclitus, 18n12, 21n24, 22n26, 23n28, 103n5

Stallsworth, Paul T., 83n103

state, 98, 160; liberal, 129, 93, 224–25

Steinmetz, David, 124n72

Strätz, Hans-Wolfgang, 179n93

Stuhlmacher, Peter, 10, 193, 225–26

Synod of Bishops, 7, 126, 168–69, 171n72

T

Taylor, Vincent, 213

Teilhard de Chardin, Pierre, 68–69

Theobald, Michael, 220–21, 226, 234n11

Thomas Aquinas, 14n31, 25, 62; on
the apostles, 85; on divine-human
cooperation, 19, 21n22, 26–27; on
doctrinal development, 144; on Gospel
historicity, 218n111; on instrumental
causality, 18–19; on the literal sense,
24n31, 134–35; on marriage, 163; on
prophecy, 17–18; on reason, 70, 162–63.
See also Benoit, Pierre; literal sense

Tracy, David, 9, 11, 13, 15, 25, 53–54, 74, 78,
103–4, 136, 237; on the Bible as "classic,"
38–42; compared with Ratzinger, 60,
64, 69, 76–77, 85–86, 94, 97–98, 142–43,
242; compared with *Dei Verbum*, 49–52;
on error in Scripture, 45; evaluation
of, 45–48; on exegesis, 42–45; and the
Heideggerian-disclosive model of
inspiration, 36–41

tradition: Abrahamic, 58–59; analogous
to language, 72, 77–80; diachronically
layered, 52, 113, 117–18, 120, 177,
192–94, 212, 224; of inquiry, 162, 229,
238–42, 246; and inspiration, 60, 85n113;
interpretive norm, 2, 32, 43–45, 48–49,
51n117, 57, 62–63, 74, 76–77, 97, 123,
129n93, 139n126, 145, 154, 157–61, 164,
219, 224; requiring a corporate subject,
63, 71–73, 75, 210; synchronically
layered, 113–115, 119–20, 224. *See also*
MacIntyre, Alasdair; Tracy, David

Trent, Council of, 27, 62, 63n38, 74,
139n126, 160–61, 167, 176, 203–4, 219,
227, 243

Tribur, Provincial Council of, 160

Treier, Daniel, 10n28

Trippen, Norbert, 110n25

Troeltsch, Ernst, 190–91

Tromp, Sebastian, 81n96, 109n22, 139n125

truth of Scripture: adequation model
of, 23–34, 42, 46; disclosure model of,
36–39, 42, 46; expressed negatively by
inerrancy, 7, 11, 103–121; expressed
positively by multivalence, 12, 103,
121–135; in the "double counterpoint"
of faith and reason, 235; symphonic,
114. *See also Dei Verbum*; Rahner, Karl;
Ratzinger, Joseph; Tracy, David

Tück, Jan-Heiner, 226n134

typology. *See* spiritual senses

U

uncertainty principle, 128–29

V

Vall, Gregory, 236

Vanhoozer, Kevin, 10n28, 238n25

Vanhoye, Albert, 35n68

Vatican I, 27, 35, 48, 74, 87–88, 94, 102,
115n39, 243;

Vatican II, 15, 57, 87, 112, 191, 243; and
the end of magisterial surveillance of
exegesis, 5–7, 104; call for Catholic–
Jewish dialogue, 35; influenced by
Ratzinger, 55, 58, 62, 66–67, 71, 189–90.
See also Dei Verbum

Vawter, Bruce, 7n18

Verbum Domini, 7

Verweyen, Hansjürgen, 54n1, 85n112,
112n31, 130n97, 144n137, 183n2

Viviano, Pauline, 229

virtue ethics, 222–23, 229, 238–39

Voderholzer, Rudolf, 58n19, 113n34,
125n76, 208n73

Vögtle, Anton, 208n77

W

Warfield, B. B., 9

Watson, Francis, 9n25, 238n23

Watson, James, 235–36

Wehr, Lothar, 220n116, 221

Weiten, Gabriel, 168nn63–64

Wicks, Jared, 5n14, 10n30, 57n15, 57n17, 58n18, 63nn35–36, 66n48, 67n49, 67nn51–52, 71nn66–68, 75n79, 91nn127–30, 93n143, 109n21, 109n23, 110nn25–27, 111n28, 112n30, 232n2.

Wilkens, Robert Louis, 174n79

Wills, Gary, 180n95

Wiker Benjamin, 129n93, 224n126

Williams, Rowan, 128n88

Wirkungsgeschichte. See effective history

Witherington, Benjamin, 148

Wittgenstein, Ludwig, 77–78

Wohlmuth, Josef, 199n49

worldview: fusion of knowledge and value, 12, 107, 108, 116, 119–20, 146, 164, 175, 177–78, 180, 190–94, 205, 214, 222, 227, 240

Wucherpfennig, Ansgar, 208n76

Y

Yeago, David, 223

ALSO IN THE SERIES

THE APOSTLE PAUL AND HIS LETTERS
An Introduction
James B. Prothro
Foreword by Fr. Thomas D. Stegman, SJ

A BIBLICAL PATH TO THE TRIUNE GOD
Jesus, Paul, and the Revelation of the Trinity
Fr. Denis Farkasfalvy, O. Cist
Foreword by Bruce D. Marshall
Edited by Fr. Thomas Esposito, O. Cist

ECCLESIAL EXEGESIS
A Synthesis of Ancient and Modern Approaches to Scripture
Gregory Vall

LITURGICAL HERMENEUTICS OF SACRED SCRIPTURE
Fr. Marco Benini
Foreword by Fr. Michael G. Witczak
Translated by Brian McNeil